A Documentary History of Modern Iraq

UNIVERSITY PRESS OF FLORIDA

Florida A&M University, Tallahassee
Florida Atlantic University, Boca Raton
Florida Gulf Coast University, Ft. Myers
Florida International University, Miami
Florida State University, Tallahassee
New College of Florida, Sarasota
University of Central Florida, Orlando
University of Florida, Gainesville
University of North Florida, Jacksonville
University of South Florida, Tampa
University of West Florida, Pensacola

A Documentary History of Modern Iraq

Edited by Stacy E. Holden

University Press of Florida
Gainesville · Tallahassee · Tampa · Boca Raton
Pensacola · Orlando · Miami · Jacksonville · Ft. Myers · Sarasota

Copyright 2012 by Stacy E. Holden
All rights reserved.
Printed in the United States of America. This book is printed on Glatfelter Natures Book, a paper certified under the standards of the Forestry Stewardship Council (FSC). It is a recycled stock that contains 30 percent post-consumer waste and is acid-free.

17 16 15 14 13 12   6 5 4 3 2 1

Library of Congress Cataloging-in-Publication Data
A documentary history of modern Iraq / Edited by Stacy E. Holden.
p. cm.
Includes bibliographical references and index.
ISBN 978-0-8130-4016-5 (alk. paper)
 1. Iraq—History. I. Holden, Stacy E.
DS70.9.D63 2012
956.704—dc23   2012009831

University Press of Florida
15 Northwest 15th Street
Gainesville, FL 32611-2079
http://www.upf.com

Contents

Introduction / 1

1. Ottoman Mesopotamia, 1903–1920 / 17

The Wedding of Regina, 1903 / 18
Lt. Col. Sir Mark Sykes on Mosul, 1906 / 21
The Young Turk Proclamation of 1908 / 24
Jafar al-Askari on Corrupt Ottoman Administration in Iraq / 25
Sultan Abdul Hamid Deposed, 1909 / 29
Tribal Rebellion near Mosul, 1909 / 30
Baghdad Petition, 1910 / 33
British Military Rule in Basra / 39
The Horrors of World War I / 42
The Proclamation of Baghdad, 19 March 1917 / 45
The War Viewed from Baghdad / 47

2. The British Mandate, 1920–1932 / 53

Iraqi Nationalism / 55
Nationalist Poetry / 61
The Revolt of 1920 / 62
Lawrence of Arabia Opposes Iraqi Mandate / 66
Winston Churchill Outlines Middle East Policy / 69
The Kurdish "Election" of King Faysal / 74
King Faysal's Coronation Speech, 1921 / 78
Shi'is Oppose (Rigged) Elections / 81

3. The Hashemite Monarchy, 1932–1941 / 89

Faysal Expresses Intention to Protect Minorities, 1932 / 90
Pan-Arab Nationalism / 93
Faysal I Promotes Pan-Arabism, 1932 / 99
The Assyrian Affair, 1933 / 102
The Bakr Sidqi Coup of 1936 / 107
Rising Anti-Semitism in Baghdad / 113
The Shi'i Celebration of Ashura / 115
Elegy to the Poor / 121

4. **Ending the Old Regime, 1941–1958 / 125**

   The Farhud / 126
   Rules for American Soldiers in Iraq during World War II / 130
   The Treaty of Portsmouth, 15 January 1948 / 133
   Intellectual Life in Baghdad / 137
   Poverty in Baghdad / 140
   The Evolution of a Communist / 143
   Law No. 1 of 1950 / 147
   The Exodus of Kurdish Jews / 148
   Life in a Shi'i Village / 154

5. **The Revolutionary Era, 1958–1968 / 160**

   American Response to Qasim's Coup d'État / 161
   Corruption and Inequality / 166
   An American View of Revolutionary Iraq / 173
   Mutiny in Mosul, March 1959 / 176
   The Social Lives of Women in Revolutionary Iraq / 182
   The Kurdish Revolt, 1961–1963 / 187

6. **Consolidating Ba'thist Power, 1968–1979 / 193**

   U.S. Response to the Ba'thist Coup, July 1968 / 194
   The Ba'thist Constitution, 1970 / 195
   The Jewish Exodus under the Ba'th / 198
   Pan-Arab Cultural Production / 206
   Women in Ba'thist Iraq / 209
   History and Ba'thist Totalitarianism / 212
   The United States Considers Assistance to Kurds, 1972 / 214
   The 1974–1975 War in Kurdish Iraq / 215
   Muhammad Baqir al-Sadr and the Principle of Social Justice / 220
   Ba'thist Response to Shi'i Protests, 1979 / 223

7. **The Iran-Iraq War, 1980–1990 / 229**

   Saddam Hussein Justifies the War / 230
   The Iran-Iraq War through a General's Eyes / 235
   The United States Supports Ba'thist Iraq / 239
   The Iran-Iraq War through a Soldier's Eyes / 244
   The Front Line / 248
   The Home Front / 254
   Al Anfal / 258
   The End of the War / 261

8. **The Persian Gulf War and Sanctions, 1990–2002 / 265**

   Ambassador April Glaspie Meets with Saddam Hussein / 267
   "Null and Void": UN SC Res 662, 9 August 1990 / 271
   "All Necessary Means": UN SC Res 678, 29 November 1990 / 272
   The Persian Gulf War Experienced in Baghdad / 273
   The Persian Gulf War Wreaks Regional Havoc / 278
   "After the Storm": Winning the War, but Losing the Peace / 281
   Denis Halliday Protests the Sanctions Regime / 285
   The Iraq Liberation Act of 1998 / 287
   The Deleterious Effects of Sanctions on Iraqi Women / 288

9. **The Invasion of Iraq, 2001–2003 / 300**

   Saddam Hussein Responds to 9/11 / 302
   Brent Scowcroft Opposes Invasion of Iraq / 303
   President Bush Argues for War / 306
   An Iraqi Elegy to Baghdad / 312
   The Battle of Nasiriyah / 315
   The Occupation of Baghdad / 320
   The Pillaging of the National Museum / 323
   Saddam Hussein Responds to Invasion / 328
   President Bush's "Mission Accomplished" Speech / 330

10. **The Occupation of Iraq under the Coalition Provisional Authority, 2003–2004 / 336**

    Civilians and the Front Line / 337
    Lt. Paul Bremer Forms a Governing Council / 339
    Women during the Iraq War / 343
    A Sunni Insurgent / 347
    Shi'i Disillusionment / 353
    The Rules of Engagement / 357
    The Coffins of Muqdadiyah / 359
    Operation Devil Siphon / 362
    The Lot of Children / 367

Secondary Source Material / 373
Acknowledgments / 375
Index / 381

Introduction

In 1903, a Baghdadi woman named Regina wed a local boy, and the story of their marriage begins this exploration of the history of Modern Iraq via primary source documents. Regina was a Jewish woman educated in a French school called the Alliance Israelite. She adhered to Western traditions, insisting, for example, on getting married in the white dress of Europeans, and not the brightly colored costume normally worn by Jewish brides in Baghdad. In doing so, she went against the wishes of her family, but Regina, touting her status as an educated woman, held firm against their pressures. Her husband, in contrast, chose to wear traditional clothes, until, that is, his young wife took control of his wardrobe and began dressing him in suits. Once they had a son, Regina, remembering the daily lessons learned at the Alliance Israelite, implemented Western concepts of hygiene, and so, much to the chagrin of her mother-in-law, she bathed her child daily. In this way, Regina was much more than a witness to Iraq's history; she was an independent agent of historical process and change.

This anthology relates the story of Iraq's long and complicated history through the stories of many different individuals like Regina, the people who actually experienced historical change and also contributed to it. Although a fairly simple tale, the story of this marriage underscores some important themes in Iraqi history. For example, Regina's story demonstrates the social influence of women, which may surprise those who conceptualize Iraq as a patriarchal society. Further, it shows the early encroachment of the West in Baghdad, a city that was, even at the turn of the twentieth century, cosmopolitan and having non-negligible ties to the outside world. It also illustrates the influence of Jewish peoples in this Islamic land, and Jews would remain an important religious minority in Iraq up until the late 1960s. The story of Regina begs the following questions: How would people in Iraq deal with encroaching Western influences? What role would minorities play in the sociopolitical and economic development of Iraq? How would Iraqis define themselves as a people and even as a nation?

This introduction provides readers with an overview of the Iraqi past and with a glimpse of the documents used to illuminate that history. This anthology follows Iraq's history from Ottoman rule in 1903 to the implementation of the Coalition Provisional Authority in 2003. In detailing the history of modern Iraq, this introduction responds loosely to the following question: How would the diverse population of this multiethnic and multisectarian state forge a coherent nation loyal to a unified state? Based on the documents collected in this anthology, it is clear that the persistence of communal identities based on ethnic and religious affiliation has undermined Iraq's struggle to forge a unified national identity.

The marriage of Regina took place just as the history of modern Iraq begins. At that time, this territory consisted of three distinct provinces in an imperial realm called the Ottoman Empire. Iraq, an area then referred to as Mesopotamia, comprised 168,000 square miles (Marr, 8). The three Ottoman provinces in Mesopotamia each centered on a principal city. There was the province of Basra in the coastal south, the province of Baghdad in the central plains, and the province of Mosul in the mountainous north. By 1903, these three provinces had been under Ottoman rule for almost four hundred years. From their capital in Istanbul, the Ottoman Sultans implemented a system of decentralized rule. In this way, they appointed *valis*, or governors, to act in their stead in the provinces.

In 1903, the three governors ruling over the Mesopotamian provinces needed to mediate the sociopolitical and economic interests of a diverse population numbering approximately 2.2 million people (Marr, 8). Then, as now, the population of this area consisted primarily of three distinct groups: Sunni Arabs, Shi'i Arabs, and the Kurds. Sunni Arabs represented 20 percent of the population, and they were found principally in the Baghdad province. The Arab-speaking Shi'is found in the coastal south represented 60 percent of Iraq's population. And the Kurds of the mountainous north represented as much as 25 percent of Iraq's population (Yildiz, 9). There were, however, also a number of smaller ethnic and religious minorities, and these included not only the Jewish community into which Regina was born but also a number of syncretic and Christian sects. Thus, the provinces were home to small groups like the angel-worshipping Yazidis of the north or the Armenian or Chaldean Christians of the south.

The Ottoman world into which Regina was born privileged Sunni Arabs, even though they were a distinct minority when compared to the Shi'i Arabs. The difference between Sunnis and Shi'is is not a spiritual one, for both subgroups follow the basic precepts of Islam set out by the Prophet Muhammad in the early seventh century. Instead, the historic division between these two subgroups, at least in Iraq, stems from a set of very temporal political considerations focused on the wielding of power within the empire. The Ottomans questioned the loyalties of Shi'is because they, unlike the Sunnis, adhered to a doctrine of the Imamate. According to Shi'i beliefs about this doctrine, clerics are conceptualized as divinely inspired and so worthy of wielding tangible political influence in this world. Such a doctrine may well lead Shi'i clerics to believe that they have the authority to question the policies and practices of rulers.

The Ottoman Empire fought several wars with Persia in the nineteenth century, and this aggravated and deepened intersectarian divisions in Mesopotamia. Many of the most influential Shi'i clerics resided in Persia (present-day Iran), an imperial territory to the east of Iraq. And so, the Ottomans kept the Shi'is out of the empire's army and administration for a set of very temporal reasons, namely they feared that Shi'i loyalties lay with the clerics and rulers in their erstwhile Persian enemy found to the east. Thus, the officer corps and state administration was filled with Sunnis, not Shi'is. Jafar al-Askari, for example, served the Ottomans with honor, even though he recognized a corruption in the administration.

The Kurds of Iraq live in the north, and they have long held secessionist aspirations. Indeed, many Kurdish tribes, like the Hamavads, fought the Ottoman army in the early twentieth century in order to avoid efforts to centralize the imperial polity. Large numbers of Kurds are also found in Syria, Turkey, and Iran, and together these lands are often called Kurdistan. These lands are mountainous, and the resulting isolation has allowed the Kurds to maintain their own language and their own cultural traditions. Most Iraqi Kurds are Sunni, but there has historically been tension with their Arab counterparts, who monopolized the structures of the state.

The diverse world into which Regina was born does not end with these three large ethnic or religious groups, for there were also a number of smaller minorities residing in the three Mesopotamian provinces of the Ottoman Empire. Presently, 3 percent of the Iraqi population is either a syncretic sect or Christian. A syncretic sect, like the northern Yazidis, a small group numbering 100,000 people, mixes elements from different religions (Ghareeb, 247). Yazidis, for example, who practice a form of angel worship, have incorporated dietary regulations from Judaism, pilgrimage practices from Islam, and eucharistic rites from Christianity (Ghareeb, 247). And many Iraqis were—and still are—Christian. These groups include: Chaldeans, Assyrians, Armenians, Jacobites, Greek Orthodox, Greek Catholics, and Latin Catholics (Marr, 17).

The overall percentage of religious minorities used to be much higher, for, as depicted in Regina's story, a thriving Jewish community once lived in Iraq. Indeed, when Regina got married in 1903, 53,000 residents of Baghdad, and this out of 150,000 total, were estimated to be Jewish (Issawi, 124). Not all Jews, however, lived in Baghdad, for at least 2.5 percent of the general population was Jewish. For example, 20,000 Jews were also ethnic Kurds, and they lived in the mountainous north (Ghareeb, 125). The slow exodus of members of this religious minority takes pride of place in this anthology, for it exemplifies modern Iraq's difficulties to forge a multiethnic and multisectarian national identity transcending communalism.

In retrospect, the world into which Regina was born seems a Golden Age in Iraqi history. The Ottomans tolerated religious diversity within their population, and many Baghdadi Jews thrived in the late nineteenth and early twentieth centuries (Ghareeb, 125). As also revealed in this anthology, Mesopotamia was becoming ever more connected to the West. Thus, Mosul, a seemingly remote corner of Mesopotamia, was visited by British diplomat Lt. Colonel Mark Sykes, who dreamed of uniting the people of these territories via a railroad. Further, the political system of the Ottoman Empire seemed poised to become liberal, which would allow for the formation of political parties transcending communal groupings based on ethnic or religious loyalties. This happened in 1908, when the Sultan Abdelhamid, under pressure by a group called the Young Turks, instituted a parliament in which members were elected within the provinces. In Baghdad, many educated elite welcomed this liberal transformation, sending petitions to the government that called for even more local control over their city. Mesopotamia, it seemed, was building the foundation necessary to develop into a stable democracy with a multiethnic national identity that would unify the diverse groups of this territory.

The West, however, began to assert a pernicious influence in Mesopotamia during World War I, and this arguably impeded the development of a multiethnic and multisectarian national identity. During World War I, the Ottomans sided with the Central Powers, which consisted of Germany and the Austro-Hungarian Empire, and not the Entente alliance, which consisted of Great Britain, France, and, eventually, the United States. The British, fearing the closure of their access to oil fields in Abadan, immediately occupied coastal Basra and set up a system of foreign rule there. The British then fought to assume control of the rest of Mesopotamia, which impoverished many people and drove them to extreme measures of survival. Lt. Gen. Sir Stanley Maude, however, who led British troops into Baghdad in 1917, promised to take into consideration the political aspirations of local residents. Indeed, after the Entente powers won World War I, Great Britain and France broke up the Ottoman Empire with the intention of creating a series of independent Arab states in the Middle East.

And so, after World War I, Mesopotamia, renamed Iraq, did indeed become a formal state, albeit one dominated by a foreign power. The West's purpose in creating states in the Middle East was not necessarily to guarantee independence to individual nations, but instead to prevent the rise of a single large imperial entity, like the Ottomans, for this would challenge European domination in the region. Thus, Europe implemented a mandate system under the auspices of the new League of Nations, whereby Great Britain, ostensibly tutoring Iraq in modern state formation, became in essence the colonial overlord of Iraq. At first, Great Britain instituted a system of direct rule over Iraq, which gave local people little say in their governance.

The Iraqi response to this policy of direct rule offers one example of the diverse peoples of these former Ottoman provinces coming together in ways that transcended communal loyalties. In the large cities, the educated elite among Sunnis and Shi'is organized joint religious ceremonies that protested British rule. In the countryside, rural tribes actively fought British troops. Iraq poets lauded these efforts to forge a single nation intent on eliminating the rule of a foreign overlord. In light of the money and manpower expended to quell this widespread revolt, some British citizens, including the celebrated T. E. Lawrence (a.k.a. Lawrence of Arabia), chastised their government for inefficient policies that did not sufficiently allow for Iraqi self-determination.

After this revolt and the criticisms from the British public, the British decided to establish a system of indirect rule in Iraq, creating, at least in appearance, a constitutional monarchy. Unfortunately, this decision would fragment the nationalist coalition and also reaffirm the primordial place of the minority Arab Sunnis in the structures of government. As colonial secretary, Winston Churchill spearheaded this initiative at the Cairo Conference of 1921, afterward telling British representatives that a constitutional monarchy offered a more efficient and less costly way to rule. He and his colleagues chose Faysal I (1885–1933) as the sole candidate to put forward in a plebiscite to legitimize a brand new royal dynasty, the Hashemites. Faysal I, a Sunni claiming descent from the Prophet Muhammad, was born on the Arabian Peninsula and had no previous ties to this place. Faysal I, however, did understand the multiethnic and multisectarian nature of Iraqi society. As embodied in his coronation speech, he promised to forge a state based on respect for all citizens regardless of their faith or ethnicity. Nevertheless, he brought with him to Iraq a Sunni cohort composed of officers trained by the Ottoman Empire, thereby perpetuating the privileged position of Arab Sunnis.

Faysal's appointment as king led to the dissolution of the nationalist movement, and communal identities began to rear their head once again in Iraq. Many Kurds, for example, wanted their own country, and so they resisted endorsing

Faysal I as the king of Iraq. At the end of World War I, and as embodied in articles 62 and 64 of the 1920 Treaty of Sèvres, Europeans had promised Kurds self-rule of their own country of Kurdistan. Such a promise, however, soon became politically inconvenient, since it required commitments of money and manpower that the British did not want to expend in forging a new landlocked state. So, the British welded Kurdistan's southern regions into northern Iraq. British officers stationed in the north then bullied Kurdish leaders to accept Faysal I as their king.

And Shi'is, too, did not want to accept the Sunni Faysal I as their king. It was clear to this majority that such a royal administration would privilege the Sunni group to which his closest advisors belonged, thereby perpetuating Sunni dominance in Iraq. For this reason, the Shi'i cleric Mahdi al-Khalisi called upon his brethren to boycott elections in the British mandate of Iraq. In response, the British engaged in policies that reaffirmed Sunni dominance of the structures of government. They sent, for example, a number of Shi'i clerics into exile, men like al-Khalisi and his son, for they feared the anti-British influence of these clerics. And so, the British mandate deliberately perpetuated Sunni dominance in the state.

Sunnis continued to dominate state institutions after Iraq gained independence in 1932. Upon independence, Faysal I again expressed an intention to protect all religious and ethnic minorities in Iraq. Nevertheless, Faysal I and many Sunnis in his administration supported a pan-Arab ideology. Pan-Arabism proposed that Arabs of Southwest Asia and North Africa should have close political and economic ties, eventually unifying as a single state. For Faysal, who came from the Arabian Peninsula, this ideology legitimized his rule over Iraq. Pan-Arabism obviously leaves out Kurds from nation-building initiatives, but it can also set aside the interests of Shi'is, who may well be culturally constructed as "Persians." According to the political scientist Malik Mufti, the Iraqi proponents of this ideology were indeed "trying to suppress particularistic identities such as those of the Shi'is, Kurds, Christians, and Jews" (Mufti, 29). Thus, pan-Arabism conceptualized Sunni Arabs as the norm and inherently provided an ideological basis for maintaining Sunni dominance within Iraq's political structures.

Pan-Arabism shaped both foreign and domestic policy in independent Iraq. Faysal I did not go so far as to propose an amalgamation of Arab states, which the former British overlord would have vetoed, but he did propose holding a pan-Arab conference in Baghdad in order to have Arab countries discuss social and cultural issues of import. The fact that the king felt compelled to run this idea through the British Embassy underscores the neocolonial role of Great Britain in Iraq. In the domestic sphere, the Hashemite monarch appointed the pan-Arab ideologue Sati' al-Husri (1880–1970) as a professor at the Higher Teachers College. From his key position in the Ministry of Education, he propagated the pan-Arab ideology to young students in the Iraqi educational system. Given the Sunni identity of the political elites who constructed these policies, the pan-Arab initiatives inherently downplayed the contributions and local identities of non-Arab Iraqi citizens.

Certainly, intersectarian political violence immediately threatened the building of a functional state and coherent nation in independent Iraq. This violence occurred in August 1933, when some Assyrians began calling for regional autonomy vis-à-vis the national state. Assyrians are a Christian people with their own Syriac language. The British had relocated about 50,000 Assyrians from Turkey to northern Iraq during World War I, because they were being persecuted for their support of the Entente powers. The establishment of these refugees brought new demographic pressures to northern Iraq, and relations with the surrounding Kurdish tribes were tense. The British decision to arm 7,500 Assyrian men, forming special military levees outside the purview of the monarchical state, increased these tensions, for the British used these Assyrian levees to quell rebellions among Shi'i and Kurdish tribes.

When Iraq became independent, the Assyrian's religio-political leader, the Mar Shimun, who feared the Sunni-dominated Hashemite state, demanded regional autonomy. Many Iraqis construed such a demand as treason, for the demands for self-determination seemed to undermine the nationalist project of the Hashemite rulers. And so the Iraqi government sent troops to the north. Bakr Sidqi (1890–1937), a Kurdish officer, led these troops. The Iraqi troops brutally repressed the Assyrians, and the army was complicit in the slaughter of unarmed Assyrian peasants who were not necessarily active in an armed struggle to secure Assyrian rights. In this way, one of the first acts of the army of Iraq was the massacre of members of a small minority group.

The Assyrians, however, were not the only ethnic or religious minority to suffer at this time at the hands of the Sunni-dominated state, and this did not bode well for the forging of a unified national identity. In 1935, the Kurds of the mountainous north revolted against the Iraqi state under the aegis of the young leader Mustafa Barzani (1903–1979). In Baghdad, a rabbi recounted rising anti-Semitism, with the police thus bogusly reporting that a memorial service was a political meeting with antistate overtones. As for the marginalized majority, meaning the Shi'is, they celebrated with particular fervor the holiday of Ashura, which, marking the Sunni-Shi'i split of 680, commemorates the battle in which

Husayn, grandson of the Prophet Muhammad, was killed along with seventy-two of his followers. In this way, it seems that the Shi'is publicly highlighted their difference from Sunnis.

The rising sectarian and ethnic sentiments of the 1930s undoubtedly contributed to the political instability that marked these interwar years. In October 1936, there was a coup against the existing government, and this was the first coup d'état in the Arab-Islamic world. This coup complicates the picture of marginalization of some ethnic minorities, for its leader Bakr Sidqi was a Kurd. He had become a national hero in 1933, when Iraqi troops violently quelled any discussion of Assyrian autonomy. Further complicating this portrait of Sunni Arab dominance, Sidqi supported Hikmat Sulayman as prime minister. Sulayman was of Turkish origins, and his family had been quite influential during the final days of the Ottoman Empire. These men both represented minority groups, and, further, they worked to integrate more Shi'is (Fattah, 176). In this way, they tried to make "a clean, if temporary, sweep of the old ruling group that had governed the country since its founding" (Marr, 46). As the historian Phebe Marr points out, the new government contained "few Arab Sunnis and not a single advocate of the pan-Arab cause on which all previous governments had been founded" (47). The cabinet that they formed, however, would resign in 1937, after Sidqi's assassination by pan-Arab officers in the army. In retrospect, this coup marked the start of the military's domination of Iraq's political life.

Indeed, only four years later, in April 1941, another coup rocked Iraq. The coup's leaders—Rashid Ali al-Kaylani (1892–1965) and a group of officers referred to as the Golden Square—held pro-German leanings. They espoused a radical pan-Arab vision, which stemmed from their desperate desire to disencumber Iraq from its neocolonial dependence on Great Britain. They overthrew the cabinet and deposed the regent Abd al-Ilah, who favored a close relationship with Great Britain. With Europe fighting World War II, Great Britain could not afford to renegotiate its binational rights and obligations. Great Britain reassumed direct control of Iraq in May 1941, and it occupied the country directly for the duration of World War II.

This Anglo-Iraqi Thirty Days War fostered increased intersectarian divisions among Iraqis. Baghdad experienced what is remembered as "the Farhud," which signifies an anti-Jewish riot of two days. Some Muslim Iraqis, it seems, though certainly not all, saw Baghdad's Jews as complicit in the British takeover. This was at least in part because Jewish merchants were responsible for 95 percent of all Iraqi imports (Ghareeb, 125). In this way, some Iraqis thought Jews would benefit from the British takeover. The two-day riot left at least 187 people dead and led to the destruction of untold amounts of property (Shamash, 209). The shock of this anti-Semitic riot led many rich Jewish families to leave Iraq.

Great Britain ended its direct occupation of Iraq soon after World War II, but this did not bring an end to the political violence that marred the postwar experiences of independent Iraq. Great Britain sought to maintain its neocolonial role in Iraq. It therefore convinced leaders in the Hashemite regime to sign the unpopular Treaty of Portsmouth in January 1948, which allowed this European power extraterritorial rights in Iraq. The postwar Hashemite regime was corrupt, so existing state institutions, though liberal in theory, did not fully allow for popular participation in the government. Increasingly, the streets, rather than the ballot boxes, became the forum in which ordinary people expressed a desire for political change.

Communists in particular found a ready ear among the impoverished masses. In postwar Iraq, poverty was on the rise, and at least one poet chastised the poor for being politically passive. Communism provided an ideology that could mobilize these masses. And according to one Communist leader, this party transcended communal affiliations, bringing together Jews, Christians, Sunnis, and Shi'is against the Hashemite corruption. Indeed, the party played a large role in the riot that followed the signing of the Treaty of Portsmouth, a tumultuous few days remembered as "al-Wathba," or "the rising." The government made a concerted effort to wipe out the intersectarian Communist party, with many leaders going into exile. Thus, the construction of a political party transcending ethnic and religious affiliation threatened the Sunni-dominated state.

Despite the promise of Communism as a cure-all for intersectarian and interethnic rivalries, anti-Semitism was on the rise in Iraq in the years following World War II. This is due in some part to the foundation of the state of Israel in 1948, a situation that led Iraq to go to war in order to preserve this land for Palestinian Arabs. In the wake of this war, which led to the trouncing of Arab troops, many in Iraq conceptualized all Jews as complicit in what they perceived as anti-Arab policies of Israel. Responding to this populist outlook, the Hashemite government, clearly looking for easy ways to appease the restless masses, decided to pass a law in 1950 that seemed to encourage Jewish migration to this new country. The passage of this law led many Jews to immigrate. Nearly all Jews in the Kurdish town of Zakho, for example, felt compelled to migrate to Israel after the passage of this law. In this way, an international war fought against Israel in 1948 acted as a catalyst for further fragmentation of Iraqi society.

Despite the formal influence of the Hashemite elite or the informal pressures of the masses, it was ultimately the back rooms of military headquarters where political change was decided. Iraq experienced another military coup in 1958, one led by Gen. Abd al-Karim Qasim (1914–1963), who intended to take Iraq out of "the pocket" of Western powers, like the former British overlord and the ascendant American superpower. This coup differed from that of 1936 and 1940, when military officers sought only to force a change in government. This coup instead aimed at razing the Hashemite monarchy. Thus, Qasim's coup was a violent affair, leading to the assassination of the entire royal family in the courtyard of their palace. Qasim then expressed an intention to establish a republic that would distribute more equitably the country's increasing oil wealth. Fearing disenfranchisement, some Arab Sunnis plotted Qasim's overthrow the next year, though the coup attempt by Abd al-Wahhab al-Shawwaf in Mosul failed to dislodge Qasim.

It was during the five-year reign of Qasim that the Iraqi state's relations with northern Kurds again broke down. Qasim's regime seemed at first to promise the further incorporation of Kurds into the Iraqi nation. Thus, Qasim allowed Mustafa Barzani, who had been exiled after a revolt in 1945, to return to Iraq. Also, Qasim appointed a Kurd to a three-man governing council (Yildiz, 16). And yet, the Iraqi government could not tolerate discussion of any autonomy around the oil-rich northern areas surrounding the northern cities of Kirkuk and Arbil. By 1961, Barzani understood that Qasim would never permit any form of Kurdish autonomy, and he withdrew his support for Qasim's republic. Instead, he decided to round up his soldiers, called *peshmergas*, and fight the Iraqi government. In this way, the policies of the reactionary government established to decrease Western influence in Iraq deepened ethnic tensions.

By the early 1960s, the Arab Ba'th Socialist Party became a force with which to contend. This party espoused a secular pan-Arab ideology that was supposed to reflect the will of all people in the Arab world, regardless of their religious belief. Indeed, the founding ideologue of the Ba'th Party, the Syrian Michel Aflaq (1910–1989), was a Christian. Aflaq argued that European powers had artificially divided the Arab nation. Thus, members of the Ba'th adhered to an anti-imperial ideology, and so opposed European and American meddling in the Middle East. In the economic sphere, the Ba'th enunciated a desire to evenly spread the wealth of the old elite fostered by colonialism. At first, it seemed that the secular Ba'th Party would incorporate Shi'is into the leadership of the party, and more than 50 percent of the party's civilian leaders were Shi'i in the early 1960s (Ghareeb, 222). Such intrasectarian power sharing did not endure, for Sunnis reasserted their dominance in the party after it took power.

The Ba'th organized two coups in Iraq during the 1960s. In 1963, the Ba'th organized a coup against the government, and the ruler Qasim was immediately executed. The Ba'th, however, at this time, ruled for only eight months, before it too was overthrown by Abd al-Salam Arif (1921–1966). It was not until 1968 that the Ba'th had enough strength to organize the coup that resulted in the thirty-five-year Ba'thist regime. The Constitution promulgated by Iraq's Ba'th Party in 1970 suggested that the party's leaders—President Ahmad Hasan al-Bakr (1914–1982) and Vice President Saddam Hussein (1937–2006)—would adhere to the basic tenets of this socialist and populist ideology, even while acknowledging the ethnic and religious diversity of Iraq.

Despite this Constitution, the Ba'th Party constructed a totalitarian state that privileged Sunni Arabs. Hussein led behind the scenes until 1979, when he assumed the presidency and became Iraq's official president. Under his aegis, the Ba'th sought to bring all aspects of the lives of its subjects under its control, including such intellectual pursuits as the writing of history. The Ba'th Party also manipulated networks of patronage in order to ensure loyalty to the state, and this policy led Hussein to improve the status of women. Although some people balked at the state's interference with daily life in Iraq, others wholeheartedly supported the Ba'th. The poet Hameed Said, for example, who was also the editor of the Ba'th's official newspaper *al-Thura*, believed wholeheartedly in a pan-Arab ideology that would bring together Arab peoples in order to block rising Israeli power in the Middle East.

It was, however, the Ba'th's absolute monopoly on violence that allowed its leaders to use fear to maintain control, and ethnic and religious minorities as well as the Shi'i majority did not fare well. In 1969, for example, two years after a crushing Arab defeat by the Israeli army, the Ba'th manufactured a spy scare that led to the public hangings of Jewish citizens falsely accused of espionage. In the wake of this tragedy, most of Iraq's remaining Jews decided to emigrate from Iraq.

Jews, however, were not the only communal group to suffer during the early years of Ba'thist rule. In the north, Barzani came to see that initial Ba'thist conciliation had been no more than a way to consolidate power. So, once again, he organized a revolt against the Iraqi state in 1974. This war led to the displacement of thousands of Kurds, who wound up in poorly provisioned Iranian refugee camps for much of the 1970s.

The Ba'th in particular targeted the beleaguered Shi'i majority, for they were beginning to organize against the injustice of the Iraqi state. Networks of patronage evolved under the Ba'th that favored Sunnis, particularly those of Tikrit, Hussein's hometown, as well as other Sunni-dominated places in Iraq's central regions. By the 1970s, Shi'is, increasingly disillusioned by Sunni sway, represented no more than 5 percent of party leaders (Ghareeb, 222). In response to this uneven distribution of power and resources, some Shi'is began to turn to religion as a means of opposing the state. Muhammad Baqir al-Sadr (1931–1980) was the most famous cleric to sway Shi'i radicals. In 1970, he became the leader of the Dawa Party, and he proposed that Iraq should be ruled as a theocracy, not as a secular Ba'thist fiefdom. In response, Hussein's Ba'th Party targeted Shi'is who used religion—particularly the Ashura commemorations—to vocalize a protest against the state.

Wars with foreign powers helped solidify Ba'thist rule, for Iraq fought two cataclysmic wars during the Ba'th's thirty-five-year rule. The Iran-Iraq War was fought between 1980 and 1988, and it killed as many as one million people. Expecting a quick victory against the newly formed Shi'i Islamic Republic, Hussein ordered the invasion of Iran on 22 September 1980. The Ba'thist president then exiled 250,000 Iraqi Shi'is, claiming that their loyalties were to the enemy polity (Ghareeb, 223). Hussein would argue that the fighting of this war saved the rest of the Islamic world from radical Shi'ism and further Islamic revolutions. A quick victory, however, was not to be. The war, which is also called the first Persian Gulf War, lasted eight brutal years. Much like World War I, soldiers fought from trenches, and their commanders ordered the use of poison gas. Fighting such a war of attrition requires a lot of manpower, and the numbers in the Iraqi army grew to staggering numbers. The Ba'th eventually felt compelled to recruit high school students to fight the war. The horrors experienced by the soldiers fighting on the front made it difficult to reincorporate veterans into civilian life, which disturbed family life and the social system of Iraq. The Iran-Iraq War ended on 20 August 1988, although the cease-fire, based on United Nations Security Council Resolution 598 (hereafter cited in the text as UN SC Res), was not signed until 1990.

This war had horrible repercussions for the northern Kurds. During the Iran-Iraq War, the secessionist aspirations of some Kurds led Hussein to fear that these northern people would assist nearby Iran in defeating Iraq. In this way, Hussein thought, they might earn their long sought political autonomy. And so, the Ba'th, in a campaign referred to as "al Anfal," targeted Kurds at the very end of the Iran-Iraq War. Thus, Hussein allowed the use of chemical weapons against Iraqi citizens. As many as 100,000 Kurds were killed and hundreds of thousands were displaced (Ghareeb, 13–14). Thus, a war with a foreign power gave this pan-Arab ideologue a means of asserting a self-serving Sunni Arab supremacy over the state government.

The Persian Gulf War was the second international war fought by the Ba'thist regime, and it took place in January and February 1991. This war started when Hussein, thinking that U.S. Ambassador April Glaspie had given a green light, decided to invade Kuwait. Hussein invaded Kuwait because the country, which refused to forgive Iraq's war debt, was overproducing oil, thereby causing international market prices to collapse. After the invasion, the United States and its allies immediately implemented Desert Shield, a defensive operation designed to protect Saudi Arabia from Iraq's expansionist ambition. President George H. W. Bush effectively used the United Nations to institute the legalities necessary to remove Iraq from Kuwait by "all necessary means." Then, on 16 January 1991, these powers, and diplomatically supported by the United States' erstwhile Cold War Soviet enemy, implemented Desert Storm to take Kuwait from the Iraqis. Thus, they immediately bombed Baghdad, the headquarters of Hussein's army, which unduly harmed the civilians in the capital city. According to Jordan's Queen Noor, this war fostered long-term instability in the Middle East, because it created a huge refugee crisis.

This refugee crisis worsened in the wake of the Persian Gulf War, because the Iraqi government violently quelled anti-Ba'thist uprisings in the Shi'i south and the Kurdish north. In the south, many disillusioned Shi'is began to take over the holy cities of Karbala and Najaf, thereby expressing their rejection of a regime that had caused them such hardship. In the north, many Kurds, with the memory of al Anfal still fresh in their minds, decided to revolt against the government. The Iraqi army, though weakened by the Persian Gulf War, still had access to the manpower and equipment, particularly armed helicopters, needed to put down these revolts. Many Kurds fled as the army began to reassert Iraqi control over their regions. The historian William Cleveland estimates that "2 million Kurds headed toward the Turkish and Iranian borders" (Cleveland, 486). American policymakers, though desiring an end to the Ba'thist regime, did not support these internal revolts, for it was beyond the purview of the diplomatic structures established by the United Nations resolutions. Once again, an international war, just as in 1941 and between 1980 and 1988, had caused Iraq's political society to fragment along ethnic and sectarian lines.

The Persian Gulf War did not really end for Iraqis with the signing of a ceasefire in February 1991, for the United Nations maintained a sanctions regime against Iraq that may have led to as many as 1.5 million deaths. The United Nations had imposed the sanctions on 6 August 1990 in order to force Iraq to withdraw from Kuwait. Thus, Iraq could import neither medicine to heal its citizens nor fertilizer needed to grow crops. The United Nations maintained the sanctions after the Persian Gulf War in order to ensure that Iraq disclosed and destroyed all weapons of mass destruction. In 1995, the United Nations would temper this resolution by allowing for the exchange of oil for food, but, given that it was the corrupt Ba'thist regime that implemented it, this program did not give respite to the general population of Iraq. The historian Charles Tripp estimates that only 500,000 people, and this out of a total population of 26 million, benefited from the Oil-for-Food Program (Tripp, 259). Protesting against this inhumane sanctions regime, Denis Halliday, the U.N. humanitarian coordinator of the Oil-for-Food Program, publicly resigned. These sanctions had a horrible effect on women and children, who were particularly vulnerable to the penury of basic food items and medicines. Some 4,500 Iraqis under the age of five years old died each month from malnutrition and preventable diseases (Ghareeb, 210). The deleterious effects of sanctions did not foster movements that would take the Ba'thist regime out of power, although U.S. policymakers hoped that it would. Thus, the American government passed the Iraq Liberation Act of 1998, which promised aid to Iraqi groups trying to oust Hussein and the Ba'th regime.

In 2003, however, the U.S.-led "Coalition of the Willing" ousted Hussein and his Ba'thist cohort from power. The American war drums began beating soon after 9/11. Iraq did not directly support al-Qaeda in these attacks, but Hussein was the only leader in the world who lauded them. President George W. Bush argued that the invasion of Iraq would assist the United States in its task to fight terrorism. Others, like the influential Brent Scowcroft, felt that this would be a distraction from targeting al-Qaeda operatives. Bush adequately made his case to the American public and their representatives, and the United States and its allies invaded Iraq on 19 March 2003.

At first, the U.S. invasion encouraged Iraqis to overcome their communal differences and act as a unified nation. Just as in 1920, poetry became a vehicle for expressing an Iraqi identity that transcended ethnic and religious communalism. Anti-Western sentiments, once again, played an important role in rhetorically bringing Iraqis together. The Iraqi exile Salah al-Hamdani published a poem that highlighted the historic victimization of the people of this land to the oppressive influence of Western powers. The Ba'thist president also called upon nationalist feeling. Hussein published a letter calling on all Iraqis, regardless of communal affiliation, to fight the forces of Halaku, a not-so-veiled reference to the Mongol hordes who invaded and occupied Baghdad in 1258.

The actual invasion of Iraq lasted no more than forty-two days. In the fighting, as in the Battle of Nasiriyah, it was difficult for U.S. soldiers to distinguish between soldiers and civilians among the Iraqi population. Nevertheless, U.S. troops occupied Iraq by 9 April, helping to tear down a statue of Saddam Hussein. Unfortunately, U.S. troops did not have orders to stop the rampant looting that followed in their wake, and as a result Iraq lost some of its most precious relics in the National Museum. Despite this inauspicious start, President George W. Bush declared a stunning victory. On 1 May 2003, President Bush gave his now infamous "Mission Accomplished" speech, whereby he declared major combat operations over and looked forward to the occupation.

The U.S. occupation, much like the British occupation after World War I, heightened ethnic and religious tensions within Iraq. The United States planned to rule directly over Iraq for the first year, and so it established the Coalition Provisional Authority under Lt. Paul Bremer. Bremer, however, as recounted in his memoirs, reproduced a communal Iraqi society in creating an Iraqi Governing Council. Thus, he appointed members based on their communal identity, not on their political leanings. In U.S.-occupied Iraq, access to power was by virtue of birth into specific communal groups, not on ability to represent overarching political interests of various popular groupings.

During this first year, an unanticipated insurgency broke out that bespoke heightened communal tensions among Iraqis. There were the Ashura bombings of March 2004, which targeted the Shi'i majority during a commemoration that distinctly reflected their unique history and culture. In the shadow of these bombings armed Shi'i groups, like the Mahdi militiamen, organized themselves and began to fight the United States. In the central region, the so-called Sunni triangle, an amorphous insurgency broke out that was, in part, an effort to oust the foreign occupier while also preserving Sunni dominance over the structures of the state. Ultimately, the insurgency became a civil war in which different communal groups vied for power and control of the government in post-Ba'thist Iraq.

And so, the first one hundred years of Iraq's formation as a modern state failed to definitively resolve the tensions between national unification and communal fragmentation. This unresolved tension arises from a variety of factors. First and foremost, the meddling of international powers has undoubtedly contributed to perpetuating a system of governance that favors communal identities. The British mandate, much like the Ottomans, privileged Sunnis, and the constitutional monarchy that they established in 1921 set the stage for the later attempts at rectifications by disadvantaged groups. The Sunni power brokers in Iraq, however, must also take their share of the blame, for all too often the leaders of this country, despite their pan-Arab rhetoric, have treated the structures of government as a personal fiefdom, raining favors down, as the Ba'th did, on members of their own communal groups. As a result, the struggle to define a unified nation and break free of communal identities is still an ongoing struggle in Iraq.

Within this complex history of events and peoples, one cannot help but wonder if our bride Regina of 1903 would recognize her homeland in the present day. Currently, there are no more than a handful of Jews who continue to reside in Iraq (Stephen Farrel, "Baghdad Jews Have Become a Fearful Few," *New York*

Times, 1 June 2008). Certainly, Regina could not have imagined that nearly all Iraqi Jews would emigrate from the country. This fact alone prevents us perhaps from trying to guess what else Regina may have thought of her homeland. Would she have been horrified by the plethora of wars and regimes that have plagued her homeland over the past 108 years? Or would she have felt sympathy for a people who proved resilient in the face of historic traumas? Certainly, she would have acknowledged the distinct political and social history of this relatively new country, one that makes Iraqi identity unique and memorable.

1

Ottoman Mesopotamia, 1903–1920

In the early twentieth century, Iraq was not an independent state. Instead, the area of present-day Iraq consisted of three provinces of the Ottoman Empire, and this imperial polity had ruled over them for nearly four hundred years. The Ottoman Empire consisted of more than twenty million people in twenty-nine provinces that spread over three continents. The three provinces in Mesopotamia, the premodern designation for the area of present-day Iraq, each centered on a principal city: Basra in the coastal south, Baghdad in the central plains, and Mosul in the mountainous north. The Ottomans, a Sultanistic dynasty legitimizing its rule through Islamic beliefs, implemented a system of decentralized rule, meaning that the Sultan appointed *valis* (governors) to act in his stead in provincial capitals. Despite this system of decentralized rule, or, more accurately, because of it, the Ottomans took pains to ensure that their provinces stayed within their political control.

And yet, centripetal forces were at work in these three provinces. In the early twentieth century, Mesopotamia consisted of 2.2 million diverse people. Of this population, 60 percent lived in rural areas (of them 17 percent were nomadic) and 40 percent lived in cities (Marr, 7). Of these, more than half were Shi'i and about 20 percent were Kurdish, with another 8 percent composed of Jewish, Christian, Yazidi, Sabaean, and Turkmen minorities (Tripp, 31). These people had little sense of having an Ottoman identity, and some of them began to attempt to exercise provincial autonomy and even independence from the central Ottoman administration in Istanbul. This was as true of the agas who led tribes in the rural areas as it was of the effendis, or urban-educated elite in the major cities.

Complicating matters, European powers, which had already colonized the Ottoman provinces of Algiers and Cairo, also exercised a substantial indirect influence within the Mesopotamian territory. They did so by developing commercial relations with the people there. The British East India Company, for example, had established contacts in Mesopotamia in the late eighteenth century, leading Great Britain to establish a consulate in Baghdad in 1802. The Great Powers, like

France, as will be seen below, also exercised influence through cultural institutions, such as schools set up for boys and girls. Germany even invited Mesopotamian soldiers to its country in order to complete their military training.

Some present-day readers might conceptualize the area of Iraq at the turn of the twentieth century as stultified and backward, but this chapter provides evidence that this region was a dynamic place connected to the outside world. This chapter begins with a description of encroaching Western influences in Baghdad. It continues with a description of Mosul by Lt. Col. Mark Sykes, a diplomat who would later sign an agreement with France that ensured that Mesopotamia was within the British sphere of influence. In 1908, the Young Turks Proclamation set up liberal institutions like elections in Iraq and throughout the Ottoman Empire. Many, like Ottoman officer Jafar al-Askari welcomed these changes. The Sultan Abdul Hamid II was deposed the next year, and another Ottoman soldier expresses ambivalence toward the event. As described herein, some landlord-sheikhs found liberal democracy inconvenient, and they fought to preserve tribal autonomy. In Baghdad, however, many welcomed the liberal transformation, sending petitions to the government to increase even more local control over their city.

The outbreak of World War I in 1914 did not put an end to Mesopotamian cosmopolitanism, though it did halt some of the political transformations taking place there. At the war's start, the British army took over Basra, and it would achieve Mosul by 1918. As documented below, a lawyer from India visited Basra during the war, and he described the increasing and very patronizing control of the British over this port. The British, however, did not easily take the rest of Mesopotamia, and an American wrote a description of Sunnaiyat, which, near Kut, was the site of one of the worst battles in this theatre of operations. British troops arrived in Baghdad in March 1917, and Lt. Gen. Sir Stanley Maude's proclamation to the people of that city promises a new Golden Age. This chapter also includes the memoir of a Baghdadi Jew who remembers the joy with which urban residents welcomed British troops.

The Wedding of Regina, 1903

Baghdad was a cosmopolitan city, and not, as could also be argued for all provincial capitals, an imperial backwater. Steamers ran up and down the Tigris-Euphrates river system. There was a postal service that allowed foreign travelers to keep in contact with their families. Telegraphs connected the people of the city to the outside world. Construction on the Baghdad Railway began in 1903, and trains would eventually run from Konya in Turkey to Baghdad. The city also had a streetcar line as well as a public library. At least fifty schools were open in Baghdad, including one run by the Carmelite Order of priests. Both boys and girls attended (Issawi, 123–25).

There were approximately 150,000 residents of Baghdad at the turn of the twentieth century, and of these, 53,000 were Jews. Thus, the Jewish community is an important component of not only the city's history but also that of Iraq. The Alliance Israelite set up a school to teach Jewish boys and girls in 1864. The Alliance Israelite is a French-Jewish organization that served Jewish peoples in Muslim lands of the Mediterranean region. This organization was a key institution of westernization in Iraq, and Europeans exercised cultural influence through it. The following is an account of one graduate taken from Aron Rodrigue's *Jews and Muslims: Images of Sephardi and Eastern Jewries in Modern Times* (Seattle: University of Washington Press, 2003). As you read the following account of this graduate of the Alliance Israelite, you should consider the following: What is the attitude of the author toward Baghdadi Jews? Why does she laud Regina? What consequences does she anticipate in regard to the education of Jewish women? What does this suggest about the role of women in the institution's commitment to a "civilizing mission"?

Baghdad, 4 February 1903

The whole city was talking about Regina's wedding. I should tell you first that Regina is one of our former students. People were saying, "Yes, Regina is *à la franca*" (the expression means "European-style"). "She is making her own trousseau with the help of a seamstress who comes from the West. She is sending for clothes from Europe, she won't accept jewelry from here, and her hair is all curled like a sheep."

The day of the ceremony people came from every part of town to see the young bride *à la franca*. As she was one of our students, I thought it important to go see her that day. The crowd was thick; with difficulty I was led through it to a room on the second floor. The young bride had just finished dressing. She looked beautiful but exhausted. "Why do you look so tired?" I asked her.

"It's because I've worked very hard, night and day, with only one person to help me." And tears began to well in her eyes.

There was a lady who was a friend of mine in the room; she came over to me and said, "Do you see how the poor thing has grown thin? Well! It's because she has had to fight; she has fought for every item in her trousseau. And it's not because her parents refused her anything, but because the things that were brought her were not to her taste. Her parents want her to buy a fabric which is too gaudy. She won't accept it. Or else it's an ankle bracelet they want her to wear. She refuses. Or else they want her to wear rouge and henna on her hands and to paint her nails black; she protests. Again today," my friend continued, "she sent for me to come to her aid. She wanted to wear her hair the way she's used to wearing it in school; they wouldn't let her do it. They were trying to force her to hang heavy gold rings on the ends of her braids. The poor girl isn't used to them; they would make her ill."

She started coming to school when she was still very young, so she has never worn them. "The poor little thing," I thought to myself. Finally the groom arrived. A rabbi gave the blessing. What a contrast there was between those two young people. In her white satin dress with a long flowing train, carrying orange blossoms, a net veil covering her face, she was altogether the European bride but for the few excessive adornments that it had been impossible not to wear.

He wore a *ziboun* (the local traditional costume) woven in gold thread, with a great cloak over his shoulders. He must not have attended the school and so had not had time to become a little civilized. But what difference does that make? Now his wife is seeing to that task. She has him wear European dress, she dines at the table with him and not in the kitchen, in contrast to all the other women in Baghdad, and against the wishes of everyone in the family, she dresses according to what she sees in the newspapers she receives.

She does not hide herself from visitors, even when they are gentlemen coming to see her husband. She has not forgotten the school, and, with the permission of her husband, she stops by from time to time to visit her former classmates. She takes as much care of her home as she does of her person. A short time after her wedding I visited her at home, and the house was clean and in good order. Even now she must often struggle to maintain what she has accomplished.

Sometimes her husband refuses all change; she is often mocked by her in-laws. From a distance, her husband's mother and sisters look upon her actions with apparent malevolence. They tell each other, "We'll see if she will be able to do this, if she really knows how to sew." They are biased against the girls from the school because the latter know how to read books, and in this place a *savante* [a learned person] (that is what people call the girls who have finished school) could never be a good housekeeper. But our former students are proving these people wrong. They have been successful in whatever changes they have undertaken in their homes, and now people are finding them sensible and capable.

Regina has a baby and she takes care of him well enough. The first few times she gave him his bath her mother-in-law ran out of the house saying that

Regina was going to kill her child. But she does not run away anymore, for she sees that the baby looks healthy. She even takes pleasure in seeing him clean and nicely dressed.

This is a student who truly has succeeded, but how much she had to go through to do it! At the same time there are others who fail in spite of their great energy. The proverb says, "The goat cannot graze beyond the length of its tether." No doubt it tries to reach farther but resigns itself when it cannot.

In the end, these first students are victims, for it is hard to live in a house where everyone looks at you with an air of defiance. The struggle against so many people joining forces against them, against their ideas, against their actions, is very difficult for these young women to endure. Nevertheless, their efforts are not lost. What they have not been able to attain for themselves, they will leave for their children to do. A new generation will begin with them. It will be more enlightened, more aware, more capable of understanding the morality taught them in the schools. Here, as in all noncivilized countries, women are very ignorant. They do not accept innovations. They are like servants in the home but they always manage to get their husbands to do what they want. This power of influence is truly extraordinary. Because it is so, once this influence starts being exercised by the young women who have studied in our schools, it will serve to improve the conditions of family life.

Lt. Col. Sir Mark Sykes on Mosul, 1906

In the years before World War I, Europe's Great Powers did not have a specific intention to colonize the Ottoman Empire. For example, many politicians in Great Britain, those belonging to the Conservative Party, intended to prop up the Ottoman Empire in order to prevent tensions between its Great Power counterparts and also to forestall Russian expansion into the Mediterranean basin, which would have upset the balance of power. For this reason, British politicians proved willing to overlook what they considered cases of misgovernment by the Ottoman Sultans. It will not be until the outbreak of World War I, when the Ottomans sided with the Central Powers (Germany and Austria-Hungary) that European politicians, particularly those in France and Great Britain, will rethink the fate of the Ottoman Empire, considering the notion of a colonial system as a useful solution to a looming power vacuum in the Middle East.

Lt. Col. Mark Sykes (1879–1919) was a key figure in the construction of British policy in Mesopotamia. He was a diplomat who traveled often to the Ottoman Empire in the years leading up to World War I. As such, his writings reflect the information that the British, politicians and public alike, received on

Mesopotamia and other areas of the Ottoman Empire. Sykes, it should be noted, was a member of the Conservative Party, so he actively sought to strengthen Ottoman control in the years leading up to World War I. This Great War, however, fostered a major rethinking of British policy. In 1916, he would, in concert with French politician François Georges-Picot, hammer out the Sykes-Picot Agreement, which secretly divvied up the Arab regions of the Ottoman Empire into distinct spheres of postwar influence. In retrospect, this agreement seems a clear indication of a Great Power desire, eventually realized through the mandate system established in the San Remo Agreement of 1920, to colonize this area.

Given Sykes's role in eking out a postwar British policy, it behooves the readers of this book to consider how this traveler-cum-diplomat conceptualized places in Mesopotamia. The following passage comes from Sykes's *The Caliphs' Last Heritage: A Short History of the Turkish Empire* (London: MacMillan and Co., 1915), 337–39. The second half of this book consists of the journal entries of Sykes, which he wrote as he traveled through various outposts of Ottoman lands. As you read the passage, you should consider the following: How does this reflect a British tendency toward a "civilizing mission"? What are the principal notions that Sykes holds toward the people of Mosul? How might this attitude have affected later policies?

> Mosul I found the same foul nest of corruption, vice, disorder and disease as I have always known it. In eight years it has made neither visible progress nor improvement. Once Mosul was a greater town than it is now, but I see no cause for regret that its filthy purlieus are less in size than they were. It is not difficult to perceive that neither art nor industry has flourished in Mosul for the last two hundred years. The new houses are as ramshackle, as insanitary, as stinking as the old; the old as ugly, as uninteresting, and as repulsive as the new. A brilliant sky gives no charm to this town of mud and mortar. Its blind alleys are narrow, evil-smelling, and as unpicturesque as those of Whitechapel; its mosques as devoid of architectural merit as a railway station. The people seem heavy, debauched, and stupefied by their surroundings. Apathy and greed are their characteristics. The shiftlessness of the Bedawi and the huckstering spirit of the pedlar combine to produce a stagnant and unpleasing personality, which ... would bode ill for the new railway. But it is well to note that Moslem and Christian alike are anxious for the railway to be built, and that most of the faults of the men of Mosul arise from their long isolation in a pestilent climate. People even tell one that agriculture is on the increase, and that in spite of raids, locusts, and lack of transport, things are a little better than they were a few years ago. I was told by a leading merchant that, taking all in all, there

was a net increase of 150 villages in the province. Yet Mosul is an evil city. By night robbers stalk untouched from house to house, and the time of rest and darkness is made fearful by the cracking of pistols and confused cries of strife. By day, drunkenness and debauchery are openly indulged in. The population is rotted by the foul distemper, corrupted and rendered impotent by drink, stupefied and besotted by vice. The degradation of the city folk is not only physical but mental. Tales are whispered of dark and hideous sorceries and incantations—the noisome stench, as it were, of the charnel-house that dead Paganism which the Cross and Mohammed have slain, but have as yet been unable to annihilate.

To my mind Mosul stands as a menace to the future of the surrounding country, and I cannot help thinking that the projectors of the new railway would do well to try to avoid the town. The standing nuisance of this sink of disease and horror will not be mitigated, but rather increased, by wealth; and if Mosul, in its present condition, becomes the chief town of a flourishing northern Mesopotamia, it will certainly contaminate the surrounding locality with the same sinister influence as Antioch of old spread over North Syria. Although the idea may appear fantastic, I would strongly suggest that it would prove in the end a gain to the investor's pocket, if the company built the railway station ten miles from the site of the present city, and so laid the foundation of a newer and cleaner Mosul, in which some attention might be bestowed to sanitary regulation and public decency. The present city is so congested, and house-building is so cheap, that the project presents really but few practical difficulties.

My last view of Mosul was typical of the whole place. Well within the city, a cluster of some three hundred houses stands by the river. This quarter is the abattoir and tannery and dyery for the whole town. Its streets are ankle-deep in decaying guts and offal; the kennels run with congealing blood and stinking dye in sluggish and iridescent streams, nauseous to behold and abominable in odour. A fume of decaying flesh hangs in the air; piles of dung, horns, and hoofs stand in the filthy alleys, while here and there the puffed carcasses of beasts, diseased and cast aside by the butchers, lie an offence against the sun. The houses are daubed with clotted filth, while naked men flit to and fro upon their noxious business. Yet, incredible as it may seem, there are families who dwell within this loathsome zone; men, women, and children inhabit these greasy dens, not from poverty or lack of better lodging, but from sheer idleness and apathy. The government has twice endeavoured to abolish this vile lair of dirt and pestilence, but on each occasion the attempt has provoked a riot.

The Young Turk Proclamation of 1908

Due to the Iraqi provinces' connections to the outside world, the incorporation of this area into the Ottoman Empire is critical for understanding the history of this place in the early twentieth century. The political life of the Ottoman Empire changed drastically in 1908. At that time, a group known as Young Turks forced the Sultan Abdul Hamid to reinstitute the Constitution. Abdul Hamid had come to power in 1876 promising to uphold constitutional reform. He was, however, an autocrat at heart, so he set aside the Constitution two years after coming to power. The Young Turks who opposed him consisted of the following groups of educated elite: immigrants living overseas, imperial bureaucrats, and a number of army officers.

Although Istanbul was thousands of miles from the three provinces of Mesopotamia—now Iraq—the proclamation had important effects here. Sarah D. Shields has studied Mosul in the late nineteenth and early twentieth centuries, and her book *Mosul Before Iraq* clarifies just how sensitive people in this region were to political changes taking place in Istanbul. In the city's hinterland, she writes that "The 1908 Young Turk Revolution in the Ottoman Empire reverberated throughout the far flung provinces, and the confusion led to increasing brigandage and insecurity in the countryside around Mosul" (Shields, 179). Concerned about precipitous political change, there was a riot in Mosul immediately following the proclamation (27). Nevertheless, a few months later, the city sent two delegates to the first Parliament, one Muslim and one Christian (61). In other words, there was a political dynamic inspired by both support for and, as will be shown in another document, opposition to the reforms issued by the Young Turks.

For this reason, it is important to analyze the reforms emanating from Istanbul. Below, you will find some of the key aspects of the Young Turks' proposed reforms. This excerpt is taken from "The Young Turks," translated by A. Sarrou, in *Civilization since Waterloo*, edited by Rondo Cameron (Itasca, Ill.: F. E. Peacock Publishers, 1971), 245–46. As you are reading it, you should consider the following questions: What are the specific reforms advocated by the Young Turks? How do these reforms affect the political ideology of the imperial structures of state? What is the role of religious minorities as conceptualized by the Young Turks?

> 1. The basis for the Constitution will be respect for the predominance of the national will. One of the consequences of the principle will be to require without delay the responsibility of the minister before the Chamber, and, consequently,

to consider the minister as having resigned, when he does not have a majority of votes of the Chamber.

2. Provided that the number of senators does not exceed one-third the number of deputies, the Senate will be named as follows: one-third by the Sultan and two-thirds by the nation, and the term of senators will be of limited duration.

3. It will be demanded that all Ottoman subjects having completed their twentieth year, regardless of whether they possess property or fortune, shall have the right to vote. Those who have lost their civil rights will naturally be deprived of this right.

4. It will be demanded that the right freely to constitute political groups be inserted in a precise fashion in the constitutional charter, in order that article 1 of the Constitution of 1293 A. H. [1876–77] be respected....

7. Turkish ... will remain the official state language. Official correspondence and discussion will take place in Turkish....

9. Every citizen will enjoy complete liberty and equality, regardless of nationality or religion, and be submitted to the same obligations. All Ottomans, being equal before the law as regards rights and duties relative to the State, are eligible for government posts, according to their individual capacity and their education. Non-Muslims will be equally liable to the military law.

10. The free exercise of the religious privileges which have been accorded to different nationalities will remain intact....

16. Education will be free. Every Ottoman citizen, within the limits of the prescriptions of the Constitution, may operate a private school in accordance with the special laws.

17. All schools will operate under the surveillance of the state. In order to obtain for Ottoman citizens an education of a homogenous and uniform character, the official schools will be open, their instruction will be free, and all nationalities will be admitted. Instruction in Turkish will be obligatory.... In official schools, public instruction will be free. Secondary and higher education will be given in the public and official schools indicated above; it will use the Turkish tongue. Schools of commerce, agriculture, and industry will be opened with the goal of developing the resources of the country....

Jafar al-Askari on Corrupt Ottoman Administration in Iraq

Jafar Al-Askari (1885–1936) was a leading politician during the British mandate and in the years immediately following independence. He was born in Baghdad, though his name refers to the Kurdish village of Askar, from which his family came. He was the son of an Ottoman officer, and he, too, became an officer. He studied at the Military School in Baghdad and the Military Staff College in Istanbul. Before World War I, the Ottoman government would send him to Germany for further training.

Al-Askari's politicization began at an early age. In the years before World War I, he belonged to the secret society *al-'ahd*. This society opposed an increasing emphasis on the Turkish identity in the Ottoman Empire, and its members wanted more rights—if not independence—for people in the Arab territories. Despite his opposition to Ottoman ideology, Al-Askari fought for the Ottomans during World War I, until the British captured him. After his escape, however, he joined the Arab Revolt of Sharif Husayn and his son Faysal. With the support of the British, most notably Lawrence of Arabia, they fought the Ottomans in order to ensure the postwar creation of an Arab state.

When the British set up a mandate in Iraq, Al-Askari returned to his homeland with King Faysal. There, he would play a key role in establishing the Iraqi military. He served as minister of defense in 1920–1922, 1930–1932, and 1935–1936. He also served as prime minister in 1923–1924 and 1926–1928. Al-Askari would be assassinated in 1936 by forces loyal to Bakr Sidqi (1885–1937), who had organized a coup.

The following excerpt describes Al-Askari's experiences in the Ottoman army just before and immediately after the Young Turk Revolution of 1908. It is taken from his posthumously published memoir *A Soldier's Story: From Ottoman Rule to Independent Iraq*, translated by Mustafa Tariq Al-Askari and edited by William Facey and Najdat Fathi Safwat (London: Arabian Publishing, 2003), 19–22 and 27–28. As you read it, you should consider these questions: What are Al-Askari's complaints about Ottoman administration? Is it possible that Al-Askari's later role in the Iraq mandate and in independent Iraq colored his memories?

> Maladministration at both central and provincial levels meant the Ottoman provinces were in constant turmoil during Abdulhamid's reign, and the government was never able to collect from them without mounting costly military campaigns. Poverty was rife, due largely to the government's mismanagement, negligence and complacency. In common with autocrats before and since, Sultan Abdulhamid never put himself to the trouble of considering the welfare of his people. He was interested only in the preservation of his life and the enhancement of his wealth, power and influence at the expense of his alienated subjects, whom he treated as if they were his worst enemies.
>
> Salaries and allowances used to be paid for only a few months of the year. I well remember how, after four years' service in the Ottoman army and just

before the new Constitution was proclaimed, I was owed 30 out of 48 months' pay. Corruption was rife, and bribery was considered neither immoral nor shameful. In administrative districts where the collection of taxes required military coercion, officers would plead with their commanders to be assigned to such campaigns so that they could extort enough money from the populace to compensate for their unpaid salaries. Officers used to approach their commanders quite unashamedly: "Our salaries are overdue," they would say. "We have wives and children at home and the Eid is coming, so please assign us to such-and-such campaign."

I myself took part with my regiment in one such campaign to the *qadha* or administrative district of Samawah. The local treasurer gave me a list of debtors from the Safran tribe who according to him owed overdue sheep tax. So I went forthwith to the tribal chief with 50 soldiers and demanded the arrears. He replied that this was impossible as his tribe was on a "tax strike": they had decided never again to pay any taxes; but that he was prepared to help me if I wanted to try to collect the money directly from them myself. I agreed to his proposal and distributed the men among the various clans of the tribe, giving each NCO a list of the taxes due in his appointed clan. I myself took 10 soldiers to find somewhere to sleep by the riverside and collect what I could from the water-wheels. We spent the night at the house of a . . . cultivator who slaughtered a lamb for us, laid before us all the delicacies he could afford and in general was most hospitable. In the morning I asked him to pay the tax on the ten ewes overdue from the previous year. He assured me that all he had was the lamb we had eaten the previous evening and that, if I did not accept the situation, he and his four sons were ready to fight us, to the death if need be, to release themselves from their miserable existence.

This made an enormous impression on me. Having gathered together the soldiers I had sent to the other clans I went back to the chief, and asked him how he dared present me with names of persons who could not possibly be in debt to the government. After much threatening and long argument he confessed that it was . . . normal for local treasury officials to demand large sums of money from sheikhs . . . such as himself, on the pretext that it had to be passed to the district and provincial governors who were supposed to send it on to Constantinople. Only by extorting such huge sums from the poor could sheikhs like him afford to lease state domains for their own cultivation. I was astonished to hear such a candid admission, as until then I had been completely unaware of such skullduggery.

This was my first practical experience of such things, a year after my graduation. The military commander was Yusuf Pasha, an honest and virtuous man of great dignity who was an old friend of my father and who, I occasionally felt, showed that he was well-disposed toward me. His headquarters were in Samawah, so I went there to see him in person and told him the whole story. He smiled and said: "Don't be dismayed or let the experience get you down. I shall see that this treasurer is severely punished." And he did . . . remove him from his post.

Before I left Samawah, there took place another curious incident that shed a revealing light on how tradesmen viewed government officials. I had been ordered to assemble a number of sailing craft for the transport of army stores to the south. I had managed to commandeer just five large *mahailahs* when the owner of one . . . came up and asked for a word in private. By way of prelude, he proffered a small cloth pouch containing five *mejidis* (gold coins), worth about 30 shillings in those days.

"What's this for?" I demanded.

"Please let us off this job, Sir. We have urgent contracts to carry grain, and this is a small gift so that you can release us. There are plenty of other boats available, Sir."

I returned the money to him, sternly stating my position: "Your proposal is illegal and I cannot accept it."

He was obviously somewhat taken aback, but he went away and came back a little later with double the amount. I saw red and shoved him away.

"Push off before I put you under arrest," I threatened.

He replied: "I don't blame you, because you're still young and innocent. Normally a quarter of this amount is enough to get ourselves out of forced requisitions like this."

This type of thing corrupted government officials and of course made the people less trusting of the authorities. . . .

After the proclamation of the Constitution in July 1908, the Ottoman government tried to put its house in better order. Salaries and allowances began to be paid on time and reforms brought a noticeable improvement to conditions in the army. Nadhim Pasha was appointed Governor of Baghdad and General Officer commanding all forces in Iraq, and brought with him a competent military staff and civilian administrators. . . . Mahmoud Shawkat Pasha was Minister of War in Constantinople and he embarked on the reform of all aspects of the Army, in particular its equipment, training and education. Several . . . army officers, chosen by competition, were sent for . . . training in Germany. I was . . . among the first group to go there—in 1910, while I was a subaltern serving in my regiment stationed in the Aadhamiyyah suburb of Baghdad, named after the famous Imam al-Aadham Abu Hanifa buried on the site of the mosque that bears his name. At the same time Lt. Nuri Al-Said, who was in the same battalion as me, passed the entrance examination to the Royal Staff College in Constantinople.

Sultan Abdul Hamid Deposed, 1909

In response to the Young Turk Revolution of 1908, some conservative Ottoman subjects initiated a countercoup on 13 April 1909. They wanted to eliminate the secularist leanings of the Young Turks and reinstate the autocratic power of the Sultan. The army, however, prevented these reactionary elements from succeeding in reversing the constitutional advancements of the Young Turks. Two weeks later, on 27 April 1909, these soldiers decided to depose Abdul Hamid II and replace him with his brother. At that time, a British traveler named Gertrude Bell was in the countryside of the Mosul region. She describes how the people of this region heard of the Sultan's deposition as well as the response of one of them. This letter is taken from a web page sponsored by Newcastle University Library (accessed 9 February 2010, http://www.gerty.ncl.ac.uk) that archives Bell's letters. As you read the passage, you should consider the date of the letter, which indicates the rapidity with which news spread in the Ottoman Empire. You should also reflect on the response of the soldier and the Arab informants to this news.

> 28 April 1909. This morning we woke up in the middle of the corn fields where we had camped and everything smelt sweet of crops and growing things. Very cheerfully we packed and breakfasted for we were only 4 hours out of Mosul and it is always exciting to reach another stage of one's journey. So we rode off and we had not been riding more than an hour before, from behind the little ridge that separated us from the town, we heard the boom of a cannon, and then another and more and more. We all looked at each other doubtfully and Fattuh said: "What is that?" but there was no one to answer. We rode on through the green corn and the smiling sunny landscape till we met an old man. I stopped and said "Why are they firing cannon in Mosul?" He lifted up his hands and said "God knows! Perhaps it is news from Stamboul [Istanbul (Constantinople)]. One man says one thing and one another. God knows what is true." We rode on a little further and met two ragged people coming down the road. Fattuh said "When did you leave Mosul?" "At first dawn" they answered. "What was happening then?" said Fattuh. "Nothing" said they "when we left, wallahi! Nothing." So we left them standing in the road with anxious faces turned toward Mosul where the cannon still boomed out from behind the hills. After a few minutes two Arabs came hurrying up behind us on their mares, one

carried a great lance. Fattuh called out "Whither going?" "To Mosul" they said. "What is your business?" said Fattuh. "We heard the sound of the cannon" they shouted back as they galloped up the hill. We were very near the top now and my soldier went with them. But just before they reached the top, a party of 4 or 5 horsemen came riding slowly over the ridge, and they stopped and talked for a moment and then they all rode back toward us. "These have news" said Fattuh. We gave the salaam and I said "What is the news?" They answered "Reshad is Sultan." "God preserve him!" said I. And so we . . . went on our way. After a minute or two my soldier said: "All the days that Abdul Hamid was Sultan we never got our pay." And that is the only native comment yet heard on the news from Stamboul.

Tribal Rebellion near Mosul, 1909

Some people in the Ottoman Empire did not welcome the Revolution of 1908, which ushered in reforms intended to foster liberal secularization. Tribal leaders in Iraq did not favor a system of political rule in which power and influence was passed through elections, because it threatened the communal basis of their own influence. And further, the Young Turks did not respect the patronage networks created by Abdul Hamid II, who co-opted local notables by giving them administrative posts. In fact, the Young Turks, organized as the dominant party the Committee of Union and Progress (CUP), were bound and determined to exercise more control over Ottoman provinces, thereby decreasing the authority of tribal sheikhs. In this way, democracy threatened the interests of tribal chiefs, who base their power and influence on communal birthright.

Ely Banister Soane was an Englishman who traveled to the Mosul province in 1909, and his account reveals the extent to which some sheikhs opposed the Ottoman system. Soane was fluent in Farsi, so he ventured to Mosul and its hinterland disguised as a Persian. One of the tribes that he encountered there was the Hamavands. They were a Kurdish tribe who moved between the area of Mosul and Persia, now present-day Iran. Soane estimated that this tribe consisted of about twelve hundred families.

Soane recounts how members of the Hamavand tribe engaged in raids against the Ottoman troops. This excerpt is taken from his memoir *To Mesopotamia and Kurdistan in Disguise* (London: J. Murray, 1912), 287–91. As you read it, you should consider the following: Who are the targets of the Hamavand ire? Can we depend on this traveler's account? Why? Why not? What effect did the acts of the Hamavands have on townsmen in this region?

In the bazaar and coffee-houses there was but one topic of conversation these days—the Hamavands. We heard rumours of their intention to raid Sulaimania, and at nights their riders came openly to the shaikhs' house to receive their orders. Once or twice they actually looted a few houses on the west side of the town. Not a soul dared venture forth. Matti used to tell me of happier times when the Christians and Kurds too used to go outside upon the low hills and spend days in the cooler air picknicking to the accompaniment of music—and I suspected, in the case of the Christians, too much 'araq. But now, to venture outside the fringe of houses upon any except the north-east side was to court robbery, if not destruction. And then the futile talk of the "ta'qib," or punishment that was to be dealt out to the tribe! We heard reports—and these seemed true—of regiments of soldiers from Anatolia and Mesopotamia collecting at Chemchemal, and judging from letters coming from Mosul and Baghdad, we were able to keep a check upon rumour, and ascertained that there were in reality some three or four thousand military, foot and "mule-riders," gathered there—to extinguish a couple of hundred rough horsemen. All these troops were kept idle by the Mosul authorities to wait for a commander, and as long as funds from the sheikhs poured into the Mosul Vali's pocket, the commander was kept engaged in pressing business elsewhere, and the Hamavands redoubled their audacity, actually raiding Chemchemal itself and killing some soldiers.

Meanwhile, the state of the district was becoming worse, for travelers were threatened not only by roving parties of ... Hamavands, but by the ... soldiery also, for the "binbashis" had consumed what little cash could be collected for their pay, and the "muhasibichis," or accountants, grew daily fatter upon sequestrated funds. Soldiers were leaving for their native places, or retiring over the frontier to Persia—taking with them their new Mauser rifles; and in Halabja a colonel commanded five half-tamed Kurdish levied men instead of his usual fifty.

Then the affair occurred which threw ridicule and despair alike upon the Turks in the district. A quarter "tabor," or about one hundred men, was ordered to replenish the Sulaimania garrison, which from a normal five hundred men had fallen to thirty-four. These were also used to convoy about seventy rifles and proportionate ammunition for distribution among the frontier posts. They started from Chemchemal, commanded by a colonel ("binbashi") and two majors (or "yuzbashi"), and accompanied by several "'askar katibi" (accountants), and other Government officials with their wives and families. Across the Chemchemal plain they saw no signs of Hamavands, though they threw out scouts, and those sent forward to reconnoiter at the Bazian cleft through the hills saw no one. Consequently they approached the break, where the sundered hill presents a V-shaped entrance to the Bazian plain, without misgiving. The place is so formed that from the Chemchemal side it is impossible to see ahead very far, as the ground rises, and the break is only about ten yards wide at the bottom, sloping up and away to the hill-tops.

When they had passed the outcrop of rock that forms the break, and the last man had entered Bazian, the hills above them suddenly rang with the shouts of the Hamavands, and from each side they raced down helter-skelter, their hill-ponies leaping cleverly down the boulder-strewn slopes. At a distance of fifty yards they opened fire, and the first to fall was a "yuzbashi." The soldiers gathered in a bunch, and the non-combatants attempted to rush back through the gap, to find themselves confronted by three or four horsemen, who fell upon them and stripped them, leading away their loaded animals. The Turks were returning the fire, but, taken at a disadvantage, made no effect upon the . . . Hamavands, who wheeled around them. Yet they held out for a little, and attempted to push forward.

In point of numbers the Turks had the advantage, and their weapons were ten-shot Mausers as against Martini carbines, but their shooting must have been of the poorest, for they only succeeded in wounding one Hamavand. Several, too, tried to break away, and were immediately picked off. In a quarter of an hour the "binbashi" fell, shot through the chest, and twelve soldiers, too, were dead, and a score wounded. The remainder cast away their arms, seeing resistance futile, and the Kurds came upon them and stripped the caravan, relieving it of all its rifles and ammunition, carrying away or tearing off the soldiers' uniforms, and looting the noncombatant passengers. There was an indescribable confusion; soldiers on foot and unarmed strove to escape on all sides, and horsemen with the shouts of a drover to his cattle rounded them up. Squads of Hamavands, driving before them mules of the defeated party, shouted at and encouraged their refractory and frightened captives. As is usual in these cases, everything was . . . done with . . . speed, and the Hamavands, infuriated by the resistance they had met with, were more merciless than usual to those whom they stripped. The men they . . . denuded, and scared the women with fierce gestures and displays of long knives to make sure of their handing over anything they might have concealed.

One of the women who had been robbed told me that some of the Hamavands had brought their wives with them, putting them behind rocks while the fight proceeded, and calling them out afterwards to enquire into the dress of the female captives more intimately than a man could have done; for in these

Muslim lands even among the wildest Kurds, a man will seldom offend a Musulman woman's modesty, and the Hamavand is a ... pious tribe, stopping ... its raiding parties to pray ... at the appointed times.

The men they left in little more than a shirt—and at last cleared off, taking with them the wife and daughter of one of the majors, whom they subsequently restored after having placed them in the care of the chief's womenfolk for a time. The remains of the caravan, twos and threes of half-naked men, and weeping women, proceeded on foot, reaching Sulaimania next day, hungry and ashamed.

It was not unnatural that the possibility of such catastrophes, and their actual occurrence, did a great deal of damage to the Turkish name, and indeed in the coffee-houses opinion was freely expressed. The Turks were jeered at, and their soldiery ridiculed. The sheikhs were rapidly becoming a terror to Sulaimania.

Baghdad Petition, 1910

In 1908, the Young Turks expressed their intention to bring about new political freedoms, including the right to form political parties. In Baghdad, some people took them at their word. According to Charles Tripp, "a variety of groups emerged in the three provinces, aimed at securing political advantage or reform" (Tripp, 21). According to this historian, there was "an explosion of journals and newspapers" as well as "the proliferation of clubs, groups and societies" (22). A "civil society" began to emerge. This term signifies that individuals formed groups outside the bounds of communal affiliations in order to pursue shared interests transcending tribal, religious, or ethnic identifications. Nevertheless, and as forefronted by Tripp, "their concerns were still those of subjects of the empire and the boundary of their political world was still effectively the boundary of the Ottoman Empire itself" (21). Certainly, however, the Young Turk Revolution of 1908 generated new ways of engaging state power.

The following document gives voice to some residents of Baghdad who, though appreciating Ottoman policies in general, did not like the specific reforms implemented by the governor Nadhim Pasha. The British embassy in Baghdad got hold of it, and the Resident John Lorimer had it translated and sent to London. Stamped "Confidential," this British agent considered it significant. As you read this document, you should consider the nature of the political concerns of the writers. What do they demand? Are their concerns local or imperial? Do the writers oppose the political structure of the Ottoman Empire? How do they conceptualize the structure of politics in the postrevolutionary era? You may be interested to know that Nadhim Pasha will be relieved of his duties in March 1911 (accessed 9 February 2010, http://www.gerty.ncl.ac.uk/letter_details.php?letter_id=1808).

> A memorandum presented to His Majesty Sultan Mohammed Rashad Khan V (may he long live); to the Right Honourable Hakki Pasha, the Prime Minister; to all the members of the Cabinet; to the Senate and Parliament; and to all Ottomans.
> To the whole Arabic press in Egypt, Syria, Tunis, America, and Constantinople; to all those who pronounce the letter "dhad" correctly (i.e. to all Arabs); and particularly to His Excellency Mahmud Shaukat Pasha, the victor of Constantinople, who is a native of Irak.
> To His Majesty the Khalif, the aristocracy, and all our brethren according to the Constitution.
> Men of tender sympathy and intelligence, is there any help for the people of Irak now that matters have reached a climax? A Nazim ("reformer") has come to us who, by his efforts, is not likely to improve our condition, but rather to make us to shirk or revolt. It need hardly be said that Irak is a country to which the attention of all Ottomans is directed, owing to the fertility of the land and the numerous rivers that run in it, and which, if properly looked after, could be made like the Garden of Eden where God created Adam.
> In the time of the Abbasite dynasty Irak attained to the highest pitch of civilization, education, and industry, and had no equal in any respect. This is a fact well known to all those who have a knowledge of history. But when the Abbasite dynasty was abolished, the schools were closed, the arts were neglected, and everything deteriorated.
> Irak was reduced to such a pitiful condition that it occasioned grief to all its well-wishers and joy to all its enemies; and it continued in that state until the time when the constitution was proclaimed, the reactionary Sultan was dethroned, and all his subordinates were degraded. Then we praised Almighty God and looked to the Committee of Union and Progress, which had taken the reins of administration into their hands. When the events mentioned above took place, we all expected that Irak would attain its former prosperous condition.... All the world was eagerly watching to see the progress which Irak would make, and how it would be turned into a land more fertile than Egypt.
> ...
> ... Nazim Pasha was appointed vali of our vilayet, commander-in-chief of the VIth Army Corps, and "reformer" of Irak, including the vilayets of Musal, Bagdad, and Bussorah. We were pleased at this appointment, as the word "reform"

sounded pleasant in our ears, and made us forget the last post which Nazim Pasha held when Abdul Hamid, in conjunction with Kamil Pasha, tried on the 31st March to overthrow the Constitution and the Committee of Union and Progress. No better man could be found for the appointment than our "reformer," the supporter of the Constitution, &c. He was made Minister of War without the sanction of Parliament, and there followed the overthrow of Kamil Pasha's Cabinet and of the arch-autocrat Abdul Hamid. . . .

Yes; the people of Irak forgot—or, rather, feigned to forget—Nazim Pasha as an autocrat. They looked to the brighter side of things, and as he came as a "reformer" they expected some good of him, and they awaited his arrival as anxiously as a good Mahommedan [sic] keeping the fast awaits the appearance of a new moon. At last His Excellency arrived with a large staff of officers . . . and a . . . reception was given to him. The people received and treated the Pasha with great respect, not because they were cowards and dreaded him, but because they did not want to interfere with his work of reform. They felt that if they interfered he would oppress the people as a preparation for justifying his shortcomings before Parliament when the time came for him to give an account of all his dealings in Irak to the nation—which time, we hope, is not far off.

The new Nazim ("reformer") arrived in Bagdad grave and self-confident. He began to make the reforms, of which mention is made hereafter, without consulting anyone.

On the day of his arrival, when he entered Bagdad, in order to show his strength and influence, he refused to receive any of the notables who came to visit him.

The first time that he presided over the Administrative Council he asked the clerk to read . . . papers to him, and all the time he kept nodding his head as if he knew all the conditions of the vilayet by divine prescience. All the members were treated like pieces of wood, he never consulted them; and when any members ventured to object he cried out, "It is settled."

A further proof of his self-confidence is the fact that, after according Suleiman Nazif Bey (the Vali of Bussorah) an enthusiastic reception on his arrival at Bagdad, he did not listen to him or ever agree to his suggestions, although Suleiman Nazif Bey was in Irak before Nazim Pasha and had more experience in its affairs. Finally they could not agree, and Suleiman Nazif Bey returned to Bussorah. This disagreement gradually assumed a bitter form, and it has turned into an enmity which exposes two vilayets to grave danger.

. . . we give below some of his reforms which may serve as a sufficient proof of his having been born an autocrat.

1. Suppression of the Arabic Language. The first reforming order which Nazim Pasha issued was that no petition or document should be submitted to Government at Bagdad or its dependencies in Arabic, and that if such documents were submitted, they should not be taken into consideration. He issued this order in the official newspaper "Zaurah." The people of Bagdad were thunderstruck . . . for they knew that most of them did not understand Turkish, and that, if they obeyed the order, their business would be delayed and their rights violated. When it was proposed in the . . . press that the language of the Kuran should be made official like . . . Turkish . . . , the press at Bagdad kept silent about Nazim Pasha's arbitrary order for fear of him.

It was only the "Rakib," of which the editor . . . is well known for his liberal ideas, that dared to criticize this Nazim's . . . reform which was contrary to common sense. He did so in a couple of well-chosen lines which caused Nazim Pasha to send him this message: "If you mean to criticize me personally, I will excuse you; but if you intend to criticize the action of the Government, I will break your neck." The editor was greatly alarmed by Nazim's fury and the official message. He became sensible that there was no freedom of the press, as provided in the Constitution; and henceforth he began to burn the incense of false eulogies before the vali. By this action Nazim Pasha gave the first blow to the Constitution of Irak.

It is one of the principal articles of the Constitution that the press should be free. The press being the mouth-piece of the people, it is through the press that the Government hears of the grievances, &c., of its subjects and is enabled to take steps for remedying them and for improving the condition of the people. Freedom of the press, which has wrought wonders in other countries, was conferred by a law passed in both Houses of Parliament after the establishment of the constitution by the sword; and it therefore cannot be violated by any person, however exalted his position. The same inviolable law also permits any person to criticize the action of any administrative official or officials, on condition of his criticism being impersonal and well founded; consequently Abdul Latif Effendi Thinaiyan was right in his criticism and ought not to have been interfered with by Nazim Pasha. . . .

3. Making Wide Streets in Bagdad. The reforms mentioned above are nothing in comparison with another great improvement which the wise Nazim ("reformer") has ordered. He saw that the streets were very narrow and old-fashioned, and not sufficiently wide for his carriage to pass. He has directed the opening out of wide streets, 20 metres broad, and he has asked for sanction to spend £T. 100,000 on the work, whereas, if he intended, to treat the houseowners fairly, he ought to have applied for £T. 2,000,000. In spite of the complaints of the people he has begun to put his plans into execution. A member of the committee informed Nazim Pasha that the inhabitants of Bagdad were all grumbling at having their houses pulled down, and suggested that a site should be chosen outside the town where a new town could be built according to the latest system, as at Aleppo and Damascus. What do you think his Excellency said? He said in a sarcastic tone, "If you go against my will, you had better not attend a committee meeting again...."

As an example of the hypocrisy of some of us, a few notables... went to the vali, Nazim Pasha, and volunteered to forego compensation for their houses which were to be taken for the streets. They aimed by their action at securing the goodwill of the vali.... This is due to their ignorance of constitutional principles, under which valis and judges are merely automata in the hands of the law. Those who have... contributed to the vali's plan lose nothing, for they are well-off; but they cause a large number of poor people to lose their... houses in the abyss which Nazim has opened. The rich lose nothing because their houses are large enough to spare a portion for this road, together with a likelihood of getting double price for the rest; but the poor will be crushed. No one can appreciate the calamity which has befallen the poor... through the... policy of Nazim except those who have visited and have seen the poverty of the inhabitants....

We have thought over the question carefully, but we cannot see that it is of any benefit to the inhabitants in general. If by opening a main street it is intended to make the city look better externally, we say that it would be better to improve the personal condition of the inhabitants first. If it is with the view of allowing plenty of room for carriage traffic, we reply that the people of Bagdad are too poor to afford carriages now, and that, when they grow rich, thanks to Nazim Pasha's reforms, it will be... to take measures to widen the streets.

Besides all this, the expenses of making the street will be a burden on the municipality of Bagdad; and the municipality will spend all its income in merely paying the interest on the money, and will not be able to spare anything for the improvement of the town.... Governments should devote the proceeds of loans to productive works so that by means of the profits, they can pay off both capital and interest." Will not Nazim... take into consideration and respect this important principle of economy?...

5. Removal of Arab Officers. The fifth of Nazim Pasha's reforms consists in the removal from the VIth Army Corps of all Arab officers—some by placing them on the retired list and others by sending them to remote places—and their replacement by Turkish officers. Wise men... took this as a sign of his bad intentions, or at least as a hint to the Arabs that he was their enemy;

notwithstanding that the Arabs, since the establishment of the constitution, have considered themselves the equals of their brethren the Turks in all civil rights, among which is employment in Government service. By Nazim's action bitter feeling has been renewed in the breasts of the Arabs, also hatred of the Turks, in spite of the allegiance which they show the Government. . . . Nazim has not been content with removing the Arab officers only; he has also begun to dismiss the civil officials one after another. . . .

We advise our Government at Constantinople not to wink at arbitrary actions which may lead to bad results, but to treat us as their equals according to the Constitution, so that we can co-operate with them in upholding the glory of Islam and of the Ottoman Khalifate. Nazim's oppressions cannot crush or kill us, whatever he and his subordinates may think, but they will cause our rich land and our strong men to be lost to the Government.

Conclusion. We meant at first to seek the assistance of the Bagdad press in presenting our complaint to the State, but Nazim permits no freedom, and again we reflected that, if we telegraphed it to Constantinople, he would intercept it. We therefore, the doctors and wise men of Bagdad, held a meeting, secretly composed this pamphlet, and sent it to Egypt to be printed and distributed.

. . . We do not wish to be anything but Ottomans, or anything but constitutionalists. We say this in order that alarmists may not accuse us of being reactionaries. . . . [W]e hereby curse all reactionaries, saying: "Damned be all who advocate the re-establishment of the era of Abdul Hamid; the curse of God and his Prophet be upon all despots, past, present, and future; the curse of God and his angels rest on those who make distinctions between the races comprising the Ottoman Empire!"

. . . Be it known to all Ministers, members of Parliament and notables, and to the press, that we are loyal supporters of Ottoman unity, and that we pray for the continuance of the Ottoman dynasty. But, if justice is not done and our complaint is not heard, we will, with the assistance of the Committee of Union and Progress who overthrew the throne of Abdul Hamid . . . overthrow the throne of Nazim Pasha, for we all hate despotism and have sworn to fight it. We do not think that there are any left amongst us who would consent to undergo further oppression after the thirty-five years' cruel reign of Abdul Hamid. . . .

Written at Bagdad this 10th day of Jamadi-al-Akhir, 1328 (corresponding to 17th June, 1910).

British Military Rule in Basra

The area of present-day Iraq was an important arena of military engagement during World War I. Fighting in Mesopotamia began at a very early date. The Ottomans declared war on the Entente powers in October 1914, and the British occupied Basra the next month. The British occupied this port city in order to protect its colony in India. They also wanted to protect the oil refineries in nearby Abadan. This last reason was made all the more important by the fact that the British had switched from coal to oil fuel in 1912. Basra had long had commercial links with India and English merchants, and the British easily occupied this city. From Basra, they would head north up the Tigris River, eventually reaching Mosul in 1918.

As shown in the following passage, the occupation of the Ottomans' Mesopotamian provinces wrought important changes for the people there. C. M. Cursetjee recorded these changes in *The Land of the Date* (1918; reprint, Reading, U.K.: Garnet Publishing, 1994), 172–75. Cursetjee was a Parsi, that is an Indian with Iranian heritage who practiced Zoroastrianism. He was sixty-nine when he traveled to the war-torn Gulf region in 1916. He was an educated man, being a lawyer trained in England. He made this voyage in order to visit his nephew, a decorated soldier in the Mesopotamian Expeditionary Force. As you read this passage, you should consider the point of view of the writer. How does his position as an Indian influence what he sees and how he presents it? What aspects of British rule does he find commendable? What aspects does he find abhorrent? How did the British occupation affect the lives of people in this port?

> Since the Turk has been thrust out, [Basra] and its environs is under the sway of a British Military Governor and for the present is governed by martial law. This is a necessity no doubt under war conditions, but it would be well if it be tempered by goodwill, tact, and practical good sense. Already the *vis inertiae* that so long brooded over the land is giving way before new activities as is seen by numerous signs of improvement and progress in many directions. Some of these signs may be trivial but it is the lifted straw that shows which way the wind blows. Anything like a reliable town police was unknown in Basra before the advent of the English. Even before sundown it was the enforced custom for all house doors to be closed and securely locked. After 4 p.m. no women of any respectability could safely venture into the streets. Roughs and foot pads abounded and had it all their own way. The police was inefficient, the courts corrupt. There was no such thing as street lighting. Sanitation was unknown, no attempt was made to make or mend roads. All this is now changed.

In Ashaar and Basra European soldiers and Indian sepoys now regularly patrol and police the streets and the river by day and night. Everybody feels and must be thankful for the security this has brought about for person and property. At night kerosene lamps well lighted are put up on posts, or hang down from hooks or brackets projecting from house walls at proper intervals and at convenient corners. The English quarter is lighted by electricity. Scavengers sweep the roads at stated times and cart away all dirt and rubbish. New roads are laid out and old ones taken in hand and turned to something like carriage-ways. Cinders and boiler sweepings from the steamships afford cheap and excellent road material, so the same is commandeered and utilized accordingly. A couple of steam rollers (when they arrive) will surely provide Basra with as good roads as could be desired. Motor-cycles, the emblem of speed and dispatch, are already to be seen in the streets of Ashaar and the Strand Road. The native Arab is already taking to the bicycle. It was amusing to see a large Arab, his flowing overgown well tucked in around his waist with sandaled-shoon, treadling a safety-cycle. Street boards showing names of streets and localities in Roman and Arabic characters are put up at obvious ends and corners and some of these names, more than most things, argue British possession in a telling way, as for instance, 'Governor's Road,' 'Emperor's Road,' 'Oxford Street,' 'Jaipur Street,' 'Crooked Lane,' 'Club Road,' 'Church Street,' 'Hyde Park Corner.' Other signs are not wanting to emphasize the new order of things. The Gymkhana and the Club are already there. The Y.M.C.A. is there as I have said before. . . . A racecourse is already there at Makina in the direction of Mergil run according to the W.I.T.C. rules, with a couple of totalisators and all the needful turf accompaniments to make horse-breeding profitable and edifying to, as providing object lessons in popular morals. The clergymen and the jockey are estimable English institutions and ever go hand in hand to indicate a British possession. Race days are instituted which the people consider and sanctify as public holidays when all Basra, Ashaar, Mohomerah, Abadan and other neighbouring places flock . . . to Makina where the hippodrome is, to take part in Basra's sport of kings.

Wherever British rule extends, prestige, that bugbear or bogie whichever you care to call it by, is of course set up as a worshipful fetish and so it is now in Basra. Orders are out and strictly enforced, according to which the *pas* must be conceded to the European, soldier or civilian cockscomb or brass-hat, chief or sub, by the aborigines of the place high or low. The *topee* or helmet is the too obtrusive symbol of foreign sway, almost to the extent . . . of Gesler's hat in the market place of Althorp. If two or three Britishers choose, as they usually do, to walk abreast in the narrow streets, the Arab or other nondescript native or stranger must willy-nilly take the wall. If some of these swells coming riding in a back-victoria, and another Victoria with 'native' gentlemen comes from the opposite way, the latter must pull up to let the all-imposing, over-exacting sahibs pass. Soldiers stand sentinels at the ends of the bridge, which connects north and south Ashaar, to prevent natives using the main or central broad passage when a sahib, the all-highest entity, is on it or about to cross; they the erstwhile owners of the country must wait or crowd on to the very narrow strip of planked footway on either side of the bridge till the sahib and even the *statutory* Anglo-Indian leisurely stalks over. The hack-driver and the *bellamchi* are required under penalties to give preference to this sort of European fare even if his conveyance is already engaged by a native. A Mr. Swayne in a volume recently placed before the public and much puffed by some too friendly critic, recommends violence as necessary and right to keep the *bellamchi* and his like in order if inclined (according to the European's fancy) to be disrespectful, or to claim more as his due than what the latter chooses to allow. He cites with approval a clergyman thrashing a native and a Russian officer throwing another into the Shat' for some fancied slight or want of the servility the lordly Westerner thinks fit to exact. The priest surely forgot the teachings of his Master and the Russian was what he is bound to be—a *kuzzak*. Yet our English author recommends these samples of Christian meekness of spirit as meet for imitation. This same sapient Englisher, wise in his own conceit, gives it as his opinion that in a country like Mesopotamia indulgence in alcohol is 'humanising in effect,' and proceeds to clinch this counsel of perfection by saying that if the prophet forbade it, 'it is worth remembering he permitted other things.' If report be trusted both alcohol as well as the 'other things' are much indulged in our new possessions on the Shat' in a way that is of course not quite on the surface. This unthinking truculence which the author above referred to so inaptly and so fatuously recommends is, I find, aptly illustrated in a cartoon of a recent issue of the *Basra Times*, where is exhibited a British subaltern or clerk in shirt-sleeves, pretending to speak to his Hindu attendant in the vernacular and misunderstanding the reply, violently kicks the unfortunate servant out of the room. This may be a comic presentment of British prowess and prestige, but is apt to lead to tragic consequences. This elegant cartoon is headed 'Budged,' and if the newcomers do not mind their ps and qs, this sort of thing might bring about their budging in earnest from the country, 'where the Arab is not' likely to be so long-suffering as the Indian. . . . Anyhow, all I and others who care to give a right thought to it can say is that the sooner such and other similar bureaucratic methods and antics for enforcing respect and upholding of prestige are discouraged and discountenanced, the better it will be for the peace and prosperity of these new provinces which the fortunes of war have added, let us hope permanently to the British Empire.

The Horrors of World War I

Although the British easily occupied Basra, the rest of their engagements in the Mesopotamian theatre would not be so easy. From Basra, the British began to move up the Tigris River. By November 1915, these troops were within fifty miles of Baghdad. Ottoman forces, however, drove the British back to Kut. There, the Ottomans besieged the British for four months, and the latter surrendered in April 1916. It is estimated that 23,000 British and Indian soldiers lost their lives in this engagement. Approximately 8,000 men surrendered, and half of them later died in labor camps. The British would need several months to regroup. They began again to conquer Kut in December 1916, definitively taking it in February 1917. From Kut, the British had a base that allowed them to continue to advance on Baghdad.

Eleanor Egan visited the site of this fighting very soon after the British conquered Kut. Egan was an American journalist writing for the *Saturday Evening Post*. She visited the frontlines in Mesopotamia in 1917 and 1918, just after the United States had entered the war on the side of Entente alliance and only months after the British had secured Baghdad. She describes her visit to Sunnaiyat in her book *The War in the Cradle of the World* (New York: Harper, 1918), 195–99. Egan's narrative does not give voice to local peoples, only British officers. The historian, however, often extrapolates information about local conditions based on the accounts told by foreigners. How does the following excerpt capture the conditions of the people living in the area of Kut? What disruptions did the war cause to local people living in this land?

> Just before we reached Kut-el-Amara we came to the battle-field of Sunnaiyat, one of the ghastliest of all the historic fields of Mesopotamia. For my benefit we banked in and went ashore. I had heard the fearful tales, and I wanted to see the fearful setting of them. I climbed the camel-thorny slope of the high Bund, and stood for a moment gazing across the far-flung network of crumbling, shell-riven trenches. That is all Sunnaiyat now is. All—except that the trenches are filled with dead men's bones. Sunnaiyat—the name of a waste place where men have suffered as men have suffered on few spots on earth....
>
> Within hearing distance of Kut, the men besieged at Kut listened to the thunder of the guns of Sunnaiyat for weeks on end—and with what prayerful hope who has the power to imagine? And it was at Sunnaiyat that the Turks

made their last desperate stand against General Maude's victorious army in 1917, the three days' battle that raged then over the already blood-drenched and historic ground being one of the fiercest and costliest fights of the whole campaign.

This was the fourth battle of Sunnaiyat, the first three having been fought in April 1916, during the course of the last tremendous effort the British made to relieve General Townshend.

It was high noon when we landed, and the sun, searching through thick sweaters and coats, burnt one's skin with a dry, prickly burning, while the wind blew penetratingly chill across the mournful waste. And I was glad of the healthy discomfort because my flesh crept with the horror of the things I saw and the things my mind was forced to visualize. The Arabs have always searched and looted the battle-fields—and they do not rebury the dead!

I have been on many battle-fields before—in France, in Serbia, in Belgium. But they were battle-fields eloquent of living love; clothed for the most part with green things and having white crosses hung with immortelles to mark the graves of the fallen who were buried where they fell. They seemed, those battle-fields, as thresholds between suffering faith and triumphant realization, and I remembered thinking in the scarred ... green fields of ... Lorraine, that I might lie down with my ear against the wholesome earth and hear God's heart beat.

But Sunnaiyat, in Mesopotamia—land of ancient battles and Cradle of the World—Sunnaiyat is gashed and ghastly, naked and piteously ashamed. To have marked the resting-places of the dead on this or on any other remote field of heroes in this unholy land would have been only to invite an even more hideous outrage. So trenches were filled and great levels were made, and one can only thank God that the British graves are left practically undisturbed.

Yet, one wants to cover the bones of the Turkish dead, too. One wants to say to them: 'Rest in Peace! Boys of a people at war with invincible human right, you fought for the triumph of your own beliefs, or as you were commanded to fight; as it was given to you to win your badges of heroism, you have won. Rest in Peace!'

Out on the edge of the intrenchments there were creeping figures bent over in eager search of the sacred ground. Arab ghouls! Not yet satisfied after so many months? No, not yet satisfied. They would pick up something and gather in an eager group to examine it in the sunlight. Nothing. They would toss it aside and go on creeping—creeping. . . .

I wonder how many of them had tossed aside the precious thing I found. It was lying near the entrance of a British trench—an old leather bayonet-scabbard all burned and blackened at the end, as though some one had been poking a fire with it. And of course, some one had. Some blessed Tommy, perhaps coaxing the coals under his supper while shells whistled over his head. He had either died or he had thrown it aside in a rush to meet the enemy hand to hand. So much of this fighting was hand to hand.

I stood and pondered over the old scabbard, looking at it and then at the fearful scene around us. And in my mind I saw two boys; one—still in the ranks fighting the great fight; the other—his head held high in the shining column of the Forever Beloved host. Which of them threw the scabbard away?

The British held this position from the first disastrous attempt to relieve General Townshend until near the end of the campaign which culminated in the capture of Baghdad, and for sheer horror and unmitigated hardship nothing could . . . surpass the thing they lived through.

The men engaged, already worn with battle, were compelled to hold on week after week without hope of respite. . . . And there was not so much as a blade of grass for them to rest their eyes upon; only the terrible desert under a pitiless burning sun. They were hemmed in by the river on one side, and on the other by a vast marsh which, when the wind was right, had a mystifying habit of moving in . . . and flooding everything, that being one of the . . . habits of the marshes that I have spoken of. They literally do blow about the desert, spreading with terrifying rapidity even before a light wind if it is steady enough. So a company might be intrenched in comparative comfort one hour in a position where it would be in danger of drowning the next, and with never a drop of rain to clear the air of the blinding . . . torturing clouds of fine dust that the desert winds always carry before them.

Nobody can tell me that the men who have fought in Mesopotamia do not deserve some special kind of recognition—which they will never get!

Leaving the British position, we walked a long way across the one-time No Man's Land—now a tangle of rubbish and rust-blackened barbed wire—and came up on the Turkish parapets. And there I saw evidence enough that the Arabs bestow their ghoulish attentions chiefly upon the Turkish dead. It is not thought that this is because the British are more respected. It is only that more of value is to be found in the Turkish graves. The British search the bodies of their own dead before they bury them. This is done . . . for what are officially listed as 'objects of sentimental value,' all such objects being returned to the family of the fallen man. But the British do not search the bodies of the enemy dead, and in their final victorious advance over this field it fell to their lot to bury hundreds of them.

So one finds a fearful story written in the tragic gullies of the Turkish position. No need to write it out. Heaps of mouldering soldier clothes and dead men's bones scattered and kicked about! Such things cause waves of shuddering nausea to sweep over the normal living human.

Yet the British have buried and reburied the dead on the field of Sunnaiyat. They have punished the Arabs and have pleaded with them. But it is an isolated field. It is far away from any connection with things as they are to-day, and there is not a human habitation within many miles of it, unless it be an Arabs' tented encampment in the desert.

I was glad enough to trudge back as quickly as possible across the miles of gashed and ghastly waste, to get back aboard our peaceful old boat, and to let myself rest in a deep deck-chair while the depth-measurers filled the evening with the monotonous sweet melody of *'Ba'hat pani!'*

The Proclamation of Baghdad, 19 March 1917

The British conquered Baghdad in March 1917. Thus, the British regrouped after the siege of Kut, re-taking the city between December 1916 and February 1917. From Kut, the British marched straight to Baghdad. Wartime in this provincial capital had been difficult. The city experienced major food shortages as well as outbreaks of cholera. These hardships were due, in part, to the fact that the British takeover of Basra in 1914 had stopped trade with Turkish-controlled Baghdad. As British troops approached Baghdad, the occupying Ottoman army abandoned their positions. For this reason, the British triumphantly marched into the city without firing a shot. Indeed, one British soldier reports that a friendly crowd gathered at Baghdad's outskirts in order to cheer the arrival of the British troops (Chandler, 99).

As soon as the British moved into Baghdad, the commanding officer Lt. Gen. Sir Stanley Maude sought to appease the local population. He did so by issuing a proclamation to the people of Baghdad. In it, he implied that the British did not seek to rule without the consent of the residents of the provincial capital. The proclamation of Lt. Gen. Sir Stanley Maude can be read at http://www.harpers.org/archive/2003/05/0079593 (accessed 7 February 2010). As you read this proclamation, you should consider the following questions: What message did Maude send to the people of Baghdad? What arguments did he use to convince Baghdadis to accept the British military presence? How did Maude use history to argue that the British conquest of Baghdad served the interests of its residents? In what ways does this proclamation seem a precursor to eventual colonization?

To the people of the Baghdad Vilayet:

In the name of my King, and in the name of the peoples over whom he rules, I address you as follows:

Our military operations have as their object the defeat of the enemy, and the driving of him from these territories. In order to complete this task, I am charged with absolute and supreme control of all regions in which British troops operate; but our armies do not come into your cities and lands as conquerors or enemies, but as liberators. Since the days of Halaka your city and your lands have been subject to the tyranny of strangers, your palaces have fallen into ruins, your gardens have sunk in desolation, and your forefathers and yourselves have groaned in bondage. Your sons have been carried off to wars not of your seeking, your wealth has been stripped from you by unjust men and squandered in distant places.

Since the days of Midhat, the Turks have talked of reforms, yet do not the ruins and wastes of today testify to the vanity of those promises?

It is the wish not only of my King and his peoples, but it is also the wish of the great nations with whom he is in alliance, that you should prosper even as in the past, when your lands were fertile, when your ancestors gave to the world literature, science, and art, and when Baghdad city was one of the wonders of the world.

Between your people and the dominions of my King there has been a close bond of interest. For 200 years have the merchants of Baghdad and Great Britain traded together in mutual profit and friendship. On the other hand, the Germans and the Turks, who have despoiled you and yours, have for 20 years made Baghdad a center of power from which to assail the power of the British and the Allies of the British in Persia and Arabia. Therefore the British Government cannot remain indifferent as to what takes place in your country now or in the future, for in duty to the interests of the British people and their Allies, the British Government cannot risk that being done in Baghdad again which has been done by Turks and Germans during the war.

But you people of Baghdad, whose commercial prosperity and whose safety from oppression and invasion must ever be a matter of the closest concern to the British Government, are not to understand that it is the wish of the British Government to impose upon you alien institutions. It is the hope of the British Government that the aspirations of your philosophers and writers shall be realized and that once again the people of Baghdad shall flourish, enjoying their wealth and substance under institutions which are in consonance with their sacred laws and their racial ideals. In Hadjaz the Arabs have expelled the Turks and Germans who oppressed them and proclaimed the Sherif Hussein as their King, and his Lordship rules in independence and freedom, and is the ally of the nations who are fighting against the power of Turkey and Germany; so indeed are the noble Arabs, the Lords of Koweyt, Nejd, and Asir.

Many noble Arabs have perished in the cause of Arab freedom, at the hands of those alien rulers, the Turks, who oppressed them. It is the determination of the Government of Great Britain and the Great Powers allied to Great Britain that these noble Arabs shall not have suffered in vain. It is the hope and desire of the British people and the nations in alliance with them that the Arab race may rise once more to greatness and renown among the peoples of the earth, and that it shall bind itself together to this end in unity and concord.

O people of Baghdad remember that for 26 generations you have suffered under strange tyrants who have ever endeavored to set one Arab house against another in order that they might profit by your dissensions. This policy is abhorrent to Great Britain and her Allies, for there can be neither peace nor prosperity where there is enmity and misgovernment. Therefore I am commanded to invite you, through your nobles and elders and representatives, to participate in the management of your civil affairs in collaboration with the political representatives of Great Britain who accompany the British Army, so that you may be united with your kinsmen in North, East, South, and West in realizing the aspirations of your race.

The War Viewed from Baghdad

Violette Shamash was two years old in 1914, so her first memories consist of life during this Great War. Shamash and her family were Jewish residents of Baghdad. In 1914, the family had only just moved into a new home, which Violette refers to as a *qasr*, or palace. Her father was a well-to-do merchant in Baghdad, and the family wanted to leave the cramped walled quarters of the Old City for Baghdad's rural suburbs. There, their palatial house was surrounded by small farms with date and fruit trees. The outbreak of the war, however, would affect her family's ability to live a normal life. She recounts how the war affected her family in her memoir *Memories of Eden: A Journey through Jewish Baghdad* (London: Forum Books, 2008), 21–24 and 61–63. As you read this account, you should consider the following: How did this war affect the different members of this family? What does this account suggest about the Young Turks' efforts to foster territorial nationalism? How may her youth affect the memories of this time, recounted more than eighty years after the war's end?

> Yes, it was the Garden of Eden all right. But we hadn't been all that long in our little orchard paradise—kings of the castle, you might say—before the Great War broke out in Europe and, distant though it seemed, its echoes began to

be heard even in our part of the world. This was, after all, the Turkish Ottoman Empire, and when Turkey became a German ally, a huge shadow fell over our lives. All across the empire, men were being conscripted into the Turkish army to fight the British, something that horrified [my father] Baba and his friends and placed them in a difficult position, for they admired England.

In 1915, our paradise came to an abrupt end. One day, to [my mother] Nana's great distress, there came a banging on the door of the *qasr* and men in Turkish uniform took Baba away. He and all the other prominent members of minority communities were being rounded up and deported to Mosul in the north of the country, near the border with Persia, on suspicion of cooperating with the enemy. Fifty or more young family men from the Jewish and Christian communities—many of them Baba's school friends, as well as two of Nana's brothers, my uncles Ezra and Moshi—made the hard journey, walking or riding mules if they could afford them, under German and Turkish guard.

It was a sad time for my mother to be left with five young children plus me, the baby, and she moved out of the *qasr* to be closer to the family and friends. Terrible hardship was experienced everywhere. Women and children were left behind, neglected and abandoned. Young men hid in attics or basements and dared not venture out on the streets. Many managed to escape to other countries, or to Basra in the south where the British had established control. Some bought their way out of service with large sums of money, although this was no guarantee against future harassment. Yet they were the lucky ones: the able-bodied Jews who had been mobilized were sent, untrained, ill-equipped and in great haste, to the front to fight for the Sultan, an ailing ruler who shared few of their traditions or values. Few ever reached it; none came back. Faced with defeat, the Turks turned on the recruits and killed them all.

Then, suddenly and inexplicably, Baba and the other deportees were allowed home—probably because the Sultan's treasury was empty and the Turks, before they faced the final curtain, were trying to get their hands on any savings that people still might have. A number of Jews, together with Muslims and Christians, were executed either because they had deserted from the army or because they could not come up with enough gold to buy their liberty. Finally, when some bankers and moneychangers grumbled about being forced to exchange their gold and silver coins for newly printed, worthless Turkish banknotes, the Turks' answer was simple: they arrested those who resisted, herded them to the Tigris, killed them and cut up their bodies before dumping them in the river in sacks. It was Tish'a-Bab, the season of mourning.

What Baba saw and heard when he came back to Baghdad made him realize what a dangerous place our isolated *qasr* would be; there was no question of our returning to it and picking up our lives again. But the city ... was no longer safe for a man of military age, and in 1916, fearing what fate might have in store for all of their countrymen, Baba and some friends decided to go into exile again, this time voluntarily. Taking gold with them, the universal passport, they ... took some mules and headed north-east, following the ancient caravan routes, aiming to cross into Persia, today's Iran, and wait the war out in Kermanshah where Baba had business contacts. It was a hazardous journey, so there was no question of taking their families with them.

It was a wrench for Baba to leave his young family again so soon, but Nana agreed it was the safest thing to do. Before leaving, he made sure that we were all safe and well looked after. There was a man who did the shopping for Nana and ran errands, someone who had known us for many years, who brought our groceries on donkey-back faithfully every morning and was paid by Baba's business secretary.... Baba also gave his secretary instructions to send him a letter every day with a sentence or signature from every one of his children. Someone always had to hold my hand so that I could add my scribble.

Accompanied by a nomad guide, Baba and his friends traveled for days before coming to the frontier where they were stopped by some Russian soldiers, allies of the British, who eyed them suspiciously and wanted to take them prisoner. Eliahu Meir, one of the party, who had fair hair and a light complexion, spoke to their officer in English, explaining that he was the group's captain—a "fact" confirmed by Baba, also in English. And so they marched away, looking confident. However, after three days making hard progress through the mountains, they were set upon by robbers who ... stripped them clean. They took all their money, possessions and clothes, leaving them with nothing but their underwear. They became lost many times, but eventually, using their common sense, they found their way and arrived at their destination, only to move on again to Hamadan where they stayed for the duration of the war....

I'm sorry that Baba was not there to witness the historic moment when the country finally fell into the hands of the British, as it was seen as such a blessing. It had been particularly hard on my mother, having to worry about Baba's safety at the same time as raising the five of us (my sisters Daisy and Marcelle didn't come along until after the war).

In 1917, as soon as it was thought safe, Baba made his way back to Baghdad. He told us the story of his escape and about life in Kermanshah and Hamadan, where he had visited the shrine of Esther and her cousin and guardian Mordekhai, the heroes of our Purim story. And then, just as we were starting to draw breath, we found ourselves turfed out of our home!

Our handsome *qasr* was one of the first buildings requisitioned by the British, who pinpointed it as particularly suitable for their needs because of its riverside location. It meant that they could unload their equipment directly from the water, using boats as transport—roads were mostly still unpaved and pitch black at night. They intended to create a military school there, and as they began to transform it, we had to move out, back to the city, where we took rented accommodation.

From the grandeur of the palace we now found ourselves in a modest house in the Kutchet el-Nasaara district, the mainly Christian quarter . . . off Rashid Street, the principal street. . . . It was where Baba's parents had their big house, after moving from Hennouni, but in contrast, ours was sandwiched in a narrow lane bustling with tradespeople and vendors trying to sell all manner of things. I never tired of looking down from the first-floor window and watching the scene below: the cobbler producing an endless stream of nails from his mouth as he hammered them into shoes; the ice-cream seller . . . shouting how refreshing his ices were; and *Abul shaadi*, the man with a monkey playing a miniature tambourine and acting the coquette, pretending to be a bride lying down on her bed. We all threw money to the monkey, which he collected in his cap and gave to his master. . . .

[W]e accepted our lot philosophically in our temporary lodging, and with Baba now safely home, things were starting to look up. In Baghdad, any literate . . . person could look forward to a career, and as most Jews had some schooling and could at least read and write, their living was virtually secure. They were in great demand as clerks and supervisors in the civil service, and surely Baba must have been tempted to go that way. But he chose instead to return to what he knew best—trading—and reactivated the business he'd had to leave so abruptly.

The British returned our property in 1919 and we were allowed to move back to the *qasr*. Originally, when we had been forced to vacate it and move to the city, the disappointment for us children had been tempered by the discovery in our rented home of a great big box of toys and games that a Turkish family had been obliged to leave behind in their haste to depart. Now, my whole family discovered something truly wondrous. We had suddenly been propelled into the 20th century: the British had wired the *qasr* with electricity—we had light! There was an electric light in every room, plus . . . electric *punkahs* (ceiling fans) that worked at the press of a button. We were totally entranced by this magic, and as life began to revert to normal, the benefits of the cooling breezes created by the fans made all the previous upheavals seem worthwhile.

Bibliography

Al-Askari, Jafar Pasha, William Facey, and Najdat Fathi Safwat. *A Soldier's Story: From Ottoman Rule to Independent Iraq; The Memoirs of Jafar Pasha Al-Askari (1885–1936)*. London: Arabian, 2003.

Australia and Great Britain. *Notes on Mesopotamia*. Melbourne: Australian Section, Imperial General Staff, 1916.

Barlow, J. A., A. Howlett, and S. H. Godfrey. *Gazetteer of Baghdad*. Simla: Government Central Press, 1915.

Budge, E. A. Wallis. *By Nile and Tigris: A Narrative of Journeys in Egypt and Mesopotamia on Behalf of the British Museum between the Years 1886 and 1913*. London: J. Murray, 1920.

Burgoyne, Elizabeth. *Gertrude Bell: From Her Personal Papers. Vol. 2, 1914–1926*. London: Benn, 1961.

Burne, A. H. *Mesopotamia, the Last Phase*. London: Gale and Polden, 1936.

Chandler, Edmund. *The Long Road to Baghdad*. New York: Cassell, 1919.

Cursetjee, C. M. *The Land of the Date: A Recent Voyage from Bombay to Basra and Back, fully Descriptive of the Ports and Peoples of the Persian Gulf and the Shat-el-Arab, Their Conditions, History, and Customs: 1916–1917*. 1918. Reprint, Reading, U.K.: Garnet Publishing, 1994.

Egan, Eleanor Franklin, and P. J. Rich. *Iraq and Eleanor Egan's "The War in the Cradle of the World."* 1919. Reprint, Lanham, Md.: Lexington Books, 2009.

———. *Persia and Turkey in Revolt*. Edinburgh, U.K.: W. Blackwood and Sons, 1910.

Fraser, David. *The Short Cut to India: The Record of a Journey Along the Route of the Baghdad Railway*. Edinburgh, U.K.: W. Blackwood and Sons, 1909.

Great Britain. *A Handbook of Mesopotamia*. London: Naval Staff, Naval Intelligence Dept., 1917.

———. *A Handbook of Mesopotamia: Prepared on Behalf of the Admiralty and the War Office*. London: The Division, 1916.

———. *Mesopotamia*. Handbooks prepared under the direction of the Historical Section of the Foreign Office, no. 63. London: H.M.S.O., 1920.

———. *Notes on Mesopotamia*. Melbourne: Australian Section, Imperial General Staff, 1916.

Hay, Rupert, and P. J. Rich. *Iraq and Rupert Hay's Two Years in Kurdistan*. Middle East classics. Lanham, Md.: Lexington Books, 2008.

Hedin, Sven Anders. *Bagdad, Babylon, Ninive*. Leipzig, GDR: F. A. Brockhaus, 1918.

Hubbard, G. E. *From the Gulf to Ararat: An Expedition through Mesopotamia and Kurdistan*. New Delhi: Asian Educational Services, 2003.

India. *Mesopotamia: Field Notes*. Calcutta: Superintendent Government Printing, 1917.

Issawi, Charles Phillip. *The Fertile Crescent, 1800–1914: A Documentary Economic History*. New York: Oxford University Press, 1988.

Leland, F. W. *With the M. T. in Mesopotamia*. London: F. Groom, 1920.
Lyell, Thomas R. G. *The Ins and Outs of Mesopotamia*. London: A. M. Philpot, 1923.
Lyon, Wallace, and D. K. Fieldhouse. *Kurds, Arabs and Britons: The Memoir of Wallace Lyon in Iraq, 1918–44*. London: I. B. Tauris, 2002.
Morad, Tamar, Dennis Shasha, and Robert Shasha, eds. *Iraq's Last Jews: Stories of Daily Life, Upheaval, and Escape from Modern Babylon*. New York: Palgrave Macmillan, 2008.
Nawab, Hamid Yar Jung. *A Trip to Baghdad. With an Appendix on the Arab Horse*. Bombay: Bombay Gazette Press, 1908.
Nunn, Wilfred. *Tigris Gunboats: The Forgotten War in Iraq 1914–1917*. London: Chatham, 2007.
Palmer, Robert Stafford Arthur. *Letters from Mesopotamia in 1915 and January, 1916*. London: Women's Printing Society, 1926.
Parfit, Joseph T. *Mesopotamia: The Key to the Future*. London: Hodder and Stoughton, 1917.
Roosevelt, Kermit. *War in the Garden of Eden*. New York: C. Scribner, 1920.
Shamash, Violette, Tony Rocca, and Mira Rocca. *Memories of Eden: A Journey through Jewish Baghdad*. London: Forum Books, 2008.
Soane, E. B. *To Mesopotamia and Kurdistan in Disguise: With Historical Notices of the Kurdish Tribes and the Chaldeans of Kurdistan*. London: J. Murray, 1912.
———. *Report on the Sulaimania of Kurdistan*. Calcutta: Superintendent Government Printing Press, 1918.
Society for Promoting Christian Knowledge (Great Britain), and National Society. *A Tommy on the Tigris: A Book for Boys*. London: For the National Society by the Society for Promoting Christian Knowledge, 1920.
Swayne, Martin Lutrell. *In Mesopotamia*. London: Hodder and Stoughton, 1918.
Sykes, Mark. *The Caliphs' Last Heritage: A Short History of the Turkish Empire*. London: Macmillan, 1915.
The Times Press. *Bombay to Baghdad: Nurses' Clubs in Mesopotamia*. Bombay: Times Press, 1918.
Warfield, William. *Bagdad, City of the Kalifs*. New York: Harper and Brothers, 1915.
———. *Journeying to Babylon*. New York: Harper and Brothers, 1915.
Wilkins, Louisa Jebb. *By Desert Ways to Baghdad and Damascus*. S.l.: Long Riders' Guild Press, 1908.
Wilson, Sir Arnold Talbot. *Loyalties: Mesopotamia, 1914–1917; A Personal and Historical Record*. New York: Greenwood Press, 1930.
Woolley, C. F., E. Noel, Mark Sykes, and Godfrey Rolles Driver. *Kurdistan and the Kurds*. London: Royal Anthropological Institute, 1919.
Wratislaw, Albert Charles. *A Consul in the East*. Edinburgh, U.K.: W. Blackwood, 1924.

2

The British Mandate, 1920–1932

Though the armistice between the Allies and Germany was signed on 11 November 1918, the postwar fate of Iraq would not be decided until spring 1920. During World War I, the British occupied the Ottoman provinces of Basra, Baghdad, and Mosul. This area had historically been known as Mesopotamia, but the British, who ruled it as a single unit, began to call it Iraq. During the war and immediately thereafter, the British exercised the policy of direct rule in the nascent political entity. This meant that they neither relied on an association with local elites nor exercised authority through extant political institutions. Instead, British officers rendered direct orders and expected them to be followed by locals. Unfortunately, most of their officers knew very little about the territory over which they ruled. As Lt. Gen. Almyer Haldane points out in his memoir, most officers with whom he worked in Iraq had come from India and just assumed that they could transfer Indian methods of colonial rule to Iraq (Haldane, 21). This would spark the ire of many of the people of Mesopotamia-cum-Iraq, for they had grown fond of the liberal institutions, like free elections, that the Young Ottomans imposed on Abdul Hamid II and his successor. In other words, significant tensions were brewing under the surface.

And these tensions would bubble over once the British announced the San Remo Agreement, which defined a definitive postwar settlement for Iraq and other places in the Middle East. France and Great Britain fashioned this postwar settlement in April 1920 at the San Remo Conference in Italy. British and French politicians decided that they would treat the Arab territories of the Ottoman Empire as separate from the lands of the Anatolian Peninsula, where Turks were the majority. Great Britain and France then split the Arab world into separate imperial spheres of influence. They created four (soon after, five) mandates, which were new political entities. France and Great Britain were to organize the administration of each of their mandated spheres of influence. Great Britain wanted to control Iraq because of its proximity to India and its potential for oil production. Besides Iraq, Great Britain was charged with administering the mandates of

Palestine and later Transjordan. (France would administer Syria and Lebanon.) According to William L. Cleveland, "the mandate system was little more than nineteenth-century imperialism repackaged to give the appearance of self-determination" (Cleveland, 164).

The British ultimately decided to impose a constitutional monarchy on the people of Iraq, albeit one that they could control. The British would hand-choose Faysal bin Hussein as king of Iraq. Once crowned king, the British ensured that Iraq had, at least in appearance, the structures of a constitutional monarchy. The first step in this process, one decided at the Cairo Conference, was the enunciation of a treaty between Great Britain and Iraq, and this was ratified in October 1922. According to the Anglo-Iraqi Treaty, Iraqis agreed to let the British appoint administrators in all eighteen of its departments—and to pay half the costs of this British Residency. In return, Great Britain promised aid to Iraq. In this way, the treaty facilitated a new system of indirect rule, whereby Iraqis appeared to acquiesce to British oversight in exchange for its aid. After the signing of the treaty, the British wanted to organize elections to a constituent assembly. In this way, the British would have (again, in appearance at least) a representative body politic, one that could rubber-stamp a Constitution that would give King Faysal significant power.

This chapter focuses specifically on the British mandate's postwar establishment in order to highlight the construction of Iraq's state institutions and the issue of political legitimacy. Gertrude Bell was Oriental Secretary, and her account of this time reveals the Islamic underpinnings of nationalist responses in Baghdad. This chapter also includes a short Iraqi poem that helped mobilize all Iraqis against the impending mandate. Urban protests contributed to a larger tribal uprising, and the memoir of a British general gives readers a ringside seat to the Revolt of 1920. Costly in money and manpower, this revolt led "Lawrence of Arabia" to oppose the mandate. Since he was not the only British citizen to oppose the mandate, Colonial Secretary Winston Churchill called for a conference in Cairo in 1921. As outlined in a speech to the House of Commons, the participants decided to establish a constitutional monarchy in which Iraqis would bear the cost of their own occupation. Wallace Lyon was an administrator in Iraq's Kurdish regions, and he recounts how he needed to coerce a local endorsement of Faysal as king. This chapter then includes the coronation speech of King Faysal. The Shi'i ayatollah Mahdi al-Khalisi made known his hatred of Faysal as a British pawn, prohibiting all his followers from participating in the elections.

Iraqi Nationalism

When the mandates were created, the British administrator Gertrude Bell was Oriental Secretary in Iraq. Unlike all too many of her colleagues, Bell was a seasoned traveler of the Arab territory. She had begun traveling in this region during the late nineteenth century, and she had met and befriended many of the Arab world's key political actors. During World War I, Bell worked for the Arab Bureau, which sent her to Basra and Baghdad. She describes the negative response of Iraqis to the San Remo Agreement in *Review of Civil Administration of Mesopotamia* (London: HMSO, 1920), 140–44. Her account provides a firsthand view of the activities of a group analyzed by historian Charles Tripp as the Independent Guard (Tripp, 39–42). As you read her account, you should consider the following: What are the components of Iraqi nationalism described by Bell? What are nationalists demanding? And what are their strategies for achieving their political goals? Who do these nationalists represent? And how do the British respond to them?

> The announcement that Great Britain had accepted the mandate for Mesopotamia was made on 3rd May. It was accompanied by a carefully considered explanation of the duties of a mandatory Power, in which stress was laid upon the fact that the ultimate goal was the development of independent institutions. The announcement spurred the nationalists to fresh activity. The claim to immediate and complete independence on the Syrian model, though it commanded the sympathy of members of the upper classes who looked to taking a leading part in the Arab State, and of men out of a job who hoped to gain a livelihood from the same source, did not make much headway in rousing the mass of the population. To that end an argument was needed which would be understood by the most ignorant and it was found in an appeal to religious fanaticism. For some time past it had been obvious to the nationalists that it would be necessary for them to present a united Islamic front. The deep prejudices which separate the Sunni and Shi'ah sects were temporarily overcome. The first symptom of rapprochement occurred in the summer of 1919, when on two occasions Sunnis attended the religious meetings which were held in memory of the deceased Shi'ah mujtahid, Saiyid Muhammad Kadhim Yazdi. But it was not till the following month of Ramadhan, which began on 19th May 1920, that the political significance of the reconciliation became apparent. Services known as Mauluds, in honour of the birth of the Prophet, were held in every Sunni and Shi'ah mosque in turn, members of both sects attending by invitation of the authorities in charge of the mosque or the heads

of the quarter in which it was situated. On some occasions the reading of the Maulud, which is distinctively a Sunni celebration, was followed by a Ta'ziyah, the Shi'ah ritual condolence on the martyrdom of Husain, but in all cases the main features of these gatherings were the political speeches and recitations of patriotic poetry which followed the religious ceremony. The Arab is peculiarly susceptible to high-flown oratory, and the frantic appeals which were made to religion, patriotism and to the Amir 'Abdullah, urging him to hasten the advent of his holy kingdom, roused extreme enthusiasm. Prominent in one of the first Mauluds was a young employee in the Auqaf [Awqaf, or religious endowments] Department, who indulged in a speech which was judged dangerous to public order. His arrest was made the excuse of a meeting the avowed object of which was to arrange for his release by force. A couple of armoured cars were sent to patrol the main street of the town, and on one of them being attacked a few shots were fired over the head of the crowd. It dispersed with all possible celerity. The casualties consisted of one blind man, who was accidentally knocked down and run over.

The leaders of the movement and organizers of the Mauluds were men of varying status and capacity. The ablest among them were two Shi'ahs, Saiyid Muhammad al Sadr, a member of a renowned family of Shi'ah divines, and Ja'far abu Timman, a Shi'ah merchant. Chief among the Sunnis were Yusuf Effendi Suwaidi, Shaikh Ahmad Daud, and 'Ali Effendi Bazirqan.

This group was officially warned that no breach in the peace would be permitted, but the civil administration considered it inadvisable to resort to extreme measures of repression. The Mauluds were allowed to continue, and those who viewed with disfavour the holding of political gatherings in mosques were afraid to refuse subscriptions to defray the expenses incurred or to fail attendance, lest they should be labeled as infidels and traitors to Arab liberty. Rumours of impending disturbance were circulated mainly through the agency of teachers in the nationalist school, with the result that the bazaar was repeatedly closed and the normal life of town interrupted. The progressive drawing in of our frontier on the Euphrates, and the attacks on Tal 'Afar and the Mosul road, gave substance to the belief that our military position was not such as would enable us to hold the tribes if they could be roused. Early in June one of the most consistent of our supporters among the tribal shaikhs near Baghdad sounded a grave note of warning, and at the same time, on the Euphrates, the paramount shaikh of the Dulaim, who had turned a deaf ear to the propaganda which had been addressed to him, solemnly declared that unless we could score some striking success he could no longer answer for his tribesmen. He urged the reoccupation of Dair; but whatever might have been the merits . . . , it was far beyond our powers of performance. While well-wishers were alarmed at our failure to put an end to tribal disorder, and by the sufferance accorded to the antics of the extremists, debates in the House of Commons and articles in the English papers were quoted . . . as evidence that the mandate was as inacceptable in London as in Baghdad.

It was under these unfavourable conditions that a declaration of future policy was made. In April, a small committee of Political Officers, presided over by the Judicial Secretary, had drawn up a scheme for the setting up of Arab institutions. It provided for a provisional constitution, including both a Council of State composed of British and Arab members with an Arab President appointed by the High Commissioner, and a Legislative Assembly chosen by election. Within a period limited to two years, the Legislative Assembly was to draw up an organic law for the permanent settlement of the country. The Acting Civil Commissioner was under no illusions as to the reception which would be accorded to this project by the extremists, but he hoped that its publication might strengthen the position of the moderates, and he was anxious that it should be issued before the fast of Ramadhan increased the existing tension. His Majesty's Government did not, however, consider that a declaration of this nature was justifiable until the terms of the mandate had been framed.

But if the scheme was not officially published, its details were universally known before the middle of Ramadhan, and the opposition which had been anticipated was not lacking. A self-chosen committee of 15 persons, styling themselves . . . appointed delegates of Baghdad and Kadhimain was formed to resist the mandate and asked for an opportunity of laying their views before the Civil Commissioner. A large body of sober-minded opinion doubted the wisdom of the programme and disapproved of the methods . . . taken to advertise it, and when, on 2nd June, Colonel Wilson invited the Delegates to meet him he extended the invitation to some 25 other persons, all . . . leading notables of Baghdad, including several Jews and Christians, neither of which communities were represented among the Delegates.

He opened the proceedings with a speech in which he expressed his regret that circumstances beyond our control had delayed the establishment of civil government in Mesopotamia, but he warned the Delegates that in encouraging disorder and inciting the population against the existing regime, they were rousing forces which would prove too strong for native institutions while in their infancy. He alluded to the proposals which had been submitted to His Majesty's Government and were already known to most of those present, and undertook to transmit to London any representations which the Delegates should make.

The Delegates presented a document in which they demanded the immediate formation of a Mesopotamian Convention elected in conformity with the Turkish electoral law, with a view to drawing up proposals for a national Arab Government as promised in the Anglo-French Declaration of November 1918. By this means, they stated, the people of Mesopotamia might attain independence. They asked ... for complete freedom of the press.

Colonel Wilson, in reply, promised that he would urge His Majesty's Government to expedite matters as much as possible, and in communicating the results of the meeting to London he proposed that the idea of a provisional Government should be discarded, and that as soon as the terms of the mandate had been formulated steps should be taken to summon a Constituent Assembly to consult on the future form of Government.

With the approval of Sir Percy Cox, who was in Baghdad for two days on his way from Tehran to London, an official announcement in this sense was sent to the leading delegates on 20th June. It ran as follows:

"His Majesty's Government having been entrusted with the mandate for Mesopotamia, anticipate that the mandate will constitute Mesopotamia an independent State under the guarantee of the League of Nations and subject to the mandate to Great Britain; that it will lay on them the responsibility for the maintenance of internal peace and external security, and will require them to formulate an organic law to be framed in consultation with the people of Mesopotamia, and with due regard to the rights ... and interests of all the communities of the country. The mandate will contain provisions to facilitate the development of Mesopotamia as a self-governing State until ... it can stand by itself, when the mandate will come to an end.

"The inception of this task His Majesty's Government has decided to entrust to Sir Percy Cox, who will ... return to Baghdad in the autumn and will resume his position on the termination of the existing military administration as Chief British Representative in Mesopotamia.

"Sir Percy Cox will be authorized to call into being, as provisional bodies, a Council of State under an Arab President, and a General Elective Assembly representative of and freely elected by the population of Mesopotamia, and it will be his duty to prepare, in consultation with the General Elective Assembly, the permanent organic law."

The Delegates replied on 30th June by repeating their request for the immediate formation of a General Council for 'Iraq. It is to be noted that this was the last occasion on which they figured as a united body. Dissensions among themselves became increasingly frequent. The rapid development of tribal disturbance detached the more moderate of the group, who were alarmed by the results of the agitation they had started and were unable to control. Even when united, the claim of the Delegates to represent the 'Iraq, or even to represent more than a section of Baghdad opinion, was manifestly untenable. The members of the Divisional Council at Basrah had on 22nd June condemned their action unanimously and expressed confidence in the British Government. In 'Amarah efforts had been made to secure support for a petition in favour of independence, but no signatories could be found and the petition was torn up. Mosul also was unrepresented. A further announcement made on 12th July had the advantage of bringing these neglected elements into play, while making provision for the immediate discussions of the Turkish electoral law, which was admittedly inapplicable to existing conditions. The announcement ran as follows:

"His Majesty's Government has authorized the Acting Civil Commissioner to invite the leading representatives of various localities to co-operate with the Civil Administration in framing proposals under which election to the General Assembly will, in due course, be held, and in making the necessary arrangements for electoral areas, the preparation of the registers of electors and other matters preliminary to the election of the General Assembly. And inasmuch as there are at present in the 'Iraq Turkish Chamber of Deputies, and who therefore have experience in matters relating to elections and in the discussion of public affairs, all these ex-Senators and ex-Deputies have been invited by the Civil Commissioner for the above-mentioned purpose. This Committee will be invited to elect a President from among their number, and to co-opt additional members from areas which, owing to the absence or death of the former Deputies, or from some other cause, are not already represented."

Among the ex-Deputies was the most prominent figure in Basrah, and perhaps in Mesopotamia, Saiyid Talib Pasha, eldest son of the Naqib of Basrah. He had returned to his native land in February 1920, after spending the years of the war in voluntary exile in India and Egypt. His renown was due largely to the determination with which he had pursued political ends under the Turkish regime, but he had undoubtedly figured before the war as the spokesman of national aspirations. . . . Since his return he had lost no opportunity of testifying to his conviction that the welfare of Mesopotamia was dependent on the acceptance of the British mandate. Together with the other ex-Deputies of Basrah and elsewhere in Mesopotamia, he did not hesitate to comply with the invitation. Nor did the ex-Deputies in Baghdad refuse to attend the Committee, though two had signed the petition of 2nd June as Delegates.

The Committee held its first meeting on 6th August, and, after a formal opening by the Civil Commissioner, elected Saiyid Talib Pasha as President. At the second meeting . . . they proceeded to the co-option of additional members and included among the number Yusuf Effendi Suwaidi, Saiyid Muhammad Sadr, and other persons known to hold extreme views. Thus constituted, the Committee could not be accused of being unrepresentative of any brand of opinion.

But the two leaders of the Delegates refused the invitation, and at the same time it became known that they intended to make a final appeal to the Baghdad mob by holding a Maulud in one of the principal mosques, followed by a demonstration in the town. Serious disorder and violence could not have failed to have resulted, and an order was issued for the arrest of Yusuf Suwaidi, Shaikh Ahmad Daud, Ja'far abu Timman and 'Ali Bazirqan. All except the second succeeded in making their escape, but the action of the Government, accompanied as it was by a proclamation forbidding the holding of further Mauluds and by strict maintenance of peace and order, restored confidence instantaneously. . . .

The flight of the three principals redounded to their discredit. Their followers had anticipated that they would glory in imprisonment in the cause of liberty, and were disconcerted by their unwillingness to assume the martyr's crown. When their houses and the nationalist school were searched, documents . . . proved that the funds collected for the school had been used for the purpose of hiring assassins with the object of removing prominent Arab personages . . . opposed to their political views. The stalwart attitude of the Arab police in Baghdad and the steadiness of Arab officials in the civil administration were . . . encouraging . . . in these difficult days.

The danger of the revolutionary tactics . . . adopted lay not . . . in Baghdad, but in their effect upon the tribes. Beyond the immediate confines of the town the population of Mesopotamia is composed of nomadic and semi-nomadic confederations, which have offered a secular resistance to ordered government. Tribal organization is a centrifugal force adverse to the formation of a unified State. The Turks had contented themselves with holding the balance by playing off one group against another and had thus succeeded in preventing any dangerous combination against themselves. The policy we pursued was to reconstruct and support the power of the shaikh, making him in turn accept responsibility for his tribe. But the measure of obedience to central authority which we demanded was far greater than that which had been expected by our predecessors. At the same time we did our best to heal the feuds and settle the ancient disputes which wrecked local peace. Thus hereditary animosities by which the Turks had profited were to a great extent, at least temporarily, extinguished.

The policy of backing the shaikh had its drawbacks. He is a petty tyrant whose misdeeds reflect on the Government which supports him. He resented any check imposed on the rapacity which he had been given a fair field to exercise, and he and his tribesmen alike resented the attempt to enforce upon them the obligations of citizenship, the preservation of order and the payment of taxes, which in the past they had successfully evaded. Nevertheless, the nature of their organization made it little likely that the tribes would take concerted action on their own initiative. It remained for the nationalists to weld together their individual grievances and their predatory instincts into a common purpose. The first success in arms facilitated the task. The tribes witnessed the withdrawal of British administration and were convinced that their efforts would, as they had been assured, drive the British out of Mesopotamia. This conviction spurred on those who had already risen and won over the half-hearted, who could not risk being left on the losing side.

The end in view was an Islamic Government, but apart from the wave of nationalist feeling, which was a world-wide consequence of the war and should not be discounted, it made a different appeal to different sections of the community. To the Shi'ah mujtahids it meant a theocratic state under Shar'iah law, and to this end they did not hesitate to preach Jihad; to the Sunnis and free-thinkers of Baghdad it was an independent Arab State under Amir 'Abdullah; to the tribes it meant no government at all. It is significant that when the shaikhs on the Tigris were pressed to join the movement they replied that they must be assured that under the new order they would not be required to pay any government dues.

Nationalist Poetry

At the time of the nationalist uprising, Iraq's Sunnis and Shi'is acted in concert, which was nearly unprecedented in the recent history of this territory. These two sects, however, as pointed out by the historian Yitzhak Nakash, needed to find a "common denominator" in their speeches and writings (Nakash, 69). This effort to find shared ground is very important in retrospect, for Iraqis subsequently considered the Revolt of 1920 as the foundational act of modern nationalism. Poetry was a cultural vehicle that could channel and disseminate shared nationalist feelings among various groups of peoples in the territory of the newly formed mandate of Iraq. Nakash excerpts a poem by Habib al-Ubaydi (d. 1963) to show how the leaders of urban nationalism manipulated themes to which both Sunnis and Shi'is could adhere. The following poem is found in Nakash's book *The Shi'is of Iraq* (Princeton: Princeton University Press: 1994), 69. As you read it, you should consider the symbols that the poet uses: How, for example, does the poet feel about the British? What, if any, role does religion play in this poem? How does the author express concepts of Arab honor?

> Set the fire O you noble Iraqis
> and wash the shame with flowing blood
> O you the people of Iraq, you are not slaves
> to adorn your necks with collars
> O you the people of Iraq, you are not prisoners
> to submit your shoulders to the chains
> O you the people of Iraq, you are not women
> Whose weapon is the tears that flow from the depth of the eye
> O you the people of Iraq, you are not orphans
> to seek guardianship [a mandate] for Iraq
> You shall no longer enjoy the water of the Tigris
> if you are content with humiliation and oppression.

The Revolt of 1920

Gertrude Bell's description of nationalists draws attention to the political life of the city, particularly the capital, but the British soon found that more pressing problems would be encountered in the countryside. It is there that the Revolt of 1920 took its highest toll. The landlord-sheikhs of the rural hinterland resented the British policy of direct rule, which challenged their authority. In other words, the landlord-sheikhs and their tribesmen were not necessarily worried about Iraqi nationalism per se. They were concerned with how British policies would affect their personal ability to control land, people, and money. These were "local motives" (Tripp, 43). Given this, opposition to the British was not coordinated from a central headquarters, but instead piecemeal, gaining momentum from opportunistic decisions on the part of tribesmen to increase their own power, and not that of all Iraqis.

The revolt began in June 1920. It was sparked by a series of arrests that the British hoped would actually prevent an uprising. By July, rebel tribes controlled the mid-Euphrates region, the heartland of this anti-imperial insurgency. As other tribes in other places perceived the successes of their erstwhile "compatriots," they too began to revolt. And so, Shi'i tribes in the south and Kurdish tribes in the north also opposed the British. Ultimately, it would take Great Britain three months to put down the revolt (Marr, 24). In doing so, the British needed to spend £40 million, a high cost for a country that had been fighting World War

I for four years. The British lost 500 troops, while at least 6,000 Iraqis lost their lives in this struggle (Tripp, 43). Despite its localized nature, this event became a founding myth of Iraqi nationalism, for it seems in hindsight that all people—no matter ethnic or sectarian persuasion—rose up in an anti-imperial struggle.

Lt. Gen. Sir Aylmer L. Haldane was a British officer who played a key role in putting down this rebellion. He had spent World War I on the western front, but was sent to command British troops in Mesopotamia in the early months of 1920. He provides a firsthand account of the initial days of the Revolt of 1920 in *The Insurrection in Mesopotamia, 1920* (1922; reprint, Nashville: Battery Press, 2005), 73–77. As you read his account, you should consider the following: Why did armed resistance break out in Rumaithah? What are the specific issues motivating rebellion? What do these motivational forces suggest about larger issues under consideration by the rebels? What is the most significant concern of British troops in fighting these rebels? And how do they resolve their problems?

> The first few days after our arrival at Sar-i-Mil were uneventful . . . but the calm was not to be of long duration, for on the 30th June an incident, trivial in itself, lighted the fire of insurrection on the Middle Euphrates.
>
> The scene of the trouble was the . . . town of Rumaithah, with some two thousand five hundred inhabitants, which stands on both banks of the Hillah branch of the Euphrates, about twenty-eight miles above Samawah. Its houses, which are mostly built of mud or sun-dried bricks, are scattered among gardens of date-groves. The circumstances which led to the outbreak were as follows:
>
> On the 25th June, Lieutenant P. T. Hyatt, the Assistant Political Officer at Rumaithah, had reported to the Political Officer of his division, Major C. Daly, that a long outstanding agricultural loan, some Rs. 800 (at that time about £100), owed by the shaikh of the Dhawalim section of the Bani Hachaim, had to be collected, and he was directed to arrest and send the defaulter to Diwaniyah. At noon on the 30th the man, Sha'alan Abu by name, was sent for, and after the necessity for payment had been explained to him, he was detained for the evening train to Diwaniyah. At 4 p.m. the retainers of the shaikh . . . took the law into their own hands, and following an example set about two weeks earlier at Samawah, fired at the political office, killed the Arab guard, and released Sha'alan. The . . . police ran away, and left the Political Officer alone.
>
> On the 25th June Major Daly had heard that the Dhawalim tribe had their flags out—showing that they considered themselves to be at war with the Government—but he decided that the wisest course was to proceed with the arrest of the defaulting shaikh. That the outbreak was not purely local may be inferred from the fact that on the 1st July the railway line south of Rumaithah

was torn up in several places, and a bridge destroyed. On the same date, too, a reconnoitering train from Samawah, manned by a few sepoys of the 114th Mahrattas, under Major Kiernander of the railway service, who, as well as Flying Officer G. C. Gardiner, was a passenger traveling from Basrah to Baghdad, became engaged with a large number of insurgents, and with difficulty succeeded in returning whence they came. North of Rumaithah more railway cutting was in progress, but the rising still retained its local character.

Troops ... were, at the urgent appeal of the Assistant Political Officer, at once dispatched to the scene from Samawah. Two platoons of the 114th Mahrattas (fifty-six rifles) arrived by rail ... on the 1st July, whose commander, Lieutenant J. J. Healey, was informed by Lieutenant Hyatt that the country was very much disturbed, and a general rising of the tribesmen might be expected. Next day one company (less half a platoon) of the same regiment came from Diwaniyah, which raised the strength of the garrison of Rumaithah to one hundred and forty rifles. During the night the civilians were moved into the Political Serai, a two-storied brick building which is on the left bank of the river, and commands some fifty yards' distance the approach to the bridge of boats, beyond which, on the other bank half a mile away is the railway station. All rations that were available, which included enough for seven days for one hundred Indian soldiers, were also placed in the Serai.

On the 3rd July a company of another unit, the 99th Infantry, under Captain H. V. Bragg, which had been dispatched from Hillah on the 2nd and had left Diwaniyah at 3:30 p.m. next day, arrived and brought with it some railway personnel. This company had had an adventurous journey, during which a wooden bridge that had been burned down by the insurgents was repaired, while the Arabs interfered by firing heavily from the surrounding villages, causing some casualties among the troops and working party.

On arrival at Rumaithah, Captain Bragg, being the senior officer, assumed command of the garrison, and with his own company occupied two Arab khans or caravanserai, one on each side of the village, while the 114th Mahrattas and the non-combatants remained in the Serai. The troops at the disposal of the commander amounted to four British officers and three hundred and eight other ranks, together with two British officers and one hundred and fifty-three railway personnel and sixty Indians—in all, five hundred and twenty-seven. The task of providing food for this small force, which had only some two days' rations with it soon became a cause of anxiety.

On the 4th the first signs of the coming siege showed themselves, when it was noticed that the Arabs were constructing a trench system north-west of the town, and carrying out regular reliefs—an indication that ex-Turkish Army officers were probably in control. On this date, complaints having reached the Assistant Political Officer that the occupants of the village of Album Hessian, which is about one and a half miles south-east of Rumaithah, had taken to looting the bazaar at the latter place, and were terrorizing the inhabitants, it was decided that a reconnaissance through the bazaar in the direction of the seat of the trouble should be made. In consequence, the two platoons of the 99th Infantry, whose advance was covered by fire from the top of the two khans held by the 114th, proceeded to carry out this mission under Lieutenant Marriott of the former regiment, who was accompanied by the Assistant Political Officer. The latter urged the subaltern not to be bound by the letter of his orders, but burn the hostile village before he returned to camp. This rather rash advice was to prove costly, for owing to some delay in getting the men to advance, the Arabs, numbering it is said from fifteen hundred to two thousand, began arriving on every side. The two platoons were overwhelmed, forty-three being reported missing, or most likely killed, while one British officer, one Indian officer, and fourteen Indian other ranks were wounded. . . . The townspeople and tribesmen in the neighbourhood became unmistakably hostile, and opening fire on the khans from all quarters of the village, killed six men and wounded fourteen others. This led to the withdrawal of every one to the Serai, to which building the 114th fought their way along a wall-enclosed road over a distance of one hundred and twenty yards, escaping with the loss of two men wounded. The question of food, with the inhabitants openly hostile, now became prominent, as also that of ammunitions, which was running short, and medical requirements, which were entirely lacking. Raids were therefore planned and carried out on the bazaar, which consists of a narrow street roofed with reed matting, some two hundred and fifty yards long, running across the village from east to west with the usual ramifications. Here are numerous diminutive shops, typical of Eastern marketing centers, the majority of which are owned by dealers in grain and vendors of other food-stuffs. These raids succeeded to the extent of securing supplies sufficient for the garrison for a few days. As the process of getting water for the garrison in the Serai from the river was attended with considerable risk, and three men had lost their lives doing so, wells were dug which, though only ten feet deep, furnished a sufficient supply for the besieged. The ammunition difficulty had been reported by heliography through Samawah to Baghdad, and could only be overcome by attempting to drop a supply in boxes from aeroplanes. This was tried, [and] aeroplanes arrived and dropped three boxes. One box fell into the river, another among date-palms a hundred yards from the Serai, and the third reached its goal but fatally wounded a Naik (L/Cpl.) of the 99th Infantry and an Arab prisoner. Through the bravery of Mr.

E.W.L. Harper of the railway service, who had already distinguished himself at the repair of the burnt bridge and in the withdrawal from the village on the 4th, and who went out with two men, the box that was dropped into the river was recovered. That which fell into the date-palm grove was secured by Sepoy Hardat of the 99th Infantry, who had to climb three walls seven to eight feet high under the fire of the insurgents, and approach to within fifty yards of the houses held by them.

By the 12th, although a sortie by the 99th Infantry secured some food, supplies were again running short. A raid on a large scale, in co-operation with bombing aeroplanes sent from Baghdad, was organized ... and may be said to have saved the situation and gained time for a force to effect the relief of the garrison. On this occasion two platoons of the 114th Mahrattas acted as covering party, while the remainder of the garrison, except a small piquet, furnished with bags, tins, and blankets, collected sufficient food for twelve days, consisting of half a ton of grain, besides some sheep and chickens. The covering party were equally successful in another sense, and killed twenty inhabitants with no loss to themselves.

Lawrence of Arabia Opposes Iraqi Mandate

The Revolt of 1920 was front-page news in England, and the British readership did not vehemently throw its support behind the continued oversight of Iraq. T. E. Lawrence was the most famous opponent of the mandate. This man is better known as the celebrated "Lawrence of Arabia" who helped to organize the Arab Revolt during World War I. This revolt began in 1916, and the Arabs fought to have the right to establish an independent state after the war. The British, in their turn, supported Arab aspirations because such a revolt would be an important diversion for Ottoman troops. As the British liaison with the Arabs, Lawrence worked with many Arab men from the three Ottoman provinces of Mesopotamia. As pointed out by Charles Tripp, Mesopotamians in the Ottoman army joined this revolt in large numbers, larger than any other contingent (Tripp, 33). Jafar al-Askari, who would later develop Iraq's military, was one officer who abandoned the Ottoman cause (al-Askari, Facey, and Safwat, 113–58). For this reason, Lawrence knew and respected many men from the Mesopotamian territory. His respect for them is apparent in a letter written to the Sunday *Times* (London), 22 August 1920, p. 15. As you read it, you should consider the following: What are the specific reasons that Lawrence considers the mandate a bad idea? How does he believe that the mandate will affect Great Britain? How does he think the mandate will affect Arabs?

The people of England have been led in Mesopotamia into a trap from which it will be hard to escape with . . . honour. They have been tricked into it by a . . . withholding of information. The Baghdad communiqués are belated . . . incomplete. Things have been far worse than we have been told, our administration more bloody and inefficient than the public knows. It is a disgrace to our imperial record, and may soon be too inflamed for any ordinary cure. We are today not far from a disaster.

The sins of commission are those of the British civil authorities in Mesopotamia . . . who were given a free hand by London. They are controlled from no Department of State, but from the empty space which divides the Foreign Office from the India Office. They availed themselves of the necessary discretion of war-time to carry over their dangerous independence into times of peace. They contest every suggestion of real self-government sent them from home. A recent proclamation about autonomy circulated with unction from Baghdad was drafted and published out there in a hurry, to forestall a more liberal statement in preparation in London, 'Self-determination papers' favourable to England were extorted in Mesopotamia in 1919 by official pressure, by aeroplane demonstrations, by deportations to India.

The Cabinet cannot disclaim all responsibility. They receive little more news than the public: they should have insisted on more, and better, they have sent draft after draft of reinforcements, without enquiry. When conditions became too bad to endure longer, they decided to send out as High Commissioner the original author of the present system, with a conciliatory message to the Arabs that his heart and policy have completely changed.

Yet our published policy has not changed, and does not need changing. It is that there has been a deplorable contrast between our profession and our practice. We said we went to Mesopotamia to defeat Turkey. We said we stayed to deliver the Arabs from the oppression of the Turkish Government, and to make available for the world its resources of corn and oil. We spent nearly a million men and nearly a thousand million of money to these ends. This year we are spending ninety-two thousand men and fifty millions of money on the same objects.

Our government is worse than the old Turkish system. They kept fourteen thousand local conscripts embodied, and killed a yearly average of two hundred Arabs in maintaining peace. We keep ninety thousand men, with aeroplanes, armoured cars, gunboats, and armoured trains. We have killed about ten thousand Arabs in this rising this summer. We cannot hope to maintain such an average: it is a poor country, sparsely peopled; but Abd el Hamid would applaud his masters, if he saw us working. We are told the object of the rising was political, we are not told what the local people want. It may be what the Cabinet has promised them. A Minister in the House of Lords said that we must have so many troops because the local people will not enlist. On Friday the Government announce the death of some local levies defending their British Officers, and say that the services of these men have not yet been sufficiently recognized because they are too few (adding the ... Baghdad touch that they are men of bad character). There are seven thousand of them, just half the old Turkish force of occupation. Properly officered and distributed, they would relieve half our army there. Cromer controlled Egypt's six million people with five thousand British troops; Colonel Wilson fails to control Mesopotamia's three million people with ninety thousand troops.

We have not reached the limit of our military commitments. Four weeks ago the staff in Mesopotamia drew up a memorandum asking for four more divisions. I believe it was forwarded to the War Office, which has now sent three brigades from India. If the North-West Frontier cannot be further denuded, where is the balance to come from? Meanwhile, our unfortunate troops, Indian and British, under hard conditions of climate and supply, are policing an immense area, paying dearly every day in lives for the willfully wrong policy of the civil administration in Baghdad. General Dyer was relieved of his command in India for a much smaller error, but the responsibility in this case is not on the Army, which has acted only at the request of the civil authorities. The War Office has made every effort to reduce our forces, but the decisions of the Cabinet have been against them.

The Government in Baghdad have been hanging Arabs in that town for political offences, which they call rebellion. The Arabs are not at war with us. Are these illegal executions to provoke the Arabs to reprisals on the three hundred British prisoners they hold? And, if so, is it that their punishment may be more severe, or is it to persuade our other troops to fight to the last?

We say we are in Mesopotamia to develop it for the benefit of the world. All experts say that the labour supply is the ruling factor in its development. How far will the killing of ten thousand villagers and townspeople this summer hinder the production of wheat, cotton, and oil? How long will we permit millions of pounds, thousands of Imperial troops, and tens of thousands of Arabs to be sacrificed on behalf of colonial administration which can benefit nobody but its administrators?

Winston Churchill Outlines Middle East Policy

The Revolt of 1920 led to no small amount of political soul-searching in London, and British policymakers subsequently decided to enunciate a more coherent and more tenable policy in the Middle East in March 1921. Cairo was chosen as the venue for a conference where high-level discussions could take place. The meeting offered a "who's who" of important personages. As colonial secretary, Winston Churchill presided over the meetings. The attendees included Gertrude Bell, General Aylmer Haldane and T. E. Lawrence. Jafar al-Askari was one of two Iraqis that also came to Cairo. These leaders came up with a political formula that they believed would be acceptable to both the Iraqi people and the British public. They decided to institute a constitutional monarchy, and then have a king sign a treaty of protection with Great Britain. In this way, British policy moved from direct rule to a policy of association that took into consideration the needs and interests of Iraq's elite.

As colonial secretary, Churchill needed to sell the policy worked out in Cairo to the representatives of the British public. The following are excerpts from a speech given in the House of Commons on 14 June 1921, less than three months after the Cairo Conference convened. It is taken from *Winston S. Churchill: His Complete Speeches, 1897–1963*, edited by Robert Rhodes James (New York: Chelsea House Publishers, 1974), 3: 3095–96 and 3: 3098–102. As you read the speech, you should consider the following: What does Churchill consider the nature of the promise to the Arabs? Was it independence? How do promises to Arabs intersect with British interests? What components of British policy in Iraq are advocated by Churchill? And how does he convince his audience to accept them?

> I must take, as my starting point this afternoon, the obligations and responsibilities into which this country has entered in the Middle East, and which, in accordance with the policy of the Government, I am endeavouring to discharge. During the War our Eastern Army conquered Palestine and Mesopotamia. They overran both these provinces of the Turkish Empire. They roused the Arabs and the local inhabitants against the Turks. We uprooted the Turkish administration, and, as the Army moved forward, set up a military administration in its place. In order to gain the support of as many local inhabitants as possible, pledges were given that the Turkish rule should not be re-introduced in these regions. There is no dispute about these pledges. They were given by Lord Hardinge, by Sir Percy Cox, and by General Maude, and they were given during the War by the present Prime Minister. Secondly, in order to gain the support of the

Arabs against the Turks, we, in common with our Allies, made during the War another series of promises to the Arabs. We made them, through King Hussein and those who gathered round him, for the reconstitution of the Arab nation, and, as far as possible, for a restoration of Arab influence and authority in the conquered provinces, or, as we term them, the liberated provinces. There is no doubt about these pledges either.... Such was the position, and such were our obligations when the War came to an end.

After the fateful period of the War, we entered upon the painful period of the peace negotiations. The principles governing the disposal of the conquered Turkish provinces ... among the victorious Allies were decided by the Supreme Council sitting in Paris during 1919, and their conclusions were embodied in the Treaties of Versailles and Sèvres and in the Covenant of the League of Nations. These Treaties were approved on behalf of Great Britain by the War Cabinet of those days, and their provisions have been accepted or acquiesced in by Parliament. Under decisions arising out of these Treaties we have solemnly accepted before the whole world the position of mandatory Power for Palestine and Mesopotamia. That is a very serious responsibility.... We are at this moment in possession of these countries. We have destroyed the only other form of government which existed there. We have made the promises that I have already recited to the inhabitants, and we must endeavour to do our duty, to behave in a sober and honourable manner, and to discharge obligations which we entered into with our eyes open. We cannot repudiate light-heartedly these undertakings. We cannot turn round and march our armies hastily to the coast and leave the inhabitants, for whose safety ... we have made ourselves responsible in the most ... solemn manner, a prey to anarchy and confusion of the worst description. We cannot ... leave the ... historic ... Baghdad and other cities ... in Mesopotamia to be pillaged by the ... Bedouins of the desert. Such a proceeding would not be in accordance with the view the ... Parliament has always ... taken of its duty, nor would it be in accordance with the reputation that our country has frequently made exertions to deserve and maintain.

It is no use consuming time and energy at this stage in debating whether we were wise or unwise in contracting the obligations I have recounted. Moving this way and that way in the agony of the Great War, struggling for our lives, striking at our enemies ... we eventually emerged victorious in arms and encumbered with the responsibilities which so often attach to the victor. We are bound to make a sincere, honest, patient, resolute effort to redeem our obligations, and, whether that course be popular or unpopular, I am certain it is the only course which any British Government or British House of Commons will in the end find itself able to pursue.... I agree that the obligation is not an unlimited one; I agree that a point might be reached when we should have to declare that we had failed and that we were not justified in demanding further sacrifices from the British taxpayer; that the conditions of our finance or our military resources were such that we could do no more. That would be a very humiliating and melancholy confession to have to make, and after giving most careful and, I think, quite unprejudiced consideration to the whole subject, I do not think it would be true to say at the present time either that we have failed or that our resources do not enable us to discharge our obligations. On the contrary, I believe that, judging by all the facts before us at the present time, it is our duty to persevere, and I hope that by persevering we may find an honourable and inextravagant and . . . prosperous issue from our affairs. But if we are to succeed, if we are to avoid the shame of failure; if we are to bring our enterprises to a satisfactory conclusion, the fundamental condition . . . lies in the reduction of expenditure in these two countries to within reasonable and practicable limits. It is to that I have endeavoured to address myself in priority over other considerations. . . .

I now come to the Cairo Conference. If any saving was to be effected in this total, it was evident that the rate at which the troops should leave the country must be substantially accelerated, and that being so, a large body of troops must quit Mesopotamia before the hot weather, which is a dangerous period, instead of waiting until afterwards as had been intended. Another large body of troops also had to quit Mesopotamia after the critical period was passed. The following are the principal economies effected by the Cairo Conference. . . . It was agreed that subject to the political arrangements which are a counterpart of these reductions, and other methods which I shall mention in the course of my statement, there should be an immediate reduction of the Mesopotamia garrison from a 33 battalion to a 23 battalion scale. This reduction will be completed by the 15th July, and troops have been pouring out of the country ever since the decision was come to. We decided on a further prospective reduction after 1st October to a 12 battalion scale, and on the immediate disposal of stock and surplus military stores in Mesopotamia, with the consequent economies in storage expenses and personnel. We decided upon a reduction in the number of horses from 47,000 on the 1st April down to 17,000 by the 1st August. . . . Lastly, there is a large reduction in the number of followers and in the Indian and native labour employed by the Army. The total traceable definite saving resulting from these measures amounted to £5,500,000, and a further close scrutiny of Army Estimates has enabled us to make another saving of £1,000,000. Against these savings we have, however, to set certain other charges for the Air Force, for Arab levies, and for subsidies . . . and charges for refugees, railways, and miscellaneous civil charges. These represent a total of £2,000,000, making a total reduction of £4,500,000....

Let us now see what is the policy and what are the methods by which we hope to achieve this enormous reduction in military strength and in expenditure while at the same time carrying out our undertakings. Hitherto, in the financial argument, I have treated Palestine and Mesopotamia as one, but now the path bifurcates, and I must deal with each country separately. I will take Mesopotamia first. In June of last year, the High Commissioner for Mesopotamia was directed by His Majesty's Government to announce the early setting up of a distinctly Arab Government under an Arab ruler in Mesopotamia, or Iraq, as it is, perhaps, more convenient to call it. That declaration we have already to a great extent carried out. A provisional native Government has been in existence for a good many months. It has been formed by Sir Percy Cox under the headship of the Naqib of Baghdad, whose services, in spite of his great age, in coming forward and assisting us at this juncture, are worthy of the highest praise and recognition. A Government with British advice and assistance, and, of course, under the protection of Imperial troops, is at present administering the country. It is our intention to replace this provisional Government in the course of the summer by a Government based upon an assembly elected by the people of Iraq, to install an Arab ruler who will be acceptable to the elected assembly, and to create an Arab army for the national defense. I must now speak about the ruler. We have no intention of forcing upon the people of Iraq a ruler who is not of their own choice. At the same time, as the Mandatory Power which is put to such heavy expense, we cannot remain indifferent or unconcerned in a matter so vital to us. We should like to have the best candidate chosen, but we must in any case have a suitable candidate chosen.... I think I am right in leaving these matters entirely in the hands of Sir Percy Cox. He is a great believer in the Arabs; he is devoted to the people of Iraq; he is acquainted with every aspect of Arab politics; he is in close personal relations with most of the candidates; he is accustomed to deal with these Arab notabilities, and I hope that under his guidance the people of Iraq will make a wise and at the same time a free choice. I feel, however, that it is necessary, after consultation with my advisers—and I have tried to obtain the best experts that the British Empire can produce in these matters—I think it necessary to state quite plainly the view which the British Government takes of what would be the best choice of ruler. Broadly speaking, there are two policies which can be adopted towards the Arab race. One is the policy of keeping them divided, of discouraging their national aspirations, of setting up administrations of local notables in each particular province or city, and exerting an influence through the jealousies of one tribe against another. That was largely, in many cases, the Turkish policy before the War, and cynical as it was, it undoubtedly achieved a certain measure of success. The other policy, and the one which, I think, is alone compatible with the sincere fulfillment of the pledges we gave during the War to the Arab race and to the Arab leaders, is an attempt to build up around the ancient capital of Baghdad, in a form friendly to Britain and to her Allies, an Arab State which can revive and embody the old culture and glories of the Arab race, and which, at any rate, will have a full and fair opportunity of doing so if the Arab race shows itself capable of profiting by it. Of these two policies we have definitely chosen the latter.

If you are to endeavour so to shape affairs in the sense of giving satisfaction to Arab nationality, you will, I believe, find that the very best structure around which to build, in fact, the only structure of this kind which is available, is the house and family and following of the Sherif of Mecca. It was King Hussein who, in the crisis of War, declared war upon the Turks and raised the Arab standard. Around that standard gathered his four capable sons—of whom the Emir Feisal and the Emir Abdullah are the two best known in this country—and many of the principal chiefs and notabilities of the Arab world. With them at our side we fought, and with their aid as a valuable auxiliary Lord Allenby hurled the Turks from Palestine. Both the Emir Abdullah and the Emir Feisal have great influence in Iraq among the military and also among the religious classes, both Sunni and Shiah. The adherents of the Emir Feisal have sent him an invitation to go to Mesopotamia and present himself to the people and to the assembly which is soon to gather together, and King Hussein has accorded his son permission to accept the invitation. The Emir Abdullah, the elder brother, has renounced his rights and claims. I have caused the Emir Feisal to be informed, in answer to his inquiry, that no obstacle will be placed in the way of his candidature, that he is at liberty to proceed forthwith to Mesopotamia, and that, if he is chosen, he will receive the countenance and support of Great Britain. In consequence, the Emir Feisal has already left Mecca on the 12th of this month, and is now on his journey to Mesopotamia, where he will arrive in about 10 days. We must see how opinion forms itself and what is the view of the National Assembly when it is elected. I cannot attempt to predict the course of events, but I do not hesitate to say that, if the Emir Feisal should be acceptable to the people generally, and to the Assembly, a solution will have been reached which offers, in the opinion of the highest authorities on whom I am relying, the best prospects for a happy and prosperous outcome.

... Our object and our policy is to set up an Arab Government, and to make it take the responsibility, with ... our guidance and with an effective measure of our support, until they are strong enough to stand alone, and so to foster the development of their independence as to permit the steady and speedy diminution of our burden. . . . [O]ur policy in Mesopotamia is to reduce our commitments and to extricate ourselves from our burdens while at the same time honourably discharging our obligations and building up a strong and effective Arab Government which will always be the friend of Britain.

The Kurdish "Election" of King Faysal

In formulating a policy for Iraq and the rest of the Middle East, British politicians felt compelled to rescind some promises made to Kurds regarding autonomy. The Kurds had banked on American promises, for the United States had entered the war, in part at least, to promote self-determination among the non-Turkish minorities of the Ottoman Empire. Buoyed by the promise of self-determination, Kurds had sent representatives to the Paris Peace Conference in 1919. Their efforts to gain autonomy seemed destined for success. Article 62 of the postwar Treaty of Sèvres, signed in August 1920, calls for "local autonomy for the predominantly Kurdish areas," and Article 64 specifies that such areas include those surrounding Mosul. Thus, it would seem that the Kurds would be politically separated from Arab Iraq.

The British eventually found such promises to be highly inconvenient, and so they would set them aside. At the Cairo Conference of 1921, British officers began to perceive the inconveniences of a separate Kurdish polity. This policy would, after all, require more money and manpower—and, given its isolation, with little in return. The High Commissioner Sir Percy Cox strongly favored the incorporation of Kurds into a larger Iraqi state. And officers who disagreed with the policy were relieved of their duties (McDowall, 166). According to one Kurdish specialist, "the exigencies of creating the Iraqi state outweighed special claims for the Kurds" (167).

And so, the British quashed Kurdish aspirations and instead invited them to rubber-stamp the evolving political structures of the British mandate. Such endorsements were to include voting in favor of a constitutional monarchy with Faysal and all his descendants as king. This plebiscite took place in July 1921, and a suspiciously high 96 percent of Iraqis were in favor of Faysal assuming the role as their king. As a result, Faysal ascended the throne in August 1921. He immediately made it clear that an independent Kurdistan was not possible. He took this position to ensure a balance with southern Shi'is. Two years later, the British would sign the Treaty of Lausanne, which officially awarded parts of Kurdistan to Iraq, Turkey, and Iran.

Wallace Lyon was a British officer in Iraq between 1918 and 1944, and he was stationed in Arbil at the time of the election of Faysal. A large city fifty miles east of Mosul, Arbil is squarely in Kurdish territory. The following account of the election is found in D. K. Fieldhouse's edited memoir by Lyon in *Kurds, Arabs and Britons: The Memoir of Wallace Lyon in Iraq, 1918–1944* (London: I. B. Tauris, 2002), 92–96. As you read the following passage, you should consider the following: What is the attitude of the Kurds with whom Lyon speaks? How does the administrator overcome their trepidation? What does Lyon's story suggest about the nature of the mandate in Iraq?

> The country . . . was now divided into thirteen provinces or liways each under a mutassaraf [governor] with a British Political Officer at his elbow to advise, support and stimulate as necessary. The Minister of Interior presided over the administration and, as in all Middle Eastern countries where law and order take priority, his was the most important portfolio in the Cabinet, not least because it was he who controlled the elections.
>
> The Mosul wilayat consisted of four liways or provinces, Mosul, Arbil, Sulaimani and Kirkuk, in each of which it was my fate to spend several years and set-up was to say the least of it [uncertain].
>
> There was no peace treaty with Turkey, now rejuvenated under Mustafa Kemal, flushed with success against the Greeks, and unwilling to accept our occupation of the Mosul wilayat. Though two Kurdish uprisings and one Arab rebellion had been suppressed yet no real tribal disarmament had taken place. The [British] troops were disgruntled at the extended post-war service in a country devoid of the normal facilities for their enjoyment and where no families were allowed. The British government was naturally anxious to reduce their commitments and expenses in accordance with post-war economies. The people had no certain knowledge of what was to be the fate of their country or those who helped us to rule it, and this was especially the case for the inhabitants of the four provinces of the old Mosul wilayat still in dispute. If it came to the worst we Britishers could go home but where could they go? The Turks had hanged everyone in Kut-al-Amara who had in any way assisted us, and this was not easily forgotten.
>
> Saiyid Talib Pasha of Basra was appointed Minister of Interior. He had always been friendly to us since the troops first landed in Basra, and the legend that he had murdered no fewer than three Turkish governors was in the present circumstances all to his credit. He was also rich. The thirteen provincial governors were all ex-Turkish officials of local origin, respectable, conservative, and men who had continued to serve on the administration since the exit of the

Turkish Army. To advise, support and stimulate them a British Political Officer was attached to each. So, though nominally an adviser of Administrative Inspector [as he was now called] was without authority, yet in practice it was the British officer who had to put the tick into the new clock. There were times when a political personality or a tribal chief had to be restrained; and, as it would be asking too much of the local governor to risk a future family feud by taking the necessary action, the British Adviser stepped in and acted for him. The police were still commanded by British officers and the ultimate sanction of force by the employment of troops or aeroplanes had to be recommended by the British Political Officers and approved by their chief and the British High Commission.

During the war . . . there had been set up in Cairo a department called the Arab Bureau which was originally intended to provoke rebellion by the Arabs so as to hamper the Turkish operations and lines of communications while facilitating our own. . . . After the Armistice, however, the 'raison d'être' of the Bureau no longer existed. Hogarth returned to Oxford, leaving Miss Bell and Lawrence to plead the cause of the Arabs. Miss Bell [had] come to Baghdad as Oriental Secretary to the Civil Commissioner [in 1917] and subsequently to the High Commissioner, Sir Percy Cox. Lawrence felt himself under an obligation to the Amir Faisal, who had been ejected from Syria by the French, and in Miss Bell he had a fervent supporter, for in fact she in a platonic but nevertheless intense degree had become a worshipper of Faisal and his cause. Thus it was that the British government was persuaded to put him on the throne of Iraq by the pleadings of Lawrence and Hogarth, while Miss Bell, like St. John the Baptist, went ahead to Baghdad to prepare the way and make his path straight. To the inhabitants of Iraq and to the British officers serving there, however, this decision was not revealed. Instead an official notification was issued to the effect that the country would be ruled by a King to be elected by the people. Thus Saiyid Talib Pasha who, though Minister of Interior, was quite unaware of the plan decided that he would enter for the Royal stakes. He gave a dinner party to all the most important people, Iraqi and British alike, including the Times correspondent, and at it he told them of his intention and hopes for their support.

As soon as Miss Bell heard of this she rushed round to Sir Percy Cox, with the result that the next afternoon [17 April 1921] Saiyid Talib Pasha was arrested when leaving Miss Bell's house after a cup of tea and a friendly chat. He was bundled into an armoured car and out of the country without further palaver. Philby, to his credit be it said, was furious on hearing that his Minister had been banished, and dashed round to see Sir Percy. What sort of procedure was this? Banishing the Minister of Interior without reference to his Adviser. . . . But all Sir

Percy said was, 'I perceive that there isn't enough room in this country for both of us.' So Philby left. The next notification published the fact that the British government's candidate for the election was Amir Faisal, and to all of us Political Officers there came a top secret coded telegram instructing us to use all our influence, personal and official, to persuade the people to elect Faisal.

For me this was a tough assignment, as the great majority of the people were Kurds who cared little for any Arab prince, and like all hill men despised the dwellers of the plains. Had I been older, more experienced, or even known at the time of the dubious methods employed to confront the people with a Hobson's choice while telling the world it was a free election, I would have stood aside. But at the time I was a young military officer, tempered in war and accustomed to carry out orders without demur, but inexperienced in the wiles of politics.

The tribal chiefs and city elders were gathered together and asked to sign the petition for Faisal. An Arab prince descended from the Prophet, who had supported us in the war against the Turks from whom they were now liberated.... They were reluctant and asked about other candidates; and I was compelled to admit there was none, but that Faisal was Lloyd George's candidate, and who would know better than him? Would the British be annoyed and perhaps send out columns of troops if they didn't sign? I said I didn't know but presumed they would be disappointed. In the end after a very long, hot and tiring day, I returned to the bungalow to find two strange British Colonels had arrived for the night. They were [Colonel Kinahan] Cornwallis and [Colonel P.] Joyce [both one-time members of the Arab Bureau]; like Joshua and his companions they had come to spy out the land. Later one [Cornwallis] was to take the place of my Chief, Philby, the other [Joyce] to found the Iraqi Army. After I had checked their credentials, they asked me how the election was proceeding and I told them that as most of the inhabitants were Kurds it was no easy matter to get their representatives to sign for Faisal; however, after much persuasion, I had succeeded in carrying out the orders and as far as I was concerned the election was over. Later I heard that Major Marshall had refused to use any persuasion in the Kirkuk liwa, and as a result the people there, who were mostly of Turkish and Kurdish origins, had refused to elect Faisal. He was older, and more experienced, and he was right where I was wrong. The Sulaimani liwa was completely Kurdish, the centre of Kurdish nationalism, governed as a separate province under the British High Commissioner and consequently left out of the election; though subsequently when, for want of British support, the Kurdish aspirations faded out, it was included in the remainder of Iraq.

The coronation was arranged to follow swiftly on the 'election' and the Naqib of Baghdad, an old and saintly gentleman who commanded universal respect, was only too willing to hand over the leadership of the provisional government; and in due course all the notables of the country were summoned to Baghdad to witness the coronation of Faisal. Perhaps coronation is the wrong word, for among the Arabs there is no such thing as a crown and the ceremony consists of leading the King to his throne. This was done by the Naqib under the supervision of Sir Percy Cox, and in the presence of all the notables assembled to witness the ceremony and to pay homage to him when seated [23 August 1921]. Apart from his relations who accompanied him to Iraq, the new King's supporters were Cornwallis, Joyce, and the ex-Turkish officers of Iraqi origin and Arab blood who had been captured by us during the war and who had elected to support the Sharif's rebellion under Faisal. The most important of these were Jafar al-Askari and Nuri Pasha as-Said, and always, though often behind the scene, the faithful and ubiquitous Miss Bell.

As soon as the ceremony was over a working party arrived to dismantle the platform and throne which, stripped of its regalia, was seen to have been hurriedly put together from sections of Japanese beer crates with the stencil marks 'Asahi' and 'NAAFI' still showing on the seat. For the few junior British officers who remained behind this provided a hilarious anticlimax to the solemnity of the occasion, though as an omen it could hardly be interpreted to predict solidity for the foundation of Hashemite rule, nor its adherence to the orthodox Moslem attitude towards alcohol. But junior Army officers were not in the councils of the great and consequently did not concern themselves with political prognostications. They did not know that the King was foisted on Iraq by the British government. . . . They were not to know that the election was rigged, still less could they foresee that every subsequent election would be rigged until the final collapse of counterfeit democracy with the violent deaths of the Hashemite family and all its principal supporters [in 1958]. . . . Thus as soon as the King had been crowned, the orders came for consolidation of the country by showing the flag.

King Faysal's Coronation Speech, 1921

The British chose Faysal bin al-Hussein (r. 1921–1933) as the new king of Iraq. His credentials, in the eyes of British politicians, were impeccable. Faysal's family claimed descent from the Prophet Muhammad, a lineage that inherently supported his political legitimacy. Also, he was the son of Sharif Hussein bin Ali, leader of the Arab Revolt in 1916. As such, he had proven an ally of the British in their cataclysmic struggle against the Turks. After World War I, he had been slotted to be king of Syria, but the French reneged on this deal. With Faysal out of a job, Winston Churchill and other British politicians sought him out as king of Iraq even though he had never traveled to Mesopotamia. They believed that his Arab nationalism and sharifian lineage would overcome such shortcomings.

The coronation was held in Baghdad, the capital city, on 23 August 1921. Faysal intended for the date of the coronation to call on religious symbolism. Thus, it came four days after the celebration of 'id al-adha, the feast of the sacrifice and the most important holiday in the Islamic calendar. It also coincided with the Shi'i feast of Ghadir, which, according to a British official, is "held to commemorate the day on which the Prophet nominated his son-in-law Ali as master of the people" (Rush, 10: 697). The British invited fifteen hundred Iraqis to the coronation, each province sending twenty-five delegates, and these were seated according to their place in the sociopolitical hierarchy.

Faysal's coronation speech provides insight into the king's perception of the Iraqi nationhood. The following speech is taken from *Records of the Hashimite Dynasties: A Twentieth Century Documentary History,* edited by Alan de L. Rush (Cambridge: Archive Editions, 1995), 10: 698–99. As you read the speech, you should consider the following: What message does Faysal try to convey in terms of Iraq's relationship with Great Britain? How does his speech address peoples of different sects or ethnicity? Does Faysal emphasize one group over others? How so?

> I offer my thanks to the generous nation of 'Iraq for the swearing of its free allegiance to me and for proving thereby its affection for me and confidence in me. I pray the Almighty to give me success in elevating the state of this dear country and this noble nation so that its ancient glory may be restored and that it may maintain a high place among rising and progressive nations.
>
> It is incumbent on me on this historical occasion on which the people of 'Iraq have demonstrated their affections for our Hashimite family to recall the noble part played by my father, His Majesty King Husain. He raised the Arab standard of war on the side of the Allies and roused the Arabs without any other motive than their liberation and the firm establishment of the racial independence which they had desired for centuries.
>
> I also regard it as my bounden duty to call to mind on this occasion the splendid spirit of those of Arabia's sons who rose and sacrificed themselves with the heroes of the Allied Armies for the sake of their country. May the memory of them be everlasting. Peace be upon them. . . .
>
> My duty today also calls me to express my gratitude to the British nation for having come to the assistance of the Arabs during the critical time of the war

and for the generous expenditure of its wealth and sacrifice of its sons in the cause of Arab liberation and independence. It is in confident reliance on that British friendship and support which has been given in the past and promised in the future that I have now come forward to take upon myself the affairs of this country.

I thank the Provisional Government for its zealous services and His Excellency the High Commissioner for his sincere friendship and the Great British Government for its reception of me as King of the Independent State of 'Iraq to which high office I am called by the direct will of the Nation.

Oh! beloved people of 'Iraq, this country was formerly the cradle of civilization and progress, the center of science and learning, but owing to the calamities and disasters of the past it had become devoid of comfort and prosperity. Security had disappeared and anarchy prevailed, the work of man had declined and nature gained the mastery. The waters of the two rivers ran waste to the sea; land was left barren which had once been green and fruitful and the desert encroached on cultivated lands so that the towns which were able to resist destruction became like oases in the desert.

This is a painful truth with which we are now faced, and any nation which desires to rise must recognize plain facts. It is for the purpose of overcoming these obstacles that the nation has risen and it was to revive such a land of desolation that we entered the great war.

If the saying is true that a people follow the religion of its King then my religion is to realize the wishes of the nation and to set the pillars of this kingdom on a foundation of a strong religious principle and to establish a civilization on a true basis of science and nobility of character: I rely first on God and the spirit of the Great Prophet and then on you, oh people of 'Iraq.

As I have repeatedly stated to you before, the progress of this country is dependent on the assistance of a nation which can aid us with men and money, and as the British nation is the nearest to us and the most zealous in our interests we must seek help and co-operation from her alone in order that we may reach our goal as speedily as possible.

If again, as we say, the people are of the religion of their king, it follows that the King must also follow the religion of his people. It is in proportion to the completeness of this union that progress will ensue. We of all nations are in the greatest need of self-help within the limitations of peace and good order. I will spare no effort to profit by the qualities of every man of the nation irrespective of religion or class. All to me shall be equal. There shall be no distinction between townsmen and Bedouin; for me the sole distinction shall be that of knowledge and capacity. The whole nation is my party and I have no other. The interests of the country as a whole are my interest and I have no other.

My first task will be to proceed with the elections and the convocation of the Constituent Assembly. The nation should understand that it is this Congress that will in consultation with me draw up the Constitution of its independence on the basis of democratic government and define the fundamental principles of political and social life. Finally, it will conform the Treaty which I shall lay before it regarding the relations which are to exist between our Government and the Great British Government. Furthermore, the Congress will establish the freedom of religion and worship so that all men may follow their own law and religion provided it does not conflict with security and public morals.

It will also enact certain Judicial Laws which will safeguard the interests of foreigners and ensure them against any interference with their religion, race or language and will guarantee equity of commercial dealing with the foreign countries. In this connection I am fully confident that in consultation with Sir Percy Cox who has proved his friendship to the Arabs in a manner which will ever live in their affectionate memory, we shall please God reach our goal.

I appeal to you for union and co-operation, deep deliberation and insight. You must seek knowledge and must work, and may God help us and grant us success.

Shi'is Oppose (Rigged) Elections

From the first, many Shi'i leaders and their followers opposed the institutions of the mandate. Charles Tripp suggests that this opposition emerged because the British placed the administration of Iraq in Sunni hands (Tripp, 55–56). Faysal, for example, was Sunni. But, and perhaps more important, the British favored the Sunni officers who had served with them in the Arab Revolt. These were the same Sunnis who had been favored by the Ottomans, so Sunni dominance began to become self-perpetuating. When British administrators began to draw up plans for elections to a constituent assembly in 1922, the opposition among many groups of Shi'i reached a fever pitch.

Ayatollah Mahdi al-Khalisi was one of the most vocal Shi'i leaders to oppose the British in general and the elections in particular. He would produce a religious decree against participation in these elections. As a result of his influence, Faysal and his British protectors would exile him to Iran. Al-Khalisi's son, who was also exiled, wrote an account of his father's life, which Pierre-Jean Luizard translated to French as *La vie de l'ayatollah Mahdî al-Khâlisî par son fils* (Paris:

Editions de La Martinière, 2005), 261–66. As you read the following translated accounts, you should consider the following: Why does al-Khalisi oppose elections? What strategies does he use to ensure that elections do not take place? What does he want in place of the mandate? Does al-Khalisi oppose democracy?

> The accursed administration exiled me on 4 Muharram 1341 [28 August 1922], and it did so deliberately intending to destroy my father. But my physical distance from him only amplified his determination and his courage to fight to defend the glory of Islam and the independence of Iraq.
>
> The English counted on the fact that the Ayatollah al-Khalisi would be frightened. They had, after all, separated him from his son and threatened him with his own exile. They hoped that this would convince him not to oppose them. And so, they announced the election of the representatives of the Constituent Assembly with the objective of having this assembly legitimize the treaty. They wanted to force Iraq to accept the bonds of servitude, but the country was refusing such servitude with a strength borne only of despair. Ayatollah al-Khalisi demanded national elections that were truly free. Some very serious events, however, would confirm that this was not possible. Indeed, the agents of the English will force the people to elect the candidates of the English. Although faced with the unfailing determination of the population, who wanted to obtain respect for its rights, the English officers would use all the means of repression at their disposal. They wanted Iraqis to submit to their will.
>
> Thus, their planes will begin to fly through the Iraqi sky and to release their bombs in every place where the candidate of the English was not a frontrunner. Thus, fifty-six bombs will hit a ceremonial funeral procession for Hussein (ahs) in Daghghara. Also, some important fighting will take place throughout the country, as in Rumaytha, which is in the Gharraf, and elsewhere. The Ayatollah al-Khalisi encouraged the people in this and ordered them to stay firmly attached to the Book of God, to His Prophet, and to His Messengers. As for the people, they stayed firmly attached to their liberty. But the English wanted nothing more than to subjugate Iraq and to make Iraqis totally dependent on them.
>
> When the situation got worse, the people called on the Ayatollah al-Khalisi and other scholars as well as the leaders of the Gharraf, and they asked the following (and here I paraphrase):
>
> "With our thanks to Their Excellencies the hujjatulislam Shaikh Muhammad Mahdi al-Khalisi, Sayyid Abu l-Hasan al-Isfahani and Mirza Husayn al-Na'ini: Patriotism and religion lead us to present our requests to the government and to demand that it takes certain measures. Since the government has not

responded to our requests, we have broken our relations with it. The 'councilor of Muntafik' [that is, the English Governor of the province of Muntafik, as he was called in official terminology] then answered with his planes, which subjected us to hellfire. Our infirm elderly and our newborns were decimated. But the English did not succeed in obtaining even the smallest concession with their savagery. Right now, all the routes to our town are cut, as well as the telegraph. Two days ago, they sent from Nasiriyya a detachment of at least eighty cavaliers who are preparing to confront the Azayrij tribe. But their route crossed that of the Khafaja tribe, which annihilated them. The Azayrij tribe then annihilated what remained of this detachment. And thus, now, thanks to God, we are united as we never were before. Certain cities, like Nasiriyya and Shatra, are exposed to our attacks and surrounded. The enemy planes do not cease to fall from the sky, and they are brought down by our guns. We hope that you indicate to us the path to follow and that you tell us what we must do these days."

Thus, the tribes began an immense protest against the acts committed by the English officers. They sent letters to the High Commissioner and to Faisal and described to them the extortion of the population. The tribes expressed to them their desire for peace, but they also put the English on their guard. The tribes let them know that if they persisted in violating their rights and imposing war on them, then they would defend themselves.

During these troubled times, Faisal's stomachache healed, but his psychological malady and his shame grew worse. He formed a Government with, at its head, the most criminal and odious of God's creatures. Abd al-Muhsin al-Sa'adun was the most evil of all the traitors produced by the Arab race. The treaty was hardly proclaimed before he began to run for the Constituent Assembly as a candidate of the English. The Ayatollah al-Khalisi gave up hope of seeing the English cede liberty to the Iraqis. His greatest fear was that this assembly would come to order, that it would recognize all that the English wanted, and that an Iraqi representation would approve this ignominious situation. Thus, the English, the usurpers of Iraqi rights, would obtain a veneer of legality and legitimacy to their proposals, even though these same signaled the death of Iraq.

Henceforth, there was no other alternative than to prohibit participation in the elections. This prohibition would forefront the illegitimate character of the elections until such as time as God willed the Iraqis to reject such illegitimacy. Ayatollah Khalisi published an edict that formalized this ban, and the entire community of Islamic scholars—except those who hid their English leanings behind Muslim appearances—followed this edict. Thus, the entire population refused to participate in the elections. Faced with this challenge, the infidel government found no other solution than to outlaw the order prohibiting the elections. But the rumor of this ban was already widespread, and the Iraqis thus posed this question:

"In the name of God the Most High,

"To Their Excellences our ulama and our hujjatulislam, may God long gratify us with your presence!

"We were informed that you, in accordance with your religious function and your spiritual direction, prohibited the entirety of Iraqi umma [Muslim community] from participating in these elections, which are, you argued, harmful to the community. We were also informed that you prohibited the providing of any type of assistance in these elections. We were also informed that you likened such rendering of aid to a war against God and His Messenger. We ask you, with all the respect that you inspire as councilors of what is just, to show this clearly in order that we conform to your sacred orders to which God ordered us to comply. May God accord you a long life!—15 Rabi al-Awwal 1341" [5 November 1922]

Ayatollah al-Khalisi wrote the following response:

"In the name of God, the Merciful Benefactor in whom I place my confidence.

"Yes, we promulgated an order prohibiting the elections to the entirety of the Iraqi umma. Whoever will be a candidate in these elections or will participate in them or will render assistance to them thus defies the will of God and His Messenger. The All Powerful says it perfectly in His glorious book: 'Don't you know that the one who defies God and His Messenger will be condemned to eternal hellfire in which he will find himself in ultimate disgrace.' May God preserve you all from this fate.—25 Rabi al-Awwal 1341 [15 November 1922], the humble Muhammad Mahdi Kazimi al-Khalisi, may God pardon him."

Sayyid Abu l-Hasan al-Isfahani and Mirza Husayn al-Na'ini—as well as most ulamas—took inspiration from him and will write the same thing as Ayatollah al-Khalisi.

The English prevented the publication of these fatwas in the newspapers, so thousands of copies of them will be made. Everywhere, these copies will be posted to the walls and the doors in the public places and the mosques. The souks will close in most regions of the country on 25 Rabi al-Thani [14 December 1922] and some rather large protests will take place. The confrontation between the English ... and the Iraqis worsened even more, and the government lost nearly all its hope that it could realize the plan propagated by the English. Once more, it tried to conciliate Ayatollah al-Khalisi. Some members of the government will even request an order allowing for my return to Iraq. They hoped thus to be able to earn the benevolence of Ayatollah al-Khalisi. But Ayatollah al-Khalisi declared, "If he returns to Iraq as a conqueror, yes, for he is my son. Nevertheless, I do not wish to see a son, one whom the English authority forcibly exiled, returned to Iraq with the government's consent. That will never come to pass! If he returns, it should be because this authority will be forced to allow him to return, just as it forcibly expelled him."

In hearing these words, their last hope of coaxing him disappeared into thin air. Henceforth, they knew that all the gold in the world would not make him change his mind one iota. Henceforth, they knew that neither misfortune nor pressure would be able to weaken his determination. Indeed, the fact that Iraq lay between life and death made him all the more strong. Such a condition will render these men disappointed and defeated.

To compel the population to go and vote, they will resort, though in vain, to all the means in their possession, from persuasion to violence. They will go back to the Ayatollah and request from him the conditions upon which he would order the people to participate in the elections. He said that, "the people would only be satisfied with the application of the following measures:

1) The annulment of the treaty and the proclamation by the English of the independence and freedom of Iraq.
2) The announcement by the new government that they will not make military service compulsory.
3) The return of all exiles, the liberation of all prisoners and the complete freedom of the press.
4) The creation of a Ministry of Foreign Affairs for Iraq."

Following this announcement, the executive committees of all the clandestine parties in Iraq will publish a communiqué that enunciates terms that are nearly identical.

The English will react to this with an extraordinary violence. They clearly desire to eradicate all opposition throughout Iraq, and to do so in the name of this deceitful government. There were no crimes or atrocities that it would not commit. But their extortion will only increase the refusal, the rejection and the pride of Iraqis. The English will even spread a rumor that the Ayatollah al-Khalisi and the entirety of the Islamic scholars have declared that it is licit to participate in the elections. At the same time, they will begin to restrain the movement of the people, especially toward the holy cities, in order that the ulama are not able to deny these lies. But the Iraqis will see through these bans to freely circulate and will succeed in getting in contact with the ulama to whom they pose the following question:

"To Their Excellencies our ulama and our ayatollahs, may God accord to them His Blessings!

"You have previously ordered a ban on the elections. Does this ban remain in place? Or is it lifted? Please inform us of the truth of the matter."

Sayyid Abu al-Hasan al-Isfahani and Mirza Husain al-Na'ini will respond with the following:

"... Yes, we previously promulgated a ban on the elections, and this ban was neither annulled nor modified. It is as legitimate today as it was before."

—15 Shawwal 1341 [31 May 1923]

the humble Abu al-Hasan al-Isfahani al-Musawi

"... Yes, we had formerly ordered a ban on the participation in the elections and all Muslims believing in God and the Last Judgment should provide all assistance necessary to carry out this order. This order is as it was, and it has not been changed or invalidated."

—17 Shawwal 1341 [2 June 1923]

the humble Muhammad Husain al-Gharawi al-Na'ini

After these two fatwas as well as some others, the Ayatollah al-Khalisi wrote:

"In the name of God, the Merciful Benefactor, in whom I place my confidence.

"Yes what the hujjatulislam and the ayatollahs formerly ordered remains legitimate, and to disobey it is a rebellion against God, comparable to comparing oneself to God."

—the humble Muhammad Mahdi al-Kazimi al-Khalisi. . . .

As soon as it was signed, thousands of copies of this fatwa were sent to all regions . . . and affixed to the walls and doors of mosques and public places. Tensions worsened again between the population, on the one side, and the English and their agents, on the other side. The tension reached its peak, but the English no longer saw any means to convince the people to submit themselves to them and to compel them to accept slavery.

Faisal's position in the middle of all this turmoil was surprising. His position illustrates his personal vice, his complete absence of moral values, and his lack of pride in either his religion or his status. Nothing mattered to him more than showing his importance to the English. Nothing mattered to him more than demonstrating to them his capacity to subjugate Iraqis to their will. Nothing mattered to him more than making them understand by concrete means that they needed him to vanquish Iraq and to deceive the country.

Bibliography

Al-Askari, Jafar Pasha, William Facey, and Najdat Fathi Safwat. *A Soldier's Story: From Ottoman Rule to Independent Iraq; The Memoirs of Jafar Pasha Al-Askari (1885–1936)*. London: Arabian Pub., 2003.

Bell, Gertrude Margaret Lowthian. *Letters: Selected by Lady Richmond from Lady Bell's Standard*. London: Penguin Books, 1953.

Bell, Gertrude Lowthian, and Florence Eveleen Eleanore Olliffe Bell. *The Letters of Gertrude Bell*. New York: Boni and Liveright, 1927.

Bourne, Kenneth, and D. Cameron Watt, eds. *Archive Editions: Eastern Affairs, January 1928–June 1930*. Vol. 6. New York: University Publications of America, 1986.

———. *Archive Editions: Eastern Affairs, June 1930–June 1932*. Vol. 7. New York: University Publications of America, 1986.

Burgoyne, Elizabeth. *Gertrude Bell: From Her Personal Papers*. Vol. 2, 1914–1926. London: Benn, 1961.

Cameron, Margaret Bell. *Letters from Egypt and Iraq, 1954*. Oriental Institute special publication, no. 71. Chicago: Development Office of the Oriental Institute, University of Chicago, 2001.

Casey, Robert J. *Baghdad and Points East*. New York: J. H. Sears, 1928.

Chapple, Joe Mitchell. *To Bagdad and Back*. New York: Century, 1928.

Chauncey, Alice. *Wanderings in the Middle East*. London: Hutchinson, 1925.

Cravath, Paul D. *Letters Home from India and Irak, 1925*. New York: Cravath, 1925.

Cunliffe-Owen, Betty. *"Thro' the Gates of Memory" (from the Bosphorus to Baghdad)*. London: Hutchinson, 1925.

Drower, E. S. *By the Tigris and Euphrates*. London: Hurst and Blackett, 1923.

Edmonds, C. J. *A Pilgrimage to Lalish*. London: Royal Asiatic Society of Great Britain and Ireland, 1927.

Great Britain. *Military Report on Iraq*. London: HMSO, 1923.

Great Britain. *Military Report on Iraq: Area 2 (Upper Euphrates)*. Iraq: War Office, 1924.

Guyer, Samuel, and Joseph McCabe. *My Journey Down the Tigris: A Raft-Voyage Through Dead Kingdoms*. London: Unwin, 1925.

Hamilton, Archibald Milne. *Road Through Kurdistan: Travels in Northern Iraq*. London: Tauris Parke Paperbacks, 2004.

Haldane, Sir James Aylmer Lowthrope. *The Insurrection in Mesopotamia, 1920*. 1922. Reprint, Nashville: Battery Press, 2005.

Hill, Roderic Maxwell. *The Baghdad Air Mail*. New York: Longmans, Green, 1929.

Hoare, Samuel John Gurney. *A Flying Visit to the Middle East*. Cambridge, England: University Press, 1925.

Iraq. *Maps of Iraq, with Notes for Visitors*. London: Waterloo and Sons, 1929.

Ising, Walter K. *Among the Arabs in Bible Lands*. Mountain View, Calif.: Pacific Press Pub. Association, 1924.

Jarman, Robert L. *Political Diaries of the Arab World: Iraq; Vol. 1 1920–1921*. Cambridge: Cambridge University Press Archive Editions, 1998.

Mackay, Dorothy Mary Simmons. *The Ancient Cities of Iraq*. Baghdad: Book Shop, 1926.

Main, Ernest. *In and Around Baghdad*. Baghdad: Times Press, 1930.

Maxwell, Donald. *A Dweller in Mesopotamia, Being the Adventures of an Official Artist in the Garden of Eden*. London: John Lane, 1921.

Powell, E. Alexander. *The Last Home of Mystery*. New York: Century, 1929.

Rinehart, Mary Roberts. *Nomad's Land*. New York: George H. Doran, 1926.

Rosen, Friedrich. *Oriental Memories of a German Diplomatist*. New York: Dutton, 1930.

Rush, Alan de L. *Recording Iraq, 1914–1966, Vol. 3 1921–1924*. Cambridge University Press Archive Editions, 2001.

———. *Records of the Hashimite Dynasties: A Twentieth Century Documentary History; Vol. 10 Part One Syria The Reign of King Faisal Part Two Iraq The Reign of King Faisal I*. Cambridge: Cambridge University Press Archive Edition, 1995.

Shah, Ikbal Ali. *Westward to Mecca: A Journey of Adventure through Afghanistan, Bolshevik Asia, Persia, Iraq and Hijaz to the Cradle of Islam*. London: H. F. and G. Witherby, 1928.

Stark, Freya. *Beyond Euphrates: Autobiography, 1928–1933*. London: J. Murray, 1951.

Tuson, Penelope, and Emma Quick, eds. *International and Regional Treaties and Agreements: Iraq, Kuwait*, vol. 1 of *Arabian Treaties, 1600–1960*. London: Cambridge Archive Editions, 1992.

3

The Hashemite Monarchy, 1932–1941

In Iraq, the mandate system lasted only ten years. Negotiations for Iraqi independence began in 1929, and the discussions between British and Iraqi politicians led to the signing of the Anglo-Iraqi Treaty Alliance in June 1930. Through this treaty, Great Britain maintained a neocolonial relationship with Iraq, meaning this foreign power retained its influence but not the expense of maintaining the country. Article I of this treaty, for example, requires Iraq to consult Great Britain about its foreign policy. Article V assures British troops access to Iraqi soil, while also providing two air bases for the Royal Air Force (RAF). Iraq, in turn, was required to seek all military aid from its former colonial overlord. This treaty, which was scheduled to last twenty-five years, was the basis on which Iraq entered the League of Nations in October 1932.

Great Britain ceded to Iraq a constitutional monarchy, albeit one riddled with contradictions and problems. Thus, Iraq had liberal institutions. There was a bicameral Parliament, for example, as well as regular elections. The executive, however, here signifying the king, was the dominant branch, for that allowed the British to continue dealing with only one man. King Faysal I was a savvy man, and so he understood that he must negotiate with the British. The smooth operation of this system, however, depended too much on the charisma of this one man. Faysal I died the next year, and neither his son Ghazi (1933–1939) nor Ghazi's successor the regent Abdulillah (1939–1958) had the late king's ability to balance the interests and networks that composed Iraq's sociopolitical life.

In retrospect, the first decade of Iraqi independence did not bode well for the future of this country. In 1933, Iraq experienced the Assyrian Affair, in which Christians living in nearby Mosul were systematically massacred—and with the acquiescence, if not active participation, of the Iraqi army. In August of that year, three hundred Assyrians would be killed at the hands of their own government, leading the international community to question Iraq's ability to govern itself. Hikmat Sulayman (1889–1964) gave the order that led to this massacre, while Gen. Bakr Sidqi (1890–1937) carried it out. The Assyrians sought autonomy from the central government, so most Iraqis considered these two men heroes. Together, they would further destabilize the regime in 1936, when Sidqi organized a coup d'état that resulted in the appointment of Sulayman as prime minister. In retrospect, this is the moment when the army, which grew from 12,000 men to 43,000 between 1932 and 1941, began to play a key role in Iraq's governance (Tripp, 76).

The readings in this chapter highlight the problems of nation-building in order to show the difficulties of incorporating the different ethnic and religious minorities into Iraq's political system. Faysal I recognized this problem, and so this chapter begins with a proclamation declaring the state's intent to protect the rights of ethnic and religious minorities. And yet, as seen in an excerpt by pan-Arab ideologue Sati' al-Husri, the government supported a pan-Arab political ideology that implicitly championed Sunni Arabs. Faysal I expressed his intention to hold a pan-Arab conference in Baghdad, and the British filed a report on this incident. This chapter then provides a firsthand account of the Assyrian Affair by a British officer stationed in Mosul. The chapter then provides a description of Iraq's first coup by General Bakr Sidqi, with the ambassador of Great Britain stating that the military forced the resignation of the Iraqi government in 1936. Zionism was an important movement in Palestine that changed the way the Muslim majority regarded their Jewish counterparts, so this chapter also includes a description of rising anti-Jewish sentiments in Baghdad. The chapter also describes the Shi'i celebration of Ashura, thereby providing a window into the political and religious life of a marginalized religious majority. Since the poor were also a marginalized group, this chapter closes with an elegy to the nonpoliticized economic majority of Iraq.

Faysal Expresses Intention to Protect Minorities, 1932

Iraq was—and still is—a diverse country consisting of many different ethnic and religious groups. The most important ethnic division in the country is between Arabs and Kurds, with the latter located primarily in the mountainous north. Based on present-day estimates, Arabic speakers constituted about 80 percent of the population, while Kurdish speakers made up 20 percent. Most Kurds are Sunnis, but the Arabs are divided between Sunni and Shi'is. Even though Shi'is are the majority, representing 60 percent of the population, Sunni Arabs, like Faysal I and his cohort, traditionally wielded the preponderance of power. Other minorities represented about 8 percent of the population, and they consist of Christians, Jews, and the syncretic Yazidis (Marr, 12–18). According to historian Phebe Marr, these groups are a "diverse medley of peoples who have not yet been welded into a single political community with a common sense of identity" (12). According to her colleague Charles Tripp, "sectarian and communal identities were often important in shaping people's responses to ... various issues" (Tripp, 75).

Upon independence, however, Faysal I expressed an intention to ensure that ethnic and religious minorities were protected in independent Iraq. The following is the "Declaration of the Kingdom of Iraq, Made at Baghdad on May 30th, 1932, on the Occasion of the Termination of the Mandatory Regime in Iraq, and Containing the Guarantees Given to the Council by the Iraqi Government" (accessed 20 September 2008, http://www.solami.com/UNGA.htm). This document provides insight into both the problems of establishing an Iraqi nation as well as the initial intentions of the state, before communal factionalism corrupted state institutions. Based on this document, you should consider the following: What were the social and political values promoted by the independent government? And how would you describe Iraq's official national identity in 1932?

Article 2: 1) Full and complete protection of life and liberty will be assured to all inhabitants of Iraq without distinction of birth, nationality, language, race or religion. 2) All inhabitants of Iraq will be entitled to the free exercise, whether public or private, of any creed, religion or belief, whose practices are not inconsistent with public order or public morals. . . .

Article 4: 1) All Iraqi nationals shall be equal before the law and shall enjoy the same civil and political rights without distinction as to race, language or religion. 2) The electoral system shall guarantee equitable representation to racial, religious and linguistic minorities in Iraq. 3) Differences of race, language or religion shall not prejudice any Iraqi national in matters relating to the enjoyment of civil or political rights, as, for instance, admission to public employment, functions and honours, or the exercise of professions or industries. 4) No restriction will be imposed on the free use by any Iraqi national of any language, in private intercourse, in commerce, in religion, in the Press or in publications of any kind, or at public meetings. 5) Notwithstanding the establishment by the Iraqi Government of Arabic as the official language, and notwithstanding the special arrangements to be made by the Iraqi Government, under Article 9 of the . . . Declaration, regarding the use of the Kurdish and Turkish languages, adequate facilities will be given to all Iraqi nationals whose mother tongue is not the official language, for the use of their language, either orally or in writing, before the courts.

Article 5: Iraqi nationals who belong to racial, religious or linguistic minorities will enjoy the same treatment and security in law and in fact as other Iraqi nationals. In particular, they shall have an equal right to maintain, manage and control at their own expense, or to establish in the future, charitable, religious and social institutions, schools and other educational establishments, with the right to use their own language and to exercise their religion freely therein.

Article 6: The Iraqi Government undertakes to take, as regards non-Moslem minorities, in so far as concerns their family law and personal status, measures permitting the settlement of these questions in accordance with the customs . . . of the communities to which those minorities belong. The Iraqi Government will communicate to the Council of the League of Nations information regarding the manner in which these measures have been executed.

Article 7: 1) The Iraqi Government undertakes to grant full protection, facilities and authorization to the churches, synagogues, cemeteries and other religious establishments, charitable works and pious foundations of minority religious communities existing in Iraq. 2) Each of these communities shall have the right of establishing councils, in important administrative districts, competent to administer pious foundations and charitable bequests. These councils shall be competent to deal with the collection of income derived therefrom, and the expenditure thereof in accordance with the wishes of the donor or with the custom in use among the community. These communities shall also undertake the supervision of the property of orphans. . . . The councils referred to above shall be under the supervision of the Government. 3) The Iraqi Government will not refuse, for the formation of new religious or charitable institutions, any of the . . . facilities which may be guaranteed to existing institutions of that nature.

Article 8: 1) In the public educational system in towns and districts in which are resident a considerable proportion of Iraqi nationals whose mother tongue is not the official language, the Iraqi Government will make provisions for adequate facilities for ensuring that in the primary schools instruction shall be given to the children of such nationals through the medium of their own language; it being understood that this provision does not prevent the Iraqi Government from making the teaching of Arabic obligatory in the said schools. 2) In towns and districts where there is a considerable proportion of Iraqi nationals belonging to racial, religious or linguistic minorities, these minorities will be assured an equitable share in the enjoyment and application of sums which may be provided out of public funds under the State, municipal or other budgets for educational, religious or charitable purposes.

Article 9: 1) Iraq undertakes that in the liwas of Mosul, Arbil, Kirkuk and Sulaimaniya, the official language, side by side with Arabic shall be Kurdish in the qadhas in which the population is predominantly of Kurdish race. In the qadhas of Kifri and Kirkuk, however, in the liwa of Kirkuk, where a considerable part of the population is of Turcoman race, the official language, side by side with Arabic, shall be either Kurdish or Turkish. 2) Iraq undertakes that in the said qadhas the officials shall, subject to justifiable exceptions, have a competent knowledge of Kurdish or Turkish as the case may be. 3) Although in these qadhas the criterion for the choice of officials will be, as in the rest of Iraq, the efficiency and knowledge of the language, rather than race, Iraq undertakes that the officials shall ... be selected, so far as possible, from among Iraqis from one ... of these qadhas.

Article 10: The stipulations of ... this Declaration, so far as they affect persons belonging to racial, religious or linguistic minorities ... constitute obligations of international concern and will be placed under the guarantee of the League of Nations. No modification will be made in them without the assent of a majority of the Council of the League of Nations.

Pan-Arab Nationalism

As made apparent in the previous document, Iraqis needed to forge a national community upon achieving independence. There were two distinct leanings in this regard. Some believed that Iraq had a distinctive national identity proscribed by its specific boundaries and the shared experiences of its people. These were the Iraqi nationalists. Others believed that Iraq's fate and identity were inherently linked to those of other Arab peoples. These were the Arab nationalists. It is not surprising to find there were many of these latter in the government of independent Iraq, for its politicians were, after all, often Sunni officers from a disparate set of provinces of the Ottoman Empire, like Syria or Palestine.

Sati' al-Husri (1882–1968) was an influential pan-Arab thinker. As a cosmopolitan and well-traveled man, he was a typical Ottoman (though he would never admit it). His family was from Aleppo in Syria, but he was born in Yemen. He grew up, however, in Istanbul. After the Young Turk Revolution of 1908, he would work for the Committee of Union and Progress (CUP) as an educator of no small influence. Under their aegis, he was sent to work in Syria, his homeland. There, he became involved in the Arab Revolt during World War I. He would move to Iraq when Faysal became king of this new country.

Al-Husri is largely responsible for the educational system in Iraq during the first twenty years of the country's history. Under Faysal, and still during the British mandate, he would act as Director General of Education, a highly influential role in a country that was just beginning to set up a standardized system of education. He would continue to influence the educational system of independent Iraq, when he acted as the director of the Higher Teachers' Training College, a position that he would hold until 1937. To promote his pan-Arab ideals, al-Husri imported intellectuals from other parts of the Arab world to teach in Iraqi schools. He also tried to prevent the establishment of local schools outside the purview of his pan-Arab curriculum (Dawisha, 85). The anti-British officers who would organize the coup of 1941 would be very influenced by his pan-Arab thinking. For this reason, al-Husri went into exile in Syria after the collapse of the government set up by these officers.

According to Sylvia G. Haim, al-Husri is "the man who did most to popularize the idea of nationalism among the literate classes of the Arab Middle East" (Haim, 42–43). For al-Husri, his position in education offered a means of inculcating national values. Given al-Husri's undeniable influence on the political life of independent Iraq, as well as other places in the Arab-speaking world, it is of critical importance to study his ideas and thoughts on pan-Arabism. Sati' al-Husri published little while in Iraq, so this selection, written in 1944, postdates the years covered in this chapter. Still, it represents the thinking of this pan-Arab ideologue as he used the education system to establish political values among the young. As you read this text, you should consider the following: What makes a person Arab? What role does Islam play in Arab identity? What are the strengths and weaknesses of this ideology in the promotion of a political identity in Iraq?

> I have read and heard many opinions and observations concerning Muslim unity and Arab unity, and which is to be preferred. I have been receiving for some time now various questions concerning this matter: Why, it is asked, are you interested in Arab unity, and why do you neglect Muslim unity? Do you not see that the goal of Muslim unity is higher than the goal of Arab unity, and that the power generated by Muslim union would be greater than that generated by Arab union? Do you not agree that religious feeling in the East is much stronger than national feeling? Why, then, do you want us to neglect the exploitation of this powerful feeling and to spend our energies in order to strengthen a weak feeling? Do you believe that the variety of languages will prevent the union of the Muslims? Do you not notice that the principles of communism, socialism, Freemasonry, and other systems unite people of different languages, races, countries, and climates; that none of these differences have prevented them from coming to understanding, from drawing nearer to one another, and from agreeing on one plan and one creed? Do you not know that every Muslim in Syria, Egypt, or Iraq believes that the Indian Muslim, the Japanese Muslim, or the European Muslim is as much his brother as the Muslim with whom he lives side by side? Whence, then, the impossibility of realizing Muslim union? Some say that Muslim unity is more powerful than any other and that its realization is

easier than the realization of any other.... Some pretend... that... Arab union is a plot the aim of which is to prevent the spread of Muslim union, in order to isolate some of the countries of the Muslim world and facilitate their continued subjugation. What is your opinion of this allegation?...

The essential point which has to be studied and solved when deciding which to prefer, Muslim unity or Arab unity, may be summarized as follows: Is Muslim unity a reasonable hope capable of realization? Or is it a utopian dream incapable of realization? And assuming the first alternative, is its realization easier or more difficult than the realization of Arab unity? Does one of these two schemes exclude the other? And is there a way of realizing Muslim unity without realizing Arab unity? When we think about such questions... we have... to define... what we mean by Muslim unity and by Arab unity and to delimit without any ambiguity the use of the two expressions.

It goes without saying that Arab unity requires the creation of a political union of the different Arab countries the inhabitants of which speak Arabic. As for Muslim unity, that naturally requires the creation of a political union of the different Muslim countries, the inhabitants of which profess the Muslim religion, regardless of the variety of their languages and races. It is also well known that the Muslim world includes the Arab countries, Turkey, Iran, Afghanistan... parts of India, the East Indies, the Caucasus, North Africa, as well as parts of Central Africa, without considering a few scattered units in Europe and Asia, as in Albania, Yugoslavia, Poland, China, and Japan. Further, there is no need to show that the Arab countries occupy the central portion of this far-flung world.

Whoever will examine these evident facts and picture the map of the Muslim world, noticing the position of the Arab world within it, will have to concede that Arab unity is much easier to bring about than Muslim unity, and that this latter is not capable of realization, assuming that it can be realized, except through Arab unity. It is not possible for any sane person to imagine union among Cairo, Baghdad, Tehran, Kabul, Haiderabad, and Bukhara, or Kashgar, Persia, and Timbuctoo, without there being a union among Cairo, Baghdad, Damascus, Mecca, and Tunis. It is not possible for any sane person to conceive the possibility of union among Turks, Arabs, Persians, Malayans, and Negroes, while denying unity to the Arabs themselves. If, contrary to fact, the Arab world were more extensive and wider than the Muslim world, it would have been possible to imagine a Muslim union without Arab union, and it would have been permissible to say that Muslim union is easier to realize than Arab union. But as the position is the exact opposite, there is no logical scope whatever for such statements and speculations. We must not forget this truth when we think and speak concerning Muslim unity and Arab unity. The idea of Muslim unity is, it is true, wider and more inclusive than the concept of Arab unity, but it is not possible to advocate Muslim unity without advocating Arab unity. We have, therefore, the right to assert that whoever opposes Arab unity also opposes Muslim unity or for the sake of Muslim unity, he contradicts the simplest necessities of reason and logic.

Having established this truth, to disagree with which is not logically possible, we ought to notice another truth which is no less important. We must not forget that the expression "unity," in this context, means political unity; and we must constantly remember that this concept of Islamic unity greatly differs from that of Muslim brotherhood. Unity is one thing and affection another, political unity is one thing and agreement on a certain principle another. To advocate Muslim unity, therefore, is different from advocating the improvement of conditions in Islam and different also from advocating an increase in understanding, in affection, and in cooperation among Muslims. We can therefore say that he who talks about the principle of Muslim brotherhood, and discusses the benefits of understanding among the Muslims, does not prove that Muslim unity is possible. Contrariwise, he who denies the possibility of realizing Muslim unity does not deny the principle of Muslim brotherhood or oppose the efforts toward the awakening of the Muslims and understanding among them. What may be said concerning the ideal of brotherhood is not sufficient proof of the possibility of realizing Muslim unity. Further, it is not ... logical to prove the possibility of realizing Muslim unity by quoting the example of Freemasonry or socialism or communism, because the Freemasons do not constitute a political unity and the socialist parties in the different European countries have not combined to form a new state. Even communism itself has not formed a new state, but has taken the place of the Czarist Russian state. We have, therefore, to distinguish quite clearly between the question of Muslim brotherhood and that of Muslim unity, and we must consider directly whether or not it is possible to realize Muslim unity in the political sense.

If we cast a general glance at history and review the influence of religions over the formation of political units, we find that the world religions have not been able to unify peoples speaking different languages, except in the Middle Ages, and that only in limited areas and for a short time. The political unity which the Christian Church sought to bring about did not at any time merge the Orthodox world with the Catholic. Neither did the political unity which the papacy tried to bring about in the Catholic world last for any length of time. So it was also in the Muslim world; the political unity which existed at the beginning of its life was not able to withstand the changes of circumstance for any length of time. Even the Abbasid caliphate, at the height of its power and glory, could not unite all the Muslims under its political banner. Similarly, the lands ruled by this caliphate did not effectively preserve their political unity for very long. Nor was it long after the founding of the caliphate that its control over some of the provinces became symbolic rather than real; it could not prevent the secession of these provinces and their transformation into independent political unity. It deserves to be mentioned in this connection that the spread of the Muslim religion in some areas took place after the Muslim caliphate lost effective unity and real power, so much so that in some countries Islam spread in a manner independent of the political authority, at the hands of missionary tradesmen, holy men, and dervishes. The Muslim world, within its present . . . limits, never . . . formed a political unity. If then, political unity could not be realized in [the] past, when social life was simple and political relations were primitive, when religious customs controlled every aspect of behavior and thought, it will not be possible to realize it in this century, when social life has become complicated, political problems have become intractable, and science and technology have liberated themselves from the control of tradition and religious beliefs.

I know that what I have stated here will displease many doctors of Islam; I know that the indications of history which I have set out above will have no influence over the beliefs of a great many of the men of religion, because they have been accustomed to discuss these matters without paying heed to historical facts or to the geographical picture; nor are they used to distinguishing between the meaning of religious brotherhood and the meaning of political ties. They have been accustomed to confuse the principles of Islamic brotherhood, in its moral sense, and the idea of Islamic unity, in its political sense. I think it useless to try to persuade these people of the falsity of their beliefs, but I think it necessary to ask them to remember what reason and logic require in this respect. Let them maintain their belief in the possibility of realizing Islamic unity, but let them at the same time agree to the necessity of furthering Arab unity, at least as one stage toward the realization of the Islamic unity in which they believe. In any event, let them not oppose the efforts which are being made to bring about Arab unity, on the pretext of serving the Islamic unity which they desire. . . . [W]hoever opposes Arab unity, on the pretext of Muslim unity, contradicts the simplest requirements of reason and logic, and I . . . say that to contradict logic to this extent can be the result only of deceit or of deception. The deceit is that of some separatists who dislike the awakening of the Arab nation and try to arouse religious feeling against the idea of Arab unity, and the deception is that of the simple-minded, who incline to believe whatever is said to them in the name of religion, without realizing what hidden purposes might lurk behind the speeches. . . .

Perhaps the strangest and most misleading views that have been expressed regarding Arab unity and Islamic unity are the views of those who say that the idea of Arab unity was created to combat Islamic unity in order to isolate some Islamic countries, the better to exercise continuous power over them. I cannot imagine a view further removed from the realities of history and politics or more contradictory to the laws of reason and logic. The details I have mentioned above concerning the relation of Muslim unity to Arab unity are sufficient . . . to refute such allegations. . . . It cannot be denied that the British . . . have humored and indulged the Arab movement. This is only because they are more practiced in politics and quicker to understand the psychology of nations and the realities of social life. Before anybody else realized the hidden powers lying in the Arab idea, and thought it wise, therefore, to humor it somewhat, instead of directly opposing it. This was in order to preserve themselves against the harm they might sustain through it and to make it more advantageous to their interests.

We must understand that British policy is a practical policy, changing with circumstances and always making use of opportunities. We must not forget that it was Great Britain who, many times, saved the Ottoman state, then the depository of the Islamic caliphate, from Russian domination. She it was who halted Egyptian armies in the heart of Anatolia to save the seat of the Muslim caliphate from these victorious troops, and she it was who opposed the union of Egypt with Syria at the time of Muhammad Ali. Whoever, then, charges that the idea of Arab unity is a foreign plot utters a greater falsehood than any that has ever been uttered, and he is the victim of the greatest of deceptions. We must know full well that the idea of Arab unity is a natural idea. It has not been artificially started. It is a natural consequence of the existence of the Arab nation itself. It is a social force drawing its vitality from the life of the Arabic language, from the history of the Arab nation, and from the connectedness of the Arab countries. No one can logically pretend that it is the British who created the idea of Arab unity, unless he can prove that it is the British who have created the Arabic language, originating the history of the Arab nation and putting together the geography of the Arab countries. The idea of Arab unity is a natural concept springing from the depths of social nature and not from the artificial views which can be invented by individuals or by states. It remained latent, like many natural and social forces, for many centuries, as a result of many historical factors which cannot be analyzed here. But everything indicates that this period is now at an end, that the movement has come into the open and will manifest itself with ever-increasing power. It will ... spread all over the Arab countries, to whom it will bring back their ancient glory and primeval youth; it will indeed bring back what is most fertile, most powerful, and highest in these countries.

Faysal I Promotes Pan-Arabism, 1932

There were indeed many benefits to Arab nationalism, or, at least, King Faysal I and his influential minister Nuri al-Said seemed to think so. The following diplomatic correspondence is from A.L.P. Burdett's *Arab Dissident Movements, 1905–1955* (London: Archive Editions, 1996), 2: 695–96. In it, Faysal tries to convince the British to let him hold a conference that would assemble representatives of Arab countries. As you read this excerpt, you should consider the following: What arguments does King Faysal I use to persuade the British to support an Arab Congress being held in Baghdad? Are there other reasons that King Faysal I might want to hold this congress? Why does the British diplomat oppose such a conference? Are there other unspoken reasons that might lead him to fear the holding of such a conference? What does this document suggest about British political attitudes in the postcolonial era?

Sir F. Humphrys to Sir John Simon
Bagdad, December 21, 1932
2. His Majesty said that he wished to ask my opinion about the proposal that an Arab Congress should be held in Bagdad. This proposal was an outcome of the growing movement among the Arab *intelligentsia* towards a closer union among all Arab peoples. Although for the next decade the chief task of the Iraqi Government would be to develop the resources of the country and to raise the standard of education and living of the people, he felt that, taking a long view of Iraq's future, the pan-Arab movement was not one which the Iraqi Government should ignore. On the north and east Iraq was overshadowed by powerful neighbours, whose growing nationalism might in the future constitute a danger to Iraq's independence. In Persia dreams of the old Sassanian Empire were being revived, and in the schools children were taught to think of Ctesiphon as the rightful capital of the Persian King of Kings. Turkey, for the moment, was a safe neighbour, but one could be sure that her old claims to ... Mosul ... might not be revived again later on. On the west, too, there would always be a threat to Iraq so long as the French remained in their present strong position in Syria. They ... once coveted Mosul and its oil. Could one be sure that they no longer dreamt of being masters of the Mosul oilfields?

3. It was true that, by virtue of her alliance with Great Britain, Iraq had nothing to fear from her neighbours at present, but he was looking ahead, and he thought that it would be unfair to Great Britain for Iraq to rely indefinitely on her support. Bearing these considerations in mind, His Majesty felt that it was necessary for Iraq to seek some means of reinforcing her position and to his mind the pan-Arab movement promised the best source of additional strength. If Iraq could rely on the support of . . . other Arab peoples, if . . . she and the Arabs of Syria could stand firmly side by side, the dangers which threatened Iraq's future integrity would be greatly diminished.

4. While . . . he believed it to be in Iraqi interests to give discreet encouragement to the Arab Congress as a means of strengthening ideas of Arab unity, he had some misgivings as to the attitude of His Majesty's Government towards . . . the pan-Arab movement and the Arab Congress. . . . [H]e wished to ask my private opinion, firstly, as to whether I thought that His Majesty's Government still entertained the same sympathy towards the Arab cause that they had shown during the war, and, secondly, whether it was likely that His Majesty's Government would regard with disfavour the holding of an Arab Congress in Bagdad.

5. I said that His Majesty's remarks and the two questions with which they had concluded raised very far-reaching considerations. I entirely agreed with him that Iraq should not rely indefinitely on British support for her safety, but I had some doubts as to whether the ideals of the movement for a closer union of Arab peoples really offered the best means of strengthening her position. Turkey, I feared, would view with misgivings any consolidation of the Arab peoples on her southern frontier; Persia, whose outlet to the sea in the south lay in an area predominantly inhabited by Arabs, would certainly be hostile to such a movement, while France, though now evidently prepared to follow in Syria the policy adopted by Great Britain in Iraq, was unlikely to relinquish her hold over the eastern littoral of the Mediterranean and would certainly be opposed to any movement aiming at the political unification of the Arabs and thereby threatening Lebanon from the east. It seemed to me, therefore, at first view, that a movement towards union with other Arab peoples, instead of strengthening Iraq's position, might very easily provoke active hostility against her among her neighbours and accentuate the dangers which His Majesty feared; dangers which were, I believed, far less real than he imagined. I did not myself share His Majesty's apprehensions that either Turkey or Persia had any designs in present circumstances on Iraqi territory, and the French clearly had their hands quite full enough already and had not, I was convinced, the least

intention of endeavouring to add to these difficulties by encroaching on Iraq. At all events, all these considerations were largely speculative and neither His Majesty nor the Iraqi Government need greatly concern themselves for the present with what was likely to happen in ten years' time. For the present their membership of the League and their alliance with Great Britain gave them a security enjoyed by few other countries in the world, and as he had himself remarked, the pressing need of the moment was to set their own house in order. The best way Iraq could serve the Arab cause was, through her own economic and cultural progress, to win back for the Arabs the prestige which they had once enjoyed among the nations of the world.

6. As regards the attitude of His Majesty's Government towards the Arabs and towards the proposal for holding an Arab Congress in Bagdad, His Majesty had, I thought, seen in British policy in Iraq clear evidence of their continued sincere sympathy with the aspirations of the Arab nation to take their legitimate place among the free and enlightened nations of the world, and it was unnecessary for me to say anything more on that point. The idea of holding a congress was quite natural and such a manifestation of a sentiment, which was well known to exist, should not give rise to any difficulties if common sense, tact and restraint were exercised by those who took part. I warned His Majesty . . . that if it were held in Bagdad the Iraqi Government would . . . become responsible if anything were said or done to give offence to their neighbours, whereas if it were held elsewhere, for example Mecca, the Iraqi Government would have no responsibility for what occurred. . . . [I]t seemed to me that if His Majesty wished to avoid embarrassment from the deliberations of the congress, the following conditions should be imposed on the organizers if it were held in Bagdad:—

The agenda of the congress should be restricted to cultural and economic questions and politics should be excluded from their discussions.

The utmost care should be taken to avoid inciting the Arabs of Syria to resort to other than peaceful means for reaching agreement with the French, and to avoid stirring up the Arabs of Palestine against the Jews.

Consideration should be paid to the susceptibilities of King Abdul Aziz-al-Saud. For example, His Majesty must not be given the impression that his position was being threatened by any member of the Hashimite family.

7. The King said that he agreed with my views, and while he could not give a positive assurance that someone might not in a speech commit an indiscretion, he felt that this was unlikely, as those who would take part were all responsible men of experience. It was the intention of the organizers to limit

... the discussions of the congress to cultural and economic questions, and he was confident that the resolutions adopted ... would conform to the conditions which I had laid down.

The Assyrian Affair, 1933

Assyrians are Middle Eastern Christians, and they were a very small and very problematic minority in Iraq. The heart of the Assyrian homeland was the Hakkari Mountains in Turkey. Nevertheless, the Assyrians sided with the Entente powers during World War I. They did so in the hope that they would later earn a homeland. At first, they fought alongside Russian forces, which were making inroads in the Anatolian Peninsula. Then, after the Bolshevik Revolution, Russian forces withdrew. Without Allied protection, the Assyrians were no more than moving targets for Ottoman forces, who massacred them. Some fled to Iran. Although the Entente alliance won the war, they were not able to fulfill their promise of a homeland, because Turkey was established as a Republic on the Anatolian Peninsula.

So, the British settled fifty thousand Assyrians in northern Iraq, close to their Anatolian home. Such an instantaneous demographic transformation breeds unrest and problems in the best of circumstances, for it places a strain on existing resources. In this instance, however, the British compounded, if you will, the problem. During the mandate era, they decided to form special armed levies composed solely of Assyrian soldiers, who had proved to be such good fighters during the war. There were twenty-three hundred men in these levies, which were a sort of "special forces." The Assyrians were called upon to put down tribal rebellions both in the Kurdish north and the Shi'i south. And the British never let the numbers of troops in the regular Iraqi army surpass those in the Assyrian Levies. For these reasons, many Iraqi people considered Assyrians British agents.

When the British gave up the mandate, the Assyrians lost their foreign protectors. Fearing reprisals after independence, many Assyrians demanded regional autonomy. The Iraqi Government opposed this idea, for it meant a loss of control of its territory. As tensions escalated, the Iraqi government decided to place the religio-political patriarch of the Assyrian community, who is referred to as the Mar Shimun, under house arrest. He had temporal authority over these people, and the Iraqi government wanted him to rescind these powers. Some Assyrians fled to Syria, but the French would not let them establish a homeland there either. So, in August 1933, many Assyrians returned to Iraq. Tensions, however, mounted, and armed Assyrians clashed with the Iraqi military (Ghareeb, 26).

The term Assyrian Affair refers to the reprisals that followed this clash, for the

Iraqi military—as well as Kurdish and Arab tribesmen—used this event as an excuse to eradicate the Assyrian community. Kurds massacred about 100 villagers in Dahuk and Zakhu. Then, the regular army killed another 315 unarmed Assyrian civilians who had gathered at the police station in a town called Sumayyil (Marr, 39). This tragedy became an international incident that led many to question whether Iraq should have received its independence. Lt. Col. R. S. Stafford was a British officer stationed in Mosul in August 1933, so he witnessed firsthand the immediate aftermath of these atrocities. As you read his account, you should consider the following: Who suffered? And what was the role of the state in this tragedy? Where does Stafford place guilt?

> I was sitting in my office on the morning of August 15th when Hikmet Beg returned. He came straight into my room in a state of collapse, for he had just come from Simmel, and even he, cynical Turk as he was, had been overcome by the horrors which he had seen. On the previous day, I had received reports that there were large numbers of Assyrian women and children in Simmel living in a state of starvation, but not a word had been said in these reports about the massacre which was the cause of this destitution, although there were other vague reports that a large number of Assyrians had been killed by the Kurds and the Irregular police—that the Army were responsible was not mentioned in any of these reports—in the mountains near Dohuk. . . . I . . . reported by telephone during the day the plight of the women of Simmel, and the Prime Minister himself telephoned to Hikmet Beg at Amadiyah instructing him to visit Simmel and see for himself what could be done for the women. So Hikmet Beg went there knowing nothing of the horror that awaited him.
>
> When Yacu's expedition went into Syria, the Assyrian villages remained untouched for several weeks, but on August 8th some Tokhuma villages, whose able-bodied men were in Syria, had been looted by Kurds from the Zakho qodha, without doubt encouraged by the Qaimaqam. When the Kurds started looting the women and children fled to Dohuk and Simmel. None of them appeared to have been seriously molested, though personal ornaments and such things were in some cases stolen. The Assyrians then began to realize what was afoot. During the next two days the Arab tribes from the right banks of the Tigris started to cross the river. Their intention was obvious. They themselves admitted that they were out for loot and they claim that they had been told what to do. Nor was this claim entirely unjustified, as the first wild cries from Baghdad suggesting the raising of the tribes against the Assyrians had reached the Arab tribesmen of the Shammar and the Jubur. In their alarm the Assyrians left their villages and fled to Simmel.

Simmel is on the main road to Zakho, about eight miles from Dohuk, under the administration of which qodha it came. It was the largest village in the neighbourhood and consisted of over one hundred Assyrians and ten Arab houses. The total population would have been about 700, most of the Assyrians belonging to the Baz tribe. . . . The headman was a strong supporter of the Mar Shimun and with fifty others had followed Yacu into Syria. These fifty were almost entirely Tiyari, hardly any of the Baz being among them. The feeling of unrest in the village increased. On August 8th the Qaimaqam of Zakho appeared with a lorry full of soldiers. . . . He entered the village and told the Assyrians to surrender their rifles, as he feared that fighting might occur between the rebel Assyrians and the Government forces, in which case the people of Simmel would be less likely to be involved if they had no rifles. . . . He assured them that they would be safe under the protection of the Iraqi flag which flew over the police post—for Simmel, being a large village, had a police post of one sergeant and four men. The Assyrians then handed in their arms, which were taken away by the troops.

Next day more troops returned, this time without the Qaimaqam, and disarmed further Assyrians who in the meantime had come in from the surrounding villages. The following day, the 10th, passed comparatively quietly. Nothing happened except that Arabs and Kurds could be seen looting neighbouring villages. They even came in and stripped the communal threshing floors on the outskirts of Simmel, where the cut barley and wheat was stacked in piles, for it was full time of harvest and the villagers were engaged in threshing and winnowing. The unarmed Assyrians could do nothing and the police did not intervene; they explained that they had no orders and that in any case their numbers were insufficient.

It was becoming quite clear now to the Assyrians what was likely to happen. Not only had they seen this looting going on, but they suddenly found they were forbidden to draw water from the village spring, being permitted only to go to the main stream, which was dirty. They knew that the Army had already shot many Assyrians. They had seen their head priest, Sada, taken out of Simmel. All day they watched the looting Arabs and Kurds. Not one of them dared to move from the neighbourhood of the police post, except one or two whose houses were near by, and who went to and fro on pathetic household tasks such as the making of bread, the last meal that many of them were destined to eat. They were in a state of deadly fear, and they spent that night in and around the police post, which is built on a small hill. They now knew only too well the sentiments which the Arabs, and particularly the Arab Army, harboured towards them, and in the small hours of the 11th... the watching Assyrians began to observe their Arab neighbours of the village starting away driving their flocks before them. This opened their eyes beyond possibility of error. They realized the trap they had been led into and they knew that they were entirely helpless.

The police sergeant ordered the Assyrians from the outlying villages to return to their homes. When they refused, saying that it was unsafe, he ordered them to leave the police post and go down to the houses in the villages below. They obeyed reluctantly. Some went to the house of Gavriel and his brother Tinan, who kept reassuring them that they would be safe and that the Government would protect them. As others were going down to the houses they suddenly saw lorries of troops and armoured cars arriving. Looking around to the police post they saw a policeman pulling down the Iraqi flag, which until then had been flying, as it had flown for years, as a symbol of the law and order under which every inhabitant of Iraq could live in safety and security. Suddenly and without the least warning the troops opened fire upon the defenseless Assyrians. Many fell, including some women and children, and the rest ran into the houses to take cover. Not a soul was to be seen in the streets. The troops well knew that there was not a rifle or revolver left in the village. An officer drove up in a car and the troops came in. This officer has since been identified as Ismail Abawi Tohalla, who comes of a well-known but by no means respectable Mosul family. He shouted to the soldiers not to kill the women and children. These were ordered to come out of the houses and go up to the police post. Many did so.

A cold-blooded and methodical massacre of all the men in the village then followed, a massacre which for the black treachery in which it was conceived and the callousness with which it was carried out, was as foul a crime as any in the bloodstained annals of the Middle East. The Assyrians had no fight left in them partly because of the state of mind to which the events of the past week had reduced them, largely because they were disarmed. Had they been armed it seems certain that Ismail Abawi Tohalla and his bravos would have hesitated to take them on in a fair fight. Having disarmed them, they proceeded with the massacre according to plan. This took some time. Not that there was any hurry, for the troops had the whole day ahead of them. Their opponents were helpless and there was no chance of any interference from any quarter whatsoever. Machine gunners set up their guns outside the windows of the houses in which the Assyrians had taken refuge, and having trained them on the terror-stricken wretches in the crowded rooms, fired among them until not a man was left standing in the shambles. In some other instances the blood lust of the troops took a slightly more active form, and men were dragged out and shot or bludgeoned to death and their bodies thrown on a pile of dead.

Gavriel, who had been mentioned in an earlier chapter as the individual who raised cheers for the Army at the Mosul meeting of July 11th, went out to plead for the Assyrians. He explained who he was, and said that his nephew, Ezra Effendi, had long been an officer in the Iraqi police. He showed his nationality papers, but these were torn in pieces before his face and he was shot in cold blood. A priest named Ismail who had taken refuge in the police post was driven out by the police, a rope tied round his neck and he was kicked down the steps and dragged away by the troops, who shot him, afterwards throwing his body on the . . . growing heap of corpses. Whilst this organized slaughter was going on, the police sergeant, who had from the beginning taken a leading part in the diabolical plot, ordered the Assyrian women to clean up the blood from the neighbourhood of the police post. The women complied, but only for a time. Suddenly they rebelled against this inhuman order and told the police sergeant to turn the machine guns on them as they would rather die. The soldiers then took the men that remained down to a ditch and went on killing until every man was dead. It was then discovered that a few men had taken refuge among the women and that some of them had hastily got into women's clothes. These were rounded up and murdered.

When there was no one left to kill, the troops took their departure. This was about two p.m., and they went off to Aloka for their midday meal and afternoon siesta. As soon as the troops had gone, the tribes, who had been interested spectators, came in and completed the looting of the houses which the soldiers had commenced. The tribes had taken no part whatever in the massacre, but as the Army were equipped with modern machine guns and no opposition, there was of course no need for any help. Later in the evening the troops came back for the police sergeant had reported by telephone that a number of Assyrian men had appeared at the police post and taken refuge there. These were hunted out and killed. The shooting went on until about sunset. In the meantime the . . . houses in the village were crowded with . . . terror-stricken women and small children. Few of them had any meal that night or for the next few days, for what grain there was in the village had been removed by the Kurds, who had also gone round the houses removing cookery utensils, bedding, and in some cases even the roof beams.

Next morning the women already distracted beyond all reason, had a further shock when they saw the Army returning, for they did not know what this might portend. The Army, however, had merely come back to bury the dead. The bodies were collected and placed in a shallow ditch. It must be remembered that the month was August with a daily sun maximum of 160 degrees Fahrenheit. According to the military report 305 men, four women, and six children were buried. . . . The burial in the shallow ditch, which was carried out most inefficiently, caused the stench under the burning son to become almost unendurable, and every fly and pestilential insect for miles around was drawn to the village. In this unspeakable atmosphere there lived for six days, one thousand terrified women and children who had seen all their male relations killed before their eyes.

The Bakr Sidqi Coup of 1936

Iraq has the dubious honor of being the first country in the Arab world to experience a coup d'état. This coup occurred in October 1936, and it is called the Bakr Sidqi Coup. General Bakr Sidqi was a career military officer in the Iraqi army, and he was the principal instigator of the coup. He believed that an authoritarian form of government—in which the army would play a large role—was a more efficient way of ruling Iraq. Politics, as they say, makes for strange bedfellows. In instituting his plans, he teamed up with liberal reformers in the Ahali group, Iraqi nationalists who wanted to see a more equitable distribution of wealth in the country. Together, these forces breached the Constitution and forced a change in the government. This coup was against the cabinet; it did not aim to eliminate the monarchy. In executing the coup, however, some soldiers shot Jafar al-Askari, the Minister of Defense. Many of the old elite, including al-Askari's brother-in-law Nuri al-Said, then went into exile.

The seasoned politician Hikmat Sulayman became prime minister, and he and his cohorts clearly sought to change Iraq's domestic and foreign policy. This group wanted to foster allies among the middle and lower classes, meaning that the old Sunni politicians would not be as influential. Indeed, there were a number of Shi'i in the government. These new leaders sought to redistribute some of Iraq's land and wealth. In terms of foreign policy, this government chose not to pursue Arab nationalism; instead, it held onto an Iraq-First policy that shifted the foreign orientations of Iraq. Iraq borders Iran and Turkey, two critical non-Arab countries. The politicians in charge facilitated better relations with them, even going so far as to join the regional alliance of Sadabad Pact, which brought together Iran, Turkey, Iraq, and Afghanistan.

These policies, however, were unpopular among Arab nationalists and landlord-sheikhs, so the coup would not lead to enduring change. Bakr Sidqi would be assassinated ten months later, when he was on his way to visit Turkey. Hikmat

Sulayman could not control the army, whose officers made it clear that they would not take his orders. As a result, the government of reformers resigned. Although the coup did not bring enduring results, this coup is critical in understanding Iraqi history. As pointed out by historian Phebe Marr: "Opening the door to the misuse of power by the military, the coup of 1936 was followed by a series of less overt but continuous military interventions behind the scenes, which became the most marked feature of political life in the years between 1936 and 1941" (Marr, 49).

The British ambassador and his staff were very eager to know the outcome of the coup, an act that they deplored. Robin Bidwell has put together a collection of British documents that includes a British account of the coup in *British Documents on Foreign Affairs: Reports and Papers from the Foreign Office Confidential Print (Series B: Turkey, Iran, and the Middle East, 1918–1939)* (s.l.: University Publications of America, 1985), 12: 16–20. As you read this account of the coup, you should consider the following: What are British attitudes toward the coup? Are they different from attitudes toward specific individuals?

Sir A. Clark Kerr to Mr. Eden
Bagdad, November 2, 1936

2. To all but what must have been a very small group of people, the morning of Thursday, the 29th October, was nothing but the beginning of a normal Bagdad day. The Afghan Minister for War had just arrived and had been met at the station with appropriate ceremonial. Ministers, secure in office, were at their desks and about their ordinary business (which, at this season, begins at a very early hour), when . . . eleven aeroplanes flew over the town. There was nothing remarkable about their appearance, because it is the habit of the Iraqi air force to make the day's routine flights about this time. But they were flying lower than usual, and were seen to be dropping leaflets. . . . It was a manifesto appealing to the King, in the name of the army, to dismiss the Yasin Cabinet and to set up a new Administration under Hikmat Sulaiman. It called upon Government officials to leave their offices until the new Cabinet was formed, and it foreshadowed the possibility that the army might . . . take forcible measures. It was signed by General Bekr Sidqi, who described himself as "Commander of the National Forces of Reform."

3. The movement had been carefully planned and the secret well kept. Bekr Sidqi had chosen a moment when all but two battalions of the Iraqi army were gathered in the neighbourhood of Qaraghan, on the road to the Persian frontier, for the purpose of their annual divisional training. Of the two remaining battalions, one was on the Euphrates and the other was at Mosul. Bagdad,

stripped of troops, lay open and defenceless. The Chief of the General Staff, General Taha-al-Hasimi, the brother of the Prime Minister, was in Angora on his way back from Europe. The air force had been called from Hinaidi to Qaraghan the day before without attracting special attention.

4. At about a quarter to 10 I received a message from King Ghazi asking me to go to see him. I lost no time in doing so. I found His Majesty in a state of great nervousness. He told me that he had had bad news which had taken him rudely by surprise. He assumed that I had already seen the leaflet, but there was more than that. Hikmat Sulaiman had brought him a letter from Bekr Sidqi and Abdul Latif Nuri, the generals commanding the two divisions now engaged in manoeuvres, which made the same demands as those in the leaflet, and which added that, if King Ghazi did not acquiesce in them, Bagdad would be bombed from the air in three hours' time. His Majesty described the helpless condition of the capital and asked for my advice, making it clear to me that he thought that any idea of resistance should be dismissed. I asked him whether he had said or done anything which might give colour to the belief that the movement had his approval. He assured me that he had not. I asked whether he felt that his authority was strong enough to check the movement if he allowed it to become known that he was opposed to it. He said that he did not think so. I asked if he had consulted his Ministers. He said that he had seen Yasin Pasha . . . and had found him half minded to resign. I . . . made to His Majesty a few obvious remarks about the disastrous consequences that had in most countries followed the excursion into politics of the army, and I advised him to lose no time in getting into touch with the two generals and in stopping them from making anything like a triumphal entry in Bagdad, the possible effects of which I did not care to forecast. This suggestion seemed to commend itself to him.

5. At this moment Yasin and Nuri arrived. Yasin showed no signs of emotion. Nuri was clearly on the edge of an explosion. The whole situation was quickly re-examined. Yasin admitted at once that he, too, had been taken by surprise. He was aware that some sections of public opinion were hostile to his Government, but the last thing he had foreseen was that attack would come from the army, least of all from Bekr Sidqi. He said that he had just had a conversation by telephone with Bekr Sidqi, and had asked him what all the fuss was about. He had explained that he was ready to resign directly since he knew that he no longer enjoyed King Ghazi's confidence, but His Majesty had given him no indication that this confidence had been lost. Bekr Sidqi had replied that the movement, of which he was at the head, was being carried out with the knowledge and the approval of King Ghazi. Here His Majesty winced a little,

and denied with emphasis the truth of this statement. Yasin then began to weigh up the chances of resistance. There was clearly still a lot of battle left in him. He glanced at and rejected an idea that King Ghazi, with the Government, should abandon Bagdad and withdraw to the provinces, where they would have time to gather together some forces with which to meet the army. King Ghazi then suggested that, if Yasin Pasha resigned, he might be able, as time went on, to procure the fall of his successor, and His Majesty hinted that such a fall would be agreeable to him. Meanwhile, Yasin had been pulling his forelock, which is always a sign that he finds himself in a difficulty. He then suggested that, before he was called upon to make a decision, His Majesty should send for Hikmat and enquire what his intentions were. If Hikmat could show that they were generally in the interests of the country, Yasin would willingly yield up his place. King Ghazi then asked that Hikmat should be sent for, and, somewhat to my surprise, I learned that he was already waiting in the palace. . . . [T]he time had come for me to withdraw, and I did so. . . .

6. When I reached the Embassy, I was told that a flight of five aeroplanes had dropped four bombs in the neighbourhood of the "sarai." The shooting had been good. Three bombs had fallen near the Prime Minister's office and the Ministry of the Interior, and one in the river. It was now about midday. Yasin and Nuri did not come to the Embassy, and at 1 o'clock I heard that the Government had resigned and that the usual Iradah had been issued empowering Hikmat to form a Cabinet. . . . Meanwhile, I had got into touch with the Air Officer Commanding and discussed with him the defence scheme and how best to put it into effect in the event of serious trouble breaking out in the capital. After that there was nothing to be done but to wait upon events.

7. By about 5 in the evening the first advance units of Bekr Sidqi's force began to reach Bagdad unobtrusively and without incident, and by 7 o'clock he was in the "sarai" with Hikmat Sulaiman. Shortly afterwards, I received a message from the new Prime Minister to the effect that his Cabinet had been formed, and that he wished to maintain the present friendly relations with His Majesty's Government and hoped to have the support of the Embassy. As . . . alarmist reports were reaching me about the state of the town, I drove through the main streets, where everything appeared to me to be quiet and normal. An organized demonstration of welcome to Bekr Sidqi's troops round about the North Gate had, it seems passed off without incident.

8. That evening I was giving one of my dull routine dinner-parties. In the middle of it I was told that Nuri had slipped across the river in a row-boat and had come in by the water gate. Nuri, however, had been seen and recognized by the sentry. He was in a state of acute nervous excitement. He told

me that after I had left King Ghazi that morning, His Majesty had sent Jafar-al-Askari to the two generals with a letter and instructions to try to dissuade them from coming into Bagdad. When Jafar reached the advance guard, he had been met by Ismail-al-Tohallah (the man who carried out the massacre at Simmel), who had taken Jafar off the main road into the desert and had shot him. Nuri had had this information from one Ahmed-al-Manassifi, the secretary to the Ministry of Defence, whom he had now brought with him to the Embassy. In his turn Ahmed had had it from Bekr Sidqi and his officers. But there was more than this. It was the intention of a group of these officers that night to murder Yasin, Rashid Ali and Nuri himself. Nuri had been able to warn Yasin, who was now in hiding in the town, but he had not been able to get in touch with Rashid Ali....

9. It seemed to me that no time should be lost in getting into touch with the new Prime Minister, in acquainting him with the plot and in using such influence as I might have to prevent its being put into effect. For this purpose I asked Mr. Edmonds to come at once to the Embassy, and I explained the situation to him. At my request he went immediately to Hikmat's house with a message from me to the effect that murders such as I understood now to be planned, coming on top of the shooting of Jafar-al-Askari, which I should be obliged to report to you, would create so deplorable an impression in London that I could not foresee the consequences. The first would probably be the rupture of relations with His Majesty's Government. At the same time I urged the Prime Minister to take instant measures to protect the lives of the three men concerned. It was about 1 o'clock when Mr. Edmonds returned, with an emphatic assurance from Hikmat that he would not allow any of the late Ministers to be harmed, and that he was taking the precaution of posting police guards on their houses.... [H]e expressed ... horror at the murder of Jafar, adding, however, that he was in no way responsible for it.... The fault lay with the King for his thoughtlessness in allowing Jafar to go to meet the army in its present temper....

11. Early on the morning of the following day, the 30th, I received a visit from Mr. Edmonds, who came with a message from the Prime Minister which reiterated his assurances of friendliness and his wish that I should co-operate with him. The urgency of satisfying myself beyond a doubt that Yasin, Nuri, and Rashid Ali should be put beyond the reach of danger prompted me to ask him to receive me, and I called upon him in the course of the morning. I was with him for about two hours. I went to him, I confess, full of prejudice, and I found myself, somewhat to my dismay, disarmed by his obvious desire to be friendly and by earnestness and the apparent sincerity with which he begged for my

support. The assurance which he gave me of his belief in the necessity of close and friendly relations between His Majesty's Government and Iraq and his desire to have help and guidance from myself left, on the face of them, nothing to be desired. He forestalled the observations which I was about to make concerning the folly and the dangers of the way in which he had come into office by saying that he himself could see what was in my mind. There was no one who regretted these circumstances more than himself, or who appreciated more than he did the dangers inherent in the part played by the army, but he could promise me that his first preoccupation would be to put the army back into its proper place. He would not remain a day in office if he failed to do this. I was not, however, deterred from saying what I had meant to say, and I said it with all frankness, and added that the whole circumstances of his coming into office would be bound to make the worst possible impression in London. I said that His Majesty's Government could hardly fail to assume that what, in fact, had been set up in Iraq was a military dictatorship, and that I should welcome any sign that he could give me to show this was not so. He again assured me that he hoped and believed that, if he were given time, he would be successful in his efforts to make the army revert to its normal functions, and he again said that, if he were not successful, he would not remain in office. I then spoke of the murder of Jafar, and he said, with obvious sincerity, that he was as shocked and as grieved as I. He also deplored the dropping of bombs in Bagdad, which had resulted in the injury of several innocent people. I went on to explain that the main object of my visit to him had been to satisfy myself that he was taking adequate measures to protect the lives of members of the ex-Cabinet. He begged me to believe that he was doing everything possible. He said that he would have liked to have been able to give me a guarantee of their safety, but that he regretted that he could not do so while feeling ran so high in Bekr Sidqi's force. He had thought, and I instantly agreed, that the best course would be to get them quietly out of the country as quickly as possible. He had been in touch with Yasin and Rashid Ali. The attitude of Yasin had given him some moments of anxiety because that morning Yasin had thrown open his house and had received visits from representatives of some of the Euphrates tribes, but he had now heard that, as a result of a visit to King Ghazi, Yasin had consented to go and take Rashid Ali with him. Hikmat was therefore making arrangements for them to leave Bagdad that night. Every precaution would be taken for their safety.... He had not, however, been able to get into contact with Nuri, and he was somewhat concerned about this. It had occurred to him that it might be possible that I could do so (he clearly knew that Nuri was in the Embassy, but was too good-mannered to show it). If by any chance I were able to do so, it would be a help to him if I could advise Nuri also to leave Iraq and could make arrangements for his departure.

12. I spent most of the rest of the day with Nuri, who was in a distressing state of nervousness, but so soon as plans were concluded with the Air Officer Commanding for his departure by aeroplane to Egypt, he recovered his spirits and he began to talk freely, if still a little wildly, about the crisis. [H]e was insistent in the expression of the belief that King Ghazi was privy to Bekr Sidqi's movement, and that he said that this was also the conviction of Yasin. I had watched King Ghazi very closely while he . . . was discussing the affair on the morning of the day before, and I am bound to say that I, too, gained the impression that it came as no surprise to His Majesty. . . .

14. A copy of Bekr Sidqi's manifesto is enclosed herein. . . .

Inclosure:

"To the Noble Iraqi Nation,

"The army, which is composed of your sons, has lost patience with the present Government, who have been concerned only with their own personal interests disregarding the public welfare. The army has therefore appealed to His Majesty the King to dismiss the present Cabinet, and to replace it by another composed of sincere citizens under the leadership of Sayid Hikmat Sulaiman, who is held in the greatest esteem and respect by the public.

"By this appeal we have no desire except to improve your condition and the country's welfare, and we have therefore no doubt that you will co-operate with your brothers, the personnel of the army and their officers, with all your power—as the power of the people is always supreme.

"To our brother officials we say: We are only your brothers and colleagues in the service of the State, which we all wish to be one having regard for the interests of the public. We expect you to do your duty by non-co-operation with the oppressive Government, and by leaving your offices until a new Cabinet . . . is formed. It is possible that the army may be compelled to take certain forcible measures, through which harm might unavoidably come to those who do not conform with this sincere appeal."

—AL FARIQ BEKR SIDQI, Commander of the National Forces of Reform

Rising Anti-Semitism in Baghdad

Comprised of three provinces in the Ottoman Empire, Iraq had historically consisted of a diverse religious and ethnic population. And so, the people in the three Mesopotamian provinces, as in the rest of the Ottoman Empire, had always been tolerant in regard to the Jewish population. Indeed, many European Jews in the late nineteenth and early twentieth centuries had sought refuge from European anti-Semitism within Ottoman borders. When Iraq became an independent country in 1932, 2.5 percent of the population of Iraq was Jewish. In Baghdad, however, the political and commercial center of this newly formed country, a full 25 percent of the city's residents were Jewish.

The lot of these Jewish residents would begin to change drastically in the 1930s, which saw the rise of Zionism. Zionism is a political movement dating to the late nineteenth century, and it was established in order to address the anti-Semitism on the European continent. To do so, it sought to establish a Jewish homeland in what was then the Ottoman province of Palestine. Immigration to Palestine began almost immediately, albeit in small numbers. The movement gained impetus during World War I, when the British issued the infamous Balfour Declaration in support of the establishment of a Jewish homeland in Palestine. Immigration to Palestine increased during the interwar years, putting no small burden on the people already living there, since there were scarce resources to go around. Indeed, mass Jewish immigration during the interwar years led local Arabs, Muslims, and Christians to revolt against the British system between 1936 and 1939.

These events in Palestine had dire repercussions for Iraqi Jews, and there was rising anti-Semitism in Baghdad in the 1930s. The Arab Revolt captured the imagination of many Iraqis, who shared the anti-British sentiments underpinning the angst of Palestinian Arabs. As a result of this revolt, the Mufti of Jerusalem went into exile in Baghdad, where he began to incite feelings against Jews, who, in his opinion, were all equally culpable in regard to the untenable situation for Arabs in Palestine. Making matters worse, Germany, now under Nazi control, sent diplomats to Iraq, and they spewed anti-Semitic Nazi venom. This Nazi ideology appealed to many Iraqis, who saw a champion against the neocolonial Great Britain. These three conditions all fed into the thinking of pan-Arab ideologues.

And so, Jews in Baghdad began to feel less secure in their native land, and this even though very few of them supported Zionism. On the whole, the Jewish community in Baghdad felt that its core identity was Iraqi, not Jewish per se, and there was no real immigration to Palestine at this time. Nevertheless, and in retrospect, there were signs that the conditions of Iraqi Jews were changing. The following letter from a teacher at the Alliance Israelite expresses concern at a growing sense of Jewish insecurity in Baghdad. The letter can be found in Aron Rodrigue's *Jews and Muslims: Images of Sephardi and Eastern Jewries in Modern Times* (1993; reprint, Seattle: University of Washington Press, 2003), 277–78. As you read the letter, you should consider the following: What has given rise to anti-Semitism according to the author? Is the government promoting tolerance or anti-Semitism? How so? What does the author suggest in regard to Jewish loyalties and national feelings?

> Baghdad, 23 April 1936
>
> Events in Palestine have had their repercussions on the spirits of the people here. Every day the Arab newspapers devote long articles to the violent activities of the Jews in Palestine and to the so-called massacres of Arabs. The Jews here have asked the Minister to order the press . . . not to arouse pointless hatred against the Jewish population in this country. We would like to hope that this request will be taken into consideration and that we will not have reason to lament the consequences of this campaign of incitement and hatred which the press has been conducting over the last few days.
>
> We cannot deny that the situation is becoming difficult. Anything that the Jews here may do has become suspect. The slightest gesture is labeled Zionist or antipatriotic. And yet God knows the Jews in Baghdad are far from entertaining any Zionist ideas. Here are a few examples of the way our actions and gestures are being viewed and interpreted:
>
> . . . [T]he leader of the community, *Hakham* Sassoon, organized a religious ceremony in memory of Mrs. Farha Sassoon, of the David Sassoon family in London, who was recently deceased. This ceremony was held in the courtyard of our school.
>
> A few days afterward we learned that the police had written up a statement in which the school was charged with holding a meeting without authorization. . . . In order to release myself of all responsibility, I was obliged to give proof that the ceremony had been organized by the head of the Jewish community and that it was he who had issued the invitations. It would have been quite serious had I been charged with the responsibility for this affair in light of the fine which the tribunal had imposed last year as a result of the reception we had given for students at the school. . . .
>
> You must have heard that a short time ago the president of the community of Basra was sentenced to fifteen days in jail for having assisted several Jewish emigrants, some of whom, it was said, did not have valid passports.
>
> M. Laredo

The Shi'i Celebration of Ashura

The majority of people in Iraq, about 60 percent, were Shi'i, and yet they, too, were much like a marginalized minority. Their status as such had begun in the

Ottoman era. In the early nineteenth century, the Sunni Ottomans fought the Shi'i Persians. Since Shi'is have a very hierarchical structure of religio-political power, the Sunnis kept Shi'is within Mesopotamia out of seats of power. The Ottomans had feared that the Shi'i imams of Persia would be able to influence Shi'is in Mesopotamian areas bordering Persia. Then, the British had continued to privilege the Sunnis that were already established in the military, the former Ottoman officers. Thus, upon independence, the Sunnis dominated the state's administrative system; and the Shi'is suffered political and economic deprivation (Ghareeb, 222).

Given this marginalization, the holiday of Ashura has often been used as a historical passion play with great contemporary significance. Ashura falls on the tenth day of Muharram, which is the first month of the Islamic calendar's lunar year. It is a day of mourning that commemorates the martyrdom of the Prophet Muhammad's grandson at the hands of fellow Muslims. In 680, the Umayyad dynasty claimed the right to rule the expanding Islamic world, but some thought that power should be passed through the Prophet's bloodline. Umayyad forces massacred Hussein and seventy-two of his followers at Karbala, and this date marks the start of the Sunni-Shi'i split. Given the lower status of Shi'is in Iraq, the commemoration of this holiday often has special political overtones that speak to injustice in the present.

In the late 1930s, the British traveler H. V. Morton witnessed the Shi'i commemoration of Ashura in Baghdad. He described this event in *Middle East: A Record of Travel in the Countries of Egypt, Palestine, Iraq, Turkey and Greece* (New York: Dodd, Mead, 1941), 186–92. As you read his description, you should consider the following: What are the components of the Shi'i commemoration of Ashura? How does the author want you to feel about the Shi'is? What can you trust as accurate in the author's account? And what can't the author tell you?

> I found myself forbidden, like any Seventeenth Century "Christian Dog," from entering the Shia mosques in Baghdad. It was the first week in Muharram, the opening month of the Moslem year, a time when Shias flagellate themselves, cut their heads with knives, and achieve a condition of religious ecstasy which culminates in the passion play commemorating the death of Mohammed's grandson.
>
> I stood outside the mosques and watched the lowering crowds of men which passed in and out, each mosque like a hive about to swarm. A fanatical crowd devoid of humour is a terrible spectacle, especially when you are detached from the object of its obsession. These men were terrifying in their single-mindedness. They were men not humbled by grief, but made savage

and revengeful. Looking at them, I realized how quickly a human sacrifice must have cleared the air in pagan times; for these Shias, whether they were aware of it or not, wanted blood....

The great Shia festival takes place during the first ten days of Muharram, a time when the faithful celebrate the death of Husein at Karbala with all manner of morbid austerities. Baghdad at this time is full of pilgrims who, as they work up to the emotional climax of their pilgrimage, march through the streets at night whipping themselves. It would be as unsafe for a Sunni Moslem as it would be for a Christian to enter their mosques or to encounter their processions.

Having made friends with several local Christians, members of the ancient Chaldean Church, I told them of my desire to witness a procession of the flagellants, and one of them agreed to take me to the house of a friend in a back street of Baghdad from whose windows we could watch the Shias pass from one mosque to another. He promised to call for me at eight o'clock that evening and take me there.

It was dark when we set out, but crowds filled the main street, for Baghdad has contracted the Western habit of aimless night sauntering, the result, probably, of electricity and of a new clerkly class unwearied by physical labour. Leaving the main street, we walked through narrow lanes in which our steps were hushed. Some alleys were like the Shambles in York. The houses leaned together, thrusting forward their top stories until only a knife-cut of sky lay overhead; and the lanes meandered so confusingly that they might have been designed by a flock of crazy sheep. After dark something of the mystery of old Baghdad returns to haunt the sleeping alleys of the old city. For the first time I felt that it would be possible to see the Caliph passing on some night adventure, or, glancing up, to see the dwarf, so dear to Eastern story, peeping from behind a lattice.

The men encountered in these lanes were not the capped and collared *effendis* of the main street: they were silent men who passed with a bat-like scrape of heelless slippers, giving a sidelong glance, as they went by, from the shelter of their head-coverings. Sometimes a long, yearning wail of Turkish gramophone music would sound from beyond a blank wall, and I went on with the knowledge of life packed away there, of people sitting together as if in ambush.

My guide halted before one of the blank walls and knocked on a door. We heard the sound of feet descending a flight of stairs, and a voice on the other side asking who it was. At once the door was opened, to reveal not the eunuch which the street suggested, or the merchant in turban and silk caftan, but a young man in a black coat, a pair of striped trousers, and black patent-leather shoes.

Speaking good English, he led the way up a flight of stone stairs to a room leading off a galleried courtyard. Two divans, upholstered in Persian fabrics and fitted with white antimacassars, faced each other under the unshaded electric bulbs. A few Chinese pictures hung on the walls, and a number of knick-knacks were dotted about on bamboo tables. The most spectacular was a stuffed cobra strangling a mongoose; it stood on a side-table, very realistic and horrible, providing that touch of India which I was beginning to look for everywhere in Baghdad.

A smiling, dark girl of about eighteen, wearing a poppy-red dress, rose from the divan where she had been sitting in an attitude of formal expectancy, and shyly shook hands. She was our hostess. Although she had not left school for long, she was too timid to exercise her knowledge of English; but now and then she would contribute the words "yes" or "no" to the conversation, which we greeted with polite applause until she cast down her eyes and turned as red as her dress.

A servant brought in a tray of tea, English biscuits, oranges, and sweet limes.

We sat talking of the Shias whom they, as Christians, deplored as dangerous and fanatical persons, and they told me of the physical mortification endured by the sect every year during Muharram. The body-beaters, which we should see passing down the street that night, were the commonest of the flagellants. Every night for ten nights they would march from one mosque to another, beating themselves. There were others who scourged themselves on the back with chains. The most savage mortification was the head-cutting which takes place on the morning of the tenth day of Muharram.

My host had seen this at Najaf and also in Baghdad. He told me that all kinds of people took part in it, but the Turcomans were the most violent performers, sometimes slashing too hard and killing themselves. There were several men in the Government office in which he worked who occasionally got a day's leave to join the head-cutting procession.

I asked my host to tell me how the head-cutting is done. He said that a band of men, who for days have been dwelling on the gory emotionalism they are about to enjoy, would gather at the mosque.

"In Karbala or Najaf," he said, "you can see these men for days whispering to the swords which they carry about in their arms, polishing and sharpening them."

Arriving at the mosque, they form a circle and revolve round a leader, working themselves into a state of emotional excitement by uttering the names of

Ali, Hasan, and Husein, until, suddenly, the leader gives a great cry and brings down his sword on his head. As soon as the others see the blood they go mad. With cries and shouts of "Husein!," "Ali!," "Hasan!," they cut their heads until their white robes are stained everywhere with blood.

They then go off together in twos and parade the town, cutting and slashing until the blood falls in the gutter and spurts on the walls of the houses. Spectators, hearing the cries and the sound of the swords on skulls, and seeing the streaming blood, begin to cry and give the mourning wail, and sometimes people who have nothing to do with the orgy lose all control, and pulling out penknives or scissors begin to stab at their arms and wrists until the blood flows.

While he was describing this, we heard, far off, a dull, rhythmic sound.

"They are coming!" said my host. "We must go up."

He led the way up a flight of stairs to a little bedroom overlooking the street. Some one switched on the light, but he turned it off at once, asking if I minded sitting in the dark. It was better, he said, not to attract attention to ourselves. As the room protruded for a yard or so into the lane, sitting in the window was rather like being in a box at the opera. I could have touched with a cane the head of any one passing below. The buildings rose dark and mysterious, and the lane twisted away out of sight, merging itself into another as dark, as narrow, probably as serpentine. The only light came from a booth let into the opposite wall, where an old man sat cross-legged among a chaotic assembly of cigarettes and tobacco. I was aware of something pleasantly adventurous and exciting in sitting concealed in the dark, watching the shrouded figures in the lane below, the customers suddenly appearing in the glow of the booth and going off again into the darkness. At intervals came a queer sound, growing gradually nearer, as if a thousand nurses, taking their time from the matron, were delivering in rhythmic chastisement a thousand resounding smacks on the posteriors of a thousand children. But as it came nearer, we heard the fierce, grief-stricken background of this sound—the sound of men groaning, crying, and shouting. The noise then became horrible. There came into view, swaying down the lane, the strangest procession I have ever seen. Boys and young men came first, holding banners which, with true Eastern inconsequence, slanted this way and that. Behind them were men bearing on their shoulders the poles of palanquins on which rested boat-shaped clusters of lights. The dark lane now blazed with the moving orange glow of paraffin flares. Behind these lights, eight abreast, came rank after rank of men naked to the waist, the sweat of their austerities clammy on their faces and shining on their brown bodies. They were like a regiment of half-naked soldiers marching as captives to their doom.

Each company was preceded by a leader, and above each company one of the strange, barbaric boats swayed in the smoke and yellow light. The companies halted every few yards and the leaders faced them, crying out: "Husein!" A deep, agonized wail immediately rose from hundreds of voices. "Hasan!" Another wail. Then, in a rhythmic Arabic chant, the whole company would shout:

"Welcome, O Husein,

When you enter Karbala."

At the beat of each word the men lifted their arms in unison and brought them smack against their naked chests. Some chests were bleeding, a revolting sight; others were swollen with weals which would soon become wounds; and as they beat themselves, their eyes gazed fixedly ahead from faces pale and terrible in the torchlight, like the faces of martyrs on their way to the stake.

Their soldierly bearing, the perfect rhythm of their arms, the timed responses, their implicit obedience to their leaders, were a contrast to the disorder of the dipping banners and swaying boats. Those breast-beaters were like men transfigured in some sorrowful dream, and in their fanatical eyes was something of the anguish of Husein, parched and wounded on the plain of Karbala.

As I looked at those hundreds of faces, men old and young, men with hairy chests of bulls, men smooth and slender, men with beards, and others with the clean-shaven faces of boys, I wondered why human beings should behave like that for the good of their souls, and from what dark jungle of antiquity such spectacles had their beginning.

Surely this beating of the body, and the cutting with knives, was the sight that Elisha saw on Carmel, when the priests of Baal "cried aloud, and cut themselves after their manner with knives and lancets, till the blood gushed upon them." A writer of one of the books of the Old Testament might have called this strange, savage sorrow for the death of Husein one of the last sins of Babylon. As I looked at the faces and wounded bodies, and the sailing tabernacles of light, I felt that I was watching something which had happened long ago in this country, when the altars of Baal and Ashtoreth were smoking on the ziggurats.

About a thousand men passed by, and the sight of their reddened torsos and the sound of their chant became monotonous, for each group was in every way like its predecessor. Now and again an added vigour was given to the breast-beating when women, standing in the street or gazing from behind latticed windows, would set up the twittering funeral cry, and at the sound men would beat themselves with renewed frenzy.

The last group disappeared down the lane, and I felt that never in my life should I forget the "lil-hala, lil-hala" of their wailing chant, which had sung itself into my brain. I rose to go. My host switched on the light and said that it would not be wise to venture into the streets until the Shias had reached their mosque. Those kind people produced more tea, more biscuits and sweet limes; and, with the clock nearly at midnight, I went through the now silent lanes back to my bed.

Elegy to the Poor

Poetry provides insights into social issues of this time as well as national politics. Indeed, the historian Halah Fattah has called poetry "that indispensable window onto the Iraqi soul" (Fattah, 183) And in Iraq, poetry was more than an aesthetic and intellectual movement; it was often political in its intent. In the 1930s, modern poetry continued to follow the traditional form developed over the course of hundreds of years, but it began to treat new and more radical themes. Thus, it no longer promoted Bedouin traditions of the premodern past, but instead sought to inform people of the deep-seated changes in the social and political life of the nascent state. In this way, the collapse of the Ottoman Empire and the setting up of the mandate were earth-shattering events that led poets to put pen to paper in new ways. After World War II, poets would become even more radicalized, for they broke away from traditional forms of poetry, known as the *diwan*, in order to express themselves in free verse (Ghareeb, 184).

Muhammad Mahdi al-Jawahiri (1900–1997) was a famous Iraqi poet in the 1930s and 1940s. He was born a Shi'ite but considered himself an Iraqi nationalist. Thus, he did not count himself among those espousing pan-Arab ideals. For this reason, he often found himself at odds with members of the government. Sati' al-Husri, for example, would fire him from his post as teacher after he published a poem lauding an Iranian (that is, Persian) summer resort (Dawisha, 86). Al-Jawahiri did favor the Bakr Sidqi Coup of 1936, but this regime jailed him the following year for criticizing it. Al-Jawahiri wrote in a traditional style, and not free verse, but he treated new and radical themes. Salma Khadra Jayyusi insists that he was an example of an artist famous for "inciting public emotions against political decadence and compromise" (Jayyusi, 79). By 1956, al-Jawahiri felt so distanced from the Hashemite regime that he left Iraq in order to live in Syria.

In the following poem, al-Jawahiri analyzes the lot of the poor. He criticizes both the poor and their privileged political leaders. It is a translation by Issa Boullata and John Heath-Stubbs and can be found in Salma Khadra Jayyusi's *Modern Arabic Poetry: An Anthology* (New York: Columbia University Press, 1987), 80–81. As you read it, you should consider the following: Who is the intended audience for the poem? Who does the poet criticize? And why? How does this poem provide insight into daily life in Iraq?

> Sleep, You hungry people, sleep!
> The gods of food watch over you.
> Sleep, if you are not satiated
> By wakefulness, then sleep shall fill you.
> Sleep, with thoughts of smooth-as-butter promises,
> Mingled with words as sweet as honey.
> Sleep, and enjoy the best of health.
> What a fine thing is sleep for the wretched!
> Sleep till the resurrection morning
> Then it will be time enough to rise.
> Sleep in the swamps
> Surging with silty waters.
> Sleep to the tune of mosquitoes humming
> As if it were the crooning of doves.
> Sleep to the echo of long speechifyings
> By great and eminent power politicians.
> Sleep, You hungry people, sleep!
> For sleep is one of the blessings of peace.
> It is stupid for you to rise,
> Sowing discord where harmony reigns.
> Sleep, for the reform of corruption
> Simply consists in your sleeping on.
> Sleep, You hungry people, sleep!
> Don't cut off others' livelihood.
> Sleep, your skin cannot endure
> The shower of sharp arrows when you wake.
> Sleep, for the yards of jail houses
> Are all teeming with violent death,
> And you are the more in need of rest
> After the harshness of oppression.
> Sleep, and the leaders will find ease
> From a sickness that has no cure.
> Sleep, You hungry people, sleep!
> For sleep is more likely to protect your rights
> And it is sleep that is most conducive
> To stability and discipline.

Sleep, I send my greetings to you;
I send you peace, as you sleep on.
Sleep, You hungry people, sleep!
The gods of food watch over you.
Sleep, You hungry people, sleep!
The gods of food watch over you.

Bibliography

Al-Askari, Jafar Pasha, William Facey, and Najdat Fathi Safwat. *A Soldier's Story: From Ottoman Rule to Independent Iraq; The Memoirs of Jafar Pasha Al-Askari (1885–1936)*. London: Arabian Pub., 2003.

Benjamin, Marina. *Last Days in Babylon: The History of a Family, the Story of a Nation*. New York: Free Press, 2006.

Bourne, Kenneth, and D. Cameron Watt, eds. *Archive Editions: Eastern Affairs, December 1931–June 1933*. Vol. 8. New York: University Publications of America, 1986.

———, eds. *Archive Editions: Eastern Affairs, December 1933–June 1935*. Vol. 10. New York: University Publications of America, 1986.

———. *Archive Editions: Eastern Affairs, December 1937–September 1939*. Vol. 13. New York: University Publications of America, 1986.

———. *Archive Editions: Eastern Affairs, June 1933–May 1934*. Vol. 9. New York: University Publications of America, 1986.

———. *Archive Editions: Eastern Affairs, June 1935–December 1936*. Vol. 11. New York: University Publications of America, 1986.

———. *Archive Editions: Eastern Affairs, June 1938–June 1938*. Vol. 12. New York: University Publications of America, 1986.

———. *Archive Editions: Supplement to Eastern Affairs Volumes 1918–1939*. Vol. 15. New York: University Publications of America, 1986.

Chubb, Mary. *City in the Sand*. New York: Crowell, 1957.

Garstang, John, and Christopher Lumby. *Traveller's Handbook to Palestine, Syria and Iraq. 6th ed., Thoroughly Revised and Partially Rewritten by Christopher Lumby. With Eight Maps and Plans, by Bartholomew, Palestine Exploration Fund Map of Excavated Sites, and an Appendix with Two Sketch Maps on the Monuments and Sites of Palestine*. London: Simpkin, Marshall, 1934.

Haim, Sylvia G. *Arab Nationalism: An Anthology*. Berkeley: University of California Press, 1962.

Harris, Christina Phelps. *The Syrian Desert: Caravans, Travel and Exploration*. London: A. and C. Black, 1937.

Howard-Williams, Ernest Leslie, and Sidney Hay. *Air Over Eden*. London: Hutchinson, 1937.

MacDonald, A. D. *Euphrates Exile*. London: G. Bell, 1936.

Miller, Janet. *Camel-Bells of Baghdad*. Boston and New York: Houghton Mifflin, 1934.
Morad, Tamar, Dennis Shasha, and Robert Shasha, eds. *Iraq's Last Jews: Stories of Daily Life, Upheaval, and Escape from Modern Babylon*. New York: Palgrave Macmillan, 2008.
Morton, H. V. *Through Lands of the Bible*. New York: Dodd, Mead, 1938.
Stark, Freya. *Baghdad Sketches*. New York: E. P. Dutton, 1938.
———. *Beyond Euphrates: Autobiography, 1928–1933*. London: J. Murray, 1951.
Tagore, Rabindranath. *Journey to Persia and Iraq, 1932*. Tagore travelogues, 1. Kolkata, India: Visva-Bharati Pub. Dept., 2003.
Thomas Cook Ltd. *Cook's Traveller's Handbook to Palestine, Syria and Iraq*. London: Simpkin Marshall, 1934.

4

Ending the Old Regime, 1941–1958

The years between 1941 and 1958 are critical for understanding the coup of 1958 that put an end to the Hashemite monarchy. This period begins with a coup by Rashid Ali al-Kaylani on 10 April 1941, one that temporarily deposed the regent Abd al-Ilah. This abrupt change of a pro-British government—along with Rashid Ali's pro-German leanings—led the British to assert explicitly their neocolonial role. During the Thirty Days War that followed, the British reoccupied Iraq. It was a military occupation regarded as untenable by many anti-British Iraqis. The resulting tensions surrounding it gave rise to the anti-Semitic Farhud on 2 June 1941, an Iraqi Krystalnacht of sorts. Great Britain, however, did not remove its troops, and Iraq remained an occupied country during World War II.

The postwar era did not bring a respite for the Iraqi people. British troops ended the direct occupation of Iraq in 1946, but their country remained influential. The monarchy tried—unsuccessfully—to gain more freedom of action from the British via the 1948 Treaty of Portsmouth. This treaty was highly unpopular, and its signing led to al-Wathba (the leap), a popular uprising in Baghdad. The Iraqi Communist Party headed the demonstrations, and the rising popularity of this party led the Hashemite government to arrest its leaders in 1949.

The increase in political violence, however, was not a one-way street in which the state alone victimized Iraqi society. This postwar period also saw the rise of anti-Semitism. To placate the masses, the government adopted legislation that reflected antiminority sentiments by the majority Muslim population. In particular, the government promulgated Law No. 1, which allowed Iraqi Jews to leave the country and renounce their citizenship. Bomb attacks on Jewish targets followed the passage of this law, leading scores of Iraqi Jews to immigrate to Israel and other countries, such as India or England.

In retrospect, several trends become evident to historians analyzing the history of Iraq between 1941 and 1958. First, this period is notable for a rise in social divisions between the peoples of this state. Wartime inflation and commercial disruptions had increased the numbers of "have-nots" in the country, thereby accounting, at least in part, for the popularity of the Communist Party. Iraq, however, was also divided along sectarian lines. Jews became a target for national ire, while Shi'is often lived separately from Sunnis.

Politically, these social conditions had two political counterparts. In this period, the historian gleans the extent to which there was popular opposition to the Hashemite regime. No Hashemite monarch had the charisma of Faysal I, and the kings in this short-lived dynasty came to be seen by Iraqis as the handmaidens of Great Britain. Second, this period is witness to the failure of state institutions. Increasingly, political opposition was expressed not through formal channels, but through informal mechanisms of political activity. Such mechanisms of political opposition might be benign, such as a gathering and concomitant discussion at a coffeehouse, or more systemically malignant, such as the increasing tendency of government opposition to express itself through street riots or bomb attacks.

The readings in this chapter are designed to underscore the slow fracturing of Iraqi society. Nissim Rejwan, for example, remembers the Farhud of 1941. Given the occupation of Iraq by Allied forces during World War II, this chapter then excerpts instructions for American soldiers stationed in Iraq, which provides insight into how Westerners viewed a place that they persisted in thinking of as exotic. This chapter then addresses some of the controversial clauses of the problematic Portsmouth Treaty. Government offices, however, cannot explain all Iraqi political activity, for coffeehouses, as described by one Arab professor, were a key informal institution. Although this professor considered Baghdad a paradise, an American colleague argued in a subsequent document that poverty characterized Baghdad. A member of the Communist Party, an Iraqi Jew, would agree that poverty accounts for the increasing politicization of Iraqis. This politicization led some Iraqi officials to placate the Muslim masses by formalizing anti-Semitism, as apparent in Law No. 1 of 1950. This law's passage led to a mass exodus, and Ariel Sabar recounts his family's decision to leave Kurdish Zakho. This chapter ends with a description of life in an impoverished Shi'i village of the south in 1957, just before the coup that would end the monarchy.

The Farhud

The Jewish community has a long history in Iraq that, as its members proudly recount, dates to sixth-century Babylon. At the time of independence there were 120,000 Jews in Iraq, which represented about 2.5 percent of the country's population. In Baghdad, however, Jews were an even more significant minority, for 25 percent of the population was Jewish. Some Jews had established trade networks with Europeans, thereby profiting from increasing ties to colonial powers in the twentieth century. These Jewish merchants were responsible for 95 percent of all Iraqi imports. Other Jews, however, worked as simple tradesmen. Despite their status as a religious minority, Iraqi Jews embraced their national identity, making important contributions to national culture. Some Jews, for example, set up newspapers, while others went into national politics (Ghareeb, 124–27).

Unfortunately, the rise of anticolonialism and pro-Nazism in the 1930s threatened the Jewish community's role in the Iraqi state. The rising anti-Semitism of this time resulted in the Farhud, which refers to an anti-Jewish riot that occurred in Baghdad in June 1941. According to one Iraqi Jew who witnessed these events, the term does not easily translate, for "the word is so horrible, it has no direct English translation" (Shamash, 199). The catalyst for this riot was British intervention—the Thirty Days War—after a coup by pro-German Rashid Ali al-Kaylani. Anti-British feelings stoked the flames of this crisis, for many Iraqis, aware of the economic role played by some Jews, believed that all Jews supported this colonial power. At the end of the day, however, avarice determined the course of events, for the masses began to loot shops and homes. According to members of the Jewish community, 586 shops were looted as well as 911 homes. Even worse, this two-day riot led to 110 deaths.

And yet, as made clear in the following account, it would be wrong to attribute strong anti-Semitism among *all* Muslim Iraqis as the root cause of this riot. Born in the 1920s, Nissim Rejwan is an Iraqi Jew who grew up in a modest home in Baghdad. His account of the Farhud is taken from *The Last Jews in Baghdad: Remembering a Lost Homeland* (Austin: University of Texas Press, 2004), 128–31. As you read this account, you should consider whom Rejwan blames for this incident: Does he blame natives of Baghdad? Or outsiders? What role do Muslims play in this account? And how does this affect your understanding of the Farhud?

> The trouble started late Sunday morning, when a group of soldiers crossing the Khir Bridge to the western side of the city met a group of Jews on their way to share in greeting the crown prince. The Jews were attacked, first with blows and then with knives—and of those who couldn't run for their lives a total of sixteen were injured and one died of his wounds. As the morning progressed and the attacks became more savage, some of the civilians, passersby, and bystanders took part in the fracas—while the policemen on duty at the bridge acted as mere onlookers and did not lift a finger.
>
> Word quickly spread to the other side of the bridge, where the Jews were concentrated—and when it reached the slum areas adjoining King Ghazi Street groups began to gather. Rumors spread that the police were not interfering,

although on several occasions they fired warning shots into the air when houses were forced open and their contents looted.

Taking heart at this obvious encouragement and seeing that not only the soldiery but some of the policemen were taking part in the forages, the mobs in such destitute neighborhoods as Abu Sifain and Ras el-Tchol—where Muslims and Jews lived in close proximity—became more systematic, and by early afternoon large trucks were seen moving furniture and other household goods from one side of the city to the other. According to an official commission later appointed to investigate the events and report on them, soldiers accompanying these lorries told enquiring police officers that they were merely moving the office furniture of the Iraqi Air Force headquarters, which had moved to another address!

These forages, often accompanied by physical violence resulting in deaths and injuries, and provoking no effective reaction on the part of the police, led the governor . . . of the Baghdad Province to try to take charge himself. But when he asked the police officers on the spot why they were refraining from shooting at the attacking mobs, the reply was that "there were no orders." He got the same reply when he approached the chief of police.

It was only when he brought an order, signed by the regent, that orders were issued to fire at looters and murderers. It took over an hour to scatter the mobs and empty the streets. By that time . . . the *farhud* (the untranslatable Arabic word which best describes the events . . .) had spread throughout the poor neighborhoods in and around Ghazi Street as well as to some far districts like Al-A'dhamiyya and el-Karrada al-Sharqiyya. In this latter neighborhood, where the attacks took place only on the second day, six Jews were injured and one Muslim who tried to defend his Jewish neighbors were killed.

It is interesting to note here that Karrada and some of the more fashionable suburbs of Baghdad, where Jews constituted a majority of the inhabitants, witnessed the least trouble, some of them none at all. In many cases, armed Muslim neighbors stood guard and managed to chase away mobs intending to attack and loot.

Totally unaware of what was going on in other parts of the city, I left the house . . . after 4:00 p.m. that same Sunday and took the bus to Bab el-Sharqi, where the open-air cafes and snack bars were. . . . [M]y friends and I had a meal of kebab, chips, and salad and sat there chatting and discussing the month's events for the nth time. Although a true patriot himself, my Muslim friend Salman was pleased with the outcome of Rachid 'Ali's rebellion since the British and their allies were fighting the Nazis and Fascists. Anti-British he certainly was, but like many moderate Iraqis with left-wing leanings he was content with leaving his anti-imperialist sentiments in abeyance....

There was no indication whatever of what was going on not far from where we sat and chatted—and when it was time to leave—about 10:00 or 11:00 p.m.—we decided that the weather was too good to take a bus and walked the whole length of Al-Rashid Street on the way to our homes. During that long stroll, I began to feel that something was not quite as it should be. There was, for instance, a small group of Jewish young men who were carefully following in our footsteps.... There were also fewer buses going.

But it was only when we approached Suq el-Shorja and the adjoining way that ... I began to feel something was definitely wrong. Besides Salman and myself, there was with us a young Jewish friend whose home happened to be in an alley leading from That el-Takya to a parallel alley also leading to Al-Rashid Street. Seeing that something was wrong, we decided to walk him to the door of his home and thus took the turn to the way leading to the Jewish quarter. As soon as we took that turn, a group of about ten or twelve young men felt encouraged to do the same—but they decided to make a run of it. They knew no doubt what was going on at the other side of the city.

We duly saw our friend safely home, refusing to leave him until he was inside the house. Then Salman decided, and I did not object, that he should see me home as well. I will never forget the way in which I was let in. I had a key to the door, but the door was bolted and I could not go in. When I knocked I was asked who it was and only after assuring the people inside that it was me did they agree to come down from the roof—where Baghdadis slept in summer—and opened the door. It transpired that my people, and the family that was sharing the house with us, had got wind of what was happening and, seeing that I was so late (it was nearing midnight by the time I was home) simply gave me up for dead, killed by one of those murdering bands of agitated Muslims roaming the streets and the alleyways.

They wanted me to tell them what was happening and the terrible scenes I had presumably witnessed—and they were visibly baffled to learn that I was not even aware of the looting, killing, and raping that were taking place. I kept my cool, told them not to panic, and went to bed. But even I could not help hearing the shots fired at a distance and even some of the shouts for help.

The next morning things worsened considerably as word spread among slum dwellers and members of displaced tribes that there was a lot to be gained by joining in the fracas. I remember watching from a window groups of men clearly from out of town and hardly knowing their way about carrying bundles of loot and streaming up and down that section of our alley that led to another alleyway. Where we lived was just two or three houses before the end of a blind alley, and ours was the only Jewish household there.

I do not remember the idea having crossed the mind of any inhabitant of our house that our Muslim neighbors would so much as touch us. The most skeptical and hysterical among us express fears that our neighbors would not interfere and let the ferocious mobs do what they like . . .

They were wrong. Without even being approached, the three older sons of our aging neighbor—one of them a government official and one a student at some college or other—assured us we could rely on their protection. They were a good and well-established Baghdad family and as such they usually had some firearms. They kept watch but I don't think there was any attempt that day on the part of the mobs to attack our house, most probably because they were not even aware of the fact that Jews inhabited it.

Rules for American Soldiers in Iraq during World War II

British troops occupied Iraq for the duration of World War II, and their American allies joined them there in 1943. The presence of these soldiers wrought important changes in the political and social life of Iraq and its people. Politically, the presence of these Western forces ensured the reinstatement of pro-British politicians in the highest ranks of powers. Following the coup, and with, it would seem, the acquiescence of the British, there were retributive internments and court martials as well as summary executions. This situation, according to historian Charles Tripp, "cut the regime off from much of the articulate middle class, making [it] ever more dependent on the British" (Tripp, 57). Economically, the war caused an ever-increasing gap between the rich and the poor. Inflation and war shortages brought great wealth to those with import licenses, usually members of the Hashemite elite, but it wrought great suffering on the masses. There can be no doubt that this period in Iraqi history sowed the seeds of the monarchy's ultimate downfall in 1958.

American servicemen stationed in Iraq, however, would have been blithely unaware of the political and economic chaos in which they were unwittingly playing a role. The United States sent these soldiers to Iraq in 1943 in order to help protect the oilfields of northern Iraq. The government sent them with a book called *A Short Guide to Iraq*. The excerpts below are reprinted from the United States Army–issued *Instructions for American Servicemen in Iraq during World War II* (Chicago: Chicago University Press, 2007), 1, 3–5, 11–14, 16–17.

The book eschews discussions of the intricacies of Iraq's political and economic life, explaining instead the ins and outs of a culture that must have seemed tremendously exotic to U.S. soldiers. Although some of the information may seem basic (though not politically correct), the army can be lauded for its emphasis on a soldier's need to treat Iraqi interlocutors with respect. As you read this excerpt, you should consider the following: What aspects of Iraqi culture are explained to U.S. soldiers? What is the tone of the handbook? What does the handbook suggest about Americans' preconceived notions in regard to Iraq?

> You have been ordered to Iraq (I-RAHK) as part of the world-wide offensive to beat Hitler.
> You will enter Iraq both as a soldier and as an individual, because on our side a man can be both a soldier and an individual. That is our strength—if we are smart enough to use it. It can be our weakness if we aren't. As a soldier your duties are laid out for you. As an individual, it is what you do on your own that counts—and it may count for a lot more than you think.
> American success or failure in Iraq may well depend on whether the Iraqis . . . like American soldiers or not. It may not be quite that simple. But then again it could. . . .
> What is Iraq, anyhow? Well, it's a lot of things, old and new. It is one of the oldest countries in the world—and one of the youngest under its present government. In Baghdad, the capital city, you will see street merchants selling exactly the same kind of pottery that their ancestors sold at the time of the Arabian Nights. Not far away you will see great dams and modern refineries equal to the best you have seen in America. If you happen to be sent to the oil fields, you will discover miracles of modern engineering construction side by side with primitive refineries built 2,000 years ago and still in operation. . . .
> But don't get discouraged. Most Americans . . . who have gone to Iraq didn't like it at first. Might as well be frank about it. They thought it a harsh . . . and inhospitable land. But nearly all of these people changed their minds after a few days or weeks, and largely on account of the Iraqi people they begin to meet. So will you.
> That tall man in the flowing robe you are going to see soon, with the whiskers and the long hair, is a first-class fighting man, highly skilled in guerilla warfare. Few fighters in any country, in fact, excel him in that kind of situation. If he is your friend, he can be a staunch and valuable ally. If he should happen to be your enemy—look out! Remember Lawrence of Arabia? Well, it was with men like these that he wrote history in the First World War.

Differences? Of Course! Differences? Sure, there are differences. Differences of costume. Differences of food. Differences of manner and custom and religious beliefs. Different attitudes toward women. Differences galore.

But what of it? You aren't going to Iraq to change the Iraqis. Just the opposite. We are fighting this war to preserve the principle "live and let live." Maybe that sounded like a lot of words to you at home. Now you have a chance to prove it to yourself.... If you can, it's going to be a better world to live in for all of us....

The Moslem bible is known as the Koran and the Moslems worship in mosques (*mosks*). They are very devout in their religion and do not like to have "unbelievers" (to them you are an "unbeliever") come anywhere near their mosques. You can usually tell a mosque by its high tower. *Keep away from mosques.* Even though you may have visited mosques in Syria or Egypt, the mosques in Iraq must not be entered. If you try to enter one, you will be thrown out, probably with a severe beating. The Iraqi Moslems even resent unbelievers coming *close* to mosques. If you have blundered too near a mosque, get away in a hurry before trouble starts. The Moslem religion requires a man to pray five times a day. This is done by facing the holy city of Mecca and going through a series of prostrations. Don't stare at anyone who is praying, and above all do not make fun of him. Respect his religion as he will respect yours....

It is a good idea in any foreign country to avoid any religious or political discussions. This is even truer in Iraq than most countries, because it happens that here the Moslems themselves are divided into two factions something like our division into Catholic and Protestant denominations—so don't put in your two cents worth when Iraqis argue about religion. There are also political differences in Iraq that have puzzled diplomats and statesmen. You won't help matters any by getting mixed up in them. Moreover, if you discuss foreign politics with them, you might be maneuvered into making statements that could be interpreted as criticisms of our Allies....

Many of the Iraqis believe in the "evil eye." This is a good deal in their minds like putting a "hex" on a person is to people in parts of our country. If you stare at people, especially children, someone may think you are the possessor of an "evil eye," and are trying to put a curse on the person you are staring at. Some of the Iraqis think that the lens of a camera is an "evil eye," and you will make enemies by taking close-up snapshots and possibly wind up with a knife in your back. General views or street scenes will cause no trouble—except mosques. . . .

Moslem women do not mingle freely with men. The greater part of their time they spend at home and in the company of their families. Never make advances to Moslem women or try to attract their attention in the streets or other public places. Do not loiter near them when they are shopping. If a woman has occasion to lift her veil while shopping, do not stare or smile at her. Look the other way. These rules are extremely important. The Moslems will ... dislike you and there will be trouble if you do not treat women according to their standards and customs.

These rules apply both to the cities and towns and to the villages and the desert. The village and desert women go unveiled more often than the women in the cities and *seem* to have more freedom. But the rules are still strict. Any advance on your part will mean trouble and plenty of it. Even when speaking to Iraqi men, no mention should be made of their female relatives. The Iraqi themselves follow this custom and would resent anyone, especially a foreigner, not doing the same.

To repeat—don't make a pass at any Moslem woman or there will be trouble. Anyway, it won't get you anywhere. Prostitutes do not walk the streets but live in special quarters of the cities.

The Treaty of Portsmouth, 15 January 1948

The Treaty of Portsmouth was supposed to be a triumphant revision of the highly unpopular Anglo-Iraqi Treaty of 1930, which had qualified Iraqi independence. Thus, it eliminated, as called for by the opposition parties, a need for Iraq to consult Great Britain in regard to foreign policy decisions. This treaty, however, was highly unpopular with the political opposition and the masses. They objected to the secretive negotiations and perceived the results as a modification of the Anglo-Iraqi Treaty—and not an elimination of it. Its signing led to a spontaneous uprising known as al-Wathba. On 16 January 1948, students protested, and the police fired on the crowd. A mass uprising ensued, and, according to Phebe Marr, "a real atmosphere of civil war prevailed in Baghdad" (Marr, 65). This treaty and the concomitant opposition to it are important for two reasons. First, the signing of this treaty revealed the extent of opposition to the Hashemite regime, perceived as tied to foreign control. Second, the popular response to its signing underscored the role of political opposition in the streets, therefore outside the purview of formal political structures.

The riots led the government to reject this treaty, and yet, given the opposition to it, we should analyze the following text of this treaty as a critical marker in Hashemite history. The text of this treaty is drawn from Penelope Tuson and Emma Quick, editors, *International and Regional Treaties and Agreements: Iraq, Kuwait*, vol. 1 of *Arabian Treaties, 1600–1960* (London: Cambridge Archive

Editions, 1992), 527–35. In order to understand this document, you might consider two distinct positions in a debate focused on the pluses and minuses of this treaty as viewed by ordinary Iraqis. What articles suggest that Iraq was an equal partner that would benefit from this treaty? Why did the Hashemite government consider this treaty a boon for Iraq? Or, indeed, for the individual members of the government of Iraq? Conversely, what articles and clauses suggest that Great Britain was perpetuating its colonial role in Iraq? Where do you perceive links between foreign and domestic affairs in the Treaty of Portsmouth?

> His Majesty the King of Great Britain . . . and His Majesty the King of Iraq. . . . Desiring to conclude a new treaty of alliance with the object of consolidating the friendly relations which exist between them and of strengthening by co-operation and mutual assistance the contribution which each of them will be able to make to the maintenance of international peace and security in accordance with the provisions and principles of the Charter of the United Nations:
>
> *Article 1*: . . . A close alliance shall continue between the . . . Contracting Parties in consecration of their friendship, their cordial understanding and their good relations. . . .
>
> *Article 3*: Should either High Contracting Party . . . become engaged in war, the other High Contracting Party will . . . come to his aid as a measure of collective defence. . . .
>
> **ANNEXURE**
>
> *Article 1*: (a) The High Contracting Parties recognize the importance of air bases as an essential element in the defence of Iraq itself and of international security and as a link in the essential communications of both parties. . . .
>
> (b) In the event of either High Contracting Party becoming involved in war, or of a menace of hostilities . . . the King of Iraq will invite His Britannic Majesty to bring immediately to Iraq the necessary forces of all arms and will furnish to His Britannic Majesty on Iraqi territory all the facilities and assistance in his power, including the use of railways, rivers, ports, aerodomes and lines of communication on the same financial terms as those applicable to the forces of His Majesty the King of Iraq.
>
> (c) To maintain the Iraqi bases at Habbaniya and Shaiba at all times, whether of peace or of war, in the necessary state of operational efficiency, His Britannic Majesty will provide at these bases the necessary technical staff, installations and equipment, and subject to paragraph (c) of Article 2 below will meet the cost of such maintenance. . . .

(d) Until such time as Peace Treaties have entered into force with all ex-enemy countries, His Majesty the King of Iraq grants to operational units of the Air Forces of His Britannic Majesty free access to and use of the two air bases referred to in (c) above, it being understood that the Peace Treaties are to be deemed to be fully in force when the Allied Forces are withdrawn from the territories of all ex-enemy States. . . .

(e) His Majesty the King of Iraq agrees to permit aircraft of His Britannic Majesty in transit across Iraq freely to use the air bases of Habbaniya and Shaiba. . . .

Article 2: (a) His Majesty the King of Iraq will provide at his expense the forces necessary for the guarding of the air bases at Habbaniya and Shaiba.

(b) Day-to-day operation of the bases and their security arrangements shall be mutually arranged between the Iraqi and British Commanding Officers, who will each retain the final responsibility for the movement of the units of his own country. . . .

(e) . . . the King of Iraq will pay the cost of maintenance of all buildings and installations at the two air bases . . . occupied by or erected for the Iraqi forces. Each of the High Contracting Parties will pay the cost of new buildings provided for the sole use of his own forces.

(f) The allocation of existing installations and buildings at the air bases will be decided by the Joint Defence Board. . . . The King of Iraq may purchase the installations and buildings allotted to the Iraqi forces at a fair valuation. On the final evacuation of British forces, the Iraqi government shall either themselves take over such buildings and permanent structures at the bases as have not previously been purchased at a fair valuation having regard to the use to which they have been put, or shall afford such facilities as may reasonably be necessary to enable the Government of the United Kingdom to dispose thereof to the best advantage.

(g) His Britannic Majesty shall not be liable for any Iraqi rates and taxes in respect of the air bases or any buildings and installations therein.

Article 3: In order that the air forces of the High Contracting Parties should attain the necessary efficiency in co-operation with each other—

(i) His Britannic Majesty offers all . . . facilities at Royal Air Force air fields in the United Kingdom and in any British colony or protectorate administered by the United Kingdom as may be required by the Royal Iraqi Air Force. In particular, His Britannic Majesty offers to make available to the personnel of the Royal Iraqi Air Force the facilities of the armament training centres of the Royal Air Force in the Middle East. . . .

Article 4: (a) All Iraqi units at bases in Iraq or in the United Kingdom and any

British colony or protectorate administered by the United Kingdom whether stationed or in transit, shall be under Iraqi command.

(b) ... [A]ll British units shall be under British command.

Article 5: In the common defence of interests of the United Kingdom and Iraq a permanent joint advisory body will be set up immediately on the entry into force of this Treaty to co-ordinate defence matters between ... the United Kingdom and the Iraqi Government. ...

This body, which will be known as the Anglo-Iraqi Joint Defence Board, will be composed of competent military representatives of the two Governments in equal numbers, and its functions will include—

(a) The formulation of agreed plans in the strategic interests common to both countries,

(b) Immediate consultation on the threat of war,

(c) The co-ordination of measures to enable the forces of either High Contracting Party to fulfill their obligations under Article 3 of the Treaty,

(d) Consultation regarding the training of the Iraqi forces and the provision of equipment for them. ...

Article 6: ... The King of Iraq agrees to afford, in case of need ... all necessary facilities for the movement of units of His Britannic Majesty's Forces in transit across Iraq, with their supplies and equipment, on the same financial terms as those applicable to the forces of His Majesty the King of Iraq.

Article 7: Subject to any modifications which the two High Contracting Parties may agree to introduce in the future, the Iraqi Government will continue to extend to the units of His Britannic Majesty's Forces disposed in Iraq in pursuance of the present Treaty, or otherwise by agreement between the High Contracting Parties, the immunities and privileges which they at present enjoy in jurisdictional and fiscal matters and the existing provisions of any local legislation affecting units of the armed forces of His Britannic Majesty in Iraq. ...

Article 8: His Britannic Majesty undertakes to grant whenever they may be required by His Majesty the King of Iraq all possible facilities in the following matters, the cost of which will be met by His Majesty the King of Iraq:

(a) Naval, military and aeronautical instruction of Iraqi officers in the United Kingdom.

(b) The provision for the forces ... of the King of Iraq of arms, ammunition, ships and aeroplanes of modern pattern such as are in current use by the forces of His Britannic Majesty on a priority which, having regard to the relative needs of each force, shall treat both forces equally. ...

Article 9: In view of the desirability of identity in training and methods between his own forces and those of His Britannic Majesty, His Majesty the King of

Iraq undertakes that, should he deem it necessary to have recourse to foreign military instructors, these shall be chosen from amongst British subjects.

He further undertakes that any personnel of his forces that may be sent abroad for military training will be sent to military schools, colleges and training centres in the territories of His Britannic Majesty, provided that this shall not prevent him from sending to any other country such personnel as cannot be received in the said institutions and training centres, or for courses not available in those territories.

He further undertakes that the armament and essential equipment of his forces shall not differ in type from those of the forces of His Britannic Majesty.

Intellectual Life in Baghdad

The coffeehouse was an important institution in the political and cultural life of Iraq in the 1940s and 1950s. Iraqis did more there than drink coffee and play backgammon. The Iraqi intelligentsia met at coffee shops and discussed new ideas. Sometimes, specific artists or authors became associated with specific coffeehouses. These intellectuals, however, did not discuss only their art; they also discussed politics. Their ideas challenged the traditions of Iraq's established social and political life. There could be grave implications for Hashemite Iraq, because less-educated Iraqis also frequented these same establishments. In this way, the coffeehouse became a place where people of different statuses and social positions met and exchanged points of view. Thus, the coffeehouse could be a politically charged venue. Poor people might not be able to afford a newspaper, but they could hear the news of the day at a coffee shop. The government often placed spies in coffeehouses known for revolutionary thought. And so, historian Eric Davis argues that urban coffeehouses offered a venue for challenging the deeply entrenched Hashemite state (Davis, 94–95).

Jabra Ibrahim Jabra (1919–1994) was a Palestinian born in Jerusalem, but he became one of Baghdad's most influential intellectuals. He moved to Baghdad after the Arab-Israeli war of 1948. Educated at Cambridge University in England, he became professor of English literature in Baghdad, where he would eventually meet his wife. He was a poet and an author. Jabra left an account of his experiences in Baghdad which was later published in *Princesses' Street: Baghdad Memories*, translated by Issa J. Boullata (Fayetteville: University of Arkansas Press, 2005), 61–63. His account captures many aspects of urban life at the time, revealing the intellectual effervescence of the Iraqi capital. How would you describe the mood in Baghdad at this time? How do people associate? What class does Jabra and his friends represent? How does the answer to this previous question affect your reading of this document?

> The academic year 1949–50 was the second year after my arrival in Baghdad to work as a professor of English literature at the College of Arts and Sciences, established that year. That year witnessed my broad openness to Baghdad, and Baghdad's openness to me in a way I had never expected or dreamt of. I began to make the acquaintance of many people, both men and women, from all walks of cultural and social life as I had in the previous year, but the circles began to expand and the paths to branch in every direction.
>
> I was kept in a state of constant activity, divided between my teaching duties and the joy of meeting people. In addition, I wrote, painted, gave public lectures in various places, and sometimes translated, especially for the journal of the Iraqi Academy.
>
> The Department of English Literature in the College of Arts, where I taught, was a department I had established in the fall of 1949 with my colleague Desmond Stewart under the supervision of Dr. Abd al-Aziz al-Douri, the dean at that time. I also lectured at the Higher Teachers' College during the time Dr. Abd al-Hamid Kazim was dean, as well as at Queen Aliya College for Girls during the deanship of Mrs. Amat al-Said. The buildings of the last were across the street from the College of Arts. As for the Higher Teachers' College, it was at some distance, and so whenever I finished lecturing at Arts or Queen Aliya, I took a two-horse carriage from among the many that still filled Baghdad's streets and roads, and I relaxed on its old leather seat as the horse ambled to Teacher's College at a stimulating rhythm that brought me there in less than ten minutes. The coachman charged me no more than fifty fils (that is, one dirham—the dinar having twenty dirhams). He often suggested that he wait for me until I finished giving my lecture, in order to take me back to my base at Arts, at a charge of one more dirham.
>
> At all these colleges, I participated in the activities of the students. Extracurricular societies were established for them: there was a debating society, using Arabic and sometimes English; another society for drama; and a third for music. We often had guests attending these activities, intellectuals from the city, as well as students and professors from other colleges. In those days, I supervised a new studio at the College of Arts for those students who loved painting, and I also used to paint with them, until Professor Hafiz al-Duroubi took it over from me upon his return from England, where he had studied art. (From these amateurs, he formed the Impressionists Group two or three years later, which included some who had begun with me at the studio and who

would later become famous artists: Muzaffar al-Nawwab, Hayat Jamil Hafiz, and Abd al-Amir al-Qazzaz. They were joined by other artists, some of whom were amateurs as well and who also became famous, such as Dr. Ala Bashir and Yasin Shakir.)

Meanwhile, I continued to write short stories, essays, and poems, and I published them in *al-Adib*, a Beirut monthly magazine owned by Albert Adib, which at that time was the cause of much interest and excitement because it attracted the young and the innovative in the Arab world. I don't know how I had time that year to also give private lessons to some young men and women in my room at Baghdad Hotel. This was a tenth-grade hotel on al-Rashid Street, on the edge of the Murabbaa Neighborhood, near the popular al-Zawra Cinema. The noise of the dialogue and music of the movies in this cinema shown at the lowest prices used to reach me during the night.

My little room overlooking the inner courtyard of the hotel was hardly large enough for a narrow bed, an old sofa, a straight-backed chair, a table for writing (which I had myself bought for two dinars when I began working a year earlier), and a movable Aladdin heater that I also used to make tea and coffee in a large kettle. I decorated the walls with oil paintings that I had done in Jerusalem and Bethlehem and with some new paintings that were beginning to increase in number. That year, this room was the meeting place of many of the most well-known of Iraq's writers, artists, and professors whose ages ranged from twenty-two to thirty-two, and it daily witnessed animated discussions about what was being written and painted in Baghdad and in all the other Arab capitals—as far as their news reached us.

Among those who came to my room were Buland al-Haydari, Adnan Raouf, Husayn Mirdan, Hilmi Samara, Jawad Salim, Desmond Stewart, Khalid al-Rahhal, Nizar Salim, Abd al-Malik Nouri, Najib al-Mani, Zuhdi Jarallah, Yousuf Abd al-Masih Tharwar, and many others. We were also within a stone's throw of the Swiss Café, which offered café au lait and *cassata* ice cream and was frequented by ladies of all ages, contrary to the custom of cafés in those days. Off to one side in the café was an electric gramophone with recordings of Bach, Brahms, and Tchaikovsky for those who liked to listen to them. Next to the Swiss Café was the famous Brazilian Café, which was more traditional than the Swiss Café and could hold many visitors, most of whom were intellectuals and journalists from the educated class of the city. This café was run by a highborn Syrian man, who liked to mix with his clientele and knew them by name and offered them the best Turkish coffee in town, which was made of Brazilian coffee beans, after which the coffee shop was named. He even had someone who would roast the coffee beans and grind them for those who desired to buy coffee to take out.

Its intoxicating aroma filled the Murabbaa Neighborhood all along al-Rashid Street. (Perhaps he was the only one in Baghdad to sell fresh coffee until Captanian opened a shop nearby where I continued to buy ground coffee beans and tobacco for many years.)

Some of the writers were not happy at the Brazilian Café unless they sat on the front line chairs facing the street, which was always noisy and busy with its ever-changing scenes, people, colors, carriages, cars, and lottery ticket sellers shouting, "Five thousand dinars! Five thousand dinars!" The din did not cease until about midnight, especially because next to the café was a famous nightclub, in which Afifa Iskandar sang.

Poverty in Baghdad

The 1940s and 1950s was a period when poverty became extremely visible in Iraq. The minority of "haves" stood in stark contrast to the "have nots." World War II increased Iraqi poverty, because it caused inflation and commercial disruptions. Even after the war, however, poverty remained widespread. This was true, as pointed out by historian Phebe Marr, "even as new oil wealth was creating visible pockets of urban affluence and modernity" (Marr, 61). Some of the economic crisis stemmed from the fact that so many people left the countryside for the city. Baghdad's population grew from 145,000 in 1900 to 580,000 in 1950. People who were from outside of this society, like foreigners, had special insight into poverty since they were not "used to" seeing the same sights every day.

For this reason, we turn now to the memoirs of two Americans who lived in Iraq in 1950 and 1951. Albert V. Baez was an American sent to Iraq to teach science by the United Nations. He lived in the capital with his wife, Joan, and their three daughters (including Joan junior, the soon-to-be famous folk singer). This family lived very comfortably in Baghdad, but they were struck in particular by the poverty of the people around them. Al and his wife, Joan, recorded some of their impressions of this poverty in *A Year in Baghdad* (Santa Barbara, Calif.: John Daniel, 1988), 31–32, 71–72, and 181–83. As you read this excerpt, you should consider the following: How does the following description highlight the poverty of some Baghdadis? And what are the strengths and weaknesses of relying on an outsiders' account to understand poverty? Are there potential inaccuracies in assertions of poverty?

We lived in the old part of Baghdad at the northern end of town called Al Wazira, where the ministries of foreign countries were situated ("wazir" means "minister"). It was near the road which leads to the old mosque at Khadhimain. From Al Wazira, looking across the Tigris, you could see groves of date palms and old homes in the distance.

We lived in a neighborhood of sharp contrasts. Some of the legation buildings were of modern construction and painted white, but most were old mud-colored structures. All of them were large, and some were elegant. Yet up the street from our modern white house, people lived in huts made completely of mud except for the palmleaf roof. As we walked by them we could see women making cow dung patties and setting them out to dry to be used as fuel for cooking. This kind of work was done by women and girls. The men and the boys never touched the cow dung. There was a shortage of fuel so women and children spent hours collecting twigs and scraps of anything that could be burned, recycled, or sold. Some little children were carrying bundles larger than themselves. . . .

Seeing real poverty for the first time at such close range made a lasting impression on all of us—especially on our children. In California we had lived in a typical middle-class house in a college town, where we did not see extremes of wealth or poverty. In Baghdad, on the other hand, we were living in a neighborhood where people of affluence and influence lived right next to people living in mud huts. We noticed that children from the poor mud huts came and took food which we had discarded and had put out for the garbage man to collect. Joan dreaded doing this because a swarm of cats would leap all over her when she came out of the house.

"Look," said Joan one day, "the children are eating the rotten pomegranates I threw out this morning."

She was distressed by this contrast between our life style and theirs and one day tried to give the children some oranges. The children ran away when she approached them. They were not used to having anyone give them anything. Joan then started the practice of putting bread and other bits of food in a bundle which the children could reach by climbing but which the ever-present dogs and cats could not reach. If she put this food out at night it was gone by the crack of dawn. . . .

I [Joan] often hopped on the bus that rattled over the dirt road to Spinney's, the British grocery store about half an hour away. The bus passed the high cement walls with pointed glass on top, sealed in to impale unfortunate thieves. Children played in gutters where there was more sewage than water. Some of them sat around garbage pails eating orange and banana skins. Men squatted by the side of the road with their water pitchers. Having no toilet facilities, they used the gutter and poured water over their lower section to clean themselves, and then dropped their long skirts down. Beggars with faces and hands as brown as the rags they wore leaned on tall sticks or sat with cupped hands out. We passed mothers, usually pregnant, with babies and children barely dressed; but no matter what the age, each one had a nose-ring or earrings of pure gold. Some had tiny pearls inlaid. Gold was a sign of prestige. Many of the very poor had their strong white teeth extracted and replaced with gold. I often wondered how many times they had gone hungry for that coveted luxury.

Vendors clattered down the dusty way, some with trays of bread on their heads, calling out "Sammoun, sammoun!" Others with oranges, called "Portughal helue!" Pushing a home-made wagon with a huge oil drum nestled in it, the kerosene vendor shouted *"Nafut, nafut!"* while beating the drum with a husky stick.

I watched the little boys run behind the bus as we bumped along. If they saw me or spied one of our girls, they sprinted fast and beat the bus to the market, greeting us with their straw baskets and cheery faces. "Memsah, me Chris, Memsah." (I'm Christian.) What they were really saying was, "We'll carry anything for you for big *baksheesh*." I couldn't help pouring out my change into their hands. Nothing made their smiles broader.

Sometimes I found it hard to believe all this—the starving children, the beggars, the filth, the fat sheiks who sat in the bus and smoked, ate oranges, and spat on the floor. The rattletrap bus that surely had square wheels—I always felt bruised in the bottom by the time we arrived. Sometimes I held my breath unconsciously because of the combined smell of diesel fuel and oranges. The Iraqis eat oranges as we drink coffee and, as there are no garbage cans, they drop the peels on the floor. We stepped on them all the way down the aisle of the bus....

Early in June ... wives of the impoverished farmers who cultivated the fields for landlords carried baskets of spinach on their heads. Their children toddled after them, dragging baskets of the momentarily life-giving substance in their arms. Spinach to sell. The law even allowed these farmers to keep a small amount of their produce.

One hot, dry morning, as I [Joan] picked the little black pebbles out of our rice, I heard a low, dull-voiced "Memsah." I spun around, and there in the doorway was a tall woman. She had come in so softly on her broad bare feet that I hadn't noticed her. She looked regal in spite of unwashed hands and face, protruding pregnant stomach, and her ragged black abayah. "Memsah, *schpint*." (Memsah, spinach.)

Her face was partially covered with her unclean garment, and at her side were two expressionless small children, eyes wide and staring, noses running and mouths gaping. They held tightly to their mother's skirts and in the tall woman's arms was a small baby girl. She too stared listlessly. Not at me—not at anything. Her chin and the stained cloth that covered her tiny chest and stomach were wet with drool; her hair was henna-colored and stuck to her head in clotted lumps of mud. It was a custom to dye the hair henna from the flowering bush whose leaves, when boiled, produced a reddish colored water. After coloring the hair they managed to roll it in little circles and stick it to their heads with mud. There was a tiny gold ring pierced into one side of the wee baby's nostril. I thought to myself, how would they ever wipe that nub of a nose without her screaming with pain?

"Memsah, schpint?" The woman repeated, and she held out her basket full and heavy with fresh green leaves.

She wanted to sell it, mud and all, I thought, and why not?

"Memsah, me Chris," she dared a half a smile.

I spoke slowly. "You are a Christian?" I made the sign of the cross and pointed to her.

"Na'am," (yes), she nodded, and a flicker of hope lightened her eyes.

"This is schpint, and you want flus?"

She shook her head, "*la-la*," (no, no), and her face grew brighter as she held out her basket to me. I understood then. She was giving it to me, taking a chance that perhaps, just perhaps, I would give her something to eat in return.

"No flus?" I smiled at her, took the basket, and dumped the muddy spinach into the sink. "All right, you wait right there like a good Christian, and I'll see if there's anything . . ." I went on muttering to myself, alternately smiling at her and poking around in our family stash of canned goods. She'd surely like sweet things like peaches, pears, figs, and of course, dates. I even dared a small jar of peanut butter. I held it up to her and made "mmmmm good" noises of approval and rubbed my stomach. "Great protein," I mumbled, and shoved it into the basket along with some pistachio nuts and powdered milk. As I looked up again her face had momentarily lost its anxiety.

The Evolution of a Communist

The Communist Party was very influential in Iraq. Its history there began in the 1930s. In the 1940s, a Christian headed this party, and he rendered it the party of intellectuals. The historian Charles Tripp states that half of the members of the party were Jews, Christians, and Shi'is, thereby "indicating the appeal of the party to minorities and to shi'a still resentful of their small share of power and privilege" (Tripp, 63). This was an urban party, appealing to the intelligentsia and workers of major cities. Since the British sided with the Soviet Union during World War II, the British occupation led to a liberalization that allowed the Communist Party to evolve (Marr, 58). After World War II, the Communist Party was no longer free to operate, but it continued to be popular in Iraq. It would remain so until the late 1960s.

Sami Michael grew up in Baghdad and became an active Communist. Like Jabra Ibrahim Jabra, Michael is a novelist. He was born in Baghdad in 1926. Though Jewish, he grew up in a neighborhood consisting of Muslims, Jews, and Christians. He would flee Iraq through Iran in 1948, after the Iraqi government issued a warrant for his arrest. He fled to Iran, considering at first the possibility of going to Russia. Ultimately, however, he became a resident of Israel. There, he noticed the oft-abominable condition of Arab Jews, and he began publishing novels to convey their plight to Israeli citizens of European origins. The following account of his decision to become a Communist is found in *Iraq's Last Jews: Stories of Daily Life, Upheaval, and Escape from Modern Babylon*, edited by Tamar Morad, Dennis Shasha, and Robert Shasha (New York: Palgrave Macmillan, 2008), 66–69. As you read the account, you should consider the following: Why did Michael choose to be a Communist, and not a Zionist? Why was it dangerous to be a Communist? What does the lot of Michael and his Communist compatriots reveal about political process in Hashemite Iraq?

> I became involved in the Communist movement because it was the single attractive alternative to the political reality in Iraq at the time for me. My graduation from high school coincided with the increase in Nazi propaganda in Iraq. I remember the Farhoud clearly. I was 14 and had taken 2 of my brothers and a sister to visit my grandfather and grandmother in the old part of Baghdad. At the end of the day we took the bus back home and then I saw the masses outside, as if prepared for something. I believe ours was the last bus that passed that mob safely before it began to riot. The bus after us was stopped and Jews were taken out and slaughtered.
>
> The areas that really suffered in the pogrom were the poor areas. The army protected the middle class and the rich, and we were protected in Betaween. After it was over, we realized that the Iraqi army had saved us from further slaughter. The British army, on the contrary, sat outside the city and waited for all the rage to be taken out against the Jews before it entered the city and took control. When we woke up on the morning of June 3, the entire street was filled with Iraqi soldiers. Out of pain, anger, and embarrassment, some of the poor people emigrated immediately after to Palestine. There were only a few hundred, not more, that immigrated in '42, '43.

So the anti-Jewish riots came as a shock—hit me hard in the face. And then World War II broke out and on the way to school we saw graffiti that Hitler was destroying the "germs." I knew that they meant me, a Jew, and my generation that was coming of age then and had previously felt so secure and happy. The world around us was crumbling. The Germans were marching from victory to victory and their intention was to conquer the entire Middle East. We began worrying about the Jews in Palestine. So to think in those days about Zionism as a solution sounded not only impossible but also stupid. Furthermore, the British army wasn't gearing up to protect Iraq against the Germans but instead dug into hiding, seeking protection against a German invasion in Palestine. Yet many Jews did join the Zionist movement in Iraq starting in the early '40s.

At this stage of the war we discovered that the one and only power that managed to stop the German advance into their territory was Moscow. How did it happen that the most un-Western, seemingly weak country managed to do that? We wondered. So suddenly we admired the Russians. We didn't understand what Communism was because in Iraq we had a very weak Communist Party at the time with perhaps just a few dozen adherents and it was underground. But we heard about it.

So my friends and I began reading all we could get our hands on about Communism. It was all in English—there was nothing in Arabic about Communism. So in addition to Balzac and Shakespeare, we started reading Marx and we began translating the books into Arabic for others to understand. Then we discovered an interesting thing: we could find no books or articles published in Iraq that spoke out against anti-Semitism—except for the Communist material. So we said to ourselves: "Here is our address." Many educated people found this was the path for them: all my friends—girls and boys, men and women.

But being a Communist was very dangerous because we became a real force—a threat to the regime—as the movement grew. The government denied us licensing as a political party in 1946. In the early and mid-'40s, the Iraqi government did not recognize Zionists and Zionism as enemies in any formal way because the Zionists did not challenge the regime—they only wanted to leave Iraq. All the heroic stories about the secrecy of the early Zionist underground were made up later on. The regime knew exactly when and where the Zionists operated and who they were. And in fact the regime was pleased about the Zionists, because one Zionist is one less Communist.

The Communists became popular: we even wielded influence within the ranks of the Iraqi army and military training academies. The Communist Party became the strongest party in Iraq, despite being underground. And the most amazing thing of all was that it was a sort of Jewish-Shi'ite-Kurdish coalition against the ruling Sunni minority. It was a very strong coalition, and very popular. We were considered heroes. If I said, "I am a Communist," I was immediately protected. Every door was open to me. We had a press and we sold our newspaper, *Al-Usba*, almost openly, with the certainty that we would be protected, and we had a circulation of about 6,000.

The arrests began as early as '43, '44, and continued through '49. *Al-Usba* was banned in 1946 shortly after its founding. The prisons were full of Communist women too—even Arab girls. The Jewish Communists were charged, ironically, with the crime of Zionism as well in many cases. But we continued to function. Communists were often given 10 years to execution. And the CID [Central Intelligence Department]—also called the *Muhabarat*—which were the secret police, acted mainly against the Communists, not against the Zionists. On the contrary, it regarded the Zionists as allies. Only just before the State of Israel was established were discriminatory measures imposed against Zionists. With the establishment of Israel, the Iraqi government was glad to get rid of the Zionists and the Jews in general, and used that event as the pretext for ordering the arrests or executions of Jewish Communists.

Then came the historic period that was later expunged from history, as if it never existed. The prohibition of publicizing the events of the Communist Party as they occurred was the result of a tacit agreement between the Iraqi, British, and Israeli establishments for decades to come.

What happened was that the issue of the Baghdad axis came to life. Iraq was preparing to sign the Portsmouth Treaty, which set out terms of cooperation and alliance between Iraq and Britain and thus was essentially a pact against the Soviet Union and Communism. We took advantage of this to organize demonstrations against the treaty and against the government in late 1947. We organized mass protests with rabbis, Muslim sheikhs and vicars, and Christian leaders, and we held hands and talked about Jewish-Arab brotherhood. The movement became known as the *al-Wathba*, like an *intifada* [uprising].

Jews and Arabs fought together against the government and the Jewish community supported it in a big way—on the streets, with their wallets, ideologically. There were street battles with many fatalities. We beat the police and the army didn't interfere. It wasn't prepared to do so, and it turned down the command to fire on us. On the contrary, soldiers as individuals also participated with us. And we won. We won to the extent that the government in Iraq fled for several days. In the final stage the party's Jewish secretary and my friend, Sasson Dallal, was hanged. It was the first case from the time of Mohammed and until today that the head of the opposition in Iraq was a Jew. Several top leaders in the party were Jews as well, and I personally helped found new cells and organized officers and members of the Shi'ite community.

Law No. 1 of 1950

The denaturalization law—that is, Law No. 1 of 1950—was a major turning point for Jewish citizens of Iraq. Israel had been founded on 15 May 1948, and Iraq was among the Arab countries that declared a war with this new country the very next day. This war ended in a definitive defeat for Arab armies, which had dire consequences for Jews in Iraq (as well as in other Arab countries). The sound defeat by Israeli troops was humiliating, and many Iraqis were angered by the displacement of 750,000 Palestinian Arabs. As a result of this war, some Iraqis assumed pro-Zionist leanings on the part of their Jewish compatriots in Israel. Israeli policymakers did not help matters for Jews in Iraq, for they sent out Zionist agents to stir up pro-Israeli sentiments among the Jewish population.

Then, in 1950, Israel passed the Law of Return, which allowed all Jews to immigrate to Israel. This Israeli law meant little to Iraqi Jews of the wealthier mercantile class, for their prosperity was tied to their country of origin (Shiblak, 136). Some Jews of Iraq's poorer classes, however, began to immigrate to Israel in the hope of a better life. The historian Abbas Shiblak estimates that from three to five thousand Jews left Iraq illegally—that is, without an exit visa—between the Arab-Israeli War in 1948 and 1950. Policymakers in Iraq felt compelled to pass the denaturalization law in response to this illegal emigration (Shiblak, 141). The denaturalization law addressed the illegal emigration by offering Jews the opportunity to give up their Iraqi citizenship legally. As you read the text of Law No. 1, you should consider the following: Why did Iraqi politicians pass this law? What stipulations are made for Jews who want to remain Iraqi? Should the law have included such stipulations? Why or why not?

Passed by the Iraqi Chamber of Deputies on 2 March 1950 and by the Iraqi Senate on 4 March 1950, as Law No. 1 of 1950.

Article 1. The Council of Ministers is empowered to divest any Iraqi Jew who, of his own free will and choice, desires to leave Iraq for good of his Iraqi nationality after he has signed a special form in the presence of an official appointed by the Minister of the Interior.

Article 2. Any Iraqi Jew who leaves Iraq or tries to leave Iraq illegally will forfeit his Iraqi nationality by decision of the Council of Ministers.

Article 3. Any Iraqi Jew who has already left Iraq illegally will be considered to have left Iraq for good if he does not return within a period of two months from the date of the putting into operation of this law, and he will lose his Iraqi nationality at the end of that period.

Article 4. The Minister of the Interior must order the deportation of anyone who has lost Iraqi nationality under Articles 1 and 2 unless the Minister is convinced by sufficient reasons that his temporary stay in Iraq is necessary for judicial or legal reasons, or to safeguard someone else's officially testified rights.

Article 5. This law will remain in force for a period of one year from the date of its coming into effect and may be cancelled at any time during that period by a Royal Iradah published in the *Official Gazette*. . . .

Article 7. The Minister of the Interior will execute this law.

Supporting Arguments. It has been noticed that some Iraqi Jews are attempting by every illegal means to leave Iraq for good and that others have already left Iraq illegally. As the presence of subjects of this description forced to stay in the country and obliged to keep their Iraqi nationality would inevitably lead to results affecting public security and give rise to social and economic problems, it has been found advisable not to prevent those wishing to do so from leaving Iraq for good, forfeiting their Iraqi nationality. This law has been promulgated to this end.

The Exodus of Kurdish Jews

When the Iraqi government passed Law No. 1, domestic policymakers and foreign diplomats alike thought that no more than 10 percent of Iraq's Jewish population would renounce their citizenship (Shiblak, 145). The promulgation of Law No. 1, however, was followed by a series of bomb attacks on Jewish targets in Baghdad, including a café, a synagogue, and a car dealership owned by a Jewish man. Together, the passage of Law No. 1 and these bomb attacks "led to something approaching mass hysteria" (146). Instead of the perceived 10 percent of the Jewish population taking advantage of the law, Israel welcomed 32,453 Iraqi Jews in 1950 and 89,088 Jews the following year (142). In this way, only about 11,000 Jews remained in Iraq (Ghareeb, 127).

The family of Ariel Sabar was among those emigrating from Iraq to Israel after Law No. 1. At that time, his father Yona was twelve years old. His grandfather Rahamim came from a mercantile family that dyed wool and sold cloth. This family lived in northernmost Iraq, in a Kurdish village called Zakho. The 27,000 residents of this town included 1,471 Jews (Sabar, 15). Up until 1950—and for as long as anyone then could remember—a Muslim aga acted as their tribal protector. After the Arab-Israeli War, however, this aga, despite his best efforts, could not shield them from the new anti-Semitic feelings among some Iraqis.

Ariel Sabar and his father Yona returned to Iraq in order to explore their family's history together. This excerpt is taken from Ariel's account of his familial quest, which was published as *My Father's Paradise: A Son's Search for His Jewish Past in Kurdish Iraq* (Chapel Hill, N.C.: Algonquin Books, 2008), 89–92 and 93–96 and 104–6. As you read this excerpt, you should consider the following: How does Yona remember his father's initial reaction to the denaturalization law? How did Muslim Iraqis of Zakho respond to the Jewish immigration to Israel? How did Yona feel about leaving his village in order to move to Israel?

When I asked my father about the Denaturalization Law a few years back, I was working as a staff writer at the *Baltimore Sun* and covering the U.S. Naval Academy in Annapolis. My father said that if I wanted a parallel for the scene among Zakho's Jewish schoolchildren the day the law was announced, I should picture the midshipmen at Annapolis tossing their caps skyward on graduation day.

"We celebrated like that," my father told me. "We threw our book bags into the air, like 'To hell with these books.'"

Among the adults, however, news of the denaturalization law exposed long-buried fault lines. The penniless felt they had nothing to lose. Israel was terra incognita, but the privations couldn't be much worse than they were in Zakho. At least one thing was certain: They would no longer be the least powerful class (the poor) of a minority religious group (the Jews) among a minority ethnic group (the Kurds), in an Arab country (Iraq) that, as at least some people saw it, had all but told its Jews to get lost.

The small but powerful class of well-to-do merchants took a different view. They owned homes, stores, and land in Zakho. To leave would be to give up everything in a gamble against bad odds. They had heard enough about Israel to know that a procession of boats carrying educated Europeans had gotten there years before. They wondered about their chances of ever achieving the same levels of wealth and prestige.

It was true that the Jews lacked power in Zakho. They depended for their security on the agas' of the Sindi, Gulli, and Slivani tribes. They had to seek the agas' blessing and pay a "fee" for every Jewish marriage. They were expected to volunteer their labor when the aga undertook the occasional public works project. But was that really too high a price for freedom of trade and religion? In light of the stories some were only now hearing about the Holocaust in Europe, many Kurdish Jews felt they had it good.

Even after the 1950 Denaturalization Law made the Jewish exodus a fait accompli, Zionism was rarely more than a way to dress up more practical impulses: hopes for a better life; unease over the breakdown of Muslim-Jewish relations; a new generation's alienation from its parents; a thirst for adventure; and perhaps most important, the growing awareness that Zakho could no longer count on its isolation to beat back the wider world.

My grandfather Rahamim was thirty-three years old, and before long, when his father passed away, he would be the family's eldest male and its head. Zakho had not failed him.

In the family's general store one simmering day in the summer of 1950, eleven-year-old Yona sat on a stool in the corner and listened while his father and another Jewish storekeeper mulled over the future. Yona had brought Kocho, a little lamb Rahamim had bought for him a few months earlier, and was stroking the animal's oily wool as the adults talked.

"Let the poor go to Israel," Rahamim said, with a dismissive sweep of the hand. "They may find a better life there. If they do, good for them."

"I'm sure Israel would rather have people like us," the other storekeeper said.

"Israel will have people like us, only here in Iraq."

The merchant returned a confused look.

"I mean," Rahamim said, "that we may be of greater use to Israel as its representatives here. We could import products from Israel and sell them to Iraqis. We could be Israeli sales agents, as it were."

His friend and business partner, Hajji Ibrahim, had walked in unnoticed a few minutes earlier and had been quietly eavesdropping. Hearing this, he let out a snort.

"Yes, Rahamim," Ibrahim said, with mock solemnity. "I will start painting the sign now: 'Special discount: Delicious Israeli oranges, grown on soil freshly fertilized with Arab blood.' The Iraqis will be lining up in the street to help the struggling Israeli farmers."

"To hell with you, Hajji," Rahamim said, glaring at his friend. "What would you have me do?"

"I think you will have a hard time in Israel," Ibrahim said, soberly now. "Here, there are just a few Jews. No problem. You get together, hatch your schemes, and then make a nice living off the rest of us. But in Israel, there are only Jews. So who will you cheat?"

"Leave my store if you want to insult me," Rahamim said, though he didn't look him in the eye. "You don't know what you're talking about."

Ibrahim turned to Yona in the corner and winked. "What do you think, ma'alme butchuk? Let's ask the little rabbi. Am I right or not?"

Yona blushed. "Kocho is tired, Babba," he said, getting up. "I'm going to take him home." Yona knew better than to tangle with adults. But what Ibrahim said to his father that day would stay with him for a very long time....

On a crisp day in late October 1950, seventy Jews left Zakho. Bureaucrats from Mosul had set up desks in the synagogue to fill out the paperwork. The departees were the town's have-nots: the small-time peddlers, the porters, the beggars, nearly all of them illiterate. Most carried only the rags on their backs and perhaps a single clay bowl or half-melted candle. Clinging to their children, they crowded onto the chartered buses and rolled south toward Mosul and the unknown.

"Let them go," Rahamim sniffed. What did 70 Jews amount to in a community of 1,850?

But those seventy were like the loose thread that unravels the blanket. Fixtures of the Jewish market—the cobbler, the blacksmith, the baker—were now gone. The houses of famously boisterous families were empty and dark. The singing in the synagogue was a little quieter. In the teahouse by the river, each day brought fresh radio reports of the mushrooming exodus: eleven hundred Jews left Iraq in May; twenty-seven hundred in June; nearly forty-five hundred in October.

Later that fall, haggard-looking bureaucrats from Mosul again set up tables in Zakho's large synagogue. The line of people wound past the *gniza* cellar where Jews buried old Torah scrolls, and out the rough-cut stone entryway into the dirt alleys. Here was the bedrock of Zakho's middle-class: its storekeepers and farmers, small landowners and kosher butchers, its weavers and blacksmiths and schoolteachers. They were Rahamim's customers. They were the people he prayed with. They were the people he sipped tea with in the evening after the market closed. What would remain for him once they left?

The line inched forward. In the afternoon, when a rain started to fall, Rahamim closed his shop and joined it. Inside the synagogue at last, Rahamim saw a row of low tables stacked with papers and bulging files. There was a commotion in the corner. An old widow, known for her fondness for home-distilled arak, was grousing that she could not understand the Arabic-speaking bureaucrats.

"I will speak slowly," the young clerk said, running out of patience. "Once again, grandma, do you want to leave Iraq? And if you leave, do you promise never to return?"

"Sir," she began, slurring her words, "You must have good spies, for it is true, I loved arak."

A low rumble of suppressed laughter echoed through the sanctuary, and the old woman looked momentarily confused. But she was determined to give the young official a full answer. "But let me assure you—all of you," she said, her voice quavering with genuine emotion, "that as of next Saturday, mark my words, I will be leaving arak for good. And no, young sir, I will never go back."

This time, Rahamim and the other men, despite their presence in Zakho's holiest building, could not hold back. They gave in to a cruel fit of laughter, which vented feelings held inside for too long, things that had nothing to do with a foolish old widow.

At the front of the line, Rahamim took a form and wrote down the names and ages of all the Beh Sabaghas: his parents, his wife, his three children, and his brothers and sisters-in-law and their children. The unsmiling clerk looked up the names in the Iraqi citizenship rolls and drew a black line through them. Then he copied the names into a new ledger, under the heading "Denaturalized." Rahamim signed another set of forms with a trembling fist. The clerk marked the top page with three stamps and handed it back.

"Take this to the passport desk," the clerk said, pointing across the room. "In fifteen days, you and your family cease to be citizens of this country." . . .

The end arrived suddenly. A line of motor coaches rolled into town early one April morning, and word went out that the time had come. Under a sky still full of stars, Jewish families, anxious and bleary, dragged suitcases and children out front doors and into the cramped alleys that led to the main street.

As they crossed the bridge to the bus stop, they saw that another crowd had gotten there first: Hundreds of Muslims had lined the streets to bid their neighbors farewell. Old women raised cries of *li-li-li-li-li-li*, ululating as if a loved one had died. A troupe of child musicians played drums and flute. Teenage boys stepped forward to help with suitcases. One beggar—beloved of the townspeople, though he was slightly mad—pounded his head against a newly erected electric pole. "Where are my brothers going?" he shrieked, until people crowded in to console him. "Why are they forsaking us?"

Yona had never seen anything like it. He threaded frantically through the throng. He studied the tear-stained faces and listened to the hoarse cries. The swarm of well-wishers pressed in around him. He was jostled and tripped over the train of a woman's robe. Getting up, he realized he had lost his parents.

"Ha-ha! Little Yona! My son!" a man's voice called from behind. Yona wheeled around. Looking at him with a sad smile was the old grocer who had given him his first job, as a bookkeeper. "I was hoping I'd see you."

The man, whose beard was grayer than the last time Yona saw him, reached into his pocket and pulled out a small box of Turkish delights. "For the journey," he said. "They may not have these where you're going. So eat them slowly, to remind you of Zakho." The man had no children of his own. Looking like he might cry, he knelt to hug the boy.

Yona wanted to tell him what he had been thinking about for the last few days: that he would come back here someday soon as an Israeli fighter pilot. He would land a gleaming jet right in the center of town, and all the Kurds would pour from their houses to cheer his return. Instead he just stood there in the old man's embrace, his arms slack at his side, tears streaming.

Buses carried the Jews to Mosul, and trains carried them to Baghdad. At the airport, angry mobs pressed against the barricades, hurling curses.

"Die, kilab yahud!"

"Rot in hell!"

"Be gone!"

It was April 16, 1951. Miryam flinched at the ugly words and pulled her children against her skirt as crowds of departing Jews pressed in from all sides. A few hours later, the Beh Sabaghas reached the checkpoint where guards searched bodies and baggage for contraband.

"Boy, are you carrying anything of value?" a policeman asked Yona.

"N-n-no, sir," Yona stuttered. The man's gruff voice reminded him of the officers who had humiliated his father on their last trip to Baghdad.

"No money, no jewelry, no precious metals?" Jews were allowed to take only 50 dinars out of the country.

"No, sir," Yona said, shaking as he tried to remember his Arabic. "Nothing."

"Turn around, Jew dog," said the officer. "I don't know that I believe you."

Yona stiffened as the man's fingers crawled over his thighs and ankles, under his arms and crotch, and, then, suddenly, into his pants pockets.

"What did my son do?" Miryam asked meekly.

"Shut it, woman," the officer barked. The man withdrew three small squares of colored paper from Yona's pocket: postage stamps bearing a portrait of Iraq's handsome boy king, Faisal II. Each one was worth 1 fil, a single penny.

"What are these?" the officer growled, his face reddening.

"Sir, it was an accident. I . . . I forgot I even had them."

"Lying Jew. How dare you try to steal property from the Kingdom of Iraq?"

Miryam put her hands to the side of her head and shrieked as the officer raised his palm. "No," she shouted. "He is a boy." But she might have been talking to a wall.

The officer slapped Yona's face three times. "One smack," he said, "for each stamp."

Life in a Shi'i Village

The rural village of the 1950s was quite different from the cosmopolitan center of Baghdad. There, tribal sheiks played a major role in every aspect of life for all residents. The Ottomans, if you remember, had tried to decrease the power of these men in the nineteenth and twentieth centuries. The British, however, had reinstated tribal sheiks, endowing them with formal authority within the Iraqi state. They did this in order to foster a cost-efficient system of indirect rule. For this reason, sheiks continued to play a prominent role in the political life of Iraq once the country received independence and, arguably, even after the 14 July Revolution of 1958. Their base of power was in the countryside, where Iraqis lived in villages that had few of the amenities of Baghdad and other big cities. In addressing the town and tribe, historian Phebe Marr writes: "Instead of love of the land, loyalty to family and tribe has dominated Iraq's social and political life" (Marr, 18).

As experienced by Elizabeth Warnock Fernea, life in the village, though filled with hardships, was not without its charms. In 1956 and 1957, this young American traveled to El Nahra, a Shi'i village in southern Iraq. She did so to assist her husband—they were newlyweds—with his anthropological fieldwork. She lived in a wattle-and-daub house, though it *was* one of the few buildings in the village with electricity. She described El Nahra as a conservative place. Gender segregation was the norm, and women wore the abaya in public, with the black cloak covering them from head to toe. (Nevertheless, and as evident in Fernea's larger work, such gender segregation did not prevent El Nahra's women from playing an important role in the village's social and economic life.) Villagers took religion very seriously, and the festivals for Ashura or Id al-Adha, were celebrated with great fervor. Presiding over all this was their sheik Hamid, and he wielded nearly unquestioned authority—and fairly (though he did use his wealth to spend summers in the cool mountains of Lebanon).

This excerpt introduces some inhabitants of El Nahra to the reader. It is taken from Fernea's classic work *Guests of the Sheik: An Ethnography of an Iraqi Village* (New York: Anchor Books, 1965). As you read this passage, you should consider the following: What are the values of the villagers? What hardships are associated with village life? What strengths? Who are the Sayids? How do they live? What does this last tell you about village life?

> I was too shy simply to knock on every door along the path, but fortunately during the first days my reluctance did not matter. Mohammed invited me to call on his mother, and in his house I met many of the Sayids, six families who

were not members of the El Eshadda, but who lived with the tribe in a sort of *noblesse oblige* relationship. Because of their descent from the Prophet, the Sayids are bound to be treated with some respect, and are used as mediators in tribal disputes. In return for their services as peacemakers, the Sayids receive the protection of the tribe, and they had been given parcels of land when they first came to settle with the El Eshadda. The ancient practice of giving other special privileges to Sayids—plowing their land for free, grinding their grain without payment—was less observed now than before. But the Sayids still received alms on religious festivals, and Laila, the local seamstress, later told me she always sewed without charge for Mohammed's sister.

The Sayids had their own small mudhif on the edge of the settlement, around which their houses clustered wall to wall. The first time I visited Mohammed's family, he called for me after supper, carrying a kerosene lantern to light the way. We turned off the main road into a dark and narrow alley which wound among the low mud houses, each marked by one or two lanterns hung inside the walls. Electricity was expensive, and only the sheik and his brothers could afford it. At the end of the alley the Sayids' mudhif loomed, also lit by lantern light, and, framed within its shadowy vault, a few men sat cross-legged, smoking and playing backgammon. The slap of the wooden pieces on the game board came to us distinctly over the sound of their voices.

Ahead, in a doorway, stood the figures of two women, tall, straight and thin like Mohammed—his mother Medina and his sister Sherifa. Medina held a second lantern high. "*Ahlan wusahlan*," she said, and we crossed their dark court, where I could hear the cow munching in the corner, into a tiny room, swept clean and almost empty. I sat on a mat covered with a rug and a white sheet. Sherifa insisted that I make myself comfortable with a long pillow also covered with clean white linen. She then brought in a charcoal brazier and we sat around it, warming our hands against the cold.

They served me fruit on that first occasion, which I knew was a great extravagance for them, but afterward when I went to visit I was offered, like all their other guests, a glass of lemon tea made by brewing the skin and seeds of dried lemons (*numibasra*). Medina made it especially well.

I spent many such evenings in Mohammed's house, where I was treated almost as a relative, and where the atmosphere was relaxed and the conversation gay. The family, once well-to-do and highly respected in the community, had retained a general air of taste and dignity in spite of misfortune. They still owned 200 acres of land, but because of soil salination, a mounting problem in the area, less than twenty acres could be cultivated. Their present poverty-stricken state was mitigated by Mohammed's job with us. They were "gentility in straitened circumstances" but they were cheerful about it, and that made all the difference.

When the family land had first begun to salt up, Medina's husband had left El Nahra to find work. He had not found it, but in Kut he had found a rich sheik whose personal charity was the support of Sayids, so he had settled there, and only visited El Nahra when he was sick or needed help. Medina made the best of it. She was only forty-five, but she looked seventy, so thin that every bone in her hand was visible. Her skin was seamed and wrinkled by years of work in the hot, drying sun, her mouth shriveled into empty gums. Her black garments had been new many years ago, but she wore them as though they had been bought yesterday; she still hennaed her fingernails and outlined her eyebrows with dull blue kohl. When she was feeling poorly, which was often, she lay on a mat and her voice became the dry, cracked whine of an old, old woman. But when she felt well she sailed down the alley like a queen, her black garments flowing behind her. In the afternoon sessions in the sheik's house she was always treated with courtesy and respect. She talked animatedly and smoked, one after the other, the cigarettes offered by Selma—she was too poor to buy them herself. The women listened attentively and laughed at her jokes; she had a way of gesturing with a cigarette and tossing her head back as she talked—she had style. I never met anyone who disliked her. Women would bring her food from their own limited stores and visit her in droves when she was too sick to get up from her pallet.

Sherifa carried herself like her mother, with a dignity not always seen among the poorer people in the settlement. I was told that when Sherifa had been younger, she had been very handsome, and her husband had bought her much gold jewelry. But the man went bad, no one would explain why; he had deserted Sherifa after her baby boy died; she was now neither widow, virgin, nor divorcee, and hence had no future. Yet she was intelligent and industrious and her advice was much sought after by other women and girls. She kept chickens and sold eggs; she raised lambs in the spring and sold the meat and wool. She helped keep the family alive.

The younger brother, Abad, was twelve, ambitious and clever. He was in the sixth class at the local primary school, and at night he sat on the path under a street lamp to study his lessons, for the two lanterns in his house were not strong enough to read by.

There was an older brother, Abdul Karim, who seemed to have been born without energy. Theoretically he was a sheep trader, but few people had seen him at work. His wife, Fadhila, was vigorous and attractive, with strong arms and bright eyes; she laughed from deep inside, a loud, healthy laugh which infected even the dourest old ladies. Her greatest sorrow was that she had no children. According to local beliefs, it was always the wife who was at fault in these matters. In a society where childlessness is grounds for divorce, Fadhila, despite her health and energy, was judged inadequate as a woman and as a wife.

Fadhila and Abdul Karim lived in their own room, across the court from that of Mohammed, Medina, Sherifa and Abad. Each household was economically separate, but Fadhila and Sherifa shared the chores, bringing cans of water from the canal several times a day, sweeping the court, feeding the cow, the lamb and the chickens, baking the barley bread and doing the cooking, the dishes, the laundry. Fadhila preferred the dishes and the laundry because it gave her an opportunity both morning and evening to exchange gossip with the other women of the village who squatted along the canal, scouring their pots with the gritty silt of the bank and scrubbing their families' clothes in the muddy irrigation water.

Down the alley lived the sheik's gardener and servant, my guide, Ali, with his wife, Sheddir, and their grown son and daughter. Their house was even more modest than Mohammed's. A small court where Sheddir cooked on a Primus stove, a lean-to for the cow and chickens, an oven for bread, and one tiny rectangular room where the entire family slept on mats on the floor because they could not afford a bed. One wooden chest, its blue paint peeling, contained their few possessions. A lantern hung on a nail, and on the mud-and-straw walls of their room pictures had been pasted or tacked—pictures from magazines of Mohammed the Prophet, of a traditional Arab beauty in abayah and fringed head scarf.

Ali's salary as the sheik's gardener and servant was minute; most of what he earned was in kind. He had access to the garden to cut grass for his cow, and he always received a small share of the sheik's grapes which he could trade in the market for barley flour or rice. Ali was saving money to help his son get married. Since Ali was a poor man, only twenty pounds was needed for the bride price, the sum set by custom within the tribe and paid by the groom's father to the bride's father. The bride's father uses part of the money to help his daughter buy furniture, household goods and her trousseau. But twenty pounds was half of Ali's annual income. How, then, to hurry up the procedure? Ali's daughter was of marriageable age, too, and since paternal first-cousin marriage was the preferred marriage in any case, Ali was negotiating with one of his brothers who also had a boy and a girl. If the fathers could simply exchange children, two marriages would be made for the price of one and the family line would be assured of continuance. A fair exchange. This was the kind of strategic arrangement which many poor *fellahin* families strove for. Otherwise a man might wait ten years to get married, for it took at least that long to save the required amount.

Sheddir, Ali's wife, while cutting grass in the garden one morning, invited me to visit her, and I did, twice. After that I did not feel as free to do so, for each time I came they spent an embarrassing amount on delicacies, fruit, coffee, sweet biscuits. I knew that wherever I went in the settlement, except perhaps for the houses of the sheik and his brothers, my arrival was bound to put a strain on the family's finances. Their traditional sense of hospitality always struggled with their slim budgets, and usually hospitality won. I would protest vigorously when this happened, but it did no good, for I was only following the accustomed pattern: a guest always protested at the honors done him to show his host how much he appreciated them. So I made excuses to Sheddir and asked her to visit me instead.

Bibliography

Abd al-Qadir, Ghulam Ali Khan, and Mohibbul Hasan. *Waqai-I Manazil-I Rum: Diary of a Journey to Constantinople*. London: Asia Pub. House, Published for the Dept. of History, Aligarh Muslim University, 1968.

Al-Ghita, Ahmad Kashif. *Outline of Modern Iraq*. London: Diplomatic Press, 1949.

Baez, Joan, and Albert V. Baez. *A Year in Baghdad*. Santa Barbara, Calif.: J. Daniel, 1988.

Barzani, Massoud. *Mustafa Barzani and the Kurdish Liberation Movement*. New York: Palgrave Macmillan, 2003.

Braidwood, Linda S. *Digging Beyond the Tigris*. London: Abelard-Schuman, 1959.

A Committee of Officials. *Iraq*. Baltimore: Lord Baltimore Press, 1946.

Crowson, Ben F. *The Kingdom of Iraq*. Washington, D.C.: Crowson Institute of Global Research, 1950.

De Gaury, Gerald. *Arabian Journey and Other Desert Travels*. London: Harrap, 1950.

Field, Henry, Stephen Hemsley Longrigg, and E. A. Kinch. *The Topography, Tribes and Villages along the Iraq Petroleum Pipe-Line*. S.l.: s.n., 1955.

Great Britain and Kenneth Mason. *Iraq and the Persian Gulf, September 1944*. Geographical handbook series. London: Naval Intelligence Division, 1944.

Haddad, Heskel M. *Born in Baghdad*. New York: Authors Choice Press, 1986.

Haeri, Shaykh Fadhlalla. *Son of Karbala*. Winchester, England: O Books, 2006.

Herring, Jane Penelope, and Elizabeth Morrison. *Jane Penelope's Journal: Being the Unique Record of the Voyages of a Sea Captain's Wife in the Indian Ocean and Persian Gulf in the Opening Years of the Nineteenth Century. And, Governess to King Feisal II of Iraq, 1940–1943: A Unique Glimpse of Pre-Baathist Iraq and Its Royal Family*. Cambridge, England: West Meadow Books, 1995.

Hindus, Maurice Gerschon. *In Search of a Future: Persia, Egypt, Iraq, and Palestine.* Westport, Conn.: Hyperion Press, 1981.

Iraq. *Baghdad.* Baghdad: Government Press, 1942.

———. *Iraq Today.* Lewisham, Great Britain: T. J. Hunt, 1953.

———. *Mosul and Its Neighbouring District; A Short Guide for Visitors.* Baghdad: Government Press, 1956.

Iraq Petroleum Company. *Handbook of the Territories Which Form the Theatre of Operations of the Iraq Petroleum Company Limited and Its Associated Companies.* London: Iraq Petroleum, 1948.

———. *Iraq Petroleum.* London: Iraq Petroleum, 1951.

Kazzaz, David. *Mother of the Pound: Memoirs on the Life and History of the Iraqi Jews.* New York: Sepher-Hermon Press, 1999.

Lloyd, Seton. *Ruined Cities of Iraq. Issued for the Iraq Government, Directorate-General of Antiquities.* Bombay: Indian Branch, Oxford University Press, 1945.

Morad, Tamar, Dennis Shasha, and Robert Shasha, eds. *Iraq's Last Jews: Stories of Daily Life, Upheaval, and Escape from Modern Babylon.* New York: Palgrave Macmillan, 2008.

Rejwan, Nissim. *The Last Jews in Baghdad.* Austin: University of Texas Press, 2004.

Sassoon, David Solomon. *A History of Jews in Baghdad.* Letchworth, England: D. S. Sassoon, 1949.

Thesiger, Wilfred. *The Marsh Arabs.* Penguin classics. London: Penguin, 2007.

United States. *Notes for American Visitors to Baghdad.* Baghdad: United States Office of Information and Educational Exchange, American Embassy, 1949.

Waheid, A. *The Kurds and Their Country: A History of the Kurdish People, from Earliest Times to the Present.* Lahore, India: University Book Agency, 1958.

5

The Revolutionary Era, 1958–1968

In 1958, a coup d'état by Abd al-Karim Qasim felled the monarchy, and this would be the first of four coups in ten years. Qasim and his followers did not just change the cabinet; they violently overthrew the Hashemite monarchy. Qasim intended to bring about long overdue changes within Iraq, thereby helping large numbers of poor people. Thus, he passed Law No. 30, which allowed the government to expropriate land from large holders and redistribute it to peasants. Oil income was finally beginning to flow in Iraq, and Qasim also intended to make sure that the poor, not just the traditional oligarchic elite, would benefit. As a result, the government would spend millions of dollars on housing projects in Baghdad. Despite Qasim's populist reforms, however, there was no hiding the fact that he ruled by virtue of military force.

And so, it would be military force that would end his regime, commencing a cycle of coups that marked the decade. The emerging Ba'th Party overthrew Qasim's regime in 1963, gaining control of the government only after two days of street-fighting. Its authoritarian tendencies soon made themselves known, but the Ba'th could, at that point, only maintain control for nine months. In November 1963, the more moderate Abd al-Salam Arif, a conservative Sunni, took over, but he too relied on the loyalty of the military in holding onto his power. When he died in 1966, his brother Abd al-Rahman took over the reins of power. His rule did not last long. In 1968, the Ba'th once again took power, this time definitively, ruling until 2003.

This chapter provides insight into a decade consisting of political instability amid some socioeconomic advances. The American ambassador published a firsthand account of the coup of 1958, and his description gives readers insight into U.S. responses to Qasim's radical platform. An anonymous author draws attention to the reasons for this coup, showing how the corruption of Hashemite officials affected the middle and lower classes. The politicization of Iraqis, however, was pooh-poohed by American magazines like *National Geographic*, which presented Iraq as an a-historical fantasyland. Fearing disenfranchisement, some rich Arab Sunnis plotted Qasim's overthrow. One Kurd's testimony provides a window on the failed coup by Abd al-Wahhab al-Shawwaf in Mosul in 1959. This revolt was put down, and Qasim continued with his reforms. These reforms embraced a revolution in the status of women, so this chapter includes testimony by upper-class women who benefited from new laws regarding women in the 1950s and 1960s. Despite advances in women's rights, all was not well in Iraq. The government waged a war with Kurds between 1961 and 1963. An American journalist traveled with Mustafa Barzani, leaving a firsthand account of the toll this war took on Kurdish people.

American Response to Qasim's Coup d'État

The Cold War officially came to the Middle East in November 1956. That year, the former colonial powers France and Great Britain—along with Israel—instigated the Suez Crisis, forcing the United States to support its erstwhile nemesis Egypt's President Gamal Abdel Nasser. The United States did so in order to preserve the peace and ensure that the Soviet Union did not get a foothold in the region. Two months later the U.S. President issued his eponymous Eisenhower doctrine, which allowed any Middle Eastern country to request economic or military aid to resist aggression. With this doctrine, the United States made it clear to the world that it had a vested interest in the goings-on in the Middle East. Based on this doctrine, the United States would militarily intervene in civil conflict in Lebanon in order to secure their interests in this pro-Western country. This military intervention in July 1958 had unanticipated (and unwelcome) consequences in Iraq.

In fact, this military intervention acted as a catalyst for the overthrow of the Hashemite regime by Gen. Abd al-Karim Qasim and his supporters. Qasim was a Brigadier General in the Iraqi army, and his unit was to be sent to the Iraqi border with Lebanon. Instead, his unit stopped in Baghdad and overthrew the government. Forces loyal to him killed the royal family and Prime Minister Nuri al-Said, who was trying to escape dressed as a woman. Qasim insisted that he would make Iraq a democratic country, but the coup's violence did not bode well for reform.

Waldemar J. Gallman had a ringside seat to these unfortunate events, for he was the U.S. ambassador stationed in Baghdad. Gallman had been stationed in Iraq since 1954. He recounted his memories of these dark days in Iraq in *Iraq under General Nuri: My Recollections of Nuri al-Said, 1954–1958* (Baltimore: Johns Hopkins Press, 1964), 200–218. As you read his account of the July events, you should consider the following: How did the United States respond to the revolution? What tangible decisions were made in the days following it?

> Shortly after five o'clock on the morning of July 14, I heard gunfire. I went out into the garden where I could get a view of the streets. Traffic was normal and early risers who were passing by were untroubled. The scene in the neighborhood of the Embassy was so reassuring that I concluded that the firing was part of the ceremonial send-off for the King and his party. I had just returned indoors, when a member of my staff appeared to announce that troops were firing on the Palace and Nuri's home and that mobs were gathering in the vicinity. Most Baghdadis sleep on the roofs of their homes during the summer months as did this member of my staff. From his roof he could see both the Palace and Nuri's home.
>
> I was fortunate to have been alerted in the early hours of the coup. Before other members of the staff could reach the Embassy, I had the second and last bit of good fortune for the day. About six o'clock an associate of Nuri appeared at the Embassy seeking asylum. The early morning gunfire had aroused his suspicions. His arrival fortunately coincided with the broadcasting of the decrees setting up the Republic of Iraq. He began immediately to translate them for us from the Arabic. By seven a.m. the new regime had established itself. A presidium consisting of Mohammad Mahdi Kubba, Khalid Naqshbandi, and Brigadier Najib Rubay'i had been appointed to replace the Royal Family. The names of the new cabinet . . . had been announced, many of them unknown even to our house guest. The names of prominent military men and civilians retired to private life or arrested by the new rulers, had been broadcast. Forty military officers were retired, among them the chief of staff, Rafiq Arif and the one time assistant chief of staff, Ghazi Daghistani. Many of those whose names were broadcast were later brought to trial before a special military court.
>
> Before the day was over it was clear that the small group which had planned the coup in utmost secrecy, had won a stunning success. In the weeks that followed there was no sign of organized opposition, either among the military or civilians. The new regime, it was clear from the start, could only be ousted by sudden and overwhelming force from outside.
>
> On the morning of July 15 I learned that . . . during the day there would be landings in Lebanon from the Sixth Fleet. I was afraid that this might set off anti-American demonstrations, and perhaps even lead to mobs breaking into the Embassy. I had these fears despite the fact that the Embassy was surrounded by tanks, and troops were encamped on the Embassy grounds for our "protection." I had misgivings because this force had not interfered with

the hanging at the entrance to the Embassy of a huge anti-American banner, nor with the painting on the garden walls of anti-American slogans. Instead of preventing such incitements to mob action, our protectors busied themselves with . . . searching all who came to and left the Embassy.

Our house guest agreed that if a mob should penetrate the Embassy and find him there, it would be equally hard on us and on him. He said that if a way could be devised for him to get through the cordon of Iraqi troops and tanks into the street, he knew where he could find safety.

We made a plan and carried it out successfully. We dressed him in the uniform of an Embassy chauffeur and put him behind the wheel of an Embassy car, with one of our officers in the back seat as a passenger. The car passed by the guards and beyond the tanks unchallenged, and then through the streets to the place where he felt he would be safe. There he got out and the Embassy officer brought the car back alone, the absence of his erstwhile driver escaping the notice of the guards.

Abdul Karim Qasim, the leader of the group that had executed the coup, was not widely known before July 14. At the time of the coup he was a brigade commander.

Nuri resorted to a judicious distribution of ammunition as one means to hold the army in check. When it was necessary to issue ammunition, only units trusted by him got any. Following the coup, it was learned that Nuri had . . . approved the issuance of ammunition to two brigades and ordered them to move toward Jordan. One of these brigades was Qasim's. The other was under the command of Colonel Abdul Salam Arif. The two converged on Baghdad in the small hours of July 14. The trek toward Jordan ended there. Shortly, the signal to seize power was given.

Nuri escaped from his home on the morning of July 14 just ahead of the mob. At once the radio announced a reward of ten thousand *dinars* for his apprehension. Sometime during the morning of July 15 he was discovered by soldiers disguised as an Arab woman, not far from the Embassy, and shot. After his escape from his home, he found refuge for a time with the Israbadi family, wealthy Shiahs from Kadhimain. Members of the family . . . were later tried for aiding Nuri. Seven were found guilty and sentenced to from one to five years in prison. The eighty-year-old head of the family, whose wife was killed on the street along with Nuri, received a sentence of three years. The defense of the accused, as their sentences indicate, was feeble.

The mob, which appeared suddenly on July 14 and carried out the early morning pillaging, was made up largely of youths ranging in age from twelve to twenty. Trucks, supplied by the new regime, brought many of them into

Baghdad and transported them around the city. For two days the mob, reinforced later by older hoodlums, had a free hand. Then the regime acted to put a stop to further extreme mob action. It also removed the inflammatory anti-Western signs and slogans which had bedecked the city. I think there were two reasons why the regime acted when it did. After having at first encouraged the mobs to engender at least the semblance of popular backing, it came to fear that they might get out of hand, causing deaths among foreigners and damage to their property. There was also concern over what Ba'thist and Communist leadership of the mob might lead to. Quickly on July 14, agents from both these camps took over the direction of the mob. The speed with which they moved surprised the new leaders of Iraq. . . .

When I made my first call on Prime Minister Qasim on the afternoon of July 15, the atmosphere of the city was very tense. "Down with Western Imperialism" was the cry of the street. I was told, when I asked for the appointment, that a military escort would take me to the Ministry of Defense where the meeting was to be held, and back to the Embassy. I was pleased by the choice of my military escort. He was Colonel Damanloudgi, formerly Iraq's assistant military attaché in Washington, whose American wife was once a member of our Foreign Service. During the days that followed I made a number of trips to and from the new Iraqi officials under his protection.

The Ministry of Defense was heavily guarded. I had to pass through rows of armed soldiers to Qasim's office where I found him armed too. He was tense but friendly. His first words were: "We want to be friends with the United States." I thanked him for his greeting and then, appreciating what pressures he was under, took up the business I had come to dispatch without further preliminaries. It was disposed of quickly and satisfactorily. I asked him to give me assurance that his government would protect American lives and property. This he gave instantly. I then asked for assurance that if I were instructed to evacuate American women and dependents his government would facilitate such an operation. Here he hesitated, but only momentarily. He had, he reminded me, just assured me that American lives and property would be safeguarded. He did not think further assurances were necessary. However, as I had made the request he would go further. Should evacuation be thought necessary by Washington, his government would facilitate it.

Two days later I received instruction to start evacuation. Qasim honored his assurances. He had only one reservation to make. In order to avoid giving the impression that ours was a panic exodus, he would like us to allow some days between flights, moving our people out in gradual, orderly fashion. I agreed to this.

But this was one of those times when Washington acted promptly and with zeal. Planes were chartered from a private company in such numbers and on such closely following days that any staggered, gradual evacuation as requested by Qasim was ruled out. Qasim, however, was again obliging. In spite of the embarrassment that so rapid an evacuation might cause him, he approved the crowded schedule worked out in Washington.

On the way back from the Ministry of Defense Colonel Damanloudgi took me along the most direct route leading to the Embassy. Everything went smoothly until we were about a mile from it. There we ran into a crowd milling about, gesticulating, and yelling "Nuri." Light tanks were parked on the side of the street and at a nearby intersection, and soldiers armed with automatic rifles stood on the tanks. When they began shooting over the heads of the mob, the Colonel quickly gave directions to turn into a side street and from there we proceeded in a roundabout way to the Embassy.

Earlier that day Nuri had been apprehended and shot. The mob I encountered had learned that his body was to be taken to the morgue. The mob intercepted it, mutilated it, and dragged it through the streets. While this was taking place in Baghdad, our marines were landing on the beaches of Beirut.

During a call a European colleague of mine made on Qasim a few days after the landings, he asked Qasim whether he would have struck on July 14 if American marines had been landed in Lebanon before that date. He promptly replied "No." . . .

I felt that we should, if possible, get at least two assurances before we extended recognition. One was the assurance that harassment of the Embassy would be stopped so that it could carry on its normal functions. The other was assurance that the families of the three Americans killed by the mob the day of the coup would be indemnified.

Some of the obstacles which interfered with the normal functioning of the Embassy were no more than petty annoyances such as the interminable searching and questioning of visitors and staff alike, coming in and out of the Embassy. The refusal to recognize the immunity of our diplomatic couriers and the failure to clear through customs the official supplies badly needed in the day to day work were more serious. A big problem was the interference with the freedom of movement of Embassy officials, within Baghdad . . . and around the country at large. Whenever our grievances were taken up with a top level Iraqi official there would be relief, but only temporarily. After a few days lower ranking military and civilian representatives of the government would resume their petty molestation. Once the situation got so bad that I had to appeal to Qasim himself. The trouble, of course, was not made by senior members of the government, but by the hundreds of inexperienced and zealous workers who had been brought in at the bottom.

Among the group rounded-up by soldiers at the Baghdad Hotel on July 14 were three American businessmen.... American friends ... who were also staying at the hotel witnessed their seizure.... A German businessman, seized and transported with them, but who, though beaten, managed to escape, identified the three as having been attacked and been in the truck with him. The bodies of the three Americans were never found. The Iraqi government claimed it could find no trace of them. We could only learn at the hospital to which the victims of mob action were brought, that none was brought in alive and that all bodies were mutilated beyond hope of identification. This inability to trace and identify the remains of the Americans complicated our efforts to get a settlement.

While we were working on these problems, but making no headway toward a solution, the new government was becoming more impatient about our failure to recognize it. About two weeks after the coup Foreign Minister Jumard complained to me about our "aloofness." Sixteen governments, but all from the Communist bloc or sympathetic in their political outlook, had by then extended recognition. "If you are not careful," he cautioned, "you might push the new government toward communism." Not long after this warning Britain, Turkey, Iran, and Pakistan decided to recognize the new regime. While uncertainties persisted, I felt that now the point had been reached where little could be gained by our continuing to withhold recognition. In fact, by delaying, we might find ourselves in a dangerously isolated position.

We extended recognition early in August. At the same time that I informed the Foreign Minister of our decision I told him that it was our understanding that Iraq would abide by the principles of international law with respect to the three missing Americans, presumably dead, and that compensation would be paid when valid claims had been established.

Claims were paid, but not until two years later.

Corruption and Inequality

Abd al-Karim Qasim's coup d'état promised a better life for poor Iraqis, whether in rural or urban areas. The Hashemite regime had incorporated only a small number of wealthy elite, mostly Sunni Arabs, in Iraq's political and economic life. The inequality bred by such an elitist system had led to growing unrest in Iraq. Qasim, however, expressed an intention to eliminate the self-interest that had shaped Hashemite politics.

Policies implemented by Qasim suggested this putschist was sincere in his desire to help marginalized Iraqis. Right after assuming power, Qasim passed Law No. 30 of 1958, which allowed the government to sequester the estates of large landowners in order to redistribute land to landless peasants and small farmers. This rich group of landowners consisted of less than 3,000 people (Tripp, 150). In cities, Qasim constructed 35,000 residential units to house the poor and lower-middle classes, the most famous being Madinat al-Thawra, or Revolution City in Baghdad.

The following account of life in revolutionary Iraq captures an elusive moment between regimes. The author's pessimistic view of the Hashemites is as tangible as his optimism in regard to Qasim's Republic. The author, however, is anonymous, preferring to publish under the pseudonym Caractacus. He published the following account of conditions in Iraq in *Revolution in Iraq: An Essay in Comparative Public Opinion* (London: Victor Gollancz, 1958), 29–46. As you read it, you should consider the following: How does the author illuminate possible reasons for the July 14 Revolution of 1958? What was the political system like before the revolution? And social and economic conditions? Why does the author insist that Nuri al-Said was "not of the twentieth century?" How would you compare this document with the Baghdad Petition of 1910 found in chapter 1? Based on the evidence in this document, was the 14 July Revolution justified?

> A police state supporting an edifice of corruption; this is what their own state seemed to Iraqis. There could be little doubt about this corruption. When a man's legitimate sources of income are known and are very moderate, and he begins to ... live in a large expensive house ... to spend visibly on every costly way of passing the time, to run a large car, to take his holidays abroad, there is only one probable explanation. In one such case a man originally of no great substance boasted that his house cost him £26,000 and that he sold it for £50,000; it was built on 1,700 square metres of land to which another 1,700 were added for the garden, all at £3 the metre. Everyone spoke of the growing class of new rich who were beginning to characterize Baghdad wealthy society and who despised everyone unable or unwilling to compete on the same scale. . . .
>
> Corruption seemed to begin at the royal family, with its constantly widening properties, and to spread downwards and outwards, through the Ministers and their sons and a few business men of exceptional wealth, who controlled more patronage than some of the Ministers; through the Members of Parliament and some officials to all the lesser parasites and hangers-on. Certain Ministers were ... particularly venal. One who was much envied by other businessmen ran his various businesses, it was said, on preferences he awarded himself or

that his colleagues gave him. Another was notorious for not caring how he made money, so long as he made it. A saying of the great Nuri's circulated everywhere—there were only three things he could not do and one . . . was to stop this particular Minister from thieving. (I will leave aside the other two things, which concerned equally famous—or infamous—figures.)

Ministers' sons who made fortunes were also notorious. One young fellow was a rich man within four or five years of leaving school. When one of the officers responsible for guarding the men arrested after the Revolution spoke to him, he said, "Why do you keep me here? I spent all my time on women and whisky and never touched politics." This is the worst sort of corruption, which takes its privileges for granted; indeed, these sons of over-privilege evidently did not realize that corruption is a moral deterioration that extends throughout the character, and spreads from one person to another. The same youth, when stopped by an officer of the traffic police, in the ordinary course of traffic control, at first refused to halt his car and then, when challenged, savagely assaulted the officer and later got him dismissed. It was . . . believed that all the sons of Ministers drove very fast indeed, ignored the rules of the road and were responsible for certain accidents, including one in which a professor was killed, which the police did not attempt to bring home to them. This . . . behaviour was worse than straight bribery, and it was more disturbing to the observer because it was ostentatious. All these people were heavy drinkers. One of them was a particularly dangerous man, moody when drunken and liable to pick a quarrel without cause. No one dared to stand up to him and people were often hurt in his brawling, including women. All this was widely known and it was a way of life which disgusted decent people. In the revolutionaries there was a Puritan detestation of drink and gambling and the sordid affairs associated with night clubs, of all the loose morality that followed the corruption of men in power.

The means used by one minister's son to get rich are worth a moment's attention. He held high rank in two government departments concerned with communications. In the first post he was famous for his smuggling of valuable articles, including drugs. In the second he developed a neat system of allotting priorities. When heavy goods arrived at the port of Basrah, he would allocate trucks to any merchant who made it worth his while, preventing rivals from bringing goods to Baghdad until this stock had been sold at monopoly prices. It was said that in this way iron joists, for example, could be had through one merchant only, at £95 when the normal price was £49, while full supplies, belonging to other firms, were lying in Basrah awaiting transport.

There were two particularly notorious ways of getting rich quickly, apart from the direct acceptance of bribes. The first was by means of a complex of trade monopolies. The Iraqi economy is barely industrialised, and depends largely on imported goods, especially luxuries. These include articles of a very ordinary type, toothpaste or chocolate or medicines, which are not made in Iraq; or soap, clothing, books, which are not made in sufficient quantities, as well as real luxury goods. There was a growing demand for some even of the latter, such as wrist-watches. Most foreign firms appoint sole agents for their goods, who were able to fix prices, and, indeed, to bully the public in many ways—if you could not buy a particular article it was often because the agent had forgotten to reorder, or miscalculated, or deliberately let stocks run out in order to force you to buy some similar commodity which he had overstocked. To this system was added an import-licence system by quota which completed the power of the trader to fix prices. The quotas were under the ... control of the Ministers, who, with their ... allies, took the first picking in direct trade, and, for the rest, granted licences to each trader who came to an agreement with the Ministry. The power that the small agent exercised on the public was great enough; the power of the big merchant was ... without limit. When a critic asked one Minister, himself a business man, whether it was not unheard of throughout the world to adopt a quota system without fixing prices, he replied only that fixed prices were not in the Iraqi tradition.

The harm done by this sort of corruption can be guessed when I say that the salary of a primary-school teacher varied, according to seniority, between £12 and £19 a month (and this was after salaries were raised). A new suit of clothes costs at least £20, or, for summer suits (it is impossible to wear ordinary clothes at a temperature of 120° F) a little less. Many ordinary professional people could not afford to buy new clothes at all: they dressed in imported second-hand clothes from America. It is true that a number of skilled and semi-skilled workmen drew better wages than this, though without security of employment; but a growing taste for lesser luxuries—the wrist-watches are a case in point—made worse the discontent at artificially high prices. Many professional people took on part-time jobs in the evenings. ... But Iraqi men are ... domestic in their tastes and like to spend time with their families. Their bitterness at the superfluous wealth of the new rich, acquired at the price of honesty, festered constantly.

The other form of corruption most discussed in pre-revolutionary Baghdad was based on land speculation. The good agricultural land around Baghdad was supposed by law to be given by the government to any competent farmers, in a position to cultivate it, who might present themselves. In practice it was not given to small men or even men of moderate wealth who applied, but to the Ministers and their richer allies, as well as to the royal family. Sometimes, under the pseudonymity of a company (one Minister developed a ghastly new slum under the name of a partner), these were the only new owners of the land around Baghdad. They farmed at most only a part, and speculated on the rest in jerry-built suburbs, named after their proprietors, who fixed the rents. In 1956 this scandal became so bad that a law was passed requiring the return of half the land so developed. The profiteers could well afford this; indeed, they had only to ask in the first place for twice as much as they wanted, to see their depredations legalized. Within the city boundaries there was adequate space for the housing development needed, but the municipality prevented building on any scale sufficient to alleviate the shortage, and the speculators on the outskirts were able to fix prices and rents as they pleased; the housing shortage, indeed, allowed them to force a fantastic rise in the values of houses and of building land. In one central suburb a man who had bought land at £2 10s. a metre in 1949, refused £10 for it in 1958. In a new street struck through the center of the city, roadside land for shops was sold at £228 the metre. Meanwhile, this beautiful new road added to the misery of the poor inhabitants of the slums that were pulled down. The owners were generously compensated, but the tenants had to go and live as much as ten miles away in new slums that were no improvement, and even so at higher rents than they paid before. . . .

So notorious was the corruption that the old regime thought it well—under the pressure of Egyptian radio criticism—to institute a purge committee which dismissed a number of corrupt officials, most of them lesser offenders, or men with enemies, who had done no more than follow the august example set them by the Court and the Cabinet. Small men with illustrious support, and a host of relatives and dependants of notables, continued to get away with it. Servants of Ministers were on the pay-roll of the Municipality; large numbers of policemen worked as guards and gardeners for important private houses, and were actually refused permission to go when required for police duties. Most of the public considered the police particularly corrupt. At the Revolution, it was discovered that in the Municipality, which seems, as a center of corruption, to have run the police a close second, there were three hundred employees who never came to their offices, except to collect a monthly salary. In the Ministry of Works a large number of foremen, and, in the hospitals, two-thirds of the male nurses, were said to be shadow employees, who received wages for no work. Often they were children still at school; and the wives and sisters of the notables received a number of appointments, on the same basis, from the Ministry of Education. With all this it is not surprising that the purge committee, appointed for one year, was received with cynicism. The most corrupt were untouched and the purge did not even pretend to approach the Ministers....

This superstructure of corruption was believed to rest upon an unequal distribution of wealth which no attempt was made to remedy. The greatest natural wealth of Iraq is oil. Western powers have felt that the lion's share of the reward for extracting and selling it should go to those who do the work; the Iraqis have felt that as the oil is theirs, the greater share of the profit should be theirs. People argued, as Abdul Salam Arif put it after the Revolution, that Londoners had no right to go shod at the expense of barefoot Iraqis. The oil belonged to Iraq, yet until after the Portsmouth Treaty, and until the nationalization of oil in Persia, the oil companies seemed to follow the slow and awkward policies of the British Foreign Office. With Nuri they negotiated an agreement that was far from satisfying public opinion, but went further towards doing so than anything had before. There was then set up the Development Board, to spend the money accruing to the State, in whatever ways would ... increase the ... wealth of the country.

In fact this Board did plenty of good work, particularly in the construction of various water-damming projects. Yet it was never trusted. Partly no doubt it was true that nothing Nuri did would be trusted—or even, perhaps, be examined fairly. But there was more to it than that. The increase of wealth seemed to benefit chiefly or only the rich. There were agreeable new things about in the shops, but they were not widely shared. There was no creation of industry on a scale sufficient to employ large numbers of the poor people whose miserable huts clustered on spare plots of land in the middle of the capital city, and beyond the flood embankment that surrounds it. The Board did good negative work in stopping the floods, but it did not find work for the victims of the country's changing social structure. Worst of all ... was the failure to promote industry. Forever Iraq traded its oil for American cars and other luxury goods. Money was not spent either on large-scale industrial projects or on the rationalization of agriculture, and not nearly enough was spent on health schemes and social services. The untackled health problems alone are terrifying....

The man upon whom this whole system depended was Nuri as-Said, a remarkable man, perhaps even a great man, born out of his time. Formerly a Turkish officer, he seemed like so many Arab politicians of the older generation, like King Abdullah in Jordan, for instance, to belong to the Ottoman age.... He was not thought of primarily as himself corrupt; it was claimed that, unlike his colleagues, he was not a rich man, and it is true that he did not live in grandiose splendour. He was the corruptor rather than the corrupted. It was in power that he was interested and he enjoyed playing the political game for its own sake;

he liked to manipulate the fates of nations, but not to plan the government of his own country. It is even doubtful if he felt that Iraq had more than a regional claim on his loyalties, unlikely that he thought of it as his country in any exclusive sense. In this way, like any Arab nationalist, he saw the Arab world as one and real, and its divisions as mere political conveniences; but he did so still in terms of the old Turkish empire, inhabited solely by princes and their viziers.

His power over his Ministers seems to have been little short of hypnotic. Some of these men have assured the Baghdad Revolutionary Court that documents written out by them in their own hands were entirely his composition. When he was in the room they seem to have had no will of their own, although in his absence they might criticize him and even decide on some quite different course of action. The revolutionary investigators were incredulous, but there seems to have been some truth in what the ex-Ministers claimed. Long before the Revolution it was noticed that a Minister might give a decision . . . and then reverse it overnight. It was no real secret that the reason was Nuri's contrary decision. The more intelligent or the more cynical Ministers would say . . . to certain requests that they could not reply, although . . . it was well within their competence to do so. It is no exaggeration to say of Nuri that, while he worked with zest in the field of international relations, he had nothing but contempt for his own people. . . . [H]e was . . . concerned with one thing only—to perpetuate the world into which he had been born. He was not of the twentieth century. . . .

True to the old tradition of the Turks, he knew only two ways of dealing with opponents, gifts and force. In the old days on the Bosphorus, when gifts failed there was a quiet arrest and the secret executioner. Nuri attempted a very similar method in the 1950s. While he tried to organize party support for himself, he made the existing parties and their newspapers illegal, and, when the attempt to build a party with some intellectual appeal proved a fiasco, he fell back on the support of men who needed no programme. From his point of view, his critics were interfering in the . . . business of government. It was not for ordinary citizens to have opinions about what was done by their rulers, or about what went on in their country. They must be punished. Probably he was not vindictive like Abdul Ilah. Cruelty for Nuri served a purpose. "Terror" is the technical term we use for force that reduces a country to silence through fear. If this was not his original intention, he quickly felt his way to it by trial and error. Nuri as-Said seemed to be a tyrant of the most classic and traditional kind.

An American View of Revolutionary Iraq

In the 1950s and 1960s, most Americans had trouble understanding and assessing Iraq and its people. When Qasim took over, for example, Americans did not understand why the Iraqi prime minister took Iraq out of the Baghdad Pact. This was a foreign policy treaty that, in American eyes, protected Iraq from aggression and kept it near to the West. By taking Iraq out of the Baghdad Pact, Qasim changed his country's foreign policy orientation and made it a Soviet satellite.

Such misunderstandings are not always centered on tangible decision making of foreign policy; they can be cultural. Thus, Americans expected Iraq to be a backward place deprived of all modern amenities. Such preconceived notions are part of an intellectual tradition referred to as Orientalism. As an intellectual tradition, Orientalism fosters the perception that the Muslim world is exotic, despotic, fanatical, and timeless. The way an American interprets information or understands events can be influenced by such preconceived notions.

Two scholars have analyzed such Orientalism in the famous *National Geographic Magazine*. Catherine A. Lutz and Jane L. Collins argue that the selection of exoticized images and interviews actually provides insight into American society, and not into that of the foreign place on which it ostensibly focuses. Linda Steet has drawn attention specifically to coverage of the Arab world, showing how such preconceived notions present a subjective image that seems to present Islamic people as lower on a hierarchy of cultures than Westerners would be.

Just because a journalist comes to a place with preconceived intellectual notions of a cultural hierarchy, however, does not mean that his or her article is completely tainted as a primary source. The following article by Jean and Franc Shor exhibits some Orientalist tendencies, but it also provides the reader with a time capsule. It was researched and written in the months immediately preceding and succeeding the 14 July Revolution. The article is "Iraq—Where Oil and Water Mix," *National Geographic Magazine* (October 1958): 443, 449, 473. As you read these excerpts, you should consider what a historian can and cannot accept as fact: Where do the authors show a tendency toward Orientalist preconceptions? How? And how does this article provide insight into revolutionary Iraq?

> There is an ominous air about a country on the eve of revolution. My wife Jean and I spent three months in Iraq early this year, and we felt it everywhere. Working in the Near East was nothing new to us; we have spent a great deal of time there. But this time it was different.
>
> In country villages the radios in public squares were almost always tuned to Radio Cairo and its litany of hate for the West. In Baghdad crowds complained

when we tried to take pictures anywhere but in the most modern sections of the city. And too many people with whom we talked echoed the pat phrases of anti-Western propaganda.

We had to discharge one interpreter because he began each day with a recital of that morning's tirade from Gamal Abdel Nasser's transmitter. He tried to turn every interview into a discussion of politics. We could never make him understand that our interest was in the physical, historical, and cultural aspects of his country, rather than its temporal problems.

Iraq is . . . undergoing a tremendous political upheaval. But the problems of any particular period . . . seem . . . less important when one remembers that this Land of the Two Rivers has seen 5,000 years of recorded history and that some of the world's greatest civilizations here rose, flourished, and decayed.

In the north stood Nineveh, royal residence of Sennacherib when that Biblical monarch ruled the Assyrian Empire during its golden age. South of Baghdad was storied Babylon, where Nebuchadnezzar built the Hanging Gardens, one of the Seven Wonders of the World. According to ancient Greek accounts, he built them to ease the sorrow of his homesick queen.

It was in Babylon that Daniel translated the handwriting on the wall and foretold the fall of Belshazzar's kingdom. And it was not far away, in a land called Sumer, that scribes of 5,000 years ago incised the records on clay tablets, giving us the first known writing.

The most famous of the early codes of law, Hammurabi's "eye for an eye and a tooth for a tooth," once ruled this country. And there is as much to interest the romantic as the scholar. Baghdad, the burgeoning capital, was the seat of Caliph Harun al-Rashid, and its main street still bears his name—synonymous with the tales of *The Arabian Nights*. . . .

Never did we stop to take a picture of a Kurdish family without being asked to remain for a cup of tea. Never did we ask a question which was not answered with a jest. And in As Sulaymaniyah, known as the capital of Kurdistan, we had an experience which endeared those people to us forever.

In the big suq in that city I was photographing Kurdish farmers and their produce when a towering gentleman in a brilliant green costume, standing on a two-wheeled cart loaded with vegetables, invited me to join him for a better view.

I climbed aboard and made my pictures. Through my interpreter, himself a Kurd, we exchanged pleasantries. The farmer offered to accompany me around the market. Together we circled the . . . crowded square, photographing as we went. Near the entrance we stopped for a shot of a gaily painted pushcart, laden with dime-store wares. The proprietor posed happily, and I was focusing my camera when an intruder arrived.

He was a young man in his early twenties, dressed in exaggerated Western style, with hair carefully duck-tailed behind his ears. As I started to take my picture, he began to shout the by then all-too-familiar refrain that I was only trying to show Americans how backward were his compatriots.

The proprietor looked at him in amazement.

"Who's backward?" he wanted to know. "Look at my wares; they are the most modern. I saved for years to get into business for myself. I would be proud to have Americans see my stand."

And without further ceremony he and my husky new-found friend grasped the young agitator by the elbows, hustled him to the suq entrance, and happily booted him out....

Jean and I had our own experiences with the deep dissatisfaction the Arab population of Iraq feels with its economic lot. Nearly everyone, we found, was ... self-conscious about the country's backward aspects and determined that Iraq should be presented to the world in its most modern light.

On a main street in Baghdad we found a pottery shop, where great water jars in brilliant colors made a vivid and charming display. We asked the proprietor if we could photograph him and his wares for the NATIONAL GEOGRAPHIC MAGAZINE. He would, he replied, be honored.

But while we were setting up our equipment, a crowd gathered. Two students demanded, in Arabic, to know why we wanted the picture. We explained through our interpreter.

"Don't let him do it," one shouted to the shop owner. "He just wants to show Americans how backward our country is."

The shopkeeper protested that he didn't see anything backward about his water jars, that he was, in fact, rather proud of them.

But the younger element in the growing crowd sided with the students. Water jars indicated a lack of plumbing, they said. If we wanted to take a picture, why not take one of some of Baghdad's new buildings?

I had already done that, I explained. I wanted to show all sides of Iraqi life. But the crowd's shouts took on a menacing tone, the proprietor obviously was becoming ill at ease, someone kicked my camera tripod, and one of the students spat at Jean.

Even our college-trained interpreter showed similar reactions. In the countryside, when I asked him to help me take a picture of water buffalo pulling a plow, he demurred, "Why don't you take a picture of a tractor?"

Again I explained. Draft animals outnumber tractors by the thousands to one in Iraq. National Geographic readers want to see the country as it is, not as it hopes to be. But I never got this point across.

Mutiny in Mosul, March 1959

There were some Iraqis, principally Arab Sunnis, who, due to their stake in the Hashemite regime, felt threatened by Abd al-Karim Qasim and his populist program. Such a program, after all, which promised increased integration of Iraqi groupings, seemed to threaten the old landed elite. Abd al-Wahhab al-Shawwaf was one of those who strongly disapproved of Qasim. Al-Shawwaf was the commander of the Mosul garrison, and he led a mutiny there in March 1959. His supporters were principally conservative Arab Sunni families. The mutiny in Mosul, which was supposed in fact to be a coup d'état, broke out during a rally by a leftist group of Peace Partisans on 6 March. This group included Communists and eventually 250,000 people would march in this northern city. Arab tribesmen joined in, which then encouraged Kurdish tribesmen to come to Mosul. Some Kurds helped quell the rebellion on behalf of Qasim's government; other Kurds looted. After four days of unrest, hundreds of people—perhaps as many as 2,500—would be killed (McDowall, 304). Thus, the mutiny-cum-coup became a bloody struggle along ethnic and class lines (Marr, 92–93). Historian Charles Tripp insists that this mutiny is significant because it solidified the role of riots in the street as a part of Iraq's political process (Tripp, 151).

The following provides a firsthand account of the events on the military base in Mosul. This document was submitted to the Kurdistan Democratic Party (KDP). At that time, the KDP was led by Mulla Mustafa Barzani, a man who has near-mythic proportions to many Kurds. The soldier recounting his testimony is doing so in order to document the treatment of Kurdish soldiers during the revolt. Massoud Barzani included it in his account of his father's life story in *Mustafa Barzani and the Kurdish Liberation Movement* (New York: Palgrave Macmillan, 2003), 340–43. As you read this account, you should consider the following: What is the position of the Kurdish sergeant vis-à-vis the revolutionary state of Abd al-Karim Qasim? Who is being held prisoner? What does the composition of the prison population suggest about ethnic divisions at this base? Does this document reveal any information about events outside of the barracks? Where and how?

A report by Sergeant Siddique Abd al-Aziz of the Lesser Mobilization Wing about the al-Shawwaf Conspiracy

On March 5, 1959 the Brigade issued a directive to all units of the Mosul camp to remain on alert because of Peace Supporters' arrival on March 6, 1959 in Mosul. On March 7, 1959 at 3:00 p.m., the alert was lifted and I went to the town and saw a demonstration repeating "Long Live Abd al-Karim Qasim." I went home. At 6:00 p.m., a camp Corp. came and asked me to return to the Stone Barrack in half an hour. I dressed and went to a bus stop near the Textile Factory at about 7:00 p.m. I found that buses were not running. I asked the guard and he told me that a curfew was in effect. Since the camp was very far, I called Lt. Col. Mikhael Abd al-Karim and told him that I was stranded. He told me to stay home. The next morning, March 8, 1959, I arrived at the camp in a military vehicle at 7:15 a.m. As I reached the camp shop, I found that the Stone Barracks were surrounded by guards from the Fifth Brigade. I was astounded. I asked a soldier and he told me that a number of patriotic officers had been under arrest since midnight. He added that they were looking for me. I knew that a plot against the government of Iraq was underway. I tried to escape by the back door. As I reached the stone staircase, I found guards who told me that leaving the camp was forbidden. I returned and tried to leave through the door leading to the riverside. I found it closed and guarded. I returned to the main gate and a Lance Corp. told me that the Commander was looking for me. We went together but did not find him. The traitor Lt. Kamil Ismail spotted us. He told me that I was under arrest. At this time, first Lt. Yousif Miran and Col. Salim of the Engineering Battalion entered the citadel. The traitor Lt. Kamil and his soldiers aimed their automatic rifles and ordered the two officers to drop their weapons and that they were under arrest. As Lt. Yousif Miran pulled his handgun, the traitor Corp. Mal Allah struck him on the hand with his pistol and led them to the jail. I found an opportunity to escape through the long tunnel leading to the south gate of the citadel. At the end of that tunnel, I found guards carrying automatic rifles. I went toward the river and I found the banks guarded by automatic fire from the top of the castle. Trapped. I returned, only to meet the traitor Lt. Kamil Ismail who directed his automatic rifle at me and yelled, "Didn't I tell you to wait here?" I told him that I had not moved. He ordered me to the jail. I asked, "why am I arrested? Is there an order to arrest me?" He said, "go to jail or I will shoot you." He added that "You are under arrest by the order of the Brigade Commander." I found the jail was full of patriots. Of them I remember Corps Ayyob Khalid, Khalid Taha and Hatim Ubaid, Lance Corps, Mustafa Taili, privates Jafar Abd al-Karim and Zuhair Yasin, and finally, myself of the Lesser Mobilization Wing. From the Engineering Battalion were Head Corp. Salih, sergeants Mustafa, Ahmad, Mohammed Siddique, Salah, and some others whose names I do not recall.

As I entered, they welcomed me and I greeted them all and reassured them. They said the plot is underway and here we are all in jail. Reassuringly, I told them that they were not alone and the conspiracy would not succeed, that I had seen in the adjacent room many arrested civilians, and in the next room another group of civilians, that I had heard the radio moments earlier that President Abd al-Karim Qasim is alive and well and would deal with it forcefully and decisively. They asked "Are you certain that the president is alive?" I replied, "Of course I am sure." They were somewhat reassured. Half an hour later, the door opened and the traitor Lt. Kamil Ismail was standing in the door with his automatic rifle in his hand and soldiers were lined up in two rows; each was carrying an automatic rifle. The Lt. called us to get out. As we did, we were standing between two rows of soldiers. He ordered us to move. We walked toward the gate leading to the river. We told each other that the game is about over and it was time for farewell comrades. However, before reaching the outer gate, guards climbed the . . . staircase leading to the second floor and ordered us to follow them up. We took deep breaths and climbed up the stairs. They took us to a room on the second floor, overlooking the street leading to the river and the forest of the southern side of the citadel.

About 25 of us were crammed in a small room which holds only two beds. In the next room, there were about 35 people. The majority of us were Kurds. Among us were only 3 or 4 of our Arab comrades. Our total was about 65, food and water were forbidden, lavatories were replaced with metal containers. We would ask the head guard, Lance Corp. Abd al-Jabbar of our wing, about the events. He would bring us the latest correct news. At about 4:00 p.m. of March 8, 1959, the traitor Lt. Khairullah Askr entered our room, ordered us to stand in one row and said that they were not Abd al-Karim Qasim and that they would shoot us dead. With his mouth he produced sounds imitating automatic guns. Pointing to Head Corp. Salih of the Engineering Battalion, he said, "And you, of course chief of the cell here." Salih replied, "I do not know what you mean?" The traitor said to him, "By Stalin, do you not know about the cell? Tell me how many do you command? He did not answer him. Corp. Hatim Ubaid of the Mobilization Wing asked him, "Sir what did I do?" As the traitor Lt. turned to him, I said, "Sir, only two days ago you were with us at the Mobilization seminar and we served and taught you. Are you going to shoot us for our efforts?" He lowered his rifle and said, "no, you rank officers of the Mobilization Wing do not have to worry. You are arrested for security and to control any move you might do. We will release you tomorrow at 12:00 noon, so do not worry . . ." Then the traitor left after he almost killed us. Ten minutes later, the head guard came in and gave us the good news by saying that Baghdad had learned of the conspiracy, and Shawwaf had been dismissed. We were delighted and began clapping, singing Long Live Leader Abd al-Karim Qasim until 6:30 p.m. when a car from the Engineering Battalion brought us food. Under the rice in the huge container, there were thin but strong cords and an iron saw to cut the iron bars if we needed to. Later, we agreed to cut the iron window grilles and use the ropes to go down the windows. At least 30 feet high, it would be impossible to escape without the cords. At about 9:00 p.m., I looked out the window and I found that they had put an armed guard for each window. Then, we began discussing the situation and the means that would ensure our escape and obtaining arms. In the end, we did not find any other way but to break the door and take over the rifles and lances. At 9:30 p.m., the head guard, a loyalist, was replaced by a corp. of the traitors. We realized that the game was dangerous. At 10:05 p.m., the officer on call, Major Abd al-Jabbar Abd al-Rahman of the Lesser Mobilization Wing, stopped by the guard near the windows and asked him about his duty. The guard replied, "I am guarding the windows." He told him, "Be alert and if any prisoner tries to escape through the window, you are to shoot him or stab him with your lance." The guard replied, "Yes sir." Then, Corp. Khalid Taha told me, "Did you hear what the Major said?" I said, "Yes and . . . he will be punished for this statement." We feared they would banish us at night to a faraway place. . . . [W]e decided to have four of us guard the door. If traitors attacked us, then the . . . guards would respond by a suicide attack. Thus, we would overpower them by . . . numbers; but nothing happened that night.

On the morning of March 9, 1959, we learned that the patriotic officers were still in their cell, unharmed. At 7:00 we heard the sound of machine-gun fire from the al-Ghuzlani Garrison. Then we saw two airplanes of the Fury type in the sky of Mosul. We feared that the Furies were those under the control of al-Shawwaf and his clique in Mosul. The shooting intensified and then stopped after a short while. At about 8:30 we saw four airplanes of the Villi type in the sky. We were delighted to see them, gave them a standing ovation and sang Long Live Abd al-Karim Qasim. We saw them swoop toward the headquarters of the traitor Shawwaf. There was a loud explosion, and dark smoke billowed. We knew that bold pilots scored direct hits. Shooting intensified and the noise got close to our jail (Stone Barracks). A few of us tried to break open the door, but we decided that it was too dangerous to go out since traitors were everywhere. After only fifteen minutes, we saw a mixed civilian and military demonstration marching from Dawwaseh toward the castle. They shouted "Long Live Abd al-Karim Qasim, and no leader but him, down with renegade traitors." As they approached the Works Office, guards on top of the building opened fire and killed three of them. The demonstrators moved into the Works Plaza and behind the walls. We heard a voice shouting "Do not fire, you will not escape, traitors. The dirty Shawwaf has been killed and they are dragging him through the streets. If you do not believe us, we will bring him here for you to see with your own eyes." The traitors responded with more fire. A civilian wearing a dark coat proceeded until he approached the citadel and yelled, "Soldiers do not fire at your brothers. They are from you and for you. You traitor officers, why do you insist on rebellion? You know that the conspiracy has failed, and your commander, al-Shawwaf is being dragged through the streets." They kept firing but the man continued to advance. Suddenly, the shooting stopped for about fifteen minutes, then we heard intensified shooting in the airport camp, and the noise became closer and we heard soldiers in the southern forest of the citadel. Under intense fire, many demonstrators fell in the forest near the wall and the rest retreated and moved to the east of the castle on the riverside. At this time, Lt. Col. Abd al-Majeed Abd al-Hakim al-Radhwani came to the prison door and asked, "Who is there?" We replied "Non-coms, should we break the door?" He said "No, just wait." At this very moment private first class Hussein Ahmad Abdulla of the Mobilization Wing came in carrying a picture of Abd al-Karim Qasim and said, "Brothers break the door, the Engineering Battalion is here." The Lt. Col. responded, "Under whose order?" The private told him, "My Battalion is here." We did not wait. We destroyed the door and window in the blink of an eye and took the weapons from the guards; only three rifles. I asked the guard, "Where are the guns and the munitions?" He said that the Corp. took them, and he left only five bullets per rifle. Three rank officers armed with rifles and the rest of us with pieces of wood from the broken door, we quickly moved through the space between the soldiers loyal to us and the traitors without being hit despite heavy firing. We reached a corner where soldiers had arrived before us and each of us took an automatic gun or a rifle. Six of us climbed to the top of the citadel. They were petty officer trainees late Hazim, Corp. Ayyob Khalid, and Lance Corp. late Mustafa Taili and another non com—whose name I can't recall, and myself. We took shelter behind the wall, and I was beside the late Lance Corp. Mustafa Taili. We saw someone firing from his 'Bern' machine gun into the street at the approaching demonstrators. I told the late Mustafa Taili of the fire behind him so as to warn him. Then, I fired a round and signaled to him to stop. He looked at us and turned his gun on us as if to shoot. I did not give him a second chance and opened fire until my gun was empty. I returned to get more munitions and before me were the first private Hussein Abdullah and Corp. Ayyob Khalid. On the stone stairs, two fell and rolled down. They were petty officer trainee Hazim and Lance Corp. Mustafa Taili. A riot swept us, all wanting to go back up, but some rank officers stopped us saying that it was suicide to go back up. Some of us went to release the Free Officers from prison. I was behind Corp. Khalid Taha, protecting his back as he advanced. As we approached Wing headquarters, we came under fire, and Corp. Khalid Taha stopped... and turned to me, I saw him bleeding. I asked him, Brother are you O.K.?" He said slight injury and continued toward the officers' prison. I left him and moved down to the civilians' prison. I found the door broken and prisoners leaving. I greeted them and I saw Lt. Col. Majeed al-Radhwani sitting at the door of the weapons depot, his pistol still in his hand. He stood up and greeted me and said that he broke the door of the civilian prison and that he did so and so. I replied that he did it after knowing that they failed, and he would see how we would finish them. I kept watching him until a Free Officer took him to jail.

Then, we cleared all the rooms of the stone garrison. The roof of the castle remained [to be taken] because of the intense resistance. Each rank officer occupied a section of the castle and began throwing explosives and hand grenades onto the roof to kill their resistance. We tried several times to climb to the top but failed. At about 7:30 p.m. on the evening of March 9, 1959, we saw a few persons walking on the roof toward the stairs leading down, Head Corp. Salih of the Engineering Battalion called to them, "Turn yourselves in and we guarantee your safety." They stopped at the top of the stairs. It was very dark and we could not turn on lights for fear of being seen. They said, "We are afraid if we give up, you will kill us." We said, "No not at all." Lt. Yousif Miran came and they brought a portable light. He ordered them to drop their weapons down the stairs. They did. Then we ordered them to come down. They did and they were eight rank officers, one first private, and six privates. We asked them if there was anyone remaining on the roof. They said only one; they were not certain if killed or wounded. They said that the traitor officers had left at dusk. We did not believe them and did not go up for fear of being tricked. We took them to jail and all their weapons were automatic of 'Port Saeed' type. We armed ourselves with their weapons and a private had only 20 bullets left because he did not know how to use his gun, and the bullets were in his pocket. We left the staircase under heavy guard. Rank officers split up, each controlling one section of the castle. The shooting continued until the morning of March 10, 1959. Then, we completely controlled the castle including the roof which was empty except for one killed. Having secured the citadel, some of us went to the city to command the soldiers and each cleared a section with the help of an armored vehicle and rank officers of various units. In two days, the city was well cleared.

The Social Lives of Women in Revolutionary Iraq

Abd al-Karim Qasim changed the status of women, making them the legal equals of men. In December 1959, he passed a new personal status code in order to revolutionize women's rights in Iraq. Personal status is a legal term that refers to otherwise private matters of the family. Applicable equally to both Shi'i and Sunnis, this new law—Law No. 188—made many changes to the existing religious and tribal status. It made polygamy very difficult—nearly impossible. It raised the minimum age of marriage to eighteen years old. It ensured that women had equal rights to inheritance. It protected women against arbitrary divorce. These were radical innovations, but such top-down legislation did not necessarily change attitudes overnight.

In Baghdad, however, among the upper and upper-middle classes, there was a distinct liberalizing of attitudes toward women in the 1950s and 1960s. There, cosmopolitan urbanism allowed for the exchange of new ideas about women. Further, there were better educational opportunities there than in other Iraqi cities. Nadja Sadig al-Ali recorded interviews with women who grew up in this era, and she published them in *Iraqi Women: Untold Stories from 1948 to the Present* (London: Zed Books, 2007), 95–101. As you read the following excerpt from this book, you should consider the following: What were the different dress codes that existed? What dictated the clothes women wore? How did women socialize with other people of their age? What do these accounts suggest about life in Baghdad in the 1950s?

> Throughout the various upheavals and political changes during the 1950s and 1960s, . . . the women I interviewed appear to have been enjoying active and varied social and cultural lives. Despite widely documented class differences prior to the revolution, many of the upper-middle-class women who regretted the fall of the monarchy were quite keen to play down class differences. When I asked Leila K., whose life story indicates that she was from a well-to-do family, about socializing across class lines, she became slightly defensive and told me:
>
>> Baghdad as a city was small in the 1950s. It had about half a million inhabitants. It is not a question of social level. You should not see it from a Western point of view. There were good families, but poor people lived with them. Socially there were some ranks and differences. But the ranks were not as definite as they are in Western countries. There was a house of rich people and beside it lived poorer people. But socially they always mixed, at weddings and at funerals, and because of the zakat.

Despite Leila's insistence that social class was a fluid category and that women of different social class backgrounds would mix regularly, the accounts of many women point to the contrary. Most of the contacts across social classes took place in the context of hierarchical relationships and contexts of charity and employment.

Families socialized along social class lines rather than within ethnic or religious groupings. Nour H., having enjoyed a privileged childhood in an upper-middle-class family, acknowledges that she grew up in a world very much apart from the majority of the Iraqi population:

> My father had been a surgeon during the monarchy. Politically, 1958 was bad, but socially we did not feel too much. My aunt was under house arrest, but she would still go to parties with foreigners. Her father had been an important politician during the monarchy. There was a huge gap between the rich and the poor before 1958. This is what started the revolution. But I do not think it affected our life styles much. We lived in a big house next to the Tigris. I went to an American high school. We had a . . . swimming pool. We had lots of mixed parties. I had lots of friends, and I was very sociable. Before I got married in 1967, I used to go out a lot. . . . I had lots of fun. There was a period of engagement when I used to go out with my fiancé. I used to go to clubs. I went swimming a lot at al-Mansur club. Two or three times a year we went to Beirut.

Although numerous families directly associated with the monarchy left Iraq after the revolution, many of the wealthy landowners and professional classes remained behind without changing much of their lifestyle. Despite the hardship that Nour and her family experienced at a later stage of her life, when her husband was arrested and tortured under Saddam Hussein, I could still get a flavour of her previous lifestyle, as her apartment in Amman was buzzing with women visitors stopping by. . . . Nour's house was obviously one of the lively hubs frequented by members of old well-known Iraqi families, who descended on Amman from all over the world during the summer months to meet up with friends and relatives from inside and outside Iraq.

Socially, the post-revolutionary period had been associated with a liberalization of social relations, dress codes and gender relations as a result both of policies associated with the Qasim government and of the influence of the Communist Party, which continued to mobilize large segments of the population. One obvious sign of the many social changes taking place in the context of modernization, urbanization and political mobilization was the changing dress code of women. Traditionally, Iraqi women had worn the *abaya*—a head-to-toe black cloth similar to the Iranian *chador*—over their indoor clothes, which differed according to class, age, urban or rural background and level of religiosity. In the late 1940s and 1950s, more and more urban middle- and upper-class girls and women stopped wearing an *abaya* over their Western-style clothes. Salwa, who was active in the ICP [Iraqi Communist Party], recalls that she would only wear the *abaya* in certain traditional quarters in Baghdad:

> We lived in Adhamiya. Maybe 5 per cent of our neighbours were wearing an *abaya*. Sometimes I would go secretly to Kadhimiya for political meetings. I would borrow an *abaya* from a friend. After 1958, most girls threw the *abaya* off. My mother used to wear *abaya*, and my father pressured her to stop wearing it. When we moved from Adhamiya, she finally agreed to stop wearing the *abaya*. Now, fifty-six years later, we are going back centuries.

At the time, educated husbands and fathers who embraced ideas of modernization, reform and progress, were instrumental in changing women's dress codes, as they perceived the *abaya* as a symbol of tradition and backwardness. Yet girls and women were surrounded by apparently contradictory forces, ranging from progressive to conservative, some promoting ideas related to modernization and reform, others stressing the need to remain true to one's tradition and culture. Ibtesam . . . had been encouraged by her . . . progressive and open-minded parents to walk to school without the *abaya*. In Najaf, which was much more conservative than Baghdad . . . , this was perceived to be a severe digression, even though Ibtesam had not even reached puberty:

> I went to high school in 1964. My school was close to Al-Kalante, a religious school for men. I was taller than other girls and I did not wear an *abaya*. The men from the religious college started to hit me every day. I had two braids and they used to hit them. I went every day to my mother and asked for an *abaya*. My mother refused to give it to me. I told her that I was afraid of the men hitting me. I was crying out of fear. Then I finally got an *abaya*. I would put it on when I passed the religious school and then take it off right away. I had lots of problems in Najaf because I did not wear the *abaya*. In Najaf even small girls were wearing the *abaya*. One day I visited my uncle. There was a shop selling ice. The owner said: "Who is this girl not wearing the *abaya*?" He and my uncle started fighting. I was only 7 or 8 years old. The ice shop owner said that I was not too young to wear it. They started fighting physically. I only wore the *abaya* for a few years.

Ibtesam and her family moved to Baghdad in 1966. A few months after their arrival she . . . stopped wearing the *abaya*:

We rented a house in al-Waziriya close to the *Kulliyat al-Tarbiya* [College of Education]. In Baghdad we first kept the *abaya* on. But after a few months, a friend of my father said: "Look, 'Ali. It is better for you and your daughters to take off the *abaya*. Only people from outside Baghdad are wearing the *abaya*." My father did not want to be perceived as traditional and out of touch with modern times. My mother agreed, so we all took it off. When our family in Najaf heard that we had removed our *abayas*, they sent a delegation to Baghdad to enquire whether it was really true. My mother told them: "Yes, of course, they removed their *abayas*. And if you bother us any more, I will remove mine as well and wear trousers."

As in similar situations all over the world, women in the capital wore more daring and fashionable clothes than women in the rest of the country, especially the countryside, where women continued to wear more conservative dress. In the 1960s, it was not unusual for younger women in Baghdad to wear miniskirts as it was the fashion at the time in Western countries. Several women told me about the Ba'th's attempt to restrict women's dress codes. Maysalun K. had a bad experience:

> From 1963 we started to see the changes with the Ba'th, especially after it came to power. At the time women and girls were wearing miniskirts because it was the fashion. Saddam's uncle ... issued a law stating that women should not wear miniskirts and that those who did would have their legs painted. Skirts were supposed to be ankle-length to the ground. One day, after I went to university, I went to McKenzie's bookshop in Rashid Street. I came out of the bookshop and ... three men approached me. I was wearing my skirt below my knee because I knew about this new law. But they ... started painting my legs black. It was during that time that women started to worry. . . . The mentality of the modern way of thinking was demolished.

Despite the Ba'th Party's commitment to modernization and development . . . many urban women associate the Ba'th Party with tribal and patriarchal ideologies and practices. Nour, who was also a big fan of miniskirts in the 1960s, argues though that the law did not work:

> Miniskirts in the '60s were very short. Girls continued to wear miniskirts. Some got their legs painted, but it did not stop us. We were mixing with boys at university, but there was a hint of difference after the Ba'th came to power. There were some boys who were getting more conservative.

Among the upper classes in the urban areas, especially in Baghdad, girls and women had been able to move about relatively freely, and socialized frequently with boys or men. Hana F. remembers fondly her childhood and teenage years:

> Families used to have *jurdagh* [summer huts] on the river built from reeds. Families would go there. Boys and girls would go together and play. We used to weave *karab* [part of the palm tree] with ropes and put them around us so that we would not drown when swimming in the river. People sat by the river, talking, having barbecues, singing and we were always mixed in terms of boys and girls and women and men.

Her memories correspond to those of Soraya, who was in her twenties when Hana was only a young child in the 1950s. Soraya, who had been a political activist since her high-school years, stresses that, as a young woman growing up in Baghdad, she never felt restricted or oppressed:

> From the late 1940s, when we were students, we used to wear sleeveless shirts and shorts. We would go to the club, swim, and play tennis or ping pong. Nobody would say "Don't go out!" I would just inform my parents that I was going out. We had lots of freedom. I would be home by ten. And all activities were mixed. We used to listen to classical music together, both Arabic and Western. We read a lot. I would borrow books from my older brothers and sisters. . . . Sometimes we would go to the cinema.

Not all women of upper-class background had parents as liberal and progressive as Soraya's. Several such women told me about conservative fathers and mothers, restrictions on their movement and on their socializing with boys and young men. And most parents of women from more modest social backgrounds were more concerned about traditions and their daughters' reputations. Mona stresses that she grew up being acutely aware that she was supposed to behave in certain ways different from boys and that staying away from boys was part of growing up:

> We used to play games on the roof with our neighbours or we played in the garden. We were not allowed to play on the streets. We mainly played with girls. We used to do a lot of picnics during the weekend. There was not much mixing between boys and girls after a certain age. Even later on when I got involved in politics, I made sure that I did not ruin my reputation in terms of my relationships with men.

The impression I gained from listening to the various women's accounts is that most parents of the urban middle and upper classes were quite happy for their daughters to mingle with . . . young men in the context of their studies, their social activities and, as far as was known and tolerated, their political activism. There were . . . restrictions and limitations with respect to dating, having boyfriends and choosing a marriage partner. Nour, who was studying architecture at Baghdad University in the mid-1960s, put it the following way:

> I was working on a final project with five or six boys at home. We worked on the boards in our salon and we worked day and night. But we were not allowed to go out for a date. We could study or work together. The normal way to get married was to meet your husband while studying at university, or at work after university, or through family arrangements. For me, I was introduced to my husband through friends. At least at this level of the upper and upper middle classes, Sunnis and Shi'is would intermarry, although it was more difficult between Christians and Muslims. Marriage arrangements varied from class to class. Often lower-class people would meet someone from the neighbourhood or marry a relative. But we were not allowed to go out with boyfriends.

The Kurdish Revolt, 1961–1963

At first, the Kurds welcomed the regime change. Abd al-Karim Qasim promulgated a temporary constitution that made Kurds and Arabs partners in Iraq's political life. It was a heretofore unheard of gesture that appeased some of those who wanted Kurdish autonomy. Thus, a Kurd sat with a Sunni and Shi'i in an executive Advisory Council. Qasim allowed the exiled Mustafa al-Barzani to return to Iraq, giving him a pension. In this early period, a Kurdish newspaper was even published openly.

Peaceful relations between Qasim and Barzani, however, did not last long. Barzani had long sought—and fought for—independent Kurdish power, and he began mobilizing troops. Barzani represented the disillusioned landed class, those who felt threatened by Law No. 30 on the sequestering of landed estates. (Their relations with urban Kurds could be tense.) Barzani did not feel that Qasim was meeting Kurdish demands quickly enough. In 1960, he traveled to the Soviet Union to complain of the Kurdish plight. While he was gone, Qasim encouraged Barzani's Kurdish rivals—ultimately unsuccessfully—to move against him.

As a result of this breakdown in relations, Barzani demanded Kurdish autonomy, which, of course, Qasim refused to give. A war between the government and Barzani's Kurdish forces broke out one month later, in September 1961. *Peshmergas*, the term used to refer to Kurdish forces loyal to Barzani, attacked the army. In return, Qasim ordered the bombing of Kurdish villages. As a revolt broke out, some Kurdish army officers abandoned their posts in order to join Barzani. Despite the participation of these officers, the Kurds fought using guerilla tactics. Lasting two years, this war cost countless lives and weakened Qasim's republic (Farouk-Sluglett and Sluglett, 79–82).

Dana Adams Schmidt (1916–1994) was the Middle East correspondent for the *New York Times* between 1943 and 1972. During the Kurdish Revolt, he snuck into Kurdistan on the back of a mule. His reporting from Kurdistan—published as four articles in September 1962—would win him the George Polk Award. Afterward, he would recount his trip in the book *Journey among Brave Men* (Boston: Little, Brown and Company, 1964), 172–75 and 221–24. As you read the following account of the lot of Kurds during this revolt, you should consider the following: What are the journalist's sources? How does the journalist want you to evaluate this situation? In other words, is Schmidt neutral in the conflict? What evidence do you find for your response?

> I will never forget the village of Sheile Dze, for there we spent thirteen desperately worried days. . . . The only good thing about the long delay was that it gave me an opportunity to get to know a Kurdish village.
>
> We could settle down in Sheile Dze with our armed guard because it was in a kind of twilight zone, neither clearly inside nor outside of Barzani territory. Benefiting from the indistinctness of frontiers, it partook of both the neutral and the fighting worlds.
>
> Most of the men of Sheile Dze were away with the fighting forces. The twenty houses that were their homes might have been the original for the story about the crooked man who lived in a crooked house, et cetera. In these poor houses nothing was ever straight. Apo explained that they lacked tools for making boards smooth and straight. Thus the poles that support the roof were all knotted and twisted. The boards of a door were of different lengths, uneven and bent. The ladder they made for climbing up to the roof was lopsided and lacking several rungs. The windows were not quite square. The houses were built of uneven stones loosely fitted together, roofed over with crooked beams, branches and earth. Two or four houses were usually backed up against one another and the roofs joined so as to make a single surface.

The effect was picturesque, but the drafts in wintertime must be formidable.

All the houses bore painted dates with the letters DDT indicating the times when they were sprayed by Iraqi government DDT teams. The most recent date seemed to be in the summer of 1960. Now the flies and mosquitoes—but mostly the flies—were obviously avenging their former suppression.

We were well enough protected at night, for the villagers supplied us with good mosquito nets suspended on poles (crooked ones, of course) attached to the four corners of two iron bedsteads. The bedsteads were the only ones in the village. By day the flies were ever-present, buzzing around our ears and nipping at our ankles. Now I understood why the Kurds like those thick woolen stockings: they protect ankles and legs not only from thorns and briars but from biting flies.

Our host here was Mohammed Sadoula, who was given this land by the Iraqi authorities when he came as a refugee from Turkey thirty years ago. Sadoula devoted nearly full time to looking after us. I suspect that it was for him a welcome excuse for avoiding work. He provided the beds and bedding and we were fed from his kitchen.

Sadoula's village was very poor and we tried to minimize the burden of our presence on him and the other villagers by ordering meat, sugar and other staples from neighboring villages. We also had a few luxuries of our own which Ahmed obtained for us just before his departure. We sent his order in to Hoshewi's headquarters, from where a courier went south into Iraqi government territory—to Arbil in this case, I believe—and there delivered the things to us as surely as any American department store. These luxuries included the Nescafé, several cans of an extremely sweet and sticky Australian jam, some boxes of English biscuits, some canned New Zealand cheese, some toilet paper, and most remarkable of all a set of gleaming white bedsheets for me. I don't suppose that anyone in Sheile Dze has slept between sheets before or since. . . .

That night he [Barzani] sat with us during supper and for several hours afterward. He talked a good deal of politics, and I discovered that he had a firmly entrenched anti-British complex. He found British machinations at the bottom of most of the Kurds' misfortunes. Thus, he believed the British had a secret agreement with the Soviet Union under which the Russians were to supply arms to Kassem [Qasim], and an agreement with Kassem under which he would pretend to threaten Kuwait, in order to distract attention from the Iraqi government's offensive against the Kurds. He believed also that Ali Amini's government in Iran was pro-American and under American influence, because, while it was in office, he had succeeded in sending several men into Iran for hospital treatment. The ensuing government under Premier Alam was pro-British and under British influence, he believed, because, while it was in office he had not succeeded in sending any more men to Iran.

But Barzani had a soft spot for the Americans, at least when talking with me. In his speculations he was always willing to give the Americans the benefit of the doubt.

As often happened, we had only a few hours of sleep before we were awakened to move to the small town of Hiran in the Khushnaou valley, which had just been taken by the Kurdish forces. This proved an extraordinary military movement. Although I had not realized it, a large part of the hard core of Barzani's forces had been camped in the mountains around us. With hundreds of armed men and pack animals spread out ahead and behind and all around us, we moved through the night along the top of a broad and long ridge, from which we could see on our left the very high peaks of Iran and on our right the bright lights of Shaqlawa and other smaller localities in the valley below. By the light of the moon, as far as I could see, the Kurdish revolutionary army was on the move.

At dawn I was disappointed to learn that one of Barzani's aides had ordered us to camp all day in the village of Bindar at the head of a valley leading down to the plain, where we would find Hiran. It was thought safer for us to wait until dark before we moved on again. But this was a bad miscalculation, as it turned out. For reasons which I could never understand—because camping inside a village was contrary to all the Barzani principles—we bedded down in dry irrigation ditches shielded by thick shrubbery and a thick terrace wall only fifty or sixty feet from the village fountain.

I extracted my portable typewriter from our baggage and made myself comfortable in a ditch to do something exceptionally unnecessary and pleasant. Knowing that our days together would soon be ended, I was writing a little note to Apo Jomart, telling him what a great man he was and how much I esteemed him when the planes came over. First a British Fury, then two Soviet-built MIG's. The Fury dropped four bombs spaced evenly and harmlessly across the mountainside, each leaving a crater about fifteen feet wide and eight feet deep. Then the MIG's firing cannon. And the Fury again, spraying the village and its surrounding with 30 mm. machine-gun fire.

As I hugged the earth under the terrace wall I was aware of an instant of silence after the MIG's passed over and then screams of women and children and the sound of many people scrambling over rocks. And then abrupt silence, broken off by the rattle of the machine gun when the Fury returned. And renewed screaming and scrambling. I looked up and saw a soldier standing a few feet away from me, blood streaming down his face. Dazed, he sat down on the ground and I rose unhelpfully to my feet and took his picture.

Then I scrambled up through the irrigation channels to the village fountain, where another soldier had been stretched out, his face quite ghostly white, his throat making gurgling noises. He seemed to be dying. Ahmed Tofiq was already there, wiping the man's face and instructing a soldier to fan him with a leafy branch to keep off the flies. The village meanwhile had burst into mad activity. A fence of tangled branches near the fountain had started to burn and Ahmed shouted to some villagers to bring water. They ignored him.

All over this village of about fifteen houses distraught people were rushing about, carrying things. A man stood in the doorway of a house that had been hit by cannon fire with the body of a little girl about six years old in his arms. Behind him a woman was moaning in pain. Apparently unable to decide whether to carry the little girl away or go back to help the moaning woman the man just stood in the doorway.

The ever-resourceful Ahmed told him to put the child down and went into the house to see what he could do for the wounded woman. Her legs were bleeding. A jagged hole about six feet in diameter, apparently made by a cannon shell, let sunlight into the house.

Somebody said there was a "doctor" in a neighboring village. Ahmed told the man to take a mule and to get the doctor. But the man demurred. He said the child was dead and there was nothing the doctor could do for his wife. A female relative had bandaged her legs, and within minutes she was up and herding her surviving children toward the grassy mountainside along with the other women and children in the village.

Not many minutes after the attack the village was quite empty, except for a very old woman who remained in a doorway upbraiding an old man who appeared to be her husband. I photographed them. The man smiled inanely while the old woman muttered furiously. The dying soldier remained by the fountain with another soldier fanning him. Someone had put a piece of gauze over his face. Several mules splattered with blood were driven by. They had been injured by flying fragments of bombs or stones.

The results of this raid were one child dead, one soldier dead, two soldiers injured, and two or three villagers injured.

This sort of thing was commonplace all over northern Iraq in the summer of 1962. The day we were bombed at Bindar eight other villages in parallel valleys leading down into the Khushnaou valley in northern Iraq were also attacked.

Bibliography

Baly, Denis. *Iraq.* Newport, R.I.: Budek Films and Slides, 1968.

Barzani, Massoud. *Mustafa Barzani and the Kurdish Liberation Movement.* New York: Palgrave Macmillan, 2003.

Caractacus. *Revolution in Iraq: An Essay in Comparative Public Opinion.* London: Victor Gollancz, 1959.

Dickson, Mora. *Baghdad and Beyond.* London: Dennis Dobson, 1961.

Edmonds, C. J. *A Pilgrimage to Lalish.* London: Royal Asiatic Society of Great Britain and Ireland, 1967.

Educational Services. *Land and Water in Iraq.* S.l.: Educational Services, 1964.

Farrington, Jay A., and Carole Chaney Farrington. *Baghdad Letters: An American Couple in Iraq, 1966–1967.* Bloomington, Ind.: 1stBooks, 2003.

Forbes, Colin D. *Innocent in a Revolution.* Lewes, Sussex: Book Guild, 1999.

Haeri, Shaykh Fadhlalla. *Son of Karbala.* Winchester, England: O Books, 2006.

Hansen, Henny Harald. *Daughters of Allah: Among Moslem Women in Kurdistan.* London: Allen and Unwin, 1960.

Harrison, David L. *Footsteps in the Sand.* London: Benn, 1959.

Iraq. *Irak: 60 Color Slides.* Baghdad: State Organization for Tourism, 1960.

Iraq. *Land of Two Rivers.* Baghdad: Directorate-General of Guidance and Broadcasting, 1960.

Mallowan, Agatha Christie. *Come Tell Me How You Live.* New York: HarperCollins, 1999.

Metti, Jemil. *Perception Wars: Iraq from the Outside In.* Philadelphia, Pa.: Xlibris, 2008.

Morton, H. V. *Middle East: A Record of Travel in the Countries of Egypt, Palestine, Iraq, Turkey and Greece.* London: Methuen, 1941.

Rawi, Nuri, Latif Ani, and Qamar Hasnain. *Iraq in Pictures.* Baghdad: Wizarat al-Thaqafah wa-al-Irshad, 1966.

Rowland, Howard. *Taking on the Middle East: A Young Man's Bizarre Odyssey in an Ancient Land.* Pacific Grove, Calif.: Park Place Publications, 2007.

Sousa, Ahmed. *An Illustrated Handbook of Iraq.* Baghdad: Ministry of Guidance, 1962.

Stafford, R. S. *The Tragedy of the Assyrians.* Piscataway, N.J.: Gorgias Press, 2006.

Stark, Freya. *East Is West.* Toronto: Transatlantic Arts, 1982.

6

Consolidating Ba'thist Power, 1968–1979

Iraq's Arab Ba'th Socialist Party organized a coup d'état on 17 July 1968, replacing the government of Abd al-Rahman Arif. There are many factors that contributed to the Arif regime's downfall. The government, for example, was fighting a war with Kurds in the north, and this destabilized the regime. Further, Arif had created networks of patronage that heavily favored a very narrow group, namely his own Sunni al-Jumayla tribe (Fattah, 207). Factors contributing to the Ba'th's overthrow of the Arif government, however, included more than just widespread domestic discontent with the regime. In June 1967, the Arab world suffered a humiliating defeat in the Six Day War with Israel, and this wreaked political havoc in Iraq. Under Arif, Iraq had remained neutral in this struggle, and Iraqis and the officers in the army were unhappy with this (Fattah, 208).

The Arab Ba'th Socialist Party espoused a populist ideology, but it did not necessarily have widespread support at the time of the coup. The political party of the Ba'th had been created in Syria in 1941, and its principal ideologue was Michel Aflaq, a Christian. It was a secular party that theoretically welcomed people of different faiths. It was pan-Arab in its orientation, meaning that it intended to draw together all states—viewed as artificial constructions—of the Arab-speaking world. Since European powers had artificially divided the Arab nation, the party enunciated anti-imperial ideas. In the economic sphere, the Ba'th sought a socialist program that would spread the wealth of the old elite fostered by colonialism. In this way, the Ba'th sought to be a mass movement. Ba'thism flourished throughout the Middle East, though in Iraq it would remain a relatively small movement until the end of the 1960s. The historian Hala Fattah notes, "Baathist ideology was sufficiently vague and adaptable to accommodate a number of disparate elements in the Iraqi population" (209).

Leaders of Iraq's Ba'th Party would ultimately eschew many of the ideology's basic tenets. The two key actors in the Ba'th Party during its first ten years of rule would be President Hasan al-Bakr and Vice-President Saddam Hussein, who took over for al-Bakr in 1979. These men were, as identified by Charles Tripp, "nominally Baathist," meaning they privileged national priorities over the pan-Arab goals (Tripp, 186). Hussein, in particular, exercised primordial influence in Iraq, beginning to forge what one historian calls the "Saddamist State" by the 1970s (Dawisha, 211). Such a state was based on highly personalized networks of patronage, whereby the Ba'th privileged certain groups, most notably Sunnis from Tikrit, hometown of Bakr and Hussein. In retaining power, the Ba'th had to neutralize its political rivals—Communists, Shi'i clerics, and Kurds—and it did so by relying on mechanisms of political violence that pitted the state against opposition groups.

This chapter provides insights into both the carrots and the sticks used by the Ba'th Party to control life in Iraq. It begins with a memo from the U.S. State Department, which reflects an ambivalent American attitude toward the coup. It then turns toward the promulgation of the Constitution of 1970, which reveals Iraqi mutations of Ba'thism. The Ba'th Party, however, had no intention of adhering to the rule of law. As recounted by Saeed Herdoon, the Ba'th manufactured a spy scare and executed a number of Jews after trials with predetermined outcomes. Despite such terror, some Iraqis supported Ba'thist rule. And so, this chapter includes a pan-Arab poem by Hameed Sa'id, editor of the *al-Thaura* newspaper. Afterward, a speech by Saddam Hussein reveals the extent to which the Ba'th—at least, in these early years—sought to break Iraqi patriarchy by encouraging women to assume a larger role in the workforce. The Ba'th Party also targeted youth, so this chapter includes reflections on the teaching of history by Saddam Hussein. This chapter then reveals a U.S. State Department memo in which the United States decides to support Kurds in 1972 in their struggle against the Iraqi state. Hineer Saleem describes the second Kurdish-Iraqi War of 1974–1975, which ultimately left the peoples of the north disillusioned with the United States. During these years, Shi'ism became a political movement, so this chapter includes an excerpt of the writings of the influential Shi'i cleric Muhammad Baqir al-Sadr. Since the Ba'th targeted Shi'is, the chapter ends with a firsthand Shi'i account of the sister of a man arrested for participating in an Ashura commemoration in Karbala in 1979.

U.S. Response to the Ba'thist Coup, July 1968

Given the subsequent international dimensions of the Ba'thist putsch, one should analyze the immediate American response to this event. The Cold War inevitably shaped U.S. responses to events in the Arab-Islamic world. High up on the list of the United States' policy priorities was the protection of Israel after the

Six Day War of June 1967. In this regard, American decision makers were cautiously optimistic as they analyzed the new regime. They favorably compared its leaders and their rhetoric to that of the militarized Ba'th regime in Syria, which had placed itself fully within the Soviet camp in order to have access to weapons so as to continue fighting the United States' Israeli ally. As you read the following document, you should consider the following: What leads U.S. policymakers to feel optimistic in regard to the Ba'thist regime? Why does the author of this document consider the resolution of the Kurdish question key?

Washington, July 22, 1968
Memorandum from John W. Foster of the National Security Council Staff to the President's Special Assistant (Rostow)
SUBJECT: A Clearer Picture of the Iraqi Coup

While you were gone, the situation in Iraq became much clearer. The new government could still be a little harder for us to deal with than the old—if we ever have a chance to deal with it—but if we had to have a Baathist government there, this is probably the best we could expect.

The Baathists are from the right-wing of the party—the opponents of those in control in Syria—and non-Baathists are playing a major role in the new government. The Syrians had nothing to do with the coup; in fact, one of the most interesting questions raised by the coup is whether the Iraqi example will encourage the moderate Syrian Baathists now in exile to take a crack at the Syrian regime.

The inability of the Aref government to deal with Iraq's domestic problems was the reason—or excuse—for the coup, and the new government is talking mainly about economic reforms, eliminating corruption and solving the Kurdish problem. They have made the usual statements about Zionism, Imperialism and Arab unity, but so far there have been no indications that Iraq's foreign policy will become more radical. It's too early to know whether there will be progress on a Kurdish settlement or more trouble—a key determinant of how free Iraqi troops will be to menace Israel.

Until we see these people in action, we won't know for sure what problems we might face, but there seems to be less cause for concern over anything radically different.

The Ba'thist Constitution, 1970

The Ba'th Party enacted a Constitution two years after its coup d'état in July 1968, and this Constitution would remain in effect until Coalition Forces occupied

Iraq in 2003. According to historian Phebe Marr, the Constitution "defined the locus of power in the new regime" (Marr, 142). The Ba'th established a Revolutionary Command Council (RCC) as well as an executive, legislative, and judicial branch of government. The president, Ahmad Hasan al-Bakr until 1979, was to head the RCC. As Marr also points out, the Constitution led to the "enshrining of the principle of the one-party state" (143). Despite these self-serving components of the new Constitution, the very act of its promulgation seemed to signal to Iraqis and to the international community that the Ba'th would follow the rule of law. The Ba'th did not do so, but the Constitution still provides an important glimpse of Iraqi mutations of Ba'thism, for it addressed a fragmented Iraqi society.

The following excerpt from the Constitution reveals the ideological leanings of the government as well as the relations between state and society. This excerpt is taken from a translated copy of the Constitution in Majid Khadduri's *Socialist Iraq: A Study in Iraq Politics since 1968* (Washington, D.C.: Middle East Institute, 1978), 183–98. As you read excerpts from this Constitution, you should consider the following: What are the ideological intentions enunciated in this document? Do you perceive any inconsistencies or problems? And, based on readings from secondary textbooks or subsequent documents, did the Ba'th Party live up to its enunciated codified intentions?

Part One: The Republic of Iraq

Article 1. Iraq is a Sovereign People's Democratic Republic: its principal aim is to achieve the United Arab State and establish the Socialist System.

Article 2. The People is the source of authority and its legitimacy.

Article 3. . . . (b) The land of Iraq is an indivisible unit and no part of it shall be relinquished.

Article 4. Islam is the religion of the State.

Article 5. (a) Iraq is part of the Arab Nation. (b) The people of Iraq is formed of two principal nationalities, the Arab nationality and the Kurdish nationality. This Constitution shall recognize the rights of the Kurdish people and the legitimate rights of all minorities within the unity of Iraq. . . .

Article 7. (a) Arabic is the official language. (b) The Kurdish language, in addition to the Arabic language, shall be the official language in the Kurdish Region.

Article 8. . . . (c) The area whose majority of population is from Kurds shall enjoy autonomy. . . .

Part Two: Social and Economic Bases of the Republic of Iraq

Article 10. . . . [E]very citizen shall perform fully his duty towards society and that society shall ensure to the citizen his full rights and freedoms. . . .

Article 12. The State shall undertake planning . . . and guiding the national economy in accordance with the following aims: (a) Establishing the socialist system on scientific and revolutionary principles. (b) Achieving Arab economic unity. . . .

Article 15. . . . [T]he properties of the public sector shall have special inviolability, which the State and all citizens have to maintain and guarantee their security and protection. Any subversion or attack on it shall be regarded as an attack on the structure of society and a violence to it. . . .

Part Three: Basic Rights and Duties

Article 19. (a) All citizens are equal before the law, without distinction on the basis of race, origin, language, class or religion. (b) Equal opportunities for all citizens shall be guaranteed. . . .

Article 20. (a) The accused is innocent until he is declared guilty by judicial procedure. (b) The right to defense is sacred in all processes of investigation and trial in accordance with the provisions of the law. . . .

Article 22. (a) The dignity of Man is guaranteed. Any kind of physical or psychological torture shall be prohibited. (b) No one may be arrested, detained, imprisoned or searched except in provisions of the law. (c) Homes are inviolable. They may not be . . . searched except as specified by the law.

Article 23. Privacy of mail, telegraphic and telephone correspondence shall be guaranteed, and it shall not be violated except for reasons of public security. . . .

Article 24. No citizen shall be prevented from travel outside the country or from returning thereto and no restriction shall be imposed on his moving and residence inside the country except in the cases defined by the law.

Article 25. Freedom of religion, beliefs and exercise of religious ceremonies shall be guaranteed, provided that this freedom shall neither contradict the provisions of the Constitution . . . nor violate morality and public order.

Article 26. The Constitution shall guarantee freedom of opinion, publication, meeting, demonstration, forming of political parties, unions and societies in accordance with the aims of the Constitution and within the limits of the law. . . .

Article 28. Education shall aim at raising and developing the general cultural level, developing the scientific thinking, encouraging the spirit of research, fulfilling the requirements of economic and social development programmes, creating a free nationalist and progressive generation . . . which takes pride in its people, its homeland and its legacy, sympathizes with the rights of all its nationalities and opposes the doctrines of capitalism, exploitation, reaction, Zionism and colonialism in order to achieve Arab unity, freedom and socialism.

...

Article 36. Any activity which contradicts the aims of the people defined in this Constitution and any act of conduct aiming at undermining the national unity of the masses of the people, provoking racial or sectarian or regional bigotry among their ranks, or violating their progressive gains and achievements, shall be prohibited.

The Jewish Exodus under the Ba'th

The Six Day War and the subsequent rise of the anti-Zionist Ba'th Party renewed tensions between Iraqi Jews and the government as well as their Muslim compatriots. During the Six Day War, Israel tripled its territory, thereby humiliating Arab armies. Within one year, the Ba'th took power, and its leaders found it convenient to use Jews as a scapegoat for their nation's ills. "Manufactured spy scares," according to Charles Tripp, provided a means to engage in "purges in the civil service and the officers corps" (Tripp, 188). The Ba'th restricted the movement of Jews by freezing their accounts, firing them from their jobs, and blocking their mail. On 27 January 1969, the Ba'th government hanged nine Jews publicly in Liberation Square. From then on, it was only a matter of time before most remaining Iraqi Jews decided to emigrate from Iraq.

In this passage, Saeed Herdoon (1936–2007) remembers the terror of Ba'thist rule. Herdoon was thirty-two years old when the Ba'th regime took power. He had wanted to leave Iraq as early as 1951, but he stayed at his father's request. At first, he did not regret his decision to stay. He refers to the period of 1958 to 1963 as a "real golden age of Iraqi Jews." The good intersectarian relations of these times, however, would not endure. The Six Day War created tension between Herdoon and some of his close Muslim friends. And Herdoon knew two of the Jews hanged by the Ba'th. The following is an interview excerpted from *Iraq's Last Jews: Stories of Daily Life, Upheaval, and Escape from Modern Babylon,* edited by Tamar Morad, Dennis Shasha, and Robert Shasha (New York: Palgrave Macmillan, 2008), 130–38. As you are reading the excerpt, you should consider the following: Who is in prison? And why? What does the list of prisoners suggest about Ba'thist power? And finally, why are Kurds and Iranians helping Jews emigrate in the early 1970s?

At Passover in 1969 I was arrested and imprisoned for nearly six months. I was in my office in the central business district. Three of Saddam's men barged into the office and began to collect the identity cards of everyone there. They separated the Jews from the non-Jews, then gave back the cards of the non-Jews and escorted them out. Five of us, all Jewish men, were left inside. The officers confiscated files and typewriters which they forced us to carry outside and into their cars. They blindfolded us and put us in the car. We remained covered with those same dirty blindfolds for the next two weeks.

We were taken to a police station, guided upstairs, and seated on the floor next to ten others and ordered not to talk. We waited all day and slept at night on the concrete floor. We were given some bread and tea and taken in groups of two to the bathroom. It tore me apart knowing that my family was certainly in agony worrying about me and my brother-in-law, Joseph Zilkha, one of the co-owners of the business who was arrested as well, leaving behind my sister and their three small children. One night I bribed a guard—with a very big sum equal to three months of his salary—to take a personal item I had in my pocket to my family so they would know I was alive. He returned with a note in my sister's handwriting that read, "We are well and working to help you."

Then they interrogated each one of us. . . . [M]y blindfold was removed. The officer told me that I was not the target of the investigation—their targets were the co-owners, Joseph Jangana and Joseph Zilkha. I didn't believe it—it was just a ploy to get me to talk. They were after our company's connections abroad: if the company held any foreign accounts that the state was not aware of, the authorities could convict us of betraying the nation. He threatened me by alluding to the torture devices in the room, iron chains, and machines that were used to pull limbs from bodies. I was . . . told to write a personal statement. I wrote and wrote but the officer found nothing in there that he was looking for, gave up, blindfolded me again and sent me back to the room with the other men.

After two weeks, we were taken to another location and I was put in a dark six-foot by six-foot cell where two other men were already confined. This became my home for the following months. There were no mattresses and no windows or light of any kind. I learned from one of my cellmates, two Muslim men from Basra, that we were in Saddam's personal prison beneath the amphitheater of the royal palace which the Ba'ath Party named "Prison of the End" to celebrate the end of the monarchy. That cellmate had been there for three months and was a source of reassurance for me. I had nothing to do with my time but worry about my fate and . . . about my younger brother, because if he were arrested, my parents would be left without further protection. I was terrified knowing that nine Jewish men had been publicly hanged only a few months before. I also knew that newspapers often ran front-page stories in which government officials announced that a prisoner had "escaped" but in truth we in the Jewish community knew that he had been killed. We had heard rumors that sulfuric acid was used to dissolve the bodies quickly in order to leave no trace of wrongdoing.

We were allowed to use the bathrooms once a day in the morning. To try to explain the stench ... is impossible. The toilets would not flush so they remained overflowing with urine and feces for months. Finally the guards had to put bricks on the ground around the toilet so we could stand on them when we used the toilet.

We were not allowed to speak, and those who broke the rules suffered harsh consequences, so we were terrified to communicate with one another. Soon after I arrived I learned that Yitzhak Dallall, an acquaintance of mine, was in the cell next to me. I saw him in the mornings during our trips to the bathroom, but he looked at me as if ready to say something, yet stayed silent. Finally, after three weeks, he managed to ask me whether I knew anything about his family's well-being. He had been taken four months earlier and was agonizing about whether they were alive or dead. It took me two weeks until I was able to answer him: I told him that they were all right and working towards his release. [Months later, days after Herdoon's release, Dallall was hanged ...]

My other cellmate was a 14-year old Bedouin shepherd from the desert. He told me he had been taken prisoner because of fears that he had witnessed a guard disposing of a body. A few weeks after I arrived, he was taken for questioning and it was decided that he would be released. Upon hearing this news, he stood in the hallway and yelled out, "God bless you all! I hope all of you will join me!" In doing that, he broke the rule prohibiting speaking, and was killed the same night.

Each man in the prison had his own tragic story, and although we were not allowed to speak, we managed to find ways to communicate and thus learn about each other. One story that I recall vividly is of a man who had been a successful doctor and had recently built a house for his young wife and newborn infant. The house happened to be in a place where Saddam was planning to confiscate all properties around his palace [now the area in the "Green Zone"]. Just as the house was completed, he was approached by one of Saddam's men who asked him to move. The man refused to sell his house. Soon after, guards broke into the doctor's home in the middle of the night and took him, his wife, and their baby and put them in a car. They were driven to a remote area and as the car sped up, his wife and baby were thrown out of the car to their deaths. He was brought to prison. This educated, cultured man quickly lost his mind: he used to sit in the corner of his cell, shaking back and forth as he recited the details of his tragedy over and over. After a short while, he was found dead in his cell.

Another story I recall is of the right-hand man to the former minister of finance in the previous regime. Anyone with ties to the former regime was imprisoned after the 1968 Ba'ath Party coup. He had been . . . loyal to his boss, so no means of torture could get him to say anything negative about the minister. After being tortured for several days, he was chained to a wall directly across from my cell. Bound and naked, he was forced to drink gallons of water and his penis was tied with a string to prevent him from urinating. For about 36 hours I sat in my cell and listened to his cries of agony and watched him become poisoned by his own urine. He died, but his body revealed no external harm—one of the clever tricks of his torturers.

The stories go on and on. Up to three times a week, Saddam held what became to be known as "torture parties." Drugged and drunk, Saddam and his thugs randomly selected prisoners in the middle of the night and brought them to a room where they tortured prisoners until the brink of death. Saddam and his men put electric shocks on their eyelids, pulled out their teeth, and hung them from the ceiling by their hands, which were tied behind their backs. When the prisoners were brought back to their cells, they were barely alive, bloodied and unable to stand. One man used a metal can to cut off large pieces of flesh that were left dangling from his legs. Some of the prisoners died shortly after their ordeal.

The food was horrendous. The guards served it out of buckets and there were no utensils or cups so we had to find our own ways of consuming the meager and disgusting fare unless we wanted the guards to serve us with their dirty hands. I refused to eat most of the time, and my weight dropped dramatically . . . by thirty pounds.

One day, guards circulated throughout the prison and took notes on each prisoner. When they got to me, they asked me what school I had attended and I told them Frank Iny. The officer turned to his partner and said, "That school graduates all the spies who spy against Iraq!" I worried that if the guard wrote down "spy" next to my name, that would spell my death. In Saddam's . . . legal system, even if I were given a court hearing and were able to protest the accusation, the judge would look down on the paper and say, "But it says right here that you *are* a spy!" But by a twist of fate, I never had my day in court.

After many long months like this, I and 14 others from what they called the "merchant group" were taken into another part of the palace. At first I was terrified that we were being taken for interrogation, but it turned out that we were put in more comfortable quarters, allowed to speak freely, could finally shower, and were fed half-decent food. We could even order food and receive packages from our families. My first package contained a change of clothing. Then I realized how much weight I had lost because my pants practically fell right off me. We were allowed to get our first exercise in months by walking around our room. Yet I was still suspicious.

One day an officer came with a note from my sister saying the family is fine and they were praying for our well being [of Herdoon and Joseph Zilkha]. Apparently, after months of standing outside the Ministry of Defense building, she managed to talk to a high-ranking officer who agreed to send the note to us. The officer then asked me if I wanted to talk to her. I didn't know how to react at first but followed him into his enormous office inside the luxurious royal palace, which was filled with paintings of Saddam. He asked for my sister's phone number, but I told him we had no phone because after the Six Day War all the telephones in Jewish homes had been disconnected. I gave him the number of the Muslim Shiite family across the street from my home and he dialed. No one answered. One night the next week he took me . . . to try again, and my neighbor answered. The neighbor ran across the street in his pajamas and woke up my parents, who rushed over to speak with us. We were only allowed to say hello and to let them know we were alive and well. . . . [O]ther prisoners were allowed to make calls but few succeeded in making contact because of the phone confiscations.

Since I had been given the daily task to water the dusty yard around the prison cells, I often overheard other inmates' conversations. In the cell next to mine, the former head of Iraq's military academy was being held. Saddam's men often . . . tortured this man at night and brought him back to his cell on a stretcher in the morning. Ironically, the same men who did this were officers this man had trained himself, so they would salute him out of habit in the morning and bring buckets of water to relieve his pain. And the strange pattern continued like that.

One day when I mustered up the courage to ask a guard if I could call home again, he asked me, "Do you want to call or would you rather go home?" He told me and some others including Joseph that we would be going home the next day. Anxious and stimulated, we couldn't sleep that night and the next morning the head of the prison, who we met for the first time, told us, "You are going home. But you didn't see anything, you don't know where you were, you didn't hear anything, and you will never tell anyone what happened here. If you do, it will be your end." They drove us to another building where we saw many other Jewish men who we knew and were told we had to arrange a 5,000 dinar bail—an amount equivalent to a modern four-bedroom house in Baghdad. But no Jew could post such a bail because the government wouldn't accept bail from a Jew. We sat there for days not knowing what to do. During this time our family visited us. The meeting was an incredibly difficult moment for all of us: one of happiness but great uncertainty and fear that we would never return home after all. My family succeeded in arranging bail for the two of us with the help of . . . lawyers who took a 10 percent cut. In this manner many of us were released. We arrived home in September, 1969, haggard thin, and weak, but alive.

The government had confiscated the business and after my experience I knew we had to leave Iraq—that we had no future here. So I spent the following months planning our escape. It was hard work convincing my parents to leave, especially my father. He said, "Why don't you go and I'll come after you in a little while. I have things to finish here." I said, "No! We are all going together."

On March 17, 1970, there was a cease-fire between the Kurds and the Iraqis in a war that had been going on for nine years. In the summer, people started traveling again to the north, the beautiful, mountainous Kurdish area. I went there by taxi to look for someone who could help smuggle us out. I spent some nights there and arranged with a Kurdish man to help us and we settled on a date and agreed on a fee equivalent to $5,000. Ten days later, I went back to meet him again to discuss the final arrangements, set the departure date, and bring him some gifts.

On the day on which we were supposed to leave, a friend who also happened to be in touch with the same smuggler came to my mother and left a message for me from the smuggler. The message was: "Don't come. It's too dangerous now." But we were already prepared to go and couldn't imagine staying another day. I was afraid we'd miss the opportunity to leave altogether. So we decided to go, rent a room in a hotel, and stay there until we found a way out, even with another smuggler if need be.

A friend of mine, Eli Dannoos, came with us. Eli had moved from Iraq to London but had come back to Iraq to visit his sick father. He was sitting in the office of his friend and my neighbor Charles Horesh when the authorities came to arrest Charles. Just because Eli was there, they took Eli too. The two of them and many others were put in Kasr al Nahaya, accused of spying for Israel. The Iraqis set up mock trials for the men, including Charles, which were broadcast on TV and radio for the whole nation to watch. Eli was released. His release, I believe, was meant to show that the Iraqi judicial system was just. Those other nine men were the ones who were hanged on January 27. But Eli meanwhile had witnessed and experienced all the torture and investigations. More than a year after his release, he was still suffering from the psychological trauma of what had happened to him.

He came to visit me at my house on the morning we planned to escape. He was visibly shaken and perpetually looking over his shoulders. We were sitting in the garden and my mother was serving coffee. He asked me with tears of desperation in his eyes if there was a way for him to escape from Iraq. Although we were preparing to go at that moment we were afraid to tell anyone that we were leaving. The Jews always kept their travel plans a secret, even from friends and relatives; a person didn't tell his own brother his plans if the brother wasn't coming along. But Eli was so sad and hopeless that I decided to tell him about my plans to escape that night. I said, "Eli, are you ready to leave today?" He looked at me and said, "What do you mean?" I repeated my question. He suddenly understood. "Yes," he answered. I said, "Go find a Kurdish taxi driver and arrange with him to take you to the north." I told him where to find such a driver and designated a point at which to meet us in the north. Eli had a girlfriend whom he wanted to marry, so he ran to get her and find a rabbi. He took the two of them to his father's bedside and Eli and his girlfriend got married. . . .

We left at midnight with just a few small bags in hand, locked the door to the house, and left quietly in a taxi. We weren't able to liquidate our assets or ship our belongings. My sister and her husband, Joseph, and their three children were in one car; his business partner and his wife and their children in another; and other relatives, my parents and I in other cars. It was a long caravan. We met Eli and his wife on the way to the north. At one point we had to pass a security checkpoint and a guard stopped us and took all of our identity cards. Because Joseph and I had been released from jail on bail we were probably listed as having been imprisoned, and our names were identifiably Jewish, so we thought: "This is the end. We're going to be arrested again, and now with the whole family." The soldier went to make a call and kept his eyes on us at the same time. Miraculously, he returned and gave the cards back to us and let us go. Forty-eight hours later, after we arrived in Tehran, we heard that a group of Jews were caught at the same checkpoint and sent back to Baghdad.

For our safety, we did not talk with each other, only when absolutely necessary with our immediate families. We pretended we didn't know each other because we didn't want to bring attention to our large group and raise eyebrows about why such a large group was on vacation together. We were drinking coffee in a coffee shop when suddenly three Land Rover jeeps stopped nearby. Several Kurds stepped out and started asking us if we were ready to leave to cross over to Iran. . . . We didn't know whether we should trust them. We looked at each other warily. It felt like a dream, not reality. And then one man nearby, also a Jew from Baghdad, said that these were the people with whom he had arranged to escape, so we mustn't fear. We breathed a sigh of relief—until the Kurdish man said, "OK, we'll take the women and the children first." To give them the women and the children! It was very scary. But this Jewish man swore to us that we were in good hands. So the women and children left in the jeeps. After about twenty very long minutes, the Kurds came back and took the rest of us in several trips. I was in the last group. They took us to a mountainous area and we began walking—49 people, including children and elderly.

Eventually we were brought to a tent and told to sit and rest on a carpet. Several Kurds began serving us in a way that we couldn't believe. They brought each of us a towel and water to wash our faces, cold water to drink, tea, and coffee. It was unbelievable, surreal. For each one of us, they brought a tray with chicken, meat, and vegetables. I didn't know why they were being so gracious; none of us could figure it out. We ate and thanked them, and again they came with towels and water and tea, and when it was about 11 o'clock at night, they said, "It's time for you to go." They took us from that area in the Land Rovers to a building made out of mud with many rooms lit with lanterns.

They divided us up into the rooms. We were sitting on the floor covered with carpets when suddenly about eight Kurdish "freedom fighters" came in—they called them *pishmorga*, which means in their language "to fight until death." They fought the government for years for Kurdish freedom from Iraqi rule. The apparent leader of the group said, *Salaam alechum* (Hello) and sat down. We didn't know who he was. He talked with us so nicely, and it was clear that he was a very highly educated person. "Are there more Jews like you in Baghdad who wish to escape from Iraq?" he asked. By that point, we all trusted him and his friends. You didn't have to probe to figure out whether to trust a Kurd or not. They were honest and friendly with the Jews. So we began giving him the names and addresses of whomever we knew, though none had telephone service. . . .

Then he asked, "Are you going to Israel?" We all became silent and grew pale. It was, for all intents and purposes, forbidden to say aloud the word "Israel" at that time. Even though we trusted him, we hesitated. We were in shock and didn't know how to answer. I finally looked at him and said, "Yes," and waited for his reaction. He didn't say anything. He just stood up and started shaking all our hands. He said it was time to go and that we were close to the border. Then he asked us: "Did any one of us"—he meant the Kurds—"ask you for a fee to help you? Because if so I will cut off his head." He continued, "I ask because in every nation, there are some weak, cheap people." Nobody admitted to paying any smugglers.

Then I stood up to shake his hand and thanked him, and he clenched my hand and said, "There is no reason to thank me. Israel gave us training, arms, medicine, and any kind of help that we needed in our war against the Iraqis. If Israel had merely publicized the news about our war and our mission, it would have been enough for us, but they did so much more. So we are very grateful to Israel, to the Jewish people. What we are doing now for you is the least we can do to reciprocate." And then I understood that this was Idris al-Barazani, the son of the head of the Kurds [Moustafa al-Barazani]. . . .

Soon after he left, we met Oddil Dallall, the widow of Yitzhak Dallall who had been with me in prison and was executed. She suddenly appeared in our room in this building—she had gotten there independently. She came to me shaking. She was worried that Iraqi intelligence officers were following her. So I promised her that we would not leave without her but until then she must pretend that she didn't know us so that we wouldn't be caught by one of these officers. But in the end I realized there were no intelligence officers—she was just traumatized by what happened to Yitzhak and had become paranoid.

We climbed into the jeeps. The drivers gave a signal with a flashlight to the Iranian border guards who opened the gate. . . . On the Iranian side we stayed at a small motel. Early in the morning a bus belonging to the Jewish Agency picked us up. We had a 12-hour bus journey followed by a 12-hour train ride to Tehran. Oddil still believed that she was being followed and couldn't fall asleep and was still shaking. So I gave her a tranquilizer—valium. I sat next to the door of the rail car and told her to go to sleep and that I would protect her. She didn't react. So I put my leg on the seat and said, "Sit on my leg. If I move from here, you will wake up." That worked.

We arrived at a hotel in Tehran at which the Jewish Agency had organized for us to stay and there we met some of our friends who had crossed over from Iraq before us. . . . We stayed in Tehran for about three weeks. I met relatives there who had been living in Tehran for years whom I didn't know I had and who had heard that we were there and came to visit us at the hotel. From there we went to Israel.

Pan-Arab Cultural Production

The Ba'th Party took a hard-line stance vis-à-vis Israel. "By adopting a radical stance toward Israel," historian Eric Davis asserts, "the Ba'th was able to both garner popular support, especially among the officer corps and the urban middle classes, and distinguish itself from the 'Arif regime" (Davis, 158). Iraqis felt great sympathy for the Palestinian plight, especially after the Six Day War, which had tripled the size of Israel and left hundreds of thousands of stateless Palestinian refugees. By supporting the Palestinians, Iraqi Ba'thists could purport to be supporting their party's original pan-Arab ideals.

Hameed Sa'id was an ordinary Iraqi who wholeheartedly supported the Ba'thist regime. He was twenty-seven years old when the Ba'th took power. He would work as editor-in-chief of Ba'thist Iraq's major newspaper, *al-Thaura*. In this way, he would help spread Ba'thist propaganda. Sa'id, however, was not adhering to the party due to self-serving aims. He truly believed in the Ba'ath's pan-Arab mission. Thus, after the assassination by the Israeli state of Palestinian activist Ghassan Kanafani (1936–1972), he wrote the following poem. This poem, titled "Dying at the Edge of Death," can be found in Salma Khadra Jayyusi's *Modern Arabic Poetry: An Anthology* (New York: Columbia University Press, 1987), 398–99. As you read the poem, you should consider the following: What are the lines that anchor the verse solidly in the pan-Arab camp? What is referenced in the description of "Mongol horses"? Why did the poet dedicate this poem to the Palestinian Kanafani? How does the poet use history in the service of Ba'thism?

DYING AT THE EDGE OF DEATH

To Ghassan Kanafani, the Witness
Here is the scene: She follows him.
He follows her. The soldier patrols
the square. And the gypsy man shudders.
She continues her watch.
On the road perhaps he will be waylaid.
But he was made to take this role,
the part of him who pursues the dream.
The royal guards must detect him.
He is lost, and
he is lost to her.

In the streets of Madrid, Jerusalem removes
her blouse. She is naked and hungry.
Looking out the windows in the evening
Madrid recognizes her and closes

all the doors.
Fear drinks the glass of sweet wine.
And Madrid drinks the blood of her own children.
He is lost. And she walks.
But the birds fear her
since her loss, and curse
their own nests.

Wherever he has been she follows now
to ask about him.
Any distinguishing marks?
Oh, don't you know? He crossed the sea
without a ship. He burned all his cards.
He died. And no one in al-Sumainah* grieved.
No one wept for him. No one dug his grave
with spearheads. The spearheads lie mute
in the museum showcases.
He sinks his eyes into them.
The spears turn into books.
O Arab homeland, chained with sands,
take a page out of this book of spearheads
and ward off the Mongol horses that stand ready.

I gather your letters and scatter them.
I see you hesitate,
postponing your promises.
Come toward me.
I will show you the boundaries,
The edges of your hands,
of your chains.

Those who wake up with her
wander with her from coffeebar
to coffeebar.
In the night they wipe her face,
scent it, and sleep beside her.

Women in Ba'thist Iraq

It may come as some surprise to learn that Saddam Hussein spearheaded a Ba'thist initiative to guarantee women's right to education and subsequently to work. According to Nadje al-Ali and Nicola Pratt, such policies served very practical economic and political purposes. First, they allowed the Ba'th Party to make up for a labor shortage within the booming economy of the 1970s. Second, they allowed the Ba'th to recruit more members (al-Ali and Pratt, 31). In making women economically independent, the Ba'th could also break traditional patriarchal networks. And so, the Ba'th would court the loyalties of women.

The General Federation of Iraqi Women was founded in 1968, and it was the principal vehicle through which women participated in the public sphere. It was a branch of the Ba'th Party. As such, it promoted women's education and employment. Despite the existence of such an institution, the historian Eric Davis insists, unfortunately, that the Ba'th never fostered a real transformation in patriarchal gender relations or the status of women (Davis, 263).

In 1971, Saddam Hussein gave the following speech to members of the General Federation of Iraqi Women. The title of the speech is "Women—One Half of Our Society." In reading this excerpt, you should consider the following: What is Saddam Hussein's vision of women's rights? Who is the guarantor of women's rights? Is it the state? Or the people? Does Hussein address the public or the private sphere? What are the arguments that he uses to convince Iraqis of a need to impose a new set of rights on women?

> Sisters, Your Congress is a prominent event in the life of our people and our country. Throughout the pre-Revolution years, the women's organization (of the party) had various militant duties and specific forms of struggle in which women joined men in the political and social fields. There was no organizational framework capable of absorbing and expressing the aspirations of millions of Iraqi women and mobilizing their energy in the fight against imperialism and Zionism and in the struggle for freedom and a better life....
>
> Despite conditions which wasted much of their potential, women in our country have truly played a noble and prominent role in our people's struggle for freedom from imperialism, dictatorship and reactionary regimes and for achieving the pan-Arab aims of unity, liberty and socialism.
>
> During the 1920 revolution in which our people gave their response to the British colonial occupation, and during the mass uprisings against the imperialist pacts and alliances, the unjust legislation and conditions and the corrupt, reactionary dictatorships, women took part and played a role which gave an

example of courage and initiative and inspired bravery and enthusiasm in the hearts of the strugglers.

The women's organization took a leading part in building up our Party and its struggle to defeat the enemies of the people and achieve the Revolution. During the difficult period of the struggle when our colleagues were subjected to intense terror, the Women's Organization of the Arab Ba'th Socialist Party undertook the active task of maintaining contact between the leadership and all Party organizations as well as between those comrades who had been arrested and those outside prison.

The women's organization was also a mobilizing force among the people, channeling their . . . anger against the methods of imperialism. In every part of the homeland, the Iraqi woman fought hard for her place in society until she achieved encouraging progress which inspires pride and confidence.

Thousands of girls are entering schools every year and thousands of women go to work in factories, schools, hospitals and state establishments, apart from the great productive role performed by women in the rural areas.

Education of women is not restricted in our country to the primary stages, nor has women's employment been restricted to minor responsibilities. Iraq's five universities include a large proportion of female students and a number of women have acquired high qualifications in medicine and engineering. Some women are now teaching in the universities. Women in Iraq have also reached high positions in the government and become ministers and directors-general. Others are . . . working in such fields as the judiciary, the arts, research and journalism.

For the first time in the history of our country, Iraqi women, after the Revolution, occupied leading posts in the trade unions. . . .

The complete emancipation of women from the ties which held them back in the past, during the ages of despotism and ignorance, is a basic aim of the Party and the Revolution. Women make up one half of society. Our society will remain backward and in chains unless its women are liberated, enlightened and educated.

Freedom is based on enlightenment, science and an understanding of the national characteristics of the country as well as on respect for the interests of the masses and the responsibilities of the fight against imperialism and Zionism. It must aim at the attainment of the national and Pan-Arab objectives. Such a freedom will be able to harness the potential of women in such a way that will lead to the building up of a . . . unified country that is both strong and advanced.

We are all—in the Party and the Government, and in the social organizations—expected to encourage the recruitment of more women to the schools, government departments, the organizations of production, industry, agriculture, culture, information and all other kinds of institutions and services.

We are called upon to struggle tirelessly against all the material and psychological obstacles which stand in our way along this path.

The obstacles which stand in the way of women in the various areas of life are greater than those which are facing men. This fact makes it incumbent on all the awakened elements in society to support woman in her natural and legitimate endeavor to occupy her place in society.

Those who still look on women with the mentality and ideas of the ages of darkness and backwardness do not express the aspirations and ambitions of the Revolution. They are at variance with the principles of the Party which are essentially based on freedom and emancipation. Indeed, they are in opposition to every true desire for progress.

The Revolution is a leap towards an enlightened freedom which is placed at the service of the people and of the progress of mankind in general. It cannot be a genuine revolution if it does not aim at the liberation of woman and the development of her material and cultural conditions.

Those with a despotic and overbearing attitude who appoint themselves as guardians of woman and place artificial barriers in the way of her emancipation and full participation in society are not rendering their country and their people any service. They are in fact doing harm to their homeland and their people. They are trying, consciously or unconsciously, to dissipate their people's potential and hinder its progress.

The women of our country are the descendants of the immortal Arab women who fought valiantly side by side with their menfolk, wrote the poetry of chivalry and glory, and participated in the great Arab heritage of civilization. Thanks to their ... commitment to the Revolution and the ... interests of the masses, and their correct understanding of the national characteristics of our ... heritage, the Arab women, together with their Kurdish sisters and all other women of Iraq, are capable of following a correct path and playing their pioneering role in the construction of the revolutionary society.

The struggle against the camp of imperialism, Zionism and reaction, with all their modern means of science and destruction, requires committed, educated and free human beings. Any segregation of women or anything less than their full participation in society deprives the homeland of half of its citizens and half of its intellectual ... and fighting potential.

An enlightened mother who is educated and liberated can give the country a generation of conscious and committed fighters. What a crime it would be against the younger generation if women were deprived of their rights to freedom, education and full participation in the life of the community!

History and Ba'thist Totalitarianism

The Ba'th Party constructed a totalitarian state. In such a political system, the state, usually led by a single charismatic ruler, subordinates all aspects of its citizens' lives to the authority of a highly centralized government. The state holds a monopoly on the institutions of violence, so it can physically impose its views on society. According to Akram Fouad Khater, however, "one of the most striking aspects . . . is not the use of physical violence to achieve its goals and to minimize opposition but rather the attempt to shape citizens' views about a broad range of subject" (Khater, 263).

Toward this end, the Ba'th targeted youth, the next generation of its subjects, inculcating loyalty to the highly personalized fiefdom in which they lived. According to Eric Davis, "If the regime could convince Iraqi youth to view communists and other Iraqi nationalists as alien, disloyal, and intent on harming Iraq, and it could simultaneously shape the categories through which they viewed the past, present, and future, than the Ba'th's rivals would find it extremely difficult to mobilize the younger generation" (Davis, 157–58).

Teaching history is a way of shaping the values of a totalitarian state's subjects, and the Ba'thist regime made a concerted effort to rewrite history. In terms of domestic politics, the Ba'th expunged from the record any achievements by Communists, its main political rival (Davis, 157). In terms of foreign policy, the Ba'thist state emphasized Iraq's Mesopotamian and Arab Islamic history, thereby fostering a sense of cultural superiority over Syria and Egypt, which vied for leadership in the Arab world (158). History became a political tool devoid of intellectual rigor, and the Ba'th denied historians opportunities for rigorous debates.

Saddam Hussein addressed the need for the Ba'th Party to control history in a speech in the 1970s. The following excerpts from the speech are translated by Akram Fouad Khater and found in his anthology *Sources in the History of the Modern Middle East* (Boston: Houghton Mifflin, 2004), 264–65. As you read the speech, you should consider the following: What aspects of history does Hussein emphasize? What reasons does he give for emphasizing them? How would the emphasis serve the Ba'th Party?

[S]everal things should be taken into consideration in modern curriculums: age, the educational and scientific capabilities of the students and pupils; thus one does not say the same things—in terms of content and approach—to high school students as one would say to elementary school students.

When we speak to young children, who have limited scientific understanding, we must speak about some political or historical issues that we wish for them to internalize, in the absolute without any qualifications. For example, when we speak of Arab unity we must not occupy the little student with details and to engage him in a discussion of whether we are indeed a single nation or not. It is enough to speak of the Arab as one nation assuming that to be an absolute reality, with a brief summary about the role that colonialism played in dividing the [Arab] countries and nation in order to weaken it and maintain control over it. We should also portray the path to unity through struggle in a simplified form as well. Thus, when we speak about the Ba'ath Arab Socialist Party as a leading party, we should speak about it to the children as if it is an absolute reality. As to the details of why and how it became a leading party then we can show that through a discussion about the accomplishments of the party, the role of the party in saving the Iraqi people, and through a discussion of the Revolution without fatiguing the students at this stage with complicated theoretical . . . or political analyses. This is especially the case with the generation that did not live through the period preceding the Revolution of 17–30 June, 1968. . . . Discussing the Revolution and the Arab Ba'ath Socialist Party without speaking of the dark era that preceded the revolution—in social, political, economic, cultural and military terms—will not provide [an] . . . objective context for understanding the Revolution. The June revolution is great because of the accomplishments it attained from 18–30 June 1968 until now; but it . . . appears greater when we understand what preceded the revolution. It is important to speak of the dark period which preceded the revolution . . . so that coming generations will understand the greatness of their revolution. We must avoid speaking in detail about matters that are constantly . . . changing because they will appear small in later stages. . . .

Here I find it necessary to speak, educate and concentrate on the fact that Iraq is part of the Arab nation more than speaking about the Iraqi people being part of the Arab nation. In this manner we can achieve our goal without upsetting opposing nationalist tendencies amongst the other part of our people.

In our national education we must speak about self-rule [for the minorities]. And when we address the subject of self-rule we must not get lost in too many details so as not to make the administrative structure of self a "Chinese Wall" that separates the Arab from the Kurd in Iraq. For instance, when we speak about Iraqi folklore we do not see it necessary to speak about Kurdish folklore, and another that is Arab and a third that is Turkish . . . etc. Rather, it should be presented simply as Iraqi folklore. So we would say for example: this is a dance from the South of Iraq from al-Nassiriya [an Iraqi town], and this is a dance from al-Sulaymaniya [another city] . . . Exaggerated actions to show that we care about local nationalisms [within Iraq] will cause immense harm in our short- and long-term plans. . . . To take for example our starting point, by way of imagining equality between the Arab and others, as saying that the Arab wears the *'iqaal* [one type of headdress] and the Kurd wears the *laffat* [another type of headdress] around the head . . . is a big mistake because this image will have negative psychological effects and will lead to dangerous . . . political results. Perhaps there is someone who is . . . plotting to maintain a Chinese wall that separates our people psychologically. . . .

When we speak about our people's nationalist sacrifices we must not limit our discourse to talking about political and military actions. Rather we need to point to the big sacrifices that the citizens have done, and continue to perform, in the field of production and other activities in order to build up the nation. He who endangers himself to save a machine is worthy of mentioning with pride in order to strengthen the tendency to consider work a basic tenet in the honor and progress of the nation . . . and to strengthen the tendency among the sons of our people to safeguard the socialist property.

The United States Considers Assistance to Kurds, 1972

To buttress its power at home, the Ba'thist regime would place itself fully in the Soviet camp within the context of the Cold War. In January 1972, Saddam Hussein visited Moscow. The talks there led to the signing of the Iraqi-Soviet Treaty of Friendship and Cooperation in April. Only two months after the signing of this treaty—and the very same month that the Ba'th nationalized the Iraq Petroleum Company—the U.S. Department of State issued the following memo. As you read this memo, you should consider the following: What was the strategic benefit to the United States in offering aid to the Kurds? Why would the Kurds want more than money?

June 23, 1972
MEMORANDUM FOR: GENERAL HAIG
FROM: HAROLD H. SAUNDERS

SUBJECT: Background for Your Talk with Kurdish Leaders

... The attached is so easily read that I will not summarize it here. The most useful thing I can do is to point out the main considerations that would go into a decision for providing some $1.5 million monthly subsidy or "moral support" that the Kurdish leaders are looking for:

—The major view in town is that we should stay out of direct support for the Kurds. As Helms [Richard Helms] understands it, the Iranian intelligence has already committed the Iranians to paying half of the subsidy [BLACKED OUT]. In short, there is enough money in the area to do this and this is one case where we could well leave this effort to local initiative.

—The second major point to consider is that what the Kurds really want to do is to get from the US some indication of support that they can noise around the Middle East. So anything we do in the way of "moral support" cannot by its nature stay quiet because if it were to do Barzani any good he would have to tell others. This would put us semi-openly into one of the longest ongoing guerilla wars in the Middle East.

—On the other hand, there is a certain attraction to trying to help the Kurds maintain some independence of the Iraqi government so that they can keep the Soviets from helping the Baath party consolidate its rule and relationship with the Communists in Iraq. However, admitting the desirability of any reasonable effort to thwart the Soviets, the question remains whether US support is essential to the success of the effort. The Kurds have kept their position with Iranian and [BLACKED OUT] support for a number of years, and the US could well take the position that this is a case for the regional countries most interested to continue. If we provide moral support, perhaps it should be in the form of acknowledged acquiescence expressed directly to them rather than to support for the Kurds.

Your main purpose in seeing these fellows will be simply to hear them out and to enable Henry [Kissinger] to send some reflections back to the Shah after hearing their case.

I might add that I have had several feelers from some of these Kurdish emissaries and so far have turned them aside. If you would like, I would be glad to go with you to this meeting with Helms and these emissaries.

The 1974–1975 War in Kurdish Iraq

When the Ba'th first came to power, the party needed peace with the Kurds in order to secure its power. By 1974, however, the Ba'th had succeeded in consolidating its power, and so the party's relationship to Kurdish leaders began to change. That year, the Ba'thist government promulgated the Autonomy Law. This dictate confined Kurdistan to a smaller area than alluded to in earlier agreements. Further, it placed strict limitations on autonomy, thereby contradicting the March Manifesto of 1970 (Yildiz, 20–22). Mustafa Barzani refused to accept the agreement, preferring instead to call up his peshmergas, or soldiers, and fight for Kurdish rights. He believed Iran and the United States backed Kurdish aspirations. His faith in these political actors would ultimately be misplaced, for each used the Kurds in pursuit of their own national interests (McDowall, 335–41).

Hiner Saleem lived through the 1974–1975 war, and he recounts his experience in a work of autobiographical fiction titled *My Father's Rifle: A Childhood in Kurdistan*, translated by Catherine Temerson (New York: Picador, 2004), 37–41 and 48–51. Born in 1964, the author grew up in Kurdistan. He fled Iraq for Syria in the late 1970s. He would later make his home in Paris, where he began directing movies. This excerpt begins with the details of how the war began in March 1974, when there was an assassination attempt against Mustafa Barzani. It ends with the accord signed on 6 March 1975 that put an end to this conflict. The narrator of this tale would have been fourteen years old at the start of this excerpt. As you read this account, you should consider the following: How did Kurdish-Iraqi relations affect ordinary people? How did it affect social relations? Economic opportunities? How does this work provide insight into the political situation of leaders?

> One day, my father came home agitated. He . . . pulled out his Brno from under the mattress, and went back to the party headquarters, followed by my brother, his Plimout in hand. The worst had just been avoided! A delegation of religious Iraqis had gone up to the mountains to meet with our general and to give him a golden Koran as a gift; without their knowledge, it had been filled with TNT by Saddam Hussein's agents. Just as they were presenting the Koran to the general, it exploded, but miraculously he escaped unharmed, protected by the man who was serving him tea. Order was later restored. My father put his Brno away under the mattress and my brother's Plimout found its niche again above the conjugal bed. As for me, I filled baskets with figs and, against my mother's advice, went to sell them to the soldiers in the barracks to earn some pocket money.
>
> One Thursday, Cheto and I were standing behind the barbed wire of the barracks, crying out, "Figs, apricots, blackberries," when two soldiers walked toward us. They were not the young conscripts we were used to having as customers. They were older, stronger, and much tougher-looking. They were carrying truncheons and wearing the red armbands of the military police. We

wanted to turn on our heels, but they called to us, "Children, don't leave. Bring us your fruit." As soon as we were near them, they pounced on us. They insulted us as they hit us. "Children of savages.... You come here with your shitty fruit to spy on us!" They hit harder and harder, pummeling and kicking us. We were raw from their blows. Our fruit was trampled underfoot. When they had had enough, they let us run away, limping and stumbling, and shouted after us, "If you come back here, we'll cut off your heads like sheep."

When I returned to our neighborhood, I passed tearful women from our family, walking behind a coffin carried by the men, my father and my uncle in the lead. I went up to Ramo. "Who died?" "No one." "So what's this coffin for?" "It's empty." "Then why are the women crying?" "We're going to kill cousin Mushir." I asked why, but he made no reply.

When they arrived in front of his door, my father and my uncle Avdal Khan, tense, shouted "Mushir!" Our cousin climbed up on the roof to escape. My uncle called out to him, "Come and see, we've brought you your coffin."

Mushir, panicked, was stranded on the rooftop. My father added, "You've dishonored the family," and my uncle called him a collaborator and fired on him. The women were ... weeping around the coffin. Avdal Khan fired a second shot. "Why do you go to Mosul so often? To meet whom? The security people? Have you become a spy, Mushir?" Mushir, terrified, tried to hide as best he could. "I'm not a collaborator!" he yelled. My uncle broke down the door, climbed up to the roof with my father tagging behind, and caught Mushir. My father looked at him sadly. "There have been rumors about you for some time.... We didn't want to believe them.... But you were never willing to say what you're up to in Mosul. You're out of work yet you always have money. We must avenge the honor of the family...." My father was interrupted. My uncle had just fired a bullet in Mushir's knee.

He was on the verge of firing a second time but my father pushed the gun aside with his hand and addressed Mushir again. "If it's true that you're not a collaborator, here, take my gun and fire a bullet into your head! Then we'll believe you. Otherwise we'll have to kill you." Mushir ... moaned and pleaded, "I go to Mosul for business!" "What business?" my uncle shouted. My father exhorted him, "Mushir, kill yourself.... Your coffin is ready.... We'll make sure you're buried with dignity." As he tried to escape, Mushir was brought to a halt by a bullet fired by my uncle. He fell from the roof, among the women, right near his coffin.

Later it was discovered that Mushir had kept a mistress in Mosul. He had not been a traitor.

The situation was deteriorating from day to day. The number of security officers grew steadily, and the tension kept rising. Trenches were dug around our town and everyone got ready to defend their neighborhood. My father and seven other men mounted guard in a trench opposite the barracks that dominated the town on the little hill behind our orchard. They expected an imminent attack. At the slightest signal from General Barzani, they were ready to launch an assault against the Iraqi barracks. The women and children were to be grouped together in a shelter. My father immediately offered our fortress-house. "I had it built especially for a time like this." No one questioned the sturdiness of the walls in our house, but the problem was its orientation. When it was built, my father had wanted all the windows to face . . . in the direction of the orchard and the hill overlooking the house. It was a beautiful view. He couldn't have foreseen that within a few months barracks would go up on that hill, a few hundred yards in front of our windows. This was why . . . it was decided that the women and children would . . . stay at my uncle Avdal Khan's house.

I didn't want the happiness of this recent period—the joy in the freedom, the concerts, the painting—to disappear. But it was obvious the putsch leaders no longer respected Kurdish rights and Kurdish autonomy. This being the case, I wanted a gun and I wanted to join the men in the trenches. But since there weren't enough weapons to go around, I was put in charge of supplying the fighters. My father and his men were very confident. Their morale was boosted by Voice of America, which referred to us as heroes and freedom fighters. It was truly reassuring to have an ally as important as America. My father kept repeating, "We're Indo-Europeans, like the Americans!" And to reassure himself even more, he added, as his father had, "We're British." Radio Moscow was now treating us as rebels, but we couldn't have cared less: let them "march to socialism" with the Baath Party! Even kids younger than I knew the names Nixon and Kissinger, and we loved them. We stayed in our trenches for several days without anything happening. Then we were given orders to move out of the town because our tanks and airplanes were going to rid the town of all the Iraqi forces and allow us very shortly to return, victorious. When my mother asked, "Where are the tanks and planes the Americans gave us?" my father said with conviction, "They're hidden in our mountains, and the planes are sheltered in clandestine airports." All of us waited for a sign from the general to march on Kurdistan and liberate it.

That was how we left for the north, for the mountains, convinced we would return, victorious, a month later. . . .

There were air bombardments day and night, and still no planes of ours in the sky. We started to lose hope.

The headquarters withdrew even farther north and we had to abandon our house. We went to hide in two huge caves, one for women, the other for men. There were no more days or nights. . . . My father sent Morse code messages uninterruptedly from the men's cave. We were surrounded by wounded people who had to be cared for with inadequate means. Those killed in the bombings were buried immediately. I helped the nurses and slept with my father's Morse code beeping on one side and the moans of the wounded on the other. . . . [A] wounded man next to me was moaning his children's names, then . . . stopped. He had . . . died. . . .

Word went out that Iraq and Iran were about to conclude a treaty, at our expense, with Kissinger's consent.

On the Kurdish radio station, a poem was declaimed describing the heavenly beauty of our mountains and the pure water of our rivers, the Tigris and the Euphrates. But I was no longer a kid. The mountains I saw were harsh, the rivers full of worms, and the sky saturated with napalm bombs.

We received orders for the women, children, and old people to head for the Iranian frontier. We could no longer think things through rationally. . . . A mortal solitude swept over our people. We were being betrayed by the Americans as we had been previously betrayed by the Soviets. On a beautiful March day, Saddam Hussein of Iraq signed a treaty with the Shah of Iran; we were losing our last support. A long letter by General Barzani addressed to Kissinger, begging him to keep his promise, was read over our radio, but Kissinger abandoned us to our fate.

I went to the *peshmergas'* baker, but there was no longer anyone there. There was nothing but our clandestine radio station still broadcasting appeals to the entire world—Jesus, Muhammad, Gandhi, Buddha, Abraham Lincoln—to come to the aid of our people. I saw some *peshmergas* commit suicide in despair. Others wanted to hide in the mountains and resist, but the general understood we were caught in an inescapable net: the choice was between accepting defeat or extermination. We took the road of exile.

Along with other families, we piled into a truck bound for the Iranian frontier; there was no alternative. After several kilometers, we climbed out of the truck, exhausted, our bundles of belongings on our shoulders. We crossed the frontier under the supervision of the Iranian police and were herded up a small hill where we sat on our heels, surrounded by soldiers. I felt as if I were in a cemetery, with all those people around me, the crouching women in their dark dresses, their heads buried in their knees, weeping. We were annihilated, and I started to cry. We were taken to a camp made up of tents. It was a gift from the United Nations. We were refugees.

Then the men arrived, heads lowered, defeated—among them my two brothers and my father, General Barzani's personal operator. Out of fear of Savak, the Iranian secret police, we couldn't cry out against the Iranians' betrayal of us.

Dozens of refugee camps stretched along the Iranian border. We were forbidden to go out without a Savak safe-conduct. And yet this land, too, was Kurdish; it was one of the quarters of our heart according to the sketch of our young teacher in Nauperdan.... Passing by a tent, I heard a man moan: it was Timar, one of the Kurdish musicians from Syria. It started to rain; our camp became a field of mud.

The summer went by with its blazing heat, and then winter came, bitingly cold that year.

We were moved to another camp. We now lived in long sheds with small square cells giving out on a central passageway; each family was assigned a cell. Time stood still; we had nothing to do. A few boys and I would leave the shed and walk around and around inside the camps, like dogs. Once I spotted my brother Dilovan standing apart with some friend. I wanted to go up to him, but he signaled me to keep away; they were getting drunk.

Muhammad Baqir al-Sadr and the Principle of Social Justice

Iraqi Shi'is were never fully incorporated into the Ba'thist political system. This is because Shi'is believe in a doctrine of the Imamate, whereby some religious scholars are supposed to have tangible political influence within any given polity. The Ba'thist government had no interest in sharing its influence among disparate groups of Iraqis. In 1968, when the secular Ba'th Party took over, some Shi'is "had begun a series of strikes and protests in Najaf aimed at curtailing government intervention in Shii affairs" (Fattah, 217). Fearing Shi'i loyalties to a religious hierarchy, rather than the existing state structures, the Ba'th persecuted Shi'is and kept them out of the networks of state patronage in Ba'thist Iraq. Thus, and as early as 1969, for example, the Ba'th regime closed down the religious university in the holy city of Najaf (Tripp, 195). The next year, the Ba'th arrested Shi'i leaders. Such acts, however, only led to the strengthening of opposition by a majority who felt left out due to their religious beliefs and identification.

The Dawa Party of Sayyid Muhammad Baqir al-Sadr (1931–1980) was the most influential opposition group—Shi'i or otherwise—to emerge in the 1970s. This group was formed by Shi'i clerics in the mid-1950s, at the time of Abd al-Karim Qasim's coup d'état. These founding religious leaders feared that secular

Communism had become all too popular among Shi'i youth. In 1970, the young firebrand al-Sadr took over the party, although some of his clerical counterparts feared his radicalism. Under his aegis, al-Sadr continued to foster and facilitate the growth of the Dawa Party throughout the 1970s, a task for which the Ba'th arrested him several times. Ultimately, Al-Sadr and the Dawa Party advocated against the Ba'th regime, wanting instead to see a form of Islamic governance in Iraq (Tripp, 196). The Ba'th finally killed al-Sadr and his sister in 1980.

Al-Sadr published two books on Islamic jurisprudence during the course of his career as a scholar. He was very preoccupied with the creation of an Islamic economy, a potentially problematic issue in oil-rich Iraq. Al-Sadr thought that "an Islamic economics system offers the best prospects for social justice; but it is also desirable because it is independent of Western models" (Euben and Zaman, 183). Religious experts, in his opinion, should check the base and exploitive nature of secular agents. Al-Sadr's discussion of Islamic economics can be found in *Princeton Readings in Islamist Thought: Texts and Contexts from al-Banna to Bin Laden,* edited by Roxanne L. Euben and Muhammad Qasim Zaman (Princeton, N.J.: Princeton University Press, 2009), 191–93. As you read the text, you should consider the following: Why is social justice a polemical idea in the Ba'thist state of Iraq? Why would the Ba'th regime feel threatened by al-Sadr's call for an Islamic economy?

> The third component in the Islamic economy is the principle of social justice. This is embodied in Islam by the elements and ... that Islam provided for the system of the distribution of wealth in Islamic society. These enable the distribution to achieve the realization of Islamic justice and to be in harmony with the values with which it is concerned. When Islam put social justice within the basic principles from which its economic theory is composed, it did not adopt social justice in its general abstract conception, nor did it call for a form of human societies that differ in their view of social justice according to their cultural ideas and concepts about life. Rather, Islam defined and crystallized this concept within a specific social plan. After that, it was able to embody this determination in a living social reality, all of whose veins and arteries throbbed with the Islamic concept of justice....
>
> The Islamic image of social justice contains two general principles, each one of which has its own lines and particularities. The first of them is the principle of general mutual responsibility; the other is the principle of social balance. Just social values are realized within the Islamic conception of mutual responsibility and balance, and it is in them that the Islamic ideal of social justice is found.... The steps that Islam took in the course of creating the most excellent

human society during its glorious historical experiment were plain and clear with regard to its concern for its principal component of its economy.

This concern was clearly reflected in the first speech that the Prophet delivered and the first political action he took in his new state.

The great Messenger inaugurated his guiding statement—as it is reported—with this speech:

> People, make preparations for yourselves. By God, each of you should know that he will die and he will leave his sheep without a shepherd. Then his Lord will say to him: Did not my Messenger come to you and tell you? And I gave you wealth and showed preference to you. What have you prepared for yourself? Then each of you will look to the left and the right and will see nothing. You will look in front and see only Hell. Whoever is able to protect his face from the Fire . . . let him do it. Whoever does not find that, let him use a good word. For one good action will be rewarded ten times to seven hundred times. . . .

His political activity began with the making of a brotherhood between the emigrants from Mecca and the supporters from Medina, and the application of mutual responsibility between them, for the sake of the realization of the social justice that Islam aimed at.

These are the basic elements in the Islamic economy:

1. Ownership of varied kinds, in the light of which distribution is determined
2. A freedom, limited by Islamic values, in the fields of production, exchange, and consumption
3. A social justice . . . will guarantee happiness to society, and whose foundation is mutual responsibility and balance. . . .

It is a realistic economy in its goals because in its systems and laws it aims at goals that are in harmony with the nature, tendencies, and general characteristics of human reality; it always tries not to ask more than is humanly possible in its legal reckoning; and it does not take humanity soaring into high imaginary skies beyond its powers and abilities. It always determines its economic plan on the basis of a real view of man. It sets out real aims that agree with that view. An imaginary economy, like for example communism, may be content to adopt an unreal aim and set forth to attain a new humanity, purified from all tendencies of egotism and capable of distributing works and wealth among men without any need for an instrument of government to direct the distribution, a humanity secure from all kinds of disputes and strife. . . . However, this does not conform with the nature of Islamic legislation or with the realism that it is characterized by in its goals and aims.

... [I]t is also real in its method. Just as it aims at real goals ... similarly it gives a real material guarantee for the realization of these goals. It is not satisfied with the guarantees of advice and guidance, which preachers and teachers give because it means going beyond such aims to the sphere of chance and guesses. For example, when it aims at the creation of general mutual responsibility, it does not seek for this only by methods of direction and the arousal of emotion; rather, it supports it with a legal guarantee that makes its realization essential in every circumstance.

Ba'thist Response to Shi'i Protests, 1979

Juman Kubba was three years old when the Ba'th came to power in 1968, and some of her earliest memories are of Ba'thist repression. Her parents were well-to-do professionals who did not join the Ba'th party. And, according to Kubba, they were subsequently targeted by it. Her father spent more than one and a half years in prison. Her mother was fired from her job as a schoolteacher. The family maid bugged their house. The tenant to whom they rented an apartment watched over them on behalf of the Ba'thist police Alamin. And then, as described below, her brother was arrested while commemorating Ashura in 1979.

Ashura is a day of mourning for Shi'is, and the holiday's political overtones were especially strong in Sunni-dominated Ba'thist Iraq. Ashura is a holiday marking the seventh-century martyrdom of Husayn ibn Ali, the grandson of the Prophet Muhammad, at the Battle of Karbala. It takes place on 10 Muharram in the lunar calendar of the Islamic world. That day marks the moment when forces loyal to Yazid, ruler of the reigning Umayyad dynasty, massacred Husayn and his seventy-two followers. They murdered the grandson of the Prophet because they wanted to retain their power over the growing Islamic empire. This massacre led eventually to the sectarian division between Shi'is and Sunnis. Shi'is believe that Husayn ibn Ali was the rightful successor to Yazid's predecessor. Conceptualized as a battle between good and evil, contemporary celebrations, which include re-enactments and self-flagellation, often offer an implicit protest to existing political structures.

Interestingly, Kubba does not make any claims to be Shi'i in this excerpt or in the entirety of her memoirs. Nevertheless, references herein make this seem highly likely. She recorded the following memories in *The First Evidence: A Memoir of Life in Iraq under Saddam Hussein* (Jefferson, N.C.: McFarland, 2003), 121–22 and 125–27. As you read this excerpt, you should try and put it in its historic context. What else is going on in 1979 both in Iraq and in neighboring Iran? And why would the Ba'thist government subsequently target a Shi'i festival?

After all we had endured, we thought the Ba'ath terror was over. But there was more of it waiting for us. In 1979 we had yet another ordeal with the Ba'ath government. My brother Amer went to the holy city of Karbala and did not come back. During the period from the time my Dad was detained until the late 1970s, there was tremendous escalation in the viciousness and cruelty of the government and the way they dealt with any potential political opposition. People were being detained and executed by the hundreds. In fact many people vanished during this period. We heard about people who were arrested at college or school or even right in their homes. We heard about many young men who were executed. I have to say that the period of the mid and late seventies was a horrible time to be living in Iraq. So many good people were victims of these atrocities; all of them were well educated, and many were from upper class families. Every week or so we would hear about some mother whose sons were missing or detained. And later we heard about such young men being dumped as corpses at the doorsteps of their homes. They were all "shaved off" and vanished. We heard one story of a leading opposition figure by the name of Abu Esam: they threw him in an acid bath to torture him and he died screaming in the compound. We heard stories about women who were brought to the prison to be gang-raped in front of their detained husbands or fathers just to intimidate the prisoners and make them say something that they did not want to say. There were episodes where the secret police would detain someone and shoot him right there on the spot—no charge, no court order, nothing. Alamin people were allowed to kill anyone without further responsibility. I can only imagine what the trauma would be like for the families. We heard of some families who had this happen to them. The government could arrest you simply because someone "reported you" to Alamin as anti-Ba'ath, or your neighbor betrayed you and said that you bought some magazine or book which was censored by the government. In fact, books of the scholar Muhammad Baqir Alsadr, who was an antigovernment charismatic religious leader, if found in your home, were grounds for arresting an entire family and naming them as anti-Ba'ath reactionaries. It was madness. In fact we had such books at home. My brothers had bought these books in the past, before the censorship of publications became prevalent. These were not political books, as political books did not exist in Iraq. They were more books of religion and philosophy. The publication and sale of all books and magazines in Iraq were controlled by the government. Because Alsadr's books had become illegal and owning them was a crime and could jeopardize your life, we were in a dilemma. We had to get rid of these books. We decided to bury them in the dirt of the garden to hide them. My sister Zeena went out in the garden at night. She dug in the dirt and hid those books away. Later, we heard that the secret police knew about this trick, which many people were using to hide books and other materials. A friend of Zeena's told her that the secret police had come to her house and dug the whole garden up in order to find what was hidden there. They found some books . . . and they arrested her brother. . . . [M]y father was alarmed. He went out in the garden with Zeena and took out all those books that she had hidden there. We collected the books and burned them in the trash. It was such a shame that we had to burn these books to protect our lives. It was sad to see books burning in flames. The books turned into ashes. It was a somber moment. . . .

My brother Amer went to Karbala to observe the religious activities of Ashura, which many people in Iraq observed: old, young, educated, uneducated, Sunni and Shia. It was not so much an ideological thing to observe these traditions. It was socio-political. These rituals had become a vortex for anti-government sentiments. So while people were reciting their religious chants commemorating the death of Imam Hussein, who was murdered many centuries ago by a ruthless ruler of his time, some people also chanted anti-Ba'ath government slogans. The youth in Iraq had grown tired of the lack of freedom and . . . were more apt to participate in . . . activities against the government. They had no attachments or responsibilities to families, they were emotional and carefree; they demanded more freedom and political rights; and they still had their whole lives ahead and it was important that they bring about change to this repressive system.

During those events my brother was in the vicinity of the demonstrations which involved some one thousand people or so. He and the demonstrators were chanting: "God is Great. God is Great. . . ." It was peaceful and they were simply chanting slogans demanding more freedom: freedom to travel, to buy books, to talk freely and gather, to form non-governmental organizations and so on. . . . The government forces were watching for such an event; they immediately intervened and crushed this demonstration, detaining or killing dozens of people on the spot. The place was swept quickly by thousands of armed security officers. There was chaos. My brother was detained and transported to Baghdad to the main Alamin headquarters.

This demonstration and the arrests were significant in the political history of Iraq. It is known today as the Uprising of 1979. The government intervention was much more severe than that in China in 1989 in Tiananmen Square, events by which the whole world was enraged and rightfully so. Of course people in the West never heard of this event in 1979 in Iraq because all news was controlled by the government. In fact the Iraqi news service did not report such activities. We . . . knew about these events via word of mouth and from people who lived in Karbala and others who managed to escape the events. In Iraq in those days, and even today, no foreign news agencies were allowed to attend such events unless they were specifically invited by the government, and they would be escorted all the time by government officers. The government crushed political events like these before they expanded. It is sad that no one knew about it or reported it and no world leaders were enraged by it.

Amer left home Thursday afternoon and was supposed to be back Friday around noon. . . . [H]e did not come back. Fear and agony hit us. . . . My mother feared something was wrong. She said that my brother had told her he would be back as soon as the rituals were over. Also, he did not call home as he promised if there was any delay—he knew how much my parents worried about him. We spent Friday in . . . agony as it became obvious that something had gone wrong. That day was sad and gloomy. . . . I too was worried about Amer and I thought that my mother's fears were well placed. Actually, both my parents were now worried and very concerned. My Dad was usually calm and cautious and not as emotional as my Mom, but even he was worried.

My father felt defeated that his son may be in the hands of the regime. He had been planning for all my brothers to leave. But it was getting harder by the week. Every couple of weeks or so, some new law or regulation was announced that made it impossible to plan any travel or any way for young men to leave the country. Dad felt that he had failed in this task. He now just wanted to know that Amer was safe. . . . Dad was dismayed that he had failed to get Amer out sooner, with my other brothers. But because Amer was still in university, it was nearly impossible to get permission for him to leave.

My sisters and I tried to help my parents in this terror that was befalling us. We called some friends of Amer to see if they had heard from him or whether they knew anything. Their response was in the negative. They had gone to Karbala too but had come back before the events. They had seen Amer there in Karbala before they left. We were not sure whether they were telling the truth or were afraid . . . to speak on the phone. My mother could not sleep that night: She . . . cried and prayed.

The next morning, my father drove to Karbala. He did not go to Karbala that often. As he was driving to find the police headquarters, he saw some shops and homes with broken windows; glass was shattered on the streets. There were damaged cars. It was obvious that some battle had occurred. Dad had a thick feeling in his chest. He knew it was going to be bad news. He went to police headquarters. He got to the office. It was a small building and there were . . . armed men in military uniform. He explained his case and pleaded with the officers there.

"My son is missing," he told them. He came to Karbala and he is missing. I came . . . from Baghdad to look for my son."

"Oh." One officer responded. "Why was your son here, if you live in Baghdad?"

"Yes," Dad replied, "He came to Karbala to watch the Ashura processions."

The officers laughed and said, "Oh, yes, we detained many young men. They are hooligans, and they are not sincere Iraqi citizens. They were arrested and taken back to Baghdad to the main Alamin office."

Dad was shocked and enraged but he maintained his composure.

"My son is not a hooligan. He is an educated young man, he attends the university of Baghdad. He was just here to watch the events like people have done for hundreds of years. Can you show me whether his name is among those whom you arrested? How do I know otherwise whether my son was among them?"

"Look, mister," the officer said, "we do not keep records. We arrested hooligans. We shipped them to Baghdad. They will be processed in Baghdad. We do not know who they are. . . . They all deserve to die."

Bibliography

Air University (U.S.). *Survival Geography of Iraq*. Gunter Air Force Base, Ala.: Arctic, Desert, Tropic Information Center, Air University, 1969.

Al-Falaki, Safá. *Iraq on the Move*. Baghdad: Ministry of Information, 1971.

British Overseas Trade Board. *Iraq*. London: The Board, 1976.

Cordiner, Bill. *Diplomatic Wanderings: From Saigon to the South Seas*. London: Radcliffe Press, 2003.

Iraq. *Archaeological Aspects in Iraq*. Baghdad: Ministry of Information, Directorate General of Antiquities, 1971.

Iraq. *Mesopotamia Yesterday, Iraq Today*. Lausanne, Switz.: SARTEC, 1977.

Khater, Akram Fouad, ed. *Sources in the History of the Modern Middle East*. 2nd ed. Boston: Wadsworth, Cengage Learning, 2004.

League of Arab States. *The Arab World*. S.l.: Jamiyat al-Duwal al-Arabi, 1970.

Nakamura, Goro. *Dawn of New Mesopotamia: The People of Iraq*. Tokyo: Japan Press Service, 1978.

Polservice Consulting Engineers Warsaw-Poland. *Kadhemiyah Old Quarters: Detailed Plan 1: 500; Report*. Baghdad: Town Planning Office for City of Baghdad, 1974.

Ramzi, N. *Iraq, the Land and the People: Photos*. London: Iraqi Cultural Centre, 1977.

SARTEC. *Iraq, 10 Years of Revolutionary Achievements*. Lausanne, Switz.: SARTEC, 1979.

United States. *Background Notes, Iraq*. Department of State publication, 7975. Washington, D.C.: Office of Media Services, Bureau of Public Affairs, 1976.

United States. *Republic of Iraq: Background Notes*. Department of State publication, 7975. Washington, D.C.: Office of Media Services, Bureau of Public Affairs, 1971.

Young, Gavin. *Return to the Marshes: Life with the Marsh Arabs of Iraq*. London: Collins, 1977.

7

The Iran-Iraq War, 1980–1990

Saddam Hussein assumed the Ba'thist presidency in 1979, and within one year Iraq became embroiled in a cataclysmic conflict with neighboring Iran. In retrospect, the lead-up to the Iran-Iraq War actually began when two very different personalities assumed power in each combatant country. In Iraq, as already stated, the secularist Hussein assumed the Ba'thist presidency; that same year, Islamic forces replaced the Western-oriented Reza Shah Pahlavi (1919–1980) with the theocratic Shi'i Ayatollah Ruhollah Khomeini (1902–1989). Hussein and his Ba'thist cohort felt threatened by Islamic Iran. Shi'is, after all, were a majority in Iraq, so it seemed possible that Khomeini might be able to influence their behavior. This fear was heightened by the fact that some Iraqi Shi'is were beginning to form opposition groups based on religious beliefs. Fearing Shi'ism as a political force, Hussein outlawed the Dawa Party and then executed its leader Ayatollah Muhammad Baqir al-Sadr and his sister.

Iran's Ayatollah Khomeini, a charismatic figure, was justifiably incensed, and he threatened to call on Iraqi Shi'is to overthrow the secular Ba'thist regime. This, in turn, led Saddam Hussein to exile about 40,000 long-established Shi'is in Iraq, claiming their loyalties were with Iran. Ever wary, and maybe reasonably so in this case, Hussein believed that Iran would aid both the Kurds and the Shi'is in order to destabilize his regime. Given this political assessment, Hussein decided that he needed to strike at Iran before Khomeini could consolidate his power and spread Islamic revolution. As an excuse for making war on his neighbor, Hussein claimed that Iraq should have full rights to the Shatt al-Arab waterway, which was located at the head of the Persian Gulf. He would also claim that this was in fact a preventive war with Iran.

Expecting a quick victory, Hussein ordered the invasion of Iran on 22 September 1980. The war, however, which is called either the Iran-Iraq War or the first Persian Gulf War, lasted a brutal eight years. The historian Hala Fattah notes that "the Iran-Iraq War of the 1980s was the longest and costliest war ever fought between two countries" (Fattah, 223). Much like World War I, soldiers fought from trenches that were surrounded by barbed wire, and they charged the enemy with bayonets. And, also like World War I, poison gas was used as a weapon. Fighting such a war of attrition requires a lot of manpower, and the numbers in the army grew to staggering amounts. In Iraq, the military increased from 190,000 men to one million (Cleveland, 419). The Iran-Iraq War ended on 20 August 1988, although the official cease-fire was not actually signed until 1990.

The cost of the war in terms of economic development was incalculable, and the mortality rate was almost unimaginable. Regarding economic development, Iraq emerged with a staggering war debt of over $80 billion. Its only port Basra was bombed, leaving the country virtually landlocked. The economist Kamran Mofid "calculated that the total cost of the war was $452.6 billion to Iraq and $644.3 billion to Iran, based on a combination of 'damage to the infrastructure; estimated oil revenue losses; and the estimated GNP losses'" (Farouk-Sluglett and Sluglett, 271). Even worse was the unbelievable mortality rate. There were at least half a million Iraqis and Iranians—civilian and soldiers—killed in the conflict. Many who came home—at least 750,000—were wounded. Since the war ended in an absolute stalemate in which neither side gained an inch of ground, it was truly "a war without a winner" (Fattah, 223).

This chapter tries to shine a light on a catastrophic war that, quite frankly, received relatively little public attention in the United States either during it or afterward. The chapter begins with a speech in which Hussein manipulates historic and contemporary events in order to convince the Arab states of the Persian Gulf to support Iraq's efforts to fight Iranians. It next provides a view of the fighting of this war by Georges Sada, an Iraqi officer. The United States played a critical role in buttressing Iraqi forces, so this chapter includes a policy document that sheds light on the U.S. State Department's thinking. The actual war is seen through a young Iraqi soldier's eyes, one stationed in the Kurdish north. A wartime correspondent provides a horrific look at the battlefields in the south. Since this war had a significant effect on families, this chapter also includes a short story by a woman who describes a wife's effort to reintegrate her husband to civilian life. The chapter then turns to al Anfal, a term signifying the Iraqi state's efforts to eradicate the Kurdish population at the end of the war. The basis of the end of this war was UN SC Res 598, passed in 1987 and accepted in 1990.

Saddam Hussein Justifies the War

In Iraq, many people referred to the Iran-Iraq War as "Saddam's Qadisiyya." This term reflects Hussein's use of history to create a sense that the Iran-Iraq War was a continuation of tensions that had existed since the seventh century. It refers to the Battle of al-Qadisiyya, which took place in 637 (Ghareeb, 186–87). In that battle, 8,000 Arab Muslim troops thoroughly trounced 30,000 Persians fighting for the Zoroastrian Sassanid dynasty. It was fought in the region of present-day Iraq, and the Arab victory allowed for the spread of Islam in Mesopotamia. During the Iran-Iraq War, Hussein proposed that the battle against Iran was a continuation of this struggle. To underscore this interpretation, the Ba'th produced an epic film about this event, and it issued stamps with images of it. According to Ofra Bengio, "the myths woven around al-Qadisiyya are a most instructive example of the Ba'thi technique of using an event with a core of historical truth that is deeply etched into the collective memory in order to further the party's ideology of Arab nationalism" (Bengio, 173).

The use—and misuse—of history did not just occur within Iraq, as the Ba'thist government pressured its subjects to continue the fight against Iran. Hussein also tried to manipulate historic and contemporary events for his Arab neighbors, particularly those of the wealthy Gulf States. Hussein needed both the ideological support of his neighbors as well as their economic backing. The following speech demonstrates Hussein's efforts to justify the Iran-Iraq War to an international audience. Hussein presented this speech to the Organization of the Islamic Conference, which consists of fifty-seven member states from all over the world. It was given in January 1981, less than six months after the war started. As you read the speech, you should consider the following: How does Hussein explain the origins of the Iran-Iraq War? Does Hussein present Iraqi efforts as offensive or defensive? How does Hussein, heretofore a Ba'thist secularist, encourage his audience to fear a victory by the Islamic Republic of Iran? And how does he use history to foster support for Iraq's efforts?

> We pray to God Almighty now that the leaders of the Islamic States are gathered in the holy city of Mecca in the land of divine revelation and the starting point of the great message of Islam to inspire us with determination, strength and reason for the purpose of achieving the great goals for which we are gathered here, and realizing the positive results in the service of our holy religion and our believing people. . . .
>
> Any problem cannot be divorced from its historical framework. . . . The efforts to solve the present . . . conflict in a[n] . . . honourable manner require . . . understanding to the nature of the conflict and . . . of its correct historical background.
>
> The problem between Iraq and Iran goes back to more than 450 years of history. . . . It is not a mere boundary problem, nor is it a minor conflict over navigational rights. It is much wider than that, as the problem signifies itself in Iran's expansionist ambitions in the neighbouring . . . Arab areas. . . .

The new regime in Iran came to power after the fall of the Shah's regime.... Iran has achieved a... territorial gain which it benefited from at the expense of Iraq, but Iraq has not obtained what was due to it according to all the international agreements concluded before 1975, and the 1975 [Algiers] Agreement....

Our starting point was the policy of good neighbourliness and the desire to establish normal relations with Iran. But in their... arrogance, the new rulers of Iran turned away from all these initiatives. They were determined... to abuse Iraq, and expand at its expense, and go along the same hostile and expansionist path taken by the Shah of Iran. This appeared from the statements made by them, and their deeds and practices....

The basic motive behind the hostile position adopted by the new regime in Iran is the desire to expand at the expense of Iraq and the Arab countries in the Arab Gulf region and to interfere in its internal affairs. This has taken now a new cover, which is what the Iranian responsible officials term as the exportation of revolution to the neighbouring countries.

... [T]his is the policy of the new rulers of Iran which tries to export what is known as the new revolution and its principles to all Islamic countries. There is no one amongst you who does not know that they are interfering in the internal affairs of all Islamic countries....

The attitude and intentions of the Iranian regime in the ... exportation of revolution did not stop at ... statements, but passed that limit in the endeavours to transfer it to actual reality against Iraq and other Islamic countries. This took place under the direct supervision of the regime's leaders. In Qom and Tehran, specialized institutions ... were established to plot against Iraq and the neighbouring states. The plotting against Iraq was escalated through the commission of acts of terrorism and sabotage by Iranians, which the Iranian authorities helped to infiltrate inside Iraq, and assisted by Iranian residents in Iraq and individuals of Iranian descent. In fact, these groups committed during the first half of 1980 ugly terrorist acts, from which not even the Muslim praying masses in the mosques escaped. All these terrorist acts were directed from Qom, as has been established by the instructions issued ... daily to the agents of the Iranian regime from the official Iranian broadcasting stations, which included even instructions as to manufacturing local bombs.... The most cruel act of terrorism was the hurling of bombs at a ... student gathering held at al-Mustansiriyah University in Baghdad on 1 April 1980, which resulted in killing and wounding a large number of students. Similarly, [there was] the hurling of bombs on 5 April 1980 from the Iranian school in Waziriyah at the funeral procession of the martyrs who were killed at al-Mustansiriyah incident.

In this second operation, some Iranian officials of the Iranian School's teachers participated....

The rulers of Iran have not stopped at that, as they started, parallel with their sabotaging activities, to renew the life of the agent rebellious movement in Northern Iraq. The Iranian government recalled the leaders of that movement, already defeated in 1975, from the United States of America to Iran and gave them a new support, as the Shah did formerly, in all means in order to threaten Iraq's security and national unity. The Iranian government has also put a special broadcasting station at the disposal of that clique which cooperated with the Zionist entity between 1965 and 1975, as has been recognized by [Israeli President Menachem] Begin....

I have referred a while ago to the question of the Iraqi lands which Iran did not deliver to Iraq despite its long encroachment thereon, as provided by the Algiers Agreement, and how the fall of the Shah regime led to the completion of delivery. The new regime came to power and we granted it the opportunity to implement Iran's obligations. But what happened with the advent of the era of the new regime is that with the beginning of tension, the Iranian military presence in those Iraqi lands increased instead of delivering them back to Iraq. Those very areas, being areas of Iraq, became themselves the source of armed attacks on the Iraqi border region. The attacks were coupled with persistent violations of Iraqi air space by the Iranian Air Force. For example, we should like to mention to you that the number of violations of Iraqi air space by the Iranian Air Force reached 249 for the period February 1979 to September 1980. This is recorded in the official notes sent by Iraq to Iran through the Iraqi Ministry of Foreign Affairs. The number of incidents of firing across the frontiers and on the border posts and attacks thereon, artillery shelling, obstructing navigation in [Iraq's main outlet to the sea, the] Shatt-al-Arab, and shelling at civilian targets reached 244 for the period of June 1979 to September 1980.... Civilian aircraft were fired at three times and one airplane was forced by Iranian Air Force—inside Iraqi air space—to land inside Iran during the period of August 1980 to September 1980. The bombardment of economic installations including petroleum installations took place seven times during the period of January 1980 to September 1980. All these violations which ... contravene the Algiers Agreement, and any principle of normal relations with Iran, have been documented in official Notes forwarded to the Iranian government, hoping that it would abide by law and reason....

It is clear from what I have said that it was Iran which started the war against Iraq on 4 September 1980 and expanded it during the following days. Iraq has not encroached upon Iran's borders or rights, when it was forced to liberate

Iraqi lands in Zain Al-Qaws, Saif Sa'ad and Maimak and other Iraqi territories from the illegal Iranian occupation during the period 8 September to 11 September 1980. Despite the Iranian escalation and widening of the military operations, Iraq was patient throughout the whole period of 11 September to 22 September 1980, without crossing the frontiers line into Iran. Iraq's patience came to an end when Iran widened its aggression to the extent of closing [the] Shatt-al-Arab, our sole national fluvial outlet to the sea, striking at our vital economic interests and peaceful cities including oil installations and the closing of the Hormuz Straits, and gaining ample evidence as to the wider aggressive intention of Iran, when . . . Iraq became exposed to a wide military action from Iran. We were forced on that date to defend ourselves by pushing the Iranian military forces deep inside the Iranian land mass in order that our towns, population, and interests remain secure from aggression. . . .

We have emphasized to all those who have sought to stop the war and the achievement of a peaceful settlement that we have fought in response to the Iranian aggression and for legitimate rights, and that we aim at restoring those rights and achieving a just and honourable settlement to the conflict and pushing away the evil from our sovereignty and people. We have also emphasized the necessity for the prevalence of the principle of non-acquisition by force in the relations between Iraq and the Arab nation on the one hand, and Iran on the other. The lands and rights which Iran has usurped by force should be restored to their lawful owners. This is one of your . . . principles as well as being a principle of international law; a divine as well as a mundane law Iraq is . . . ready to restore the Iranian lands occupied in the war. By all this, a just . . . settlement would be achieved. Hence, the appropriate climate for the establishment of normal relations between Iran, the Arabs and Iraq, away from the expansionist inclinations and the acts of aggression would be achieved, as well as the . . . conditions for . . . the countries in the area for evolution, development . . . and real independence. . . .

Islam does not ordain disunity and strife. It does not allow breach of pledges and violation of agreements, for although the Algiers Agreement was imposed on us . . . yet had the new rulers of Iran adhered to it, we would have done the same, not because we believe the Algiers Agreement to be correct, but because we signed it for we do honour agreements while the gentlemen, the new rulers of Iran violated the 1975 Agreement and therefore there can be no return to it. Moreover, Islam does not accept the denial of the rights of others. It does not approve of fanning conflicts, enmities, the use of force and violence against Muslims without a legitimate reason. . . .

The noble religion of Islam orders us to do good deeds and not abuse, to give everyone his due rights, and that none of us should violate the other. Islam orders us to protect our neighbours, respect his rights and assist him, and not to usurp his lands, and spill the blood of his sons illegally.

The great Prophet, Muhammad ... is the last prophet and the Seal of Messengers, the book of God is clear, and the Sunna of His Prophet and His Companions is as clear as the sun. There is no new prophecy ... and there is nothing between the Muslim and his God except the Book of God and the Sunna of his Prophet.

The Iran-Iraq War through a General's Eyes

During the Iran-Iraq War, Hussein often dressed in fatigues, even though he had no military experience. Hussein, after all, had spent his youth as a Ba'thist radical and never served in the armed forces. This fact increased the importance of having a competent officers corps in order to win a victory against Iran. Hussein, however, undercut the influence of officers, fearful that they would detract from his totalitarian power. In writing about the officers during the Iran-Iraq War, the historians Marion Farouk-Sluglett and Peter Sluglett point out that "there was always the possibility that a serious rival or challenger to the president might appear from within its ranks" (Farouk-Sluglett and Sluglett, 272). To prevent the creation of national heroes, Hussein banned the media from mentioning generals by name after a victory. He also rotated generals frequently in order to ensure that they would not gain the loyalty of their troops. And he "exerted as much control as possible over the army and its commanders, which seriously hampered the conduct of war" (273).

One Iraqi general has written a description of Hussein's leadership style during the war. Georges Hormis Sada (b. 1940) was an Air Commander in Iraq's Air Force during the Iran-Iraq War. He had graduated from Iraq's Air Academy in 1959 and underwent further training in Great Britain, Russia, and the United States. Sada was an Assyrian Christian. He never joined the Ba'th Party. He retired from the Air Force in 1986 but was called back to active service during the second Persian Gulf War of 1991. At that time, Saddam Hussein ordered Sada's arrest, because he refused to contradict the Geneva Convention and kill captured American fighter pilots. After the U.S. invasion in 2003, Sada became a senior advisor to the National Security Council on the new government in Iraq. The following passage is from Sada's memoir *Saddam's Secrets: How an Iraqi General Defied and Survived Saddam Hussein* (Nashville: Thomas Nelson, 2006), 84–90. In this passage, Sada references Adnan Khayralla, who was Minister of Defense during the Iran-Iraq War. Khayralla died in 1989 in a helicopter crash that some found suspicious, given this political personality's rising popularity with the masses. As you read this passage, you should consider the following: How does Sada revise understandings of the war's start? Why is Khayralla upset by this finding? What does the passage suggest to you in terms of Hussein's style of political leadership?

Secret Information

One day in 1984, Gen. Khairallah called and asked for me to meet him privately. When I arrived, he said, "Georges, I want to discuss something with you, and I don't want a word of it to get back to Saddam." I said, "I understand. And believe me, sir, if you tell me it's strictly between us, it will remain a secret." He thanked me and shook my hand; then he asked me a question that took me by surprise. He said, "Georges, do you remember the way we attacked Iran?" I said, "Yes, sir, I remember." He said, "You remember that we were told that Iran had shut down their air space and that was a sign that they were preparing to attack us?" Again, I said, "Yes, sir. . . ."

He said, "Georges, was that true?" I said, "No, sir . . . I said at the time that merely closing your air space doesn't necessarily mean that you're planning an attack. There are many reasons why this could happen." I mentioned a few of those reasons, and then I told him, "Sir, there's another reason why I know this is the case. As you know, we captured many Iranian pilots during the war, and in the interrogations I specifically asked them, 'Why did your country close your air space?'"

"What those pilots told me," I said, "was that a group of officers in the Iranian Air Force had rebelled against the Khomeini regime, and when the plot was discovered, many of them were killed. But some of the rebels tried to make a run for it, and they were taking any plane they could get . . . and flying away. . . . To put a stop to that, Khomeini . . . had to close the Iranian air space and order the military to shoot down any plane attempting to enter or exit from Iran without permission."

. . . [A]ll air traffic had to be grounded. . . . But because of Saddam's paranoia . . . this was translated in Iraq as an act of war—as the first sign that the Iranian military was preparing to attack us. This all happened on September 17, 1980, and five days later we were ordered to launch the first strike on Iran.

That's what I told Gen. Khairallah. . . . After I explained what I found out, he said, "Georges, I want you to prepare a report for me, and you're free to use any military resources you need. I want to know for sure whether the Iranians were trying to attack us or not. Can you do that?" I told him I would be glad to do it. So he said, "How will you do it?"

I said, "It won't be hard to do, sir. I'll ... ask as many of the Iranian pilots we captured as I can, and from their answers I'll know whether or not they were prepared to make an assault on Iraq." ... [A]nd when I had ... those forms ... analyzed, it was clear that none of the Iranian pilots was prepared to fly against Iraq. There had been no training, no mission plan, no armament of the Iranian fighters with combat weaponry, and no alerts had been issued from the air command center that would have suggested that war was imminent.

When I presented this information to Gen. Khairallah, it was obvious that he was troubled by the news. He ... looked at me and said, "Georges, why did our air force commander believe we were going to be attacked? And why did he order that we carry out the first strikes?" I told him I didn't know the answer to that, but perhaps Saddam had pressed him to give a negative report in order to legitimize his decision to attack Iran.

... Saddam felt threatened by Ayatollah Khomeini and the Shiite regime in Tehran. If Khomeini continued his verbal assaults on Iraq's secular government, he might ... persuade the large Shia population in the south of Iraq to join a revolution against Saddam, and he wasn't going to let that happen. So, a preemptive strike against Iran was ... the obvious solution.

When Gen. Khairallah realized it was Iraq, in fact, who had started the war, he was ... distressed. I don't know, but he may even have gone to talk to his cousin, Saddam, about this, and if so, I'm sure he expressed his disappointment that Iraq had done such a thing. ... Adnan Khairallah had ... the moral authority of a leader, and this is probably why Saddam decided he had to get rid of this man before he, too, threatened his power. ...

Confidential Sources

I continued to wait for Khairallah outside Saddam's office for a few more minutes, and when he finally arrived, the secretary went in and told Saddam that the minister of defense and I were there.... But Saddam told him, "Send in Gen. Khairallah and tell Gen. Sada to wait."

As I sat there I wondered how long I'd have to wait, but after no more than ten minutes the secretary's telephone rang. It was Saddam telling him to send me in. So I went in and saluted the president. As I started to sit down I noticed that there were several chairs, some close and some far away from the president's desk, so I walked toward one near the back. But ... Saddam said, "No, no. Georges, you come up here." And he pointed to a chair very close to his desk, between himself and Gen. Khairallah. So I walked up to that chair and took a seat.

... Gen. Khairallah spoke directly to me, and he said, "Georges, the president is going to ask you several questions. I want you to answer these questions as the Georges we all know and trust." Suddenly, I was worried about what would come next. The meeting was beginning to sound more like an interrogation than a conversation about military matters. ... Maybe he wanted to know if Khairallah had shared some classified information about the Iran-Iraq War or something else of a more personal nature.

But Khairallah went further and said, "Georges, even if the president asks you about Adnan Khairallah, I want you to answer him honestly, as I know you will." This really puzzled me. I couldn't imagine what sort of questions Saddam was going to ask. But I remembered my conversation with Gen. Khairallah when he asked me to do the research to find out if we had attacked Iran without provocation. At that time he had sworn me to secrecy.

This was especially troubling because ... he was telling me to be honest with the president, but he had previously made me swear never to tell anyone, especially Saddam, what I found out. So I decided that if this was what Saddam was going to ask me, then I would have to say I didn't know anything about it. ... I had given Gen. Khairallah my word as a fighter pilot, so even if they killed me, I wouldn't go back on my word of honor.

But thank God he didn't ask me that. ...

Sniffing Out Rebels

Then Saddam said, "Georges, do you have any idea why I've sent for you?" I said, "No, sir, no idea at all. ..." Then Saddam asked me the question, and ... I understood what he was looking for. At that time there were people in the city of Mosul, in the north, who were becoming ... powerful, and Saddam was ... concerned that ... they were too powerful. During the Iran-Iraq War, a large number of officers in the military command staff were from Mosul, and ... all of them were Sunni Muslims.

On top of that, the army chief of staff, the intelligence chief, the chief of air force intelligence, six of the eight top air force commanders, and most of the corps, division, brigade, and unit commanders in the Iraqi Army were all Sunnis from the same area around Mosul. ... [I]n his all-consuming paranoia, Saddam had begun to wonder about this, and he realized the Muslawis could easily form a coalition to challenge his power.

Saddam would, of course, do anything to hold on to power, so he wanted to find out if any of these people might pose a threat. ... I realized that my visit to his office, along with Gen. Khairallah, was part of his ... fact-finding mission. Saddam said to me, "Georges, I want you to tell me how all these Sunnis from Mosul came to hold all the top positions in the military."

"Sir," I said, "that's an easy answer. We all know the Shia have no chance of becoming senior leaders and commanders in the military of Iraq. Since we're always fighting with Iran, which is under the control of the Shia in that country, it's only natural that the majority of our leaders would come from the ... Sunni population in Mosul and the north—and this also happens to be where our best military schools are located."

... [S]everal years earlier the army had been looking for a new base commander in [southern] Basra.... They decided the logical choice would either be me, an Assyrian Christian from Mosul, or another officer who was a Sunni from Mosul. The chief of staff said they would trust either of us more than they would trust any of the Shia officers who lived in that area. They knew we would remain loyal to the military and not simply be puppets of the political and religious groups in the south.

But Saddam ... sniffed the air, and he asked me, "Didn't you smell something in this collection of officers and commanders in the army and air force? Did you smell that these Muslawis might have a plan to start a rebellion against us?"

"No, sir," I said very seriously. "I've never heard of anything like that at all. ..."

[S]hortly after the end of the ... war, Saddam ordered a ... number of his top commanders, all ... from Mosul in the north, to be hanged. And when those executions were ... carried out, there were two pilots among them: Gen. Salem, the deputy air force commander and Gen. Hassan, who was director of operations for the air force. These were good and honest men, even though I didn't agree with them on many things.... Saddam thought nothing of killing innocent men if it served his purposes.

The United States Supports Ba'thist Iraq

Ultimately, the United States offered Iraq substantial support in fighting its war against neighboring Iran. The United States, you see, had been a strong supporter of the Shah of Iran and was, conversely, the bitter enemy of Ayatollah Khomeini, who took Iran out of the American sphere of influence. The United States, however, had broken off diplomatic relations with Iraq in 1967, fearing Iraq's placement within the Soviet sphere after the Six Day War. At first, the Iran-Iraq War may have been considered a boon to policymakers in Washington, since it effectively neutralized two anti-Western countries that each had the potential to be regional centers of power. The United States, however, eventually found it convenient to ensure that Iraq did not lose the war. It resumed diplomatic relations with Iraq on 27 October 1984. In this way, Iraq became eligible to receive U.S. aid. By 1987, the United States and Iraq signed an agreement that provided Iraq with economic and technical assistance. That same year, the United States sent naval vessels to the Gulf to protect oil tankers, and this was of great help to Iraq (Farouk-Sluglett and Sluglett, 267). In this way, Iraq had the backing and assistance of both the United States and the Soviet Union against isolated Iran.

The following document explores the thoughts of U.S. policymakers as they discuss their shifting relations with their erstwhile Iraqi enemy. The Department of State issued this memorandum on 7 October 1983, one year before the United States resumed diplomatic relations with Iraq. Written by Nicholas A. Veliotes and Jonathan Howe of the Bureau of Near Eastern and South Asian Affairs, it is titled: "Iran-Iraq War: Analysis of Possible U.S. Shift from Position of Strict Neutrality." As you read it, you should consider the strategy of U.S. policymakers: What is the policy at the time that this document is written? Why does the author advocate a change in policy? And what are the specific policy changes both rejected and encouraged by the authors?

The Present Policy

When the war began . . . our poor relations with both combatants and concern for our security interests in the Gulf led us to reinforce air defenses . . . and to block the use of air bases in the Arabian Peninsula by Iraqi aircraft to reduce the threat of expansion of the war. Our neutrality policy evolved out of this preventative reaction. . . . [T]his policy . . . has:

—avoided direct great power involvement;

—prevented spread of the war beyond the territory of the combatants to threaten Gulf oil supplies;

—contributed to the current military stalemate;

—preserved the possibility of developing a future relationship with Iran while minimizing openings for expansion of Soviet influence.

Two changes in the circumstances surrounding the war now raise the issue of whether this policy continues to best serve our objectives of stability in the Gulf and an eventual negotiated conclusion to the war which returns the parties substantially to the *status quo ante*:

—bilateral relations with Iraq have improved over the last three years while relations with Iran continue to be virtually non-existent;

—the Iranian strategy of bringing about the Iraqi regime's political collapse through military attrition coupled with financial strangulation seems to be slowly having an effect.

Iraq appears to have concluded that it must change the strategic situation or risk eventual Iranian success....

A Tilt Toward Iraq: What It Might Include

There are three areas of possible actions we might take to bolster Iraq: financial, diplomatic and military.

Financial

Iraq's annual foreign exchange expenditure... is estimated to be $12 billion for military and $6 billion for commercial imports. Its foreign exchange earnings from oil exports are running at $6 billion yearly. Financing from Saudi Arabia and the Gulf states has fallen from a rate of about $1 billion monthly... to less than half of that rate....

Increasing financial assistance to Iraq does not seem feasible.... Supporting Iraq in exporting more oil is more promising. The capacity of its pipeline across Turkey is being expanded by about 25% by work to be completed late next spring.... Iraq is working out arrangements, involving American firms, which will enable it to build a pipeline that will connect to the pipeline across Saudi Arabia to the Red Sea. However, this link cannot be completed before the end of 1984 at the earliest and, therefore, offers no early relief. Promoting a security environment in which Iraq could fairly quickly (six months) restore some oil export capacity (up to 500,000 b/d) from its damaged facilities at the head of the Gulf would provide the most immediate effective relief....

Diplomatic

The Secretary's meetings with Iraqi Foreign Minister Tariq Aziz have raised the level of visibility of our dialogue with Iraq over the last year. In your recent meetings with MFA Under Secretary Ismat Kittani, you told him directly that Iraq's defeat by Iran would not be in the U.S. interest. Contacts through Turkey have sought to reassure Iraq about the sincerity of our interest in seeing an agreed end to the fighting and our efforts to withhold U.S. military equipment from both sides; this has been only partially successful....

The initiative we are fostering in the U.N. to discourage further attacks on oil-related facilities in the Gulf aims not only at enabling Iraq to meet its financial needs by increasing oil exports—thereby vitiating Iran's strategy of economic strangulation and reducing the motivation for Iraq to escalate the war—but also at establishing an area of tacit agreement between the parties on which an eventual ceasefire could be built. . . .

Other actions we could take include:

(a) More explicit statements of support for the territorial integrity of Iraq and the survival of its present government. These would . . . confirm the Iranian regime's belief that Iraq is an instrument of U.S. policy without having any positive impact. Such statements would . . . damage Saddam Hussein's credibility among both internal and external supporters while giving a propaganda opening to Syria.

(b) Intensified efforts to assure that U.S.-controlled military items do not reach:

(1) either combatant: We do not have evidence to support the allegations of significant evasion of U.S. export controls. . . . [W]e could strongly reaffirm to our friends our opposition to provision of any U.S.-controlled equipment. This . . . would have limited military effect, but it would demonstrate to Iraq . . . our effort to keep U.S. arms out of the conflict.

(2) Iran only: This approach would reduce the force of our argument while doing little for Iraq, which does not have U.S. arms in its inventory and has ready access to alternative suppliers.

Military

There are other possible actions which could be taken to seek to affect the military balance:

(a) Seek to discourage the supply of critical equipment to Iran. While difficult to carry out because of the sensitive nature of some of the information which might have to be revealed in a determined effort and because we have only moral suasion to counter commercial incentive, such action . . . would have . . . medium-term effect on Iran's . . . capabilities. . . .

(b) Permit U.S.-controlled equipment to reach Iraq through third parties. (This assumes insufficient domestic support to be able to supply U.S. equipment directly.) New . . . types of military equipment are not needed by Iraq. Moreover, the types of equipment we could supply would be restricted by legal requirements, such as the prohibition on supplying arms through a third party which we cannot supply directly. Also, we would expect sharp resistance in Congress to establishment of any kind of arms sale relationship with Iraq. A . . . partisan position on arms supply would reduce our ability to provide leadership on initiatives . . . to try to limit and stop the fighting.

(c) We do not consider the commitment of U.S. forces to defend Iraq a serious possibility and, therefore, raise only the prospect of U.S. participation in multilateral protection of Iraqi oil export operations.... If Iran were to attack Iraqi oil installations in the Gulf again, the U.S.—in conjunction with its friends and allies—could help Iraq defend its oil export operations. The way in which we approach such a commitment would be important in determining whether we were entering into a state of war with Iran—with the domestic and international policy burdens that would imply. It would have to be done in the context of keeping the Gulf open for international oil shipments generally rather than characterized as an effort to protect only Iraqi oil exports.... The US willingness to take firm action would reassure the Gulf states of our support for their security. Such a step should also improve US-Iraqi relations, contribute to a further moderation of Iraqi policies and begin the process of restoring Iraq as a counterweight to Syrian influence.

There are some serious risks, however, associated with such action, many of which would depend on the extent of US involvement:

—Direct U.S. and multinational military support for Iraq could provoke greater escalation by Iran and further defer any improvement in the post-Khomeini period. (We would be in a position which may make direct attacks on Iran necessary to defend Iraqi facilities.) The more active the tilt, the more predictable the response.
—No matter how we attempt to portray our actions as having the general aim of keeping the Gulf open for oil shipments, they will be seen as specifically supporting Iraq in its war with Iran.
—... it may be very difficult, if not impossible, to obtain Allied and Gulf state participation in an active defense, though the French are likely to be willing to provide equipment and advisors. Nonetheless, protracted defense of Iraqi oil shipments would require staging areas in the northern Gulf and the active assistance and support of Saudi Arabia and the shaikhdoms.
—Defense of Iraqi oil facilities, even with active measures, cannot be guaranteed and would be difficult to sustain, militarily and financially, in light of numerous other worldwide military commitments.
—Congressional and public support for an overt tilt to Iraq would be difficult to obtain.
—Israel and Syria would object strongly to any US military action to assist Iraq.

Assessment

Our policy of strict neutrality has already been modified, except for arms sales, since Iran's forces crossed into Iraq in the summer of 1982. The steps we have taken toward the conflict since then have progressively favored Iraq. (We assume that other actions not discussed here, such as providing tactical intelligence, would continue as necessary.)

We believe there would be a net advantage to seeking more actively to restrict, so far as possible, all U.S.-controlled equipment transfers to both parties (which would have little or no effect on military capabilities but would strengthen our credibility with the Iraqi regime) and also acting to discourage shipment to Iran of critical equipment from non-communist sources. Other military or quasi-military options have more disadvantages than advantages. Moreover, we need to continue to be cautious about tilting so far toward Iraq that either Iraq is able to force a level of U.S. support we may not wish to provide (such as military protection of transport in the Gulf) or that we become identified with a regime whose longer-term political prospects remain uncertain. Consequently, we propose that you authorize . . . approaches to governments which have transferred U.S.-controlled equipment to Iran or Iraq, or might do so.

In addition, the qualified tilt which we have in fact practiced for over a year is again being ratcheted one notch higher through the UN approach we are pursuing to assist Iraq to resume oil exports through the Gulf. It balances our interest in seeing that Iraq is not defeated with our interest in avoiding an escalation which could draw us directly into the conflict—while doing nothing to worsen our position with respect to Iran.

More broadly, we see significant advantage in maintaining an overall posture of neutrality. What we propose here would be within such broad limits. However, this further tilt toward Iraq would . . . have the following political effects in the region:

—further improve our bilateral relations with Iraq and encourage its non-alignment;

—support our objective of avoiding Iraq's collapse before revolutionary Iran without going so far as to alarm Israel.

The Iran-Iraq War through a Soldier's Eyes

The Iran-Iraq War led to the militarization of Iraqi society. Given the war's eight-year length, young people in 1988 could not remember when their country was not at war. Young men, especially from poor families without connections, were drafted into the army at an alarming rate. Thus, the army grew from 190,000 in 1980 to one million by the war's end.

Mahmoud Albayati was in high school at the height of the war, which is when he was drafted to serve his country. He would eventually get his degree and work in the weapons industry. But he hated the Ba'thist regime. Thus, he would flee Iraq during Operation Desert Storm of the second Persian Gulf War in 1991. After, he then moved to the United States. He recounts his experiences during the Iran-Iraq War in *Out of Iraq: Escape from Saddam and Al-Qaeda* (Baltimore: PublishAmerica, 2006), 16–21. As you read his memoir, you should consider the following: How does Albayati feel about the Ba'th? And what is the cost of this war in terms of the social life of its citizens? Where is Albayati eventually stationed? And what does this reveal about the larger implications of wartime in Iraq?

> During the war with Iran (1980–1988) there was almost daily air attacks upon Baghdad. We used to hide under the stairs or rush away from the windows at first, but after a while we got used to it. We even started running outside or onto the roof of our house, just to have a look. . . . The Iranian fighter jets flew excitingly low, breaking the sound barrier. We'd learned from experience that they didn't bomb civilians (except accidentally)—besides, we'd grown so accustomed to what was happening that we'd become hardened. Children could identify all kinds of weapons and bombs: AK47, RBG7, Phantom Fighter, Russian MIG; in short, we had become transformed from normal kids to war kids. We drew tanks and war scenes instead of trees and birds. We listened for planes and explosions the way children in other countries listened to nature and animals.
>
> The government decreed that everything should serve the purpose of defeating Iran. There was no room for enemies of the country, for laxness of ideology, or for travel (in fact, all borders were sealed). The minimum punishment became death: with the maximum punishment your death combined with the death of your entire family. I remember thinking: if they could, they would have killed our souls.
>
> Then Saddam established what they termed "The People's Army." Baath party leaders stepped up enrolment, stopping people at checkpoints and signing up any who were male and able-bodied. In 1985 they took Father: he spent one year fighting Iran before he was allowed to go free. During that year we lost all financial support; and our lives were turned upside down. The army wouldn't even pay my father enough to transport him home from the war for a few days.
>
> Our family had never been rich, but things had never been as bad as this before. We were devastated; though we would have been still more devastated had we realized that the war was to last for the next eight years. In common with my friends, I came of age in a state of war, with Iraq's borders remaining

closed until 1989. The government knew that more than half the country's youth would certainly choose to leave if they could, but they needed us, not only to be cannon-fodder but to form the workforce that fuelled the machines of war.

Every day I came home from school and turned on the TV. There was only one channel; and every day the news seemed the same: coffin after coffin of dead soldiers (people's fathers, brothers, sons) accompanied by false reports of the stirring victories that our army was supposed to be enjoying. Everyone lost someone; most people lost more than one. I was still in high school but I knew that the . . . fingers of war were extending to touch me, along with everyone else during those dark days.

But the worst part was Haqy. I lost my best friend to Saddam's war machine. He had worked too many hours in my father's workshop to do well at school. When he failed the final exam to go to high school, he was sent to the front, where he didn't survive two months before being sent home in a box.

When I heard he had been killed, I felt as if a part of me had also died. I remembered the lyrics of a song he had liked to sing while he was working:

"Tell me, where were you walking in that dark night?

The hours are too long, and your days too short."

Remembering this made me long to cry, especially recalling cycling with him around the Old City, and how I'd used to call him "a bag of jokes." Yet Haqy's death also had a powerful influence on me, even aside from the simple human misery of his loss. It made me work even more fervently in school as my best chance of missing out on the war, although, even at school, we were obliged to attend military training two or three days a week. . . . More and more I retreated into the world of books, studying until my head hurt and my eyes became bloodshot. Meanwhile, my family situation got worse and worse. My mother, who lost her two brothers in the war, became sick with pain and grief. My six sisters did what they could around the house, but it was so hard for them, especially with my father's apparent indifference and selfishness. What was he thinking? . . .

My last year in high school was in 1983–84. Scud missiles still fell regularly on Baghdad, and (despite the fact that Saddam had decreed that deserters would be punished by death) many soldiers fled. The entire country seemed to be falling apart: it's hard to explain how violence and bloodshed, fear and trepidation had become part of the normal fabric of life.

One day the Baath party invited party members to come to the local soccer field. . . . [E]very high school student was . . . a party member, so we all had to go. While we watched, they pulled onto the pitch a man who had ... suffered considerable ill-treatment, calling him a coward and a traitor. Despite his feeble pleas for clemency, they put him against a wall while a four-man firing-squad dispatched him into the next world.

Realizing that we, as party members, were somehow linked to these murders, I believe that the same thought was in every mind: "I am one of them. I have to escape. This can't go on!" But, easy as it is to think such things, translating them into action is horribly difficult. It was a somber crowd that filed out of the soccer field, turning their backs on the crumpled heap that had once been a fellow citizen of Baghdad.

I had only one more year left before finishing high school, when, during the summer of 1982, the order came: everyone must join the pre-military army.

Now most fathers desperately tried to save their sons from this order, the order that most people thought would never come. Some knew some high-ranking person; others pleaded with far-flung, long-forgotten family members. But we knew no one who could help—and my father did nothing—so I had to go. I was only 15 and the AK47 gun which I was issued with was too long for me to handle properly; but such details were of no concern to the men in charge, who had almost as little respect for the lives of their soldiers as for those of the enemy.

We were sent to the middle of the desert. ... Our training included live rounds of ammunition rushing over our heads, creeping under barbed wires, being asked to "freeze" in order for soldiers to casually shoot all around our bodies, and walking thigh-deep through sewage water. But the worst part of it all was the feeling I had that my father had failed to protect me. He hadn't been there for me when I needed him.

Friday was the worst day of the week for me. All the other boys' parents used to come on Fridays to see them and give them better food and money. I waited and waited, but no one came. I finally realized my father would never come. Either he no longer cared enough, or he no longer cared at all.

When I saw the other children being hugged and given food and money from their parents I wanted to cry, but I couldn't. Soldiers can't cry ... and what teenage boy wants his peers to know that he is upset and afraid? The anger and the pain I felt fuelled my fury at my father and the government.

Of course, the other boys suffered the same harsh training that I did: many fell sick; others became depressed. After only two short weeks of training we were ordered to the battle zone, our leaders herding us into buses and trucks like so many cattle. We moved north for about five hours to a top secret destination, pausing to eat in a city called Toz Khermato, just south of ... Kirkuk. This was the first time I ate goat meat. I will always associate the taste of goat meat with ... fear.

Finally we understood our mission. We were to protect the oil pipeline from the Kurds, who continually damaged the pipes in order to strike back at the government. Our section contained some 700 men, and my subgroup consisted of eight youths who were based at the checkpoint alongside the oil pipe. This area of the country was hilly, almost mountainous: ideal country for a hiking holiday, which, of course, was not exactly our purpose! Although we did go bird-hunting one day—our youthful lightheartedness cut short when a Kurdish villager shot one of us. This was a serious reality check for us all: we might have been only high school kids, but this was still a war.

One night I was sleeping when gunfire erupted around our checkpoint. I woke up fast, sweating.

"Quick, Mahmoud! Shoot!" our leader cried, but it was too dark for me to see anything.

"Where?" I cried, from my vantage point.

"Towards the village!"

Terrified, I pointed my gun towards the village and shot, feeling snipers' returning fire sizzle past my ear. Then I put new bolts in the magazine and shot again until all answering fire ceased. Our unit dispatched twenty soldiers and by the morning it was over, though we kept checking for snipers. I went home and prepared myself to finish high school with the memory of the bullets winging past my head.

The Front Line

The southern front was arguably the most horrific place to be stationed if you were an Iraqi or an Iranian soldier, for that was the heart of the fighting around the Shaat al-Arab waterway. As a reporter for the *Wall Street Journal* as well as the *New Yorker*, Tony Horwitz had the opportunity to travel to Iraq during the Iran-Iraq War. The following account of the front line is taken from *Baghdad without a Map, and Other Misadventures in Arabia* (New York: Plume, 1992), 120–27. As you read it, you should consider the following: How do the Ba'thists use the front line as propaganda? And how do his fellow reporters respond to the horror of the front?

The telephone shook me awake at six in the morning and a voice at the other end declared, "There has been another great victory."

Half asleep, I wondered for a moment if I'd left the radio on. "Come to the airport immediately," continued the voice, which I groggily recognized from my visits to the Ministry of Information. "Today you will go to the southern front."

There were several dozen reporters already gathered at the airport, an international hodgepodge of Turks, Russians, Chinese, French, Americans and locally based Arabs.

"Where is your water?" asked one of the Iraqis, a veteran of trips to the front. I told him that I'd assumed water would be provided. "Are you kidding?" He cradled two water bottles as though they were vintage Moët. "And food—in a few hours, you will only dream of it."

Information was also scarce. Even in victory, the Iraqis rarely disclosed strategic details or even the precise location of the battlefield. "Bodies, that's all you get," said an American cameraman. A few months before, the Iraqi had driven him for six hours through the desert, then stopped at a flat plain covered with Iranian corpses. "This Iraqi guy ran ahead of us shouting, 'Here! Here! More murdered Persians!' We filmed for an hour, then they drove us back to Baghdad. I never even found out where we'd been."

Our trip was following a similar formula. During a long, unexplained delay at the airport, we inquired about the "great victory" we were being taken to see. One of our escorts responded by turning on a television, to show us a "victory tape." It was stock footage of bombs bursting and rockets flaring, with Saddam's face superimposed and a Wagnerian chorus singing in the background:

"The victory is for you, oh Saddam.
With our blood and with our soul
We sacrifice ourselves for you, oh Saddam."

Exactly how many Iraqi souls had been sacrificed in the eight-year war remained a mystery. Two hundred thousand dead was the most common estimate, a staggering toll in a nation of only sixteen million people. Certain streets of Baghdad looked the way I imagined Berlin or Paris did in the 1920s. Young amputees gathered at the Babel Cinema, leaning their stumps on crutches as they studied posters for Bruce Lee films. Veterans rolled through the souk in wheelchairs, shopping piled on their plastic legs. Driving back from Babylon, I'd passed taxis with flag-draped coffins strapped to the roof. This was how bodies were ferried home from the front. At one point casualties were so high that the Iraqis stored corpses in freezers, releasing a few at a time to avoid panicking the public by flooding the capital with coffin-laden cabs.

To bolster morale, the Iraqis also tried to carry on as though the war hadn't disrupted everyday life. "The flight time to Basra is fifty minutes," the pilot announced as we settled into the Iraq Air 737, "and our cruising altitude will be twenty-seven thousand feet." Every passenger on board was a reporter or Iraqi official. No commercial planes had flown to Basra for years.

The veneer of normality evaporated as soon as we landed at Basra, Iraq's second city, near the convergence of the Tigris and Euphrates. Green camouflage covered the terminal, and military aircraft crowded the runway. The Iraqis issued us helmets and loaded us into helicopters that swooped low over the desert to avoid detection by Iranian radar.

Wars have a way of finding inhospitable terrain. The plain east and north of Basra, the scene of most of the war's fighting, is a treeless expanse of grit and marsh, torched by searing winds. Winter was the season for slaughter. In summer, when the temperature hovered at 120 degrees, small arms became too hot to handle and tank drivers risked being cooked in their metal canisters.

Closer to the front, the landscape had been completely made over for the convenience of killing. Barrels of long-range artillery bristled out of the earth, pointing the way to Iran. Bulldozers pummeled the plain into ridges and trenches that swelled, like waves of dirt, one after another for miles. From the helicopter, the Iraqi lines resembled sand-castle fortifications that some ugly gray tide had washed over. The only scenery was a billboard showing Saddam in a pith helmet and carrying a gun, as if ready to go "over the top" and into the Iranian trenches.

The helicopters set down, and we piled into buses, then into jeeps, then hurtled toward the front. At ground level, clutching the death seat of an army jeep, the war suddenly became real. Cannons drummed the desert, each thu-*thump* throbbing through the sand and rattling the jeep's thin floor. Columns of smoke rose from the distant horizon. The driver, a vacant-eyed Iraqi soldier, stared out through a tiny space in the windshield; the rest of the glass was smeared with mud so a flash of glare wouldn't lure the Iranian artillery.

Incoming shells had pockmarked the road. Every hundred yards or so, the driver slammed the brake on the floor, swerved around a blackened crater, then hit the accelerator again, reaching eighty in time to dodge the next crevasse. Tomorrow I may die, he said with his driving; today I may as well risk it all streaking down this fractured strip of tar.

He dropped two wheels onto the shoulder to pass a mangled jeep, splayed on the road like a run-over cat. There was a mechanical whirr as the photographers behind me loaded their cameras with film.

"Bodies, *mon ami*," a French photographer said to the driver. "We must have bodies."

The American beside him chimed in nonchalantly, "What we really need is a blown-out bunker with Iranians hanging out of it and Iraqis standing on top."

He checked his light meter with a quick scan of the desert. "You know, victor and vanquished in the same shot."

The victors had told us nothing of the battle, except that it had taken place at a borderland of sand and marsh known as Majnoon. *Majnoon* is Arabic for "crazy," a prewar name referring to the region's gushing oil wells. The Iranians had captured Majnoon in 1984, and now, apparently, the Iraqis had crawled out of their trenches in a rare summer assault to "liberate" the territory.

We reached the foremost Iraqi line, a tangle of . . . bunkers topped by leaking sandbags. In front of the trenches, barbed wire and spiked metal tank traps had been laid out as a welcoming mat for oncoming Iranians. Whatever shrubs had once sprouted here had been gassed, shattered or uprooted. There was no shade from the blazing sun and nowhere to hide outside the trenches. It looked like Flanders Field, without the mud.

A bridge lay over the trench, and we drove across it, into what had been, until a few hours before, a no-man's-land between the two armies. It was now a smoldering junkyard of burned rubber and blasted metal. Flat land mines lay strewn across the dust like runaway hubcaps. At points, it looked as though a giant lawn mower had run across the plain, chewing up and spitting out jagged bits of jeep, rifle, boot, helmet, canteen and bloodied uniform. The driver turned on his windshield wipers to see through the swirling smoke and dust. And in the backseat, the photographers cleaned their lenses, resuming their grisly refrain.

"This is all very scenic," the American said, "but where are the goddamn bodies?"

The jeep clawed through a cut in the ramparts and deposited us just inside the captured Iranian line. The Iraqis had cleared their dead from the field, but the Iranians lay where they'd fallen. A lone gunner sprawled straight back from his forward post, a splotch of red blossoming across his chest and staining the sand. His eyes and mouth were open in an expression of bemusement, as though someone had just shouted "Bang, bang, you're dead!" and he'd soon leap to his feet and start playing soldier again.

A short distance away, the scene wasn't so ambiguous. One stretch of trench was a corridor of splattered flesh, bodies overlapping one another, cut down together in a torrent of gunfire. Some of the bodies were beginning to bloat, giving off a horrible stench, as if from an outhouse stuffed with rotting meat. Limbs twisted in improbable, almost yogic, contortions. One man had died clutching a gash in his groin, entrails oozing onto his thigh. Another's wounds were hidden; he seemed to be dozing comfortably with his head on the stomach of a friend, eyes closed and face tilted toward the midday sun.

Our Iraqi escorts had chosen their spot well. This bit of battlefield lay on a narrow isthmus of sand between expanses of marsh; there hadn't been much room for the Iranians to maneuver, and it was impossible to walk ten feet without coming upon more bodies. Bodies scattered amid loaves of bread, cans of Kraft cheese and an upturned teakettle, as though the predawn assault had caught the Iranians at breakfast; bodies flung like discarded clothing onto the tops of bunkers or halfway into the marsh; bodies curled up in foxholes; bodies that didn't look like bodies, just pieces fanning out from a bloody core where the shell or grenade had hit.

A Turkish journalist on his fifth visit to the front flipped open his notebook and lectured on the art of reporting war.

"First thing, always study the corpses," he said, nudging his toe against the crushed skull of an Iranian teenager. "Are they fresh? Bullets in front or back?" He inspected the blood dribbling from the corpse's nose. "I think it is fresh. If the body is black and burst-open, then maybe it is old."

He scribbled in his notebook. Bullets in front. Bodies fresh.

"Number two. Are there any signs of gas?" He plucked a mask from the dust and opened a frayed U.S. Army manual, a relic from the days when America supplied the shah's army. The manual showed G.I. Joe with a buzz cut and fatigues, demonstrating how to wear the mask. "The Iranians expected gas," the Turk continued, "but bullets were enough." He slapped his notebook shut. "With corpses you must study these things."

Letters and journals fluttered across the field, and I collected a few for a Farsi-speaking colleague to translate. Mostly, they recorded the tedium of trench warfare. "At 15:00 the enemy has added two rows of barbed wire in front of his position," read a log filled with similar entries. One soldier had passed the time doing Farsi crosswords and doodling pigs. Another filled his log with crude sketches of a woman with luxuriant curls cascading down her shoulders; an un-Islamic daydream in a country of heavily veiled females. In the margin he'd scribbled what seemed to be verses to the girl he'd left behind. "I have seen your picture and puffed your perfume and wish I could be with you always enjoying your beauty and your beautiful smell."

In a letter from Tehran to a young soldier named Jalil, each family member contributed a thought, with a sister composing a poem and a brother adding the final words. "I hope that this war is going to finish in favor of truth," he wrote. "Then all the youngsters will once again come back to the warmth of their families. And you too." The letter lay beside the warm body of a teenager who might well have been Jalil, face up on the sand, his close-cropped hair and patchy beard matted with blood. Flies crawled in his one open eye.

Many of the corpses were those of men my own age, killed in the final days of a pointless war. But I found it hard to feel any connection. What I did feel was a mad compulsion to stare. Look how fragile the flesh is! How easily a skull collapses! The whole scene wasn't so much nightmarish as numbing. What a piece of work is man! Putrid flesh and crushed bones; lunchmeat for maggots, mold for the loam.

I wasn't given long to wax Shakespearean. Soon after we arrived, Iraqi bulldozers and trucks moved in to dig fresh trenches and turn the Iranian guns around. There was no room to maneuver, and no sentiment spared for the enemy dead. One huge vehicle and then another rolled over the bodies. The corpses lurched up and jerked their arms under the weight of the wheels, as if in a final protest, before collapsing in an even spread of brains, bones, organs. A truck bogged for a moment and then churned on, leaving tread marks on the pancake of flesh.

As soon as the convoy passed, a group of Iraqi soldiers crowded atop the gore, firing guns in the air and flashing victory signs for the cameras.

"Mister, picture! Mister, picture!"

The photographers jostled for position. They had what they'd come for: victor and vanquished in the same shot.

"Shadow!" the American yelled at the Frenchman. "Get your goddamn shadow off the goddamn corpse!"

Away from the tumult, two Iraqi soldiers slumped against a bunker, sharing a cigarette. They looked exhausted but elated, suffused with the high of battlefield survivors. Their eyes glowed, their chapped lips curved into glazed, involuntary smiles. "We attacked for six, maybe eight hours," said one of the men, whose name was Mahmoud. "Then the Persians just got up and ran away." He nodded toward the corpses. Present company excluded.

Beside Mahmoud, a gray-haired man named Naim nursed a wound in his hand. His olive-drab uniform was mottled with blood, and each crease of his face was a pocket of grime. As he spoke, he spit dirt from between his teeth. "I am tired, but I am not so scared of the enemy as I was," he said, shaking his head in disbelief. "They don't fight like Iranians anymore."

Naim peered inside a pillbox, checking for corpses, then crawled halfway in to shield himself from the sun. "I do not like to see so much blood," he said. "But when the bodies are Iranian, I do not mind so much." He tipped his helmet over his eyes and didn't even stir at the celebratory bursts of gunfire unleashed for the photographers a few feet away.

The Home Front

The following is a fictional short story that brings to life the experiences of those on the home front as they welcome the soldiers in their family back to a noncombatant situation. "Iraqi fiction," notes Shakir Mustafa, "has been particularly well suited to keeping pace with troubling realities in Iraq" (Mustafa, xiii). Ibtisam Abdullah is the author of this story, which can be found in Shakir Mustafa's *Contemporary Iraqi Fiction: An Anthology* (Syracuse: Syracuse University Press, 2008), 185–90. Abdullah is not only an author of fiction, but also a journalist, so it is not surprising to find her work hinges on such a crisp description of a Baghdadi woman's wartime experiences. As you read this story, you should consider the following: Who is the narrator? What is the soldier's relationship to the mirror? What does this short story suggest about family life during the Iran-Iraq War?

> I'm alone, and it doesn't look like that's going to change anytime soon. I can put up with that. All I have learned these years is how to pass or kill time with silence. It's a profession I began to master after he went to war. Or after he was drafted. Anyway, loneliness soon followed. Mornings go on reasonably well, but evenings and nights are heavy. They wear down my shoulders and eyelids, and by night's end dim lines spread across my face. My nose alone sticks out, presiding over a landscape of features vanquished by the barriers of mute darkness. Then I slowly fall into sleep. I lull myself with sighs of relief as I repeat for the hundredth time, "There goes another long day, and tomorrow might bring something else."
>
> Hours of sleep bring some energy to my body, and I rise as soon as I wake up. Then comes the daily routine of eating breakfast, cleaning our two-bedroom house, cooking, bathing. As I work, I feel his presence as if he has never departed, and as if he'd walk in any moment and hold me in his arms. I often talk to him during meals. I place his teacup on the small table in the kitchen and talk to him. Joke with him or reproach him. His vacant seat has always seemed filled with his presence.
>
> We've been in love with each other, and the past two years of our married life have only intensified our initial passions. We were practically inseparable during evening hours whether we stayed at home or went out. The time that flies unnoticeable during the day we would seize and fill with pleasure at its end. These little pleasures died out bit by bit after he was drafted.
>
> We, or he, started to change over a period of several months. A few little things would happen when he was on leave. I would think about them for a

while and then dismiss them. I didn't want to spoil the joy of our brief reunions. The little things multiplied and came into focus with his sharper changes a few months later. He withdrew and almost seemed a different person.

Emotions have spent themselves, and silence envelopes me again. Like a dormant volcano, I can go over what happened and think about it. I think it all started with his reluctance to speak. His spells of absent-mindedness increased, and he seemed to lose touch with his surroundings. Whenever I tried to break the shell of silence around him, he'd jump, terrified; his face muscles would contract, and he'd look at me with scared suspicions.

He used to stare for long frightened moments at his face in the mirror. He'd stand close to it or retreat, all the time staring at his eyes and his paling features. Sometimes he smiled, at others he looked distressed, but whenever he realized I was watching him, he left the mirror alone and distracted himself with something else.

One night he gazed at his face in the mirror, but after some scrutiny turned to me and surprised me with a question, "What has changed in me?"

Depressed, I looked at him, wondering what to say. He repeated the question, "What has changed in me?"

"What do you think?"

"I don't know. I don't seem to know myself anymore. A strong feeling tells me I've changed. That much I'm sure of."

"What has changed? The way you do things, for instance?"

He shook his head in disagreement and said, "No, not that. I mean my face. My features. Don't you see that?"

I looked at his face for some time, the way he had been doing, and shook my head. "I don't know," I said. "Perhaps some paleness in the face."

He picked up a hand mirror and stared at it, then whispered to himself, "Yes, I'm sure I've changed. No, it's not the paleness. What I mean is that I have a different face."

I laughed, sensing how close to me he seemed at that moment. I took his head in my hands and laid it on my breasts. "It's a better face," I said, and I lifted his face to me and kissed his eyes and forehead. "I'd still love you even if the change were for the worse. Do you hear me? I'd still love you."

I don't know if he really believed me, for he said nothing, not even when I pressed him a little afterwards. He turned his back to me and left the house without saying where he was going.

The quiet and silence that fell then drowned me with past memories. Yes, he's changed, I thought. At the beginning he used to avoid talking about the war and ignored all my questions for months or gave only cryptic answers.

"What do you do there at the front?" I'd ask. "The usual," he'd say. His stony silence shielded me from a world that for him had become the usual.

"How do you spend your days there?"

"Oh, the usual."

"What's the usual?" I try to break that wall of silence.

"Oh, all these questions! But you know what the war is about, right? You read about it, right? It's on television every evening."

But during his last leave it was the war that he talked about when he talked at all. It was he who broke the silence, and with that he made a hole in the heavy bag of withdrawal he carried on his back for months. He'd talk even without my prompting, with loving embraces, his head often on my breasts. Long talks about incoming fire and engulfing flames. Smoke and explosions and dead soldiers and POWs. And the state of mental collapse that seized them in moments of weakness so devastating to both body and soul. I'd listen, not daring to interrupt. . . .

As he looked into the mirror one evening, a happy smile parted his lips. "This is me. I haven't changed. The eyes are mine, and so are the thin face, the mouth, the moustache. Everything as it used to be."

"I told you a million times," I said.

"But—"

"What, not those doubts again!"

"Well, they don't quite go away. They might contract a little like a stream of molten iron when cold water is poured on it, but they start flowing again as soon as the temperature rises again."

Indeed, I was sensing the change he underwent, as if nothing but molten iron flowed in and pulverized his insides. His eyes would squint sometimes, and their light would fade as if a curtain of dense fog separated him from the world around him. But they were also the eyes I loved so much, and they would sparkle again with dazzling radiance, like dashes of lightning emerging from dark clouds.

Oh, when those dark clouds dissipated and he was himself again! Gentle and cheerful, telling me silly stories about his fellow soldiers and what they all did when he was away. But when he was not himself, I simply waited for him. I became very much the wall he needed to lean against during those times of ebb and flow that left the psyche drained. The wall occasionally sagged and whined under his pressing pains, but didn't buckle under them. If it did, that would have broken him into pieces.

Alone, in the midst of this engulfing silence, I keep remembering his previous leave. His volatility and long hours outside the house by himself alarmed me. "You hardly spend any time with me now," I said one day.

"Oh, there's nothing there. The Baghdad I've almost become a stranger to is calling me back. The lights, the frenzy, the attractions, the streets, the hotels resounding with laughter, the extravagance displayed on faces and bodies. You have things we've forgotten. Over there, everything is calculated, light, words, singing, even silence, and the meager space for movement. Over there I'm a different being."

I was struck by his last sentence. It brought me vague fears, but I had to suppress them then. "What's the difference between the one I know here and the other over there?" I said with a calculated laugh.

"I'm in better touch with myself over there. When you see this, you'll see the difference. Two things control me there, defending what I need to defend and preserving myself, and the two cross over all the time. They make me do things I'd have shuddered to think of before." Then he said, "Would you believe it, I have no fears when the battle surges. What scares me is the lull when we stay in the trenches, the silent wait when we run out of words. The silence we sometimes try to kill with meaningless words. When the wait wears us down, we fall asleep without losing the feeling that our exhausted bodies have tiny sharp needles shot through every single cell."

On another evening, he told me, "During those quiet times one of us would explode in a fit of hysterical laughing or crying or lurch out of the underground trench; that's when the silence comes to an end. We make a move, and one of us might even try to choke the contagious frenzy that's about to spread to the rest." He also told me, "Over there I know who I am and what's at stake, to kill or be killed. But here all certainties disappear. Your quiet fills me with questions and draws me toward you and our home and the pleasures of the past. This scares me. . . ."

During his most recent leave it was only the paleness that I saw. At least this is how he looked to me when I met him at the door. A face with almost no color, like the white masks some Japanese actors wear. Lifeless or nearly so. His masks were paleness and silence. On the first day he barely moved. He was nailed to a chair in the living room, chain smoking, and completely ignored me and my anxiety. The second day was no different. He moved only when he had to and ate only a light lunch. The next four days were like that.

It was on the seventh day that he picked up the mirror and stared at his face. His features contracted, and the paleness intensified.

"What is it?" I said.

"I've changed a lot," he said almost to himself.

"You paint an exaggerated picture of your condition."

"What do you know about my condition?"

I came close to him and tried to hug him the way I did during his fits of talking. He let me hold him for a few seconds, but he stiffened when I tried to take away the mirror from him. His hands clung to it in despair. He raised his eyes to me, and there I saw the frenzied look. I pulled at the mirror, but his grip tightened.

"Are you crazy? It's just a mirror," I said.

"No, it's the truth."

His hand was still clinging to the mirror when I withdrew. His eyes widened and flashed. He raised his hand and threw the mirror at me. Its broken pieces flew all over the room. A long wound opened on my chest, and blood flowed between the two of us.

Al Anfal

At first, some politicized Kurds believed the Iran-Iraq War might be a boon for them, for it put an end to the government's policy of repatriating their communities. In this sense, the late 1970s had been hard for Kurds. In 1974 and 1975, they fought a war against the Iraqi government with the assistance of Iran. Once Iran and Iraq made peace in the Algiers Agreement of 1975, however, the Ba'thist regime could essentially decimate the Kurdish communities without reprisals. By 1978, the Iraqi government moved as many as 600,000 Kurds from their homes to resettlement communities (Farouk-Sluglett and Sluglett, 269). The Iran-Iraq War initially put a temporary end to such policies, for the government was preoccupied with its need to defeat the Islamic Republic of Iran.

Iran, however, moved the front line north in 1983, when it began to occupy Kurdish towns in Iraq, and this changed the situation for Kurds. Some Kurds saw the war as yet another important opportunity to assert their right to autonomy. As evident in Mahmoud Albayati's excerpt above, Hussein's regime sent troops to the northern regions of Iraqi Kurdistan. By 1987, Kurdish leaders were setting aside their differences and discussing an alliance with leaders in Tehran, Iran's capital. Such discussions were viewed as a distinct threat in Baghdad.

This threat led to the vicious al Anfal campaign, which was a systematic effort on the part of the Iraqi government to depopulate the north of all Kurds. This official policy began in fall 1987, when Hussein's cousin Ali Hassan al-Majid—later called Chemical Ali—became governor of the north, with all powers needed to put down Kurds. The subsequent al Anfal campaign reflects the Ba'thist effort to raze Kurdish villages, destroy Kurdish agriculture, and, in fact, eradicate the entirety of the Kurdish population. This eradication was to include not only Kurdish men fighting the government, but also the noncombatant women and children who may have had no political aspirations. Rural areas were the focus of this campaign, for the Ba'th had secured both the cities and the main highways. Al Anfal involved mass killings as well as the use of chemical weapons. At Halabja, for example, the Iraqi Air Force dropped enough chemical weapons to kill 5,000 people in one morning. The Ba'th did this in order to prevent support to Kurdish guerillas operating outside of cities. The al Anfal campaign was not recognized by the United States as a genocide (which would have then required the United States to act militarily to protect Kurds), but it had all the earmarks of such. The Ba'th destroyed nearly 4,000 villages. At least 182,000 Iraqis died at the hands of their own government, and they were targeted based on ethnicity. Another 160,000 fled through the mountains into Iran and Turkey, where they lived in insalubrious refugee camps.

Some Kurds survived and were able to tell their stories. In 2003, the American Mike Tucker traveled to Iraqi Kurdistan in order to collect the stories of Kurds. He recorded an interview with two survivors of the al Anfal campaign in *Hell Is Over: Voices of the Kurds after Saddam* (Guilford, Conn.: Lyons Press, 2004), 108–10. Tucker interviewed Hajee Omar Sharif and Issa Hajee on 13 August 2003. As you read the accounts of these survivors, you should consider the horror of being a victim of your own government. Does such testimony about al Anfal require the international community—especially the United States—to act? Or should a government have the right to rule as it sees fit?

Hajee Omar Sharif

I was born in 1923 in Satarngay. At that time, it was a nice place. The British came, now and then. They gave us little trouble; it was the Arabs, even then, who were trying to steal our land. Six times in my life, my land has been stolen by Arabs—we lost everything, each time. Six times, we have regained it.

The worst, of course, was Al Anfal.

During Al Anfal, we were imprisoned at Bayharke, like the people of Gizi and so many Kurds. My village was destroyed by Saddam Hussein's Iraqi Army—once, he personally came to my village and oversaw the destruction. In Al Anfal, I lost my brother, son, and son-in-law.

The Iraqi jets bombed us with the chemical death in Al Anfal. First, the airplanes came and bombed us with chemical weapons. Also, I saw them bomb Zinevah village. We escaped—those of us who survived—by walking through the mountains. But the Iraqi Army surrounded us in the night. They arrested us, and tied all the men's hands behind their backs. They stole all our possessions. And they took us to De Hay, a Christian village. In De Hay, the Iraqis put tanks in front of us. We were sure we were going to be massacred. It was August 1988. But they did not fire at us. They made us stand in front of the tanks for the longest time, and then they laughed at us.

Then, we were moved to Circinck, for only a day. We were very thirsty, hungry, and tired. We got no food or water. Then, they brought us to Nzarkay Castle [Dahuk prison]. For three days, they held us at Dahuk prison. The Iraqi secret police came, and separated the men from the women and children. And they tortured everyone! They tortured the men, and boys over ten years of age, the most.

Nobody could dare talk. They beat us with iron bars, stones, concrete blocks, and wooden clubs. There was no food and no water, for three days. No one could sleep—we were so afraid. The men were taken in blacked-out cars. You could not see in, through the windows. The cars returned, after three hours. The cars returned without our men.

I was judged too old to kill, so they did not drive me away. They took me, with all the women and children of our village, to Salamiyah. Over the coming years, with freedom in Iraq now a reality, Kurdish skeletons will appear all over northern Iraq. Already, they are finding the mass graves at Hatra and Hilla. Salamiyah was hell. Like all Al Anfal. All Kurdistan was hell, and Saddam was the Devil incarnate. The Iraqi Army put us in big holes in the ground. There were 300 to 400 people in each big hole. We had no toilets. There was very little food or water, and no shelter. Many of our people died daily, from dysentery and cholera and exposure. Especially the young children, and the babies. We didn't dare even look at the Iraqi soldiers or they'd torture us. After a month in the killing pit, we were moved to Bayharke. This is where I met the survivors of other massacres, such as the Gizi survivors. We were put in an open area behind barbed wire. No one could visit us, not even our relatives. The Iraqi Army surrounded us. Here, in the Bayharke prison, I met my old friend Issa Hajee. I was so shocked to see him! I was sure he died in Al Anfal.

Issa Hajee

It was a terrible time in Bayharke. But our Kurdish people were still able to smuggle in food, medicine, and blankets. People even smuggled in tents and plastic shoes. The summers were brutal, under the plastic sheets. In the winters, we had no heaters and sometimes, no blankets—the men were always giving up their blankets to the children and women. We lived in canvas tents, in the winters. Normally, five to six people died each day from exposure, diarrhea, cholera, and in the summer, heat stroke. And this was just in one small sector of the entire prison.

From my village of Beskay, twenty-four of our men were taken and killed, even before we got to Bayharke. My village, Beskay, is near Zawita. Like Hajee Omar Sharif, the Iraqis first took us to Dahuk Prison for three days of torture, and then took all the men away and murdered them. I was just as shocked to see him as he was to see me! I was sure the Iraqi Army had killed him. It was hell on earth, Al Anfal. Hell on earth.

The End of the War

By 1987, international pressure forced the United Nations Security Council to pass a resolution that called for an end to the devastating Iran-Iraq War. At first, Iraq seemed ready to accept the terms of UN SC Res 598, but Iran would not embrace it. Instead, Iran began an offensive into northern Iraq in March 1988. By April, Iraq had decided that it needed to organize a grand offensive that would allow it to take back its town of Fao in northern Iraq, and Iran had lost nearly all its captured territory by that summer. It was not until 20 August 1988, after so much more horrific fighting, that UN SC Res 598 became a basis for a cease-fire ending hostilities. That said, it would not be until August 1990, two weeks after the start of the second Persian Gulf War, that Iraq finally agreed to the full implementation of UN SC Res 598. The Iran-Iraq War therefore ended as a stalemate. The text of UN SC Res 598 provides critical insights into the fighting of the war as well as the responses to it by the international community. The Council of Foreign Relations has the text of this important resolution on its website (accessed 18 February 2010, http://www.cfr.org/publication/11200). As you read the following text of the resolution, you should consider the following: What does the international community know about the war? And did this knowledge compel the United Nations to act more decisively at an earlier date? And which clauses would Hussein have found problematic?

> The Security Council,
> Reaffirming its resolution 582 (1986),
> Deeply concerned that, despite its calls for a cease-fire, the conflict between the Islamic Republic of Iran and Iraq continues unabated, with further heavy loss of human life and material destruction,

Deploring the initiation and continuation of the conflict,

Deploring also the bombing of purely civilian population centres, attacks on neutral shipping or civilian aircraft, the violation of international humanitarian law and other laws of armed conflict, and, in particular, the use of chemical weapons contrary to obligations under the 1925 Geneva Protocol,

Deeply concerned that further escalation and widening of the conflict may take place,

Determined to bring to an end all military actions between Iran and Iraq,

Convinced that a comprehensive, just, honourable and durable settlement should be achieved between Iran and Iraq,

Recalling the provisions of the Charter of the United Nations, and in particular the obligation of all Member States to settle their international disputes by peaceful means in such a manner that international peace and security and justice are not endangered,

Determining that there exists a breach of the peace as regards the conflict between Iran and Iraq,

Acting under Articles 39 and 40 of the Charter,

1. Demands that, as a first step towards a negotiated settlement, the Islamic Republic of Iran and Iraq observe an immediate cease-fire, discontinue all military actions on land, at sea and in the air, and withdraw all forces to the internationally recognized boundaries without delay;

2. Requests the Secretary-General to dispatch a team of United Nations observers to verify, confirm and supervise the cease-fire and withdrawal and further requests the Secretary-General to make the necessary arrangements in consultation with the Parties and to submit a report thereon to the Security Council;

3. Urges that prisoners-of-war be released and repatriated without delay after the cessation of active hostilities in accordance with the Third Geneva Convention of 12 August 1949;

4. Calls upon Iran and Iraq to co-operate with the Secretary-General in implementing this resolution and in mediation efforts to achieve a comprehensive, just and honourable settlement, acceptable to both sides, of all outstanding issues, in accordance with the principles contained in the Charter of the United Nations;

5. Calls upon all other States to exercise the utmost restraint and to refrain from any act which may lead to further escalation and widening of the conflict, and thus to facilitate the implementation of the present resolution;

6. Requests the Secretary-General to explore, in consultation with Iran

and Iraq, the question of entrusting an impartial body with inquiring into responsibility for the conflict and to report to the Council as soon as possible;

7. Recognizes the magnitude of the damage inflicted during the conflict and the need for reconstruction efforts, with appropriate international assistance, once the conflict is ended and, in this regard, requests the Secretary-General to assign a team of experts to study the question of reconstruction and to report to the Council;

8. Further requests the Secretary-General to examine, in consultation with Iran and Iraq and with other States of the region, measures to enhance the security and stability of the region;

9. Requests the Secretary-General to keep the Council informed on the implementation of this resolution;

10. Decides to meet again as necessary to consider further steps to ensure compliance with this resolution.

Bibliography

Bengio, Ofra. *Saddam Speaks on the Gulf Crisis: A Collection of Documents.* Tel Aviv, Israel: Tel Aviv University, 1992.

Collins, John M. *Military Geography of Iraq and Adjacent Arab Territory.* Washington, D.C.: Congressional Research Service at the Library of Congress, 1990.

Foreign Affairs Information Management Center (U.S.). *Iraq, Post Report.* Washington, D.C.: U.S. Government Printing Office, 1981.

Gold, E. J. *Visions in the Stone: Journey to the Source of Hidden Knowledge.* Nevada City, Calif.: Gateways/IDHHB, 1989.

Horwitz, Tony. *Baghdad without a Map, and Other Misadventures in Arabia.* New York: Plume, 1992.

Hussein, Saddam. *On Current Affairs in Iraq.* Baghdad: Translation and Foreign Languages Pub. House, 1981.

———. *On History, Heritage, and Religion.* Baghdad: Translation and Foreign Languages Pub. House, 1981.

———. *On Iraq and International Politics.* Baghdad: Translation and Foreign Languages Pub. House, 1981.

———. *Revolution and National Education.* Baghdad: Dar Al-Mamun for Translation and Pub., 1981.

———. *Thus We Should Fight Persians.* Baghdad: Dar Al-Mamun for Translation and Pub., 1983.

International People's Conference for Peace. *The Iran/Iraq Conflict: Background and Facts; A Report Submitted by the Preparatory Committee for the International People's Conference for Peace, Baghdad 25–27 May 1988.* S.l.: s.n., 1988.

Khutut al-Jawwiyah al-Kuwaytiyah. *Kuwait Airways Business Guide to the Gulf.* Boston: Travel Products and Services, 1984.

Kremmer, Christopher. *The Carpet Wars: Ten Years in Afghanistan, Pakistan and Iraq.* London: Flamingo, 2003.

Mustafa, Shakir. *Contemporary Iraqi Fiction: An Anthology.* Syracuse, N.Y.: Syracuse University Press, 2008.

Randal, Jonathan C. *After Such Knowledge, What Forgiveness?: My Encounters with Kurdistan.* Boulder, Colo.: Westview Press, 1999.

Rossi, Pierre, and André Lepage. *Iraq, the Land of the New River.* Paris: Éditions J. A., 1980.

Salbi, Zainab, with Laurie Becklund. *Escape from Tyranny: Growing Up in the Shadow of Saddam.* New York: Gotham Books, 2005.

United States. *Iraq: Post Report.* Washington, D.C.: U.S. Dept. of State, 1981.

United States, and Foreign Affairs Information Management Center (U.S.). *Iraq, Post Report.* Department of State publication, 9283. Washington, D.C.: U.S. Dept. of State, 1988.

Weygand, James Lamar, and Joy Weygand. *Mesopotamia: Somewhat Irrational Iraq.* Nappanee, Ind.: Press of the Indiana Kid, 1989.

Young, Gavin, and Nik Wheeler. *Iraq, Land of Two Rivers.* London: Collins, 1980.

8

The Persian Gulf War and Sanctions, 1990–2002

On 2 August 1990, only two years after the end of the Iran-Iraq War, Iraq invaded Kuwait with the intention of annexing this oil-rich country. Saddam Hussein ordered his troops to take over Kuwait for a number of reasons. First, Hussein was angered that Kuwait and Saudi Arabia would not forgive the $60 billion debt incurred during the Iran-Iraq War. In Hussein's view, he had saved the entirety of the Sunni world from Shi'i radicalism, so all Arab countries must help pay. Second, Kuwait, despite quotas set by the Organization of Petroleum Exporting Countries (OPEC), was overproducing oil. The resulting drop in global prices meant that Iraq was losing approximately $6 billion in annual revenue, which made it even harder to pay back its war debt. Hussein spoke to the U.S. Ambassador April Glaspie on 25 July 1990, and this was the last high-level contact between the two governments before the invasion. The U.S. ambassador told Hussein that: "we have no opinion on the Arab-Arab conflicts, like your border agreement with Kuwait" (Sifry and Cerf, 68). Iraqi troops invaded the country eight days later, and Hussein announced that Kuwait would henceforth be the nineteenth province of Iraq.

Iraq, however, had grossly miscalculated American concerns in regard to the Gulf region, for the United States immediately took action to liberate Kuwait from Iraq. In the opinion of U.S. policymakers, Iraq, already a principal oil-producer in the world, would simply be too powerful to contain if it controlled oil-rich Kuwait and its coastline. This was especially true since it would give Iraq access to a sea port. (Basra, Iraq's sole port, had been destroyed during the Iran-Iraq War, leaving the country all but landlocked.) Within four days of Iraq's invasion of Kuwait, UN SC Res 661 was adopted, which imposed sanctions on Iraq in order to induce Iraq to withdraw its troops. Sanctions, however, would not be enough.

Military operations in the Gulf region can be divided into two distinct phases. At first, and with the assistance of other members of the United Nations, the

United States began to act defensively to protect its ally Saudi Arabia, an operation called Desert Shield. By 9 August, the United Nations Security Council went so far as to declare Iraq's annexation of Kuwait "null and void" (UN SC Res 662), and the exiled Kuwaiti government requested military assistance in implementing these resolutions. Exhibiting a brilliant use of multilateral diplomacy, U.S. President George H. W. Bush forged a Coalition of thirty-four countries, all of which agreed to military action against Iraq. By 29 November 1990, the United Nations Security Council authorized member states to facilitate Iraq's withdrawal by "all necessary means" (UN SC Res 678). This resolution gave Iraq until 15 January 1991 to withdraw troops and restore Kuwaiti sovereignty.

By the time the deadline arrived, 500,000 U.S. troops were stationed in the Gulf. The offensive maneuvers against Iraq began on 16 January, and these are called Operation Desert Storm. The Coalition of the Persian Gulf War began its offensive with an air war. The United States, with its superior technology, targeted military facilities in Iraq, arguing that it was the headquarters of the Iraqi military in Kuwait. Unfortunately, civilians also suffered in what has been described as "the most intensive air bombardment in military history" (Cleveland, 484). The most famous civilian tragedy during the Persian Gulf War was the striking of the Amiriyah shelter on 13 February, a bombing that killed at least 408 people, mostly women and children. The ground war in Kuwait was not launched until 24 February, and it was more a rout than a military engagement. According to William Cleveland: "Evidence released after the war revealed that the US reports grossly inflated the size and the abilities of the Iraqi military in order to justify the massive force deployed against Iraq" (484). Fighting lasted forty-two days. At the end of the war, 26,000 Iraqi soldiers as well as 3,000 Iraqi civilians were dead. The Coalition, however, which had relied on high-tech equipment lost only 148 soldiers.

Iraq accepted all terms of the cease-fire agreement, but the United Nations nevertheless decided to maintain the sanctions regime. These sanctions—as well as a sanctions committee—had been established on 6 August 1990 through UN SC Res 661. The member states of the United Nations maintained these sanctions in order to make sure that Iraq recognized Kuwait's sovereignty. They also wanted to force Iraq to eliminate weapons of mass destruction, including the chemical weapons used against its own citizens during the al Anfal campaign. The aerial bombardment of Iraq, however, had lasted six weeks. As pointed out by historian Charles Tripp, the Persian Gulf War had decimated the economic structures of Iraq even more than had occurred during the eight-year-long Iran-Iraq War (Tripp, 249). For this reason, Iraq was unprepared for the sanctions regime.

And so, there was a looming humanitarian crisis in Iraq by 1995. The government had set up a system of rations, and this prevented famine. It did not, however, prevent widespread malnutrition. The United Nations' Food and Agriculture Organization (FAO) reported that four million people, representing about 20 percent of the population, were suffering from lack of caloric intake. Iraq, unfortunately, could not effectively grow its own food because fertilizers, for which the chemical compound could be used in weapons, were among the prohibited imports. Infant and child mortality rose drastically, especially since the sanctions regime prohibited the import of many medicines. According to historian Phebe Marr, "The applications of sanctions for over a half a decade had by 1995 fundamentally changed Iraq's social and economic structure and the welfare of its population for the worst" (Marr, 268).

This chapter suggests that the long-term losses due to the Persian Gulf War, in particular, regional instability and humanitarian crisis, far outweighed the short-term gains for the United States and members of the Coalition, which so handily won the war and restored Kuwaiti sovereignty. The chapter begins with the transcript of a meeting between Hussein and U.S. Ambassador April Glaspie, in which, as interpreted by some, she seemed to give Iraq the go-ahead to resolve its conflict with Kuwait as it saw fit. Since the United Nations played such an important role in this conflict, this chapter includes two of the most critical resolutions: UN SC Res 662, which declared the Iraqi invasion "null and void," and UN SC Res 678, which allowed member states to liberate Kuwait by "all necessary means." An Iraqi resident of Baghdad then provides an account of the forty-two-day aerial bombardment of her city. After this document, Jordan's Queen Noor clarifies how the fighting fostered regional instability in neighboring countries. The end of the fighting on 28 February 1991 did not signal an end to the suffering of ordinary people, and President George H. W. Bush and Brent Scowcroft describe American responses to the failed uprisings of Shi'is and Kurds. Economic sanctions continued to be imposed by the international community, and the horrific effects of this system cannot be overstated. And so, this chapter includes a speech given to the U.S. Congress by Denis Halliday after he resigned his position in the United Nations to protest the sanctions. This speech is followed by Hadani Ditmars's article for *Ms.*, which details the horrid effects of sanctions on women and children.

Ambassador April Glaspie Meets with Saddam Hussein

On 25 July 1990, President Hussein met with April Glaspie, the U.S. ambassador to Iraq. When these two political personalities met, Iraqi troops were already gathering in the south, near the Kuwaiti border. Eight days later, apparently thinking that the United States would not involve itself in the Gulf region, Iraq invaded Kuwait. In truth, this interview is extremely controversial. It was Iraq that subsequently published a transcript of the Hussein-Glaspie interview, and the U.S. State Department will make no comment on its accuracy. Phebe Marr suggests that the meeting was called by Hussein in order to forestall American intervention and that the Ba'thist president may even have come away from the meeting feeling that he had "a green, or at least amber, light" in terms of conquering Iraq's northern neighbor (Marr, 227). An excerpt of this transcript is taken from Micah L. Sifry and Christopher Cerf's *The Iraq War Reader: History, Documents, Opinions* (New York: Simon and Schuster, 2003), 61–71. As you read the transcript, you should consider the following: Why did Saddam Hussein believe that the United States would allow for the Iraqi invasion of Kuwait? What tone does Glaspie take with President Hussein? What promises does Hussein make in regard to the looming crisis with Kuwait?

> *President Saddam Hussein:* . . . Iraq came out of the war burdened with a $40 billion debt, excluding the aid given by Arab states, some of whom consider that too to be a debt although they knew—as you knew too—that without Iraq they would not have had these sums and the future of the region would have been entirely different.
>
> We began to face the policy of the drop in the price of oil. . . . [W]hen planned and deliberate policy forces the price of oil down without good commercial reasons, then that means another war against Iraq. Because military war kills people by bleeding them, and economic war kills their humanity by depriving them of their chance to have a good standard of living. As you know, we gave rivers of blood in a war that lasted eight years, but we did not lose our humanity. . . . We do not accept that anyone could injure Iraqi pride or the Iraqi right to have high standards of living.
>
> Kuwait and the U.A.E. [United Arab Emirates] were at the front of this policy aimed at lowering Iraq's position and depriving its people of higher economic standards. And you know that our relations with the Emirates and Kuwait has been good. On top of all that, while we were busy at war, the state of Kuwait began to expand at the expense of our territory. . . .
>
> But go and look for yourselves. You will see the Kuwaiti border patrols, the Kuwaiti farms, the Kuwaiti oil installations—all built as closely as possible to this line to establish that land as Kuwaiti territory. . . .
>
> We do not accept threats from anyone because we do not threaten anyone. But we say clearly that we hope that the U.S. will not entertain too many

illusions and will seek new friends rather than increase the number of its enemies.

I have read the American statements speaking of friends in the area. . . . [I]t is the right of everyone to choose their friends. We can have no objections. But you know you are not the ones who protected your friends during the war with Iran. I assure you, had the Iranians overrun the region, the American troops would not have stopped them, except by the use of nuclear weapons.

. . . I hold this view by looking at the geography and nature of American society into account. Yours is a society which cannot accept 10,000 dead in one battle.

You know that Iran agreed to the cease-fire not because the United States had bombed one of the oil platforms after the liberation of Fao. Is this Iraq's reward for its role in securing the stability of the region and for protecting it from an unknown flood?

So what can it mean when America says it will now protect its friends? It can only mean prejudice against Iraq. This stance plus . . . statements . . . made has encouraged the U.A.E. and Kuwait to disregard Iraqi rights.

I say to you clearly that Iraq's rights . . . we will take one by one. That might not happen now or after a month or after one year, but we will take it all. We are not the kind of people who will relinquish their rights. There is no historic right . . . for the U.A.E. and Kuwait to deprive us of our rights. If they are needy, we too are needy. . . .

We clearly understand America's statement that it wants an easy flow of oil. We understand America saying that it seeks friendship with the states in the region, and to encourage their joint interests. But we cannot understand the attempt to encourage some parties to harm Iraq's interests. . . .

If you use pressure, we will deploy pressure and force. We know that you can harm us although we do not threaten you. But we too can harm you. Everyone will cause harm according to their ability and their size. We cannot come all the way to you in the United States, but individual Arabs may reach you.

You can come to Iraq with aircraft and missiles but do not push us to the point where we cease to care. And when we feel that you want to injure our pride and take away the Iraqis' chance of a high standard of living, then we will cease to care and death will be the choice for us. Then we would not care if you fired 100 missiles for each missile we fired. Because without pride life would have no value.

It is not reasonable to ask our people to bleed rivers of blood for eight years then to tell them, "Now you have to accept aggression from Kuwait, the U.A.E or from the U.S. . . ."

We do not put all these countries in the same boat. First, we are . . . upset that such disagreement is taking place between us and Kuwait and the U.A.E. The solution must be found within an Arab framework and through direct bilateral relations. We do not place America among the enemies. We place it where we want our friends to be. . . . But repeated American statements last year made it apparent that America did not regard us as friends. . . .

Ambassador Glaspie: [I]t is a great pleasure for a diplomat to meet and talk directly with the president. I clearly understand your message. We studied history at school. They taught us to say freedom or death. . . . Mr. President, you mentioned many things during this meeting which I cannot comment on on behalf of my Government. But with your permission, I will comment on two points. You spoke of friendship and I believe it was clear from the letters sent by our president to you on the occasion of your national day that he emphasizes—

Hussein: He was kind and his expressions met with our regard and respect.

Glaspie: As you know, he directed the United States administration to reject the suggestion of implementing trade sanctions. . . . I have direct instructions from the president to seek better relations with Iraq.

Hussein: But how? We too have this desire. But matters are running contrary to this desire.

Glaspie: This is less likely to happen the more we talk. . . . President Bush wanted better . . . relations with Iraq, but he also wants an Iraqi contribution to peace . . . in the Middle East . . . He is not going to declare an economic war against Iraq.

You are right. It is true what you say that we do not want higher prices for oil. But I would ask you to examine the possibility of not charging too high a price for oil.

Hussein: We do not want too high prices for oil. And I remind you that in 1974 I gave Tariq Aziz the idea for an article he wrote which criticized the policy of keeping oil prices high. It was the first Arab article which expressed this view. . . . Twenty-five dollars a barrel is not a high price.

Glaspie: [M]any Americans . . . would like to see the price go above $25 because they come from oil-producing states.

Hussein: The price at one stage had dropped to $12 a barrel and a reduction in the modest Iraqi budget of $6 billion to $7 billion is a disaster.

Glaspie: I think I understand this. I have lived here for years. I admire your extraordinary efforts to rebuild your country. I know you need funds. We understand that and our opinion is that you should have the opportunity to rebuild your country. But we have no opinion on the Arab-Arab conflicts, like your border disagreement in Kuwait.

"Null and Void": UN SC Res 662, 9 August 1990

The United Nations Security Council convened within hours of Iraq's invasion of Kuwait, and it was to play an important role in this conflict. It immediately passed UN SC Res 660, which called for "the immediate and unconditional withdrawal of all Iraqi forces" (United Nations, 167). It is notable that all the members of the Security Council—the United States, France, Russia, China, and Great Britain—expressed deep concern over this issue, with none of the infighting that had marked the Security Council during the Cold War, which had only just ended. Four days later, the members of the Security Council adopted UN SC Res 661, which imposed economic sanctions on Iraq in order to persuade this country to abandon its Kuwaiti prize. At this time, it established a Sanctions Committee, which would remain a critical institution until the U.S. invasion of Iraq in 2003 (at which time, it was finally disbanded). Iraq, however, disregarded these resolutions, and Hussein declared Iraq's "comprehensive, eternal and inseparable merger" with Kuwait on 7 August (United Nations, 16).

As a result of Iraqi aggression and Hussein's truculent stance, the United Nations Security Council passed Resolution 662. In it, member states completely undermined the legal validity of Iraq's aggression. The text of this document is taken from the United Nations' *The United Nations and the Iraq-Kuwait Conflict, 1990–1996* (New York: United Nations, 1996), 169. As you read the following text, you should decipher precisely how the Security Council foresaw this resolution fostering Iraqi withdrawal. What carrots and sticks does it offer to Ba'thist Iraq?

> The Security Council,
> Recalling its resolutions 660 (1990) of 2 August 1990 and 661 (1990) of 6 August 1990,
> Gravely alarmed by the declaration by Iraq of a "comprehensive and eternal merger" with Kuwait,
> Demanding once again that Iraq withdraw immediately and unconditionally all its forces to the positions in which they were located on 1 August 1990,
> Determined to bring the occupation of Kuwait by Iraq to an end and to restore the sovereignty, independence and territorial integrity of Kuwait,
> Determined also to restore the authority of the legitimate Government of Kuwait,
>
>> 1. Decides that annexation of Kuwait by Iraq under any form and whatever pretext has no legal validity, and is considered null and void;
>> 2. Calls upon all States, international organizations and specialized agencies

not to recognize that annexation, and to refrain from any action or dealing that might be interpreted as an indirect recognition of the annexation;

3. Demands that Iraq rescind its actions purporting to annex Kuwait;

4. Decides to keep this item on its agenda and to continue its efforts to put an early end to the occupation.

"All Necessary Means": UN SC Res 678, 29 November 1990

Over the course of the three months following the passage of UN SC Res 662, there was no sign that Iraq planned to pull its troops from Kuwait. The members of the Security Council, however, were determined to force Iraqi compliance. And so, it passed UN SC Res 678 on 29 November, giving Iraq forty-five days to withdraw before member states of the United Nations took definitive actions. At that point, the United States, with the exception of the invasion of Grenada in 1983, had not engaged in military conflict since the end of the Vietnam War in 1975. This fact may have led Hussein to gamble that the United States would not be willing to put its soldiers at risk in a war with the much more powerful Iraq. In any event, the United Nations Security Council would pass this resolution legalizing the use of force that would allow it to engage in war as of 15 January 1991. As you read the following excerpt, you should consider the parameters placed on the making of war against Iraq. Does the resolution indicate that bombing or invading Iraq would be a legal act?

The Security Council,

... Noting that, despite all efforts by the United Nations, Iraq refuses to comply with its obligation to implement resolution 660 (1990) ... in flagrant contempt of the Security Council,

Mindful of its duties and responsibilities under the Charter of the United Nations for the maintenance and preservation of international peace and security,

Determined to secure full compliance with its decisions,

Acting under Chapter VII of the Charter,

1. Demands that Iraq comply fully with resolution 660 (1990) ... and decides, while maintaining all its decisions, to allow Iraq one final opportunity, as a pause of goodwill, to do so;

2. Authorizes Member States cooperating with the Government of Kuwait, unless Iraq on or before 15 January 1991 fully implements, as set forth in paragraph 1 above, the above-mentioned resolutions, to use all necessary means to uphold and implement resolution 660 (1990) ... to restore international peace and security in the area;

3. Requests all States to provide appropriate support for the actions undertaken in pursuance of paragraph 2 above;

4. Requests the States concerned to keep the Security Council regularly informed on the progress of actions undertaken pursuant to paragraphs 2 and 3 above;

5. Decides to remain seized of the matter.

The Persian Gulf War Experienced in Baghdad

The Persian Gulf War would begin on 16 January 1991, when the United States began the aerial bombardment of Iraq. The United States did not have international authorization to invade the country, but this aerial campaign was designed to take out the military's headquarters in Iraq's capital city. Residents of Baghdad, however, like Nuha al-Radi, did not see much evidence of the precision bombing so often touted in the Western media. During the forty-two days of war, Coalition forces (but really the United States) "subjected Iraq to the most intensive air bombardment in military history" (Cleveland, 484). Al-Radi recorded her impressions of this aerial bombardment. Al-Radi is a painter, and she certainly comes from an upper-class background. The following excerpts are taken from the 2003 edition of *Baghdad Diaries: A Woman's Chronicle of War and Exile* (New York: Vintage Books, 1998), 10–11, 18–19, 32–34, 40–41, 47. As you read the following passage, you should consider the following: How did the aerial bombardment affect residents of Baghdad? How did al-Radi, herself very Western, begin to feel in regard to the United States?

Day 1

I woke up at 3 a.m. to the barrage of exploding bombs. I let out a huge groan that I can still hear. I couldn't believe that war had started. I went out on the balcony, the sky was lit up with the most extraordinary firework display—the noise was beyond description. My dog, Salvador Dali, was chasing frantically round the two houses looking up at the sky and barking furiously. I couldn't get an answer from Ma and [Aunt] Needles' phone so tried Suha who answered in a hushed voice from her shelter under the stairs, and told me to put out my lights. "What for?" I asked. "All the street lights are still on." Suha, being a fastidious and efficient person, had taped all her windows and doors against nuclear fallout, and organized the windowless room under the stairs as her shelter and stashed it with provisions. I refused to take any such precautions, but Ma insisted on it and made a variety of designs on my windows, scrimping on the last ones as she ran out of tape.

Later on I ventured outside to put out the garage light. Salvador was very nervous. Shortly after that we lost all electricity, I needn't have bothered with putting the lights out. The phones followed suit and went dead. I think we are done for, a modern nation cannot fight without electricity and communications. Thank heavens for our ration of . . . matches. . . . Why are we being punished this way?

With the first bomb, Ma and Needles' windows shattered, the ones facing the river. It's a good thing their shutters were down otherwise they could both have been badly hurt. . . .

Day 10

I say "Read my Lips," today is the tenth day of the war. . . . Where is your three to ten days swift and clean kill? Mind you, we're ruined. I don't think I could set foot in the West again. If someone like myself who is Western educated feels this way, then what about the rest of the country? Maybe I'll just go to India. I don't know if it's because we grew up there that I have such a close affinity to that country, or because they have a high tolerance level and will not shun us Iraqis.

Suha mended her bike today. . . . We rode out together and caused a sensation in the streets. . . . One guy also on a bike sidles by us and says, "Actually, I have a Mercedes at home."

"Are we in Paris?" says another.

One sour man says, "We don't have girls who ride bikes!" We yelled at him, "More fool you," and pedaled away. . . .

Tomorrow I'll be fifty years old. I feel very depressed. We're in such a mess and it's all so sad. So many people have to die, and for what?

M.A.W. says we can get electricity in one minute if we attach ourselves to Turkey or Jordan because we have a connected circuit. Yesterday we heard we may be getting it from Iran. What can they connect it to if they have bombed the stations?

Everyone talks . . . about food. While eating lunch, it's what we're having for dinner. People's freezers are beginning to empty. One goes visiting and is given a defrosting chicken and green beans to take home. We cooked up all the meat we had in our various houses. The *basturmas* that we had hung up in Dood's house are starting to stink—the whole house has begun to reek.

Hala says she will give me a bucket of water as my birthday present. . . .

Day 18

Last night M.A.W. said, "Wars must be continuous. I have got so used to eating charred food that when we finish this war we must start another." We are saving gas by cooking and heating food in the fireplace, which seems to be smoking. . . . We are baking our own bread. The favourite way is to place the unleavened dough flat on fine wire mesh, like pita bread, and bake it on an Aladdin stove. These kerosene stoves have proven their worth. They are the best heaters and now the best breadmakers. No Iraqi home is without one. People discovered that M.A.W. has . . . wire mesh and started to queue up for their share. He has it cut up and grudgingly doles it out. . . .

The birds have taken the worst beating of all. They have sensitive souls which cannot take all this hideous noise and vibration. All the caged lovebirds have died from the shock of the blasts, while birds in the wild fly upside down and do crazy somersaults. Hundreds, if not thousands, have died in the orchard. Lonely survivors fly about in a distracted fashion.

The sky is now covered with black clouds. We are fighting and confusing the enemy with our usual burning tyres. Meanwhile they use computer technology to destroy us. An astronaut on a Russian satellite said he saw huge black clouds and many fires burning across the region.

Salvador has gotten more used to the noise of the explosions, but a very loud bang still sends him chasing about distractedly. Dogs seem to sense an air raid before it begins. They tense up and start barking before we can hear anything. I wonder why they don't use them instead of radar? . . .

We've now been without water for one week. My hands and nails are disgusting. Everyone has a sooty face. No one bothers to look in the mirror any more. Needles is the only one who still looks neat and clean. Raad says that in Jadiriyah . . . they have no more day; the sky is permanently black from the smoke of the Dora refinery as it burns. It has been burning from the first day of the war. . . .

Day 27

Apparently the racket that we heard yesterday was the sound of the B-52 bombers. They sounded horrific. Menth got a bullet through the front windshield of his . . . car. . . .

Fat cats everywhere. Fat cats sleeping, or sitting in doorways; fat cats walking and crossing the streets with no fear of being run over. They of all creatures seem to be totally unmoved by what is happening around them. They have been eating to bursting point on all the leftovers from the thawing freezers.

Meat and chicken have been passed around like nuts—but the end is in sight. Salvador will have to get used to being a vegetarian quite soon. . . .

Talking about freezers, Sheikha came back yesterday to her house. She had spent the first three weeks at her daughter's house and only came back at the behest of her neighbours, who could not stand the smell coming out of her house. She put on a face mask and emptied her giant freezer. . . . [F]loating on a sea of stagnant scummy water, was an entire sheep, and bobbing around it were twenty-four chickens and sundry legs of lamb in various states of decay. Two dozen *kubbas*, sixty-eight rice patties, plus plastic bags full of stuffed vegetables, beans and peas, all of which had been frozen and put away for the hard times to come. Three whole fishes, hunks of beef, kilos of mince, loaves of bread, cakes and pastries—all had to be thrown out, adding to the diet of the bloated street animals who have never had it so good. By the way, this description of the contents of Sheikha's freezer could just as easily apply to every well-to-do household in Baghdad before the start of the war. Everyone was preparing and hoarding foodstuffs in their freezers, never imagining that they would bomb us out of electricity. . . .

Most people have run out of petrol, and it doesn't appear likely that we will be getting any more in the near future. So it's either pedaling on the bike, walking, or going by bus. Buses are still running but they are packed. A few families took precautions and hoarded petrol in tanks in their gardens—there have been many accidents. Munir U. built large tanks in Najul's garden but didn't check them for leaks. Now he says the petrol has all gone. . . . Petrol is so scarce that some dealers mix it with water. One has to buy it from a reliable source and check its colour. Pinky-mauve is the best.

Some are thinking about going to shelters for the night. Suha and I offered to go and check ours out, although I would never . . . spend the night there. The Suleikh shelter is inside Baghdad College . . . in the grounds of what used to be a monastery and vineyard in the tenth century—the monks were famous for their wine. Wish it was wine instead of war now. The shelter is a big, plain, windowless block. They are the same design all over Baghdad. . . . A claustrophobic nightmare. Inside there was low-voltage electricity, not even enough to read by. Very high ceilings. "You can register your name," said the guard at the door, "and come or not come. But if you do want to come, you must be here by six. That's when the doors shut." The doors look like massive metal walls.

My next-door neighbour and her three daughters have been going there for the last couple of nights. Her husband is stuck in Tunis and she says her daughters are less nervous and sleep better there without the noise—but it's not quite paradise. . . .

Day 34

After the rains the streets became black and shiny with great puddles that looked like oil slicks. All the black smoke descended with the rain....

Tariq Aziz has gone to Moscow, but I don't think that will help us any. Bush is fighting a dirty war.... He will continue to hammer us 'til the bitter end, he doesn't care how many Iraqis he kills. The West seems to have only three images of Arabs—terrorists, oil sheikhs, and women covered in black from head to toe. I'm not even sure that they know if there are ordinary human beings who live here....

We have a new anti-aircraft gun, a 16-millimetre or whatever, very close by. It makes a ... slow, dull, thud-like noise and adds weight to our nightly open-air concert. A modern symphony of sounds, discordant yet harmonious. At night, when the sky is covered with great big white, yellow and red flashes and our neighbourhood gun is thudding away, it is almost possible to fool oneself into thinking that one is attending a Philip Glass-like opera with an overlay of *son et lumière*. No *son* or even words yet, but in time it will be history, and they can have the whole of Iraq in which to play this light and sound in. Nobody agrees with my interpretation of our war music. Funnily enough, I cannot listen to any real music.

I don't like the siren. It's disturbing in its persistence. The dogs also get upset by that sound, and start barking the minute it goes off.

Well, Mr. Bush said no to the overtures of Tariq Aziz. I never thought he would say yes anyway. It doesn't serve his purpose. What a brave man, he passes judgment on us while he plays golf far away in Washington. His forces are annihilating us. I find it very difficult to believe that we have been so discarded by everyone, especially the Arabs. I presume that this war will be the end of so-called Arab unity—that was a farce even while it lasted. I don't think I want to call myself an Arab any more. As an Iraqi, I can choose to be a Sumerian, a Babylonian or even an Assyrian....

We had a super barbecue lunch today. A lovely day, but quite noisy—the racket is still going on even now at midnight. I can't stand the Voice of America going on about American children and how they are being affected by this war. Mrs. Bush, the so-called humane member of that marriage, had the gall to say comfortably to a group of school kids, "Don't worry, it's far away and won't affect you." What about the children here? What double standards, what hypocrisy! Where's justice?

Day 42

Defeat is a rock-bottom feeling. This morning, the forty-second day, the war stopped. They kept at us all night long, just in case we had a couple of gasps left in us. It was the worst night of the bombing of the whole war, relentless— nobody slept a wink. The noise was indescribable. We shook, rattled and rolled. Nobody could call this one a concert night, disharmony with no breathing spaces.

They say the Americans are in Nasiriya. Will they come to Baghdad? Like my dreams, will they come marching down Haifa Street?

The Persian Gulf War Wreaks Regional Havoc

All but two Arab leaders supported Coalition forces in Operation Desert Shield and Operation Desert Storm. But among the people (not the leaders), the Persian Gulf War was extremely unpopular. In some ways, it is possible to argue that the Persian Gulf War fostered the suppression of democracy in the Arab world, for the governments of Egypt and Morocco felt compelled to quell large demonstrations. As pointed out by the historian William L. Cleveland, many ordinary Arabs felt that the United States and its allies applied a double standard: These countries insisted that Iraq adhere to a U.N. resolution to get out of Kuwait (UN SC Res 662), but they did not similarly force Israel to comply with a similar resolution to get out of the Occupied Territories (UN SC Res 242). Further, the Persian Gulf War seemed to many Arabs as an excuse to impose the artificial boundaries drawn by imperial powers (Cleveland, 482).

King Hussein of Jordan, however, along with Yasser Arafat of the Palestine Liberation Organization (PLO), refused to endorse a military resolution to the Persian Gulf conflict. King Hussein had ruled Jordan since 1953, and he had always had very close relations with the United States and Great Britain. Jordan, however, shared a border with Iraq, so the king felt his country was particularly vulnerable to a military solution to this crisis. This is especially true given the demography of his kingdom. Only 25 percent of the population is ethnic Jordanian, with the rest of the 75 percent being from other polities (this last being a political term that encompasses Palestinians) in the region. For these reasons, Jordan needed peace in the region. Queen Noor is the widow of King Hussein, and she has published an account of this time in *Leap of Faith: Memoirs of an Unexpected Life* (New York: Hyperion, 2003), 327–35. As you read this passage, you should consider the following: What was King Hussein's position in regard to Iraq? In what specific ways did the Persian Gulf War affect life in Jordan?

On January 17, we learned later, Bush called King Fahd and President Mubarak to tell them the air war was about to begin, and James Baker called the Soviets. Hussein and I found out on CNN that the war had started; we sat in front of the television devastated as we watched the opening bombardment of Baghdad. The King acutely appreciated the potential consequences of the assault and the furies it would unleash. Divisions between Arab countries would be exacerbated, and extremists would bring terrific pressure to bear by depicting their governments as puppets of the West. The economic consequences would also be very grave, particularly for poor countries. Saudi Arabia's willingness to accept foreign troops on its sacred soil would be seen as a humiliation to all Arabs, especially in a region that was so sensitive to colonialism. Anti-American feelings on the streets of Jordan and throughout the region would reach an all-time high, fanned by those trying to cast the bombing of Baghdad in religious terms, as an assault by Christian and Jewish forces against Islam. My husband saw the strong possibility of these forces spiraling out of control and was heartsick at his helplessness to do anything to stop it. . . .

Just as my husband was constantly moving from the situation room . . . to the refugee camps to all the units of the army, where he made it a point to greet and encourage every soldier, I was always on the go myself. Cholera had been reported at one of our refugee camps, and we had an urgent need for more blankets and warm clothing as the winter rains began, so I devoted myself to these tasks.

With each passing day, public sentiment in Jordan became more and more supportive of Saddam Hussein. He became an overnight Arab hero when he launched his first Scud missiles into Israel on January 17. Two days later, the mood on the streets became almost euphoric when at least three Iraqi Scuds hit Tel Aviv, especially since it had happened after U.S. reports that Saddam Hussein had been effectively neutralized. Such overblown coalition claims fueled the myth that Saddam Hussein was invincible.

I clung stubbornly to the hope that it would become clear to all that war was not a solution, only a multiplier of suffering. "Successful missions," as the White House and the Defense Department described them, meant death for Iraqi civilians that we, or people close to us, knew. Those innocent victims were our neighbors. . . .

As the air war continued, every Iraqi Scud launched at Israel or Saudi Arabia raised fears in Jordan that the warheads might contain chemical or biological weapons. Some people hung litmus paper in their houses to determine if there were chemical agents in the air; others taped their windows shut. The demand for gas masks grew. . . .

Hussein's greatest preoccupation was the safety of the country. Roads into Jordan were being targeted by allied warplanes, and oil trucks carrying perfectly legal oil into our country were being bombed. A rationing system had already been put into place because of the Saudi decision to cut off our oil; cars with even-numbered license plates were allowed on the roads one day, and those with odd-numbered licenses the next, but still the lack of fuel was becoming a national crisis. So was the carnage along the highway from Baghdad to Amman, with civilian cars and trucks and buses coming under steady allied attacks with a mounting loss of Jordanian life.

The King felt he could not remain silent in light of the ongoing devastation of neighboring Iraq and its effects on Jordanians. The mood on the streets was close to boiling over at the continuing destruction of Baghdad. People were on the verge of taking matters into their own hands. He had to respond, and he did, on February 6, after a coalition bombing of Jordanian oil tankers and trucks on the Baghdad-Amman international highway killed fourteen civilians and injured twenty-six more. In an impassioned speech to the Jordanian people, he condemned the allied attack against Iraq and reaffirmed his commitment to a diplomatic solution to the crisis. He spoke stirringly of the Iraqi people and their reduction to a primitive way of life. Expressing his solidarity with the people of Iraq and of Jordan, he asked: "Which voices will win in the end? The voices of reason, peace, and justice, or the voices of war, hatred, and insanity?"

The speech had an immediate and positive impact on Jordanians, lifting their morale and muting their frustration and anger. There was an . . . audible sigh of relief throughout the country as people felt that their . . . fears were . . . understood by their leaders. My husband's stature soared in Jordan and plummeted in Saudi Arabia and in the West. The Saudis . . . wrote off Hussein as having "lost his role" in the Middle East, and the Americans vilified him. The day after the speech, phone calls and faxes poured in from American reporters, members of Congress, and even some of my friends, demanding to know why my husband had thrown his weight behind Saddam Hussein. . . .

The war ended six weeks after it began, leaving Kuwait smoldering and Iraq in ruins. American missiles . . . had destroyed electrical plants, severed telephone lines, and shattered bridges and highways, as well as factories, dams, sewage facilities, hospitals, and schools. No one knows how many civilians were killed, but the toll . . . included hundreds of women and children in the Amariya bomb shelter on February 13. Some 88,500 tons of bombs were dropped on Iraq, the equivalent of seven and a half atomic bombs the size of the one dropped on Hiroshima. By and large Iraq was reduced to a pre-industrial state, as my husband had forecast in his February speech.

Aside from Kuwait and Iraq, no country suffered more from the Gulf crisis than Jordan. Because of my husband's neutral stance in the war, the Gulf states, Kuwait, and Saudi Arabia cut off all economic aid. Because of the ongoing UN-imposed sanctions against Iraq, Jordan suffered a shattering $3 billion loss in trade revenue from our largest trading partner, Iraq. Tourism, a major source of revenue, dried up completely, as did foreign investment in Jordan. At the same time, our responsibilities increased enormously. More than 400,000 expatriates, officially called "returnees," came to Jordan after being expelled by Kuwait and Saudi Arabia.... Our population grew 15 percent overnight, putting further strain on water and housing, and adding many thousands of new students to our schools. Unemployment soared to nearly 30 percent.

On the Arab street, the war against Iraq was viewed as an anti-Arab war, no matter which governments the Western members of the coalition claimed as their allies. There was absolute certainty among the people in the entire region, including Jordan, that the war was intended to undercut Arab independence, strength, and control over its own resources, especially oil. This led some to an even greater identification with Saddam Hussein, but this was by no means a uniform phenomenon in the region; in fact, many Arabs criticized the Iraqi invasion of Kuwait. There was a general consensus, however, that the suffering of the Iraqi people was completely unjustifiable.

The humanitarian cost of the war was heartbreaking. We had made great strides in Jordan over the previous decade, achieving standards of literacy, immunization, and maternal and infant mortality rates that approximated—and in some cases exceeded—those of far more developed countries. Suddenly the crisis and the war set all that progress back. The immunization programs for which we were renowned began to lag behind schedule, leading to an outbreak of polio in poorer areas. Our schools, which had been models in the region, became impossibly crowded with the new wave of returnees, and we had to establish a double-shift schedule to accommodate them. As poverty rose, we were beginning to see signs of malnutrition.

I remember going down to the Dead Sea with my husband soon after the war ended. "We are at the lowest point on Earth," he said. "It can only go up from here."

"After the Storm": Winning the War, but Losing the Peace

The cease-fire negotiated at Safwan, an Iraqi city on the infamous "highway of death," effectively ended the war. According to Gen. H. Norman Schwarzkopf, who negotiated the cease-fire, "we had inflicted a crushing defeat on Saddam's forces and accomplished every one of our military objectives" (Schwarzkopf, 559). The cease-fire agreement went equally well, in Schwarzkopf's opinion, for the Iraqi representative agreed to all U.S. demands (564). The official end of this war, however, did not bring relief for the Iraqi people. Kurds in the north and Shi'is in the south rose up against the government, forcing severe military reprisals in those areas. President George H. W. Bush and his National Security Advisor Brent Scowcroft describe the denouement of this war from an American perspective. The following description of the end of fighting comes from their collective memoir *A World Transformed* (New York: Vintage Books, 1998), 488–90. As you read this account, you should consider the following: What are the "unresolved problems" to which the text refers? Do the authors express any regrets? If so, what are they? What do they count as the successes of this war and the ensuing peace? Why didn't the United States and its Coalition allies overthrow the Ba'thist regime?

> The end of effective Iraqi resistance came with a rapidity which surprised us all, and we were perhaps psychologically unprepared for the sudden transition from fighting to peacemaking. True to the guidelines we had established, when we had achieved our strategic objectives (ejecting Iraqi forces from Kuwait and eroding Saddam's threat to the region) we stopped fighting. But the necessary limitations placed on our objectives . . . and the lack of a "battleship *Missouri*" surrender unfortunately left unresolved problems, and new ones arose.
>
> We soon discovered that more of the Republican Guard survived the war than we had believed or anticipated. Owing to the unexpected swiftness of the Marine advance into Kuwait, the Guard reserves were not drawn south into the battle—and into the trap created by the western sweep around and behind Kuwait as we had planned. While we would have preferred to reduce further the threat Saddam posed to the region—and help undermine his hold on power—by destroying additional Guard divisions, in truth he didn't need those forces which escaped destruction in order to maintain internal control. He had more than twenty untouched divisions in other parts of Iraq. One more day would not have altered the strategic situation, but it would have made a substantial difference in human terms. We would have been castigated for slaughtering fleeing soldiers after our own mission was successfully completed.
>
> We were disappointed that Saddam's defeat did not break his hold on power, as many of our Arab allies had predicted and we had come to expect. The abortive uprising of the Shi'ites in the south and the Kurds in the north did not spread to the Sunni population of central Iraq, and the Iraqi military remained loyal. Critics claim that we encouraged the separatist Shi'ites and Kurds

to rebel and then reneged on a promise to aid them if they did so. President Bush repeatedly declared that the fate of Saddam Hussein was up to the Iraqi people. Occasionally, he indicated that removal of Saddam would be welcome, but for very practical reasons there was never a promise to aid an uprising. While we hoped that a popular revolt or coup would topple Saddam, neither the United States nor the countries of the region wished to see the breakup of the Iraqi state. We were concerned about the long-term balance of power at the head of the Gulf. Breaking up the Iraqi state would pose its own destabilizing problems. While Ozal put the priority on Saddam and had a more tolerant view of Kurds than other Turkish leaders before or since, Turkey—and Iran—objected to the suggestion of an independent Kurdish state. However admirable self-determination for the Kurds or Shi'ites might have been in principle, the practical aspects of this particular situation dictated the policy. . . . [T]he uprisings distressed us, but they also offered Saddam an opportunity to reassert himself and rally his army. Instead of toppling him as the cause of its humiliating defeat, the Iraqi military was put to work to suppress the rebellions. It was a serious disappointment.

Trying to eliminate Saddam, extending the ground war into an occupation of Iraq, would have violated our guideline about not changing objectives in midstream, engaging in "mission creep," and would have incurred incalculable human and political costs. Apprehending him was probably impossible. . . . We would have been forced to occupy Baghdad and, in effect, rule Iraq. The coalition would instantly have collapsed, the Arabs deserting it in anger and other allies pulling out as well. Under those circumstances, there was no viable "exit strategy" we could see, violating another of our principles. Furthermore, we had been . . . trying to set a pattern for handling aggression in the post–Cold War world. Going in and occupying Iraq, thus unilaterally exceeding the United Nations' mandate, would have destroyed the precedent of international response to aggression that we hoped to establish. Had we gone the invasion route, the United States could conceivably still be an occupying power in a bitterly hostile land. It would have been a dramatically different—and perhaps barren—outcome.

We discussed at length the idea of forcing Saddam personally to accept the terms of Iraqi defeat at Safwan just north of the Kuwait-Iraq border—and thus the responsibility and political consequences for the humiliation of such a devastating defeat. In the end, we asked ourselves what we would do if he refused. We concluded that we would be left with two options: continue the conflict until he backed down, or retreat from our demands. The latter would have sent a disastrous signal. The former would have split our Arab colleagues from the coalition and, *de facto*, forced us to change our objectives. Given those unpalatable choices, we allowed Saddam to avoid personal surrender and permitted him to send one of his generals. Perhaps we could have devised a system of selected punishment, such as air strikes on different military units, which would have proved a viable third option, but we had fulfilled our well-defined mission; Safwan was waiting.

One other aspect of Safwan has occasioned debate: the decision to let Saddam use his helicopters. The Iraqis claimed they needed them as the only means of communication with the various parts of the war ravaged country. Schwarzkopf was without instructions on the matter, and granted the request. Saddam almost immediately began using the helicopters as gunships to put down the uprisings. Scowcroft discussed the issue with Cheney, proposing that the authority to fly the helicopters be rescinded. Cheney and Powell felt this would appear to be undercutting Schwarzkopf, and the helicopters did not allow him to do much that he could not also do—albeit with greater effort—with artillery. Scowcroft did not pursue the issue and it was never taken to the President. In retrospect, since the helicopters were being used offensively, not for communications, Schwarzkopf would not have been undercut and . . . it might have been salutary to have rapped the Iraqis on the knuckles at their first transgression.

As the conflict wound down, we felt a sense of urgency on the part of the coalition Arabs to get it over with and return to normal. This meant quickly withdrawing US forces to an absolute minimum. Earlier there had been some concern in Arab ranks that once they allowed US forces into the Middle East, we would be there to stay. Saddam's propaganda machine fanned these worriers. Our prompt withdrawal helped cement our position with our Arab allies, who now trusted us far more than they ever had. We had come to their assistance in their time of need, asked nothing for ourselves, and left again when the job was done. Despite some criticism of our conduct of the war, the Israelis too had their faith in us solidified. We had shown our ability—and willingness—to intervene in the Middle East in a decisive way when our interests were challenged. We had also crippled the military capability of one of their most bitter enemies in the region. Our new credibility (coupled with Yasir Arafat's need to redeem his image after backing the wrong side in the war) had a quick and substantial payoff in the form of a Middle East peace conference the following year in Madrid.

Denis Halliday Protests the Sanctions Regime

The economic sanctions established in UN SC Res 661 remained in place after the war. Ultimately, the global community began to recognize the devastation these sanctions wrought on ordinary Iraqis, and people put pressure on their governments to render some assistance to them. Thus, the United Nations Security Council passed Resolution 986 in 1995. This established the Oil-for-Food Program, whereby Iraq could sell some oil on the world market in order to import supplies that would alleviate the looming humanitarian crisis. The Iraqi government wanted all sanctions lifted, so it initially rejected this truncated sovereignty. By January 1996, however, Iraq recognized its need to accept the Oil-for-Food Program. And yet, it would be another fourteen months before the first food shipments arrived. In evaluating the effects of UN SC Res 986, Phebe Marr states: "It softened but could not end, the acute humanitarian crisis so evident in 1995 and 1996, especially in food supplies and eventually in medicine, but some malnutrition remained and the fundamental causes of economic decline had not been addressed" (Marr, 283).

For many people, the Oil-for-Food Program was not enough. Denis J. Halliday, for example, was the U.N. humanitarian coordinator in Iraq. He was appointed to this position on 1 September 1997, two years after the implementation of the Oil-for-Food Program (and six months after the first shipments of food to Iraq). After one year, he resigned—and this after thirty years of service to the United Nations. He resigned in a very public manner because he wanted to broadcast widely his opposition to the sanctions regime. On 6 October 1998, Halliday gave a speech before the U.S. Congress, which is transcribed below (accessed 9 December 2008, http://www.merip.org/mer/mer209/hallid.htm). As you read the speech, you should consider the following: How does Halliday think that sanctions affected life in Iraq? Why does this lead him to resign his position? What arguments does he present for ending the sanctions regime?

> Concerned international organizations have correctly focused on the plight of Iraq's 23 million people, particularly its children. After eight years of sanctions, high levels of malnutrition and child ... mortality continue. These victims are innocent civilians who had no part ... in the decisions that led to the events that brought on United Nations sanctions in the first place. The World Health Organization (WHO) confirmed to me that the ... rate of sanctions-related child mortality for children under five years of age is from five to six thousand per month. They believe this is an underestimate, since in rural parts of Iraq children are not registered at birth, and if they die within six weeks of birth, they are never registered.

There are many reasons for these tragic and unnecessary deaths, including the poor health of mothers, the breakdown of health services, the poor nutritional intake of both adults and young children and the high incidence of water-borne diseases as a result of the collapse of Iraq's water and sanitation system—and, of course, the lack of electric power to drive that system, crippled by war damage following the 1991 Gulf War.

Many people have questioned the propriety of sustaining Security Council sanctions in the full knowledge of their devastating impact on the children of Iraq. Human rights violations in Iraq greatly trouble many of us. We see a tragic incompatibility between sanctions that are harming the innocent children and people of Iraq, and the United Nations charter, specifically the Convention on Human Rights and the Rights of the Child. The incompatibility with the spirit and letter of the charter constitutes a tragedy for the United Nations itself, and . . . threatens to undermine the UN's . . . legitimacy as a benign force for peace and human well-being throughout the world.

It is not generally reported, but sanctions have had a serious impact on the Iraqi extended family system. We are seeing an increase in single-parent families, usually mothers struggling alone. There is an increase in divorce. Many families have had to sell their homes, furniture and other possessions to put food on the table, resulting in homelessness. Many young people are resorting to prostitution. The social impact of eight years of sanctions has devastated standards of traditional behavior, evidenced by the collapse of Muslim family values. Sanctions have undermined children's and parents' mutual expectations of each other. Sanctions have forced the Iraqi people to live with humiliation. Again, the children are the hardest hit. Now they are forced to work to bring money into the family. The school drop-out rate is 20 to 30 percent. Children are now committing street crime. . . . The incidence of begging is now very common. The drop-out rate will lead to higher levels of illiteracy in a country formerly renowned for maintaining a high standard of education.

. . . [T]here is a sense of hopelessness . . . [T]rade union leaders . . . asked me why the United Nations does not simply bomb the Iraqi people . . . rather than extending sanctions which kill Iraqis incrementally over a long period. Sanctions continue to malnourish and kill. Sanctions are undermining the cultural and educational recovery of Iraq, and will not change its system of governance. Sanctions encourage . . . fanaticism. Sanctions destroy the family, undermine women's social and economic advances and encourage brain-drain. Sanctions constitute a serious breach of the United Nations Charter on Human Rights and children's rights. Sanctions are a counter-productive, bankrupt concept that has led to unacceptable human suffering. And sanctions have an impact on all of us—not only those in Iraq, but those of us outside who need to work with and look forward to Iraq's re-entry into the international community. . . .

The Iraq Liberation Act of 1998

While the Oil-for-Food Program was allowing Hussein to foster loyalty among his hand-chosen elite, a growing group of influential politicians in Washington were honing what is now termed a neoconservative doctrine. This doctrine became very influential after the dissolution of the Soviet Union in 1991. It held that the United States should construct an interventionist foreign policy in order both to protect American interests (free markets) and to spread American values (human rights). Neoconservatism was particularly influential with members of the Republican Party.

Most people who advocated this doctrine believed that a mistake had been made by leaving Saddam Hussein in power at the end of the Persian Gulf War. And so, on 5 October 1998, the U.S. Congress passed the Iraq Liberation Act of 1998. This committed about $100 million to assist opposition groups that wanted to oust Saddam Hussein. The Iraqi National Congress, headed by Ahmed Chalabi, was an umbrella organization for the exiled opposition, and the U.S. Congress meant to funnel some money to its efforts to oppose the Ba'thist regime. This law was arguably the first sign that the neoconservative agenda in regard to Iraq would ascend. The following is a summary of this piece of legislation, which does exist as a larger text (accessed 25 February 2009, http://www.iraqwatch.org). As you read it, you should consider the following: What are the means by which the United States anticipates the overthrow of Hussein's government? Was it justifiable for a state to encourage the overthrow of a rival regime? Why? Or why not?

> Iraq Liberation Act of 1998—Declares that it should be the policy of the United States to seek to remove the Saddam Hussein regime from power in Iraq and to replace it with a democratic government.
>
> Authorizes the President, after notifying specified congressional committees, to provide to the Iraqi democratic opposition organization: (1) grant assistance for radio and television broadcasting to Iraq; (2) Department of Defense (DOD) defense articles and services and military education and training (IMET); and (3) humanitarian assistance, with an emphasis on . . . the needs of individuals who have fled from areas under the control of the Hussein regime. Prohibits assistance to any group or organization that is engaged in military cooperation with the Hussein regime. Authorizes appropriations.

Directs the President to designate: (1) one or more Iraqi democratic opposition organizations that meet specified criteria as eligible to receive assistance under this Act; and (2) additional such organizations which satisfy the President's criteria.

Urges the President to call upon the United Nations to establish an international criminal tribunal for the purpose of indicting, prosecuting, and imprisoning Saddam Hussein and other Iraqi officials who are responsible for crimes against humanity, genocide, and other criminal violations of international law.

Expresses the sense of the Congress that once the Saddam Hussein regime is removed from power in Iraq, the United States should support Iraq's transition to democracy by providing humanitarian assistance to the Iraqi people and democracy transition assistance to Iraqi parties . . . with democratic goals, including convening . . . foreign creditors to develop a . . . response to the foreign debt incurred by the Hussein regime. . . .

It should be the policy of the United States to support efforts to remove the regime headed by Saddam Hussein from power in Iraq and to promote the emergence of a democratic government to replace that regime.

The Deleterious Effects of Sanctions on Iraqi Women

Many thought that Saddam Hussein could not maintain power after being weakened during the Persian Gulf War, but the Ba'thist regime was deeply entrenched, more so perhaps with the passage of the Oil-for-Food Program. This program, asserts historian Charles Tripp, helped the Ba'thist regime, because it brought money to grease the wheels of patronage in Iraq. The money from the sale of oil went directly into the hands of the Ba'thist elite. Tripp insists that there developed a "shadow state" beyond the confines of public institutions. Networks of patronage—based on nepotism and tribalism—emerged. Hussein was the source of these networks, and he decided to whom wealth and influence would go. Tripp estimates that 500,000 residents of Iraq—this figure out of a total population of 26 million—benefited from money earned through the Oil-for-Food Program established by the United Nations in 1998 (Tripp, 259). By 2002, the Oil-for-Food Program allowed Iraq's government to export $12 billion annually, or 1.7 million barrels of oil a day (Tripp, 268).

And so, even after the creation of an Oil-for-Food Program, the negative effects of sanctions cannot be overstated. The journalist Hadani Ditmars also opposed the sanctions regime, even after the establishment of the Oil-for-Food Program. Ditmars traveled to Iraq as a journalist, and her six trips there became the basis for her book *Dancing in the No-Fly Zone: A Woman's Journey through*

Iraq (Vancouver, B.C.: Raincoast Books, 2005). The following account of Iraq, however, is taken from an article in *Ms.* (June/July 2001): 47–57. As you read the following article, you should consider the following: Why does Ditmars focus on the lives of women? How do women's experiences under the sanctions differ from those of Iraqi men? How specifically did sanctions affect the people of Iraq? How does Ditmars feel about the sanctions? Are there any inconsistencies in her presentation of information about the sanctions in Iraq?

> If you live in North America and must depend on CNN for images of Iraq, you might well think that this is a place inhabited only by the Republican Guard, Saddam Hussein, and legions of his supporters chanting patriotic slogans. Iraq, a country rich in culture and history, with more than 22 million people who are Arabs, Kurds, Muslims, and Christians, is almost always reduced to caricature: an empty desert nation inhabited only by war-mongering crazies and passive victims.
>
> If Iraqis in general are invisible to the Western eye, Iraqi women are that much harder to see. Although their presence in public life was more keenly felt before the embargo, which began 11 years ago, they are still active in many areas of society. But as a traveler to Iraq, you have to cross a threshold before you can really get inside the lives of women. In fact, the road from the Jordan border to Baghdad is conspicuously absent of any sign of womankind. From my hotel in Amman to the venerable al-Rashid Hotel in Iraq's capital, it is a blur of desert highway, roadside stands run by men, and male border guards. And once I get to Baghdad, my encounters with women feel almost clandestine. Interviews go through a Ministry of Information–assigned minder—who is a man....
>
> On this, my fourth trip to Iraq in three years, my driver and I have arrived at the border at midnight. We still have hours to go before we reach Baghdad. As the mustachioed border guards (nearly all the men seem to sport a Saddam Hussein mustache) go through my papers, I regret not being able to fly into the country. I had tried to get on a plane from Amman but was told at the last minute that the U.N. had revoked permission for anything but a "humanitarian" flight....
>
> After the standard document checking ("You, Canada?" they always ask, in disbelief, as I explain about my Arab name, my Lebanese grandmother), I am allowed into Iraq....
>
> I arrive in Baghdad at 5 a.m. and enter the al-Rashid, where a tiles mosaic likeness of George Bush and the words BUSH IS CRIMINAL grace the entranceway, so that it is impossible to avoid stepping on him as you walk in. Iraqis

believe that the mosaic's creator, Leila al-Attar—who died shortly after she completed the work, when her house was bombed during Clinton's 1993 missile attack on a residential area of Baghdad—was deliberately targeted. But everywhere else, the president on display is not Bush, but Saddam Hussein. He appears in many guises: here looking dapper in a Panama hat, there quite natty in an improbably Tyrolian cap. There had been a vogue for large sculptures of goddesses like Ishtar in the sixties and seventies, but these are now overwhelmed by presidential statues.

"The whole situation is oppressive," says Nasra al-Sadoun, editor of the *Baghdad Observer*, an English-language weekly. "So the men oppress the women more—it's natural." Al-Sadoun is casually sanguine. Her face is tough, proud, handsome, but the dark circles under her eyes betray her exhaustion; it is hard to tell whether this is recent or the result of ten years of waiting to exhale. Her husband and the father of her four children died two years ago, of a stress-related stroke. It seems that many Iraqis are dying young these days, in their early fifties, of strokes and hypertension-related heart disease. While the young suffer from malnutrition, the middle-aged suffer from seeing a country and a lifestyle they helped build crumble before their eyes.

In the 11 years since the harsh U.N. sanctions were imposed, well over 1 million Iraqis have died. Figures from UNICEF show that 5,000 to 6,000 children die monthly from sanction-related causes—mainly malnutrition, waterborne diseases, and lack of medicine. More than half of Iraq's population does not have access to clean drinking water, yet chlorine is blocked by sanctions. As much as 70 percent of Iraqi women suffer from anemia. Before the embargo, Iraq's socialized medicine and general oil wealth made obesity the biggest health issue. Today, it is infant mortality. The number one killer of children under five is dehydration from diarrhea. These problems are especially severe in the south, where birth defects and cancers in women and children have skyrocketed as well. This is the area where bombing—nearly always using depleted uranium tips—has been most intense, and where infrastructure damage and pollution are the most prevalent. The residue from the bombs is everywhere; it has leaked into the water of southern Iraq and is part of the desert dust that everyone breathes.

Due to sanctions, the value of the *dinar* has plummeted, and the majority of Iraqis have seen their lives go from comfortable to desperate, with many women forced to prostitute themselves in order to feed their families. The educational system, once the envy of the Arab world, is now in ruins. The embargo has meant that science, technology, and even literature textbooks are blocked at the border, as are chemicals for lab experiments and lead pencils.

Although a small percentage of Iraqis are enriching themselves through sanctions profiteering, selling food and medicine on the black-market and running banned supplies into the country, life for the majority remains grim. As an article in *The Economist* stated, "Sanctions impinge on the lives of all Iraqis every moment of the day." The middle class has been virtually wiped out. There is a new generation of angry, unemployed young men, increasingly drawn to the seduction of fundamentalist Islam.

When it comes to laying blame for these conditions, U.S. State Department critics allege that there are warehouses full of untouchable medicine outside Baghdad, and some U.N. officials quoted in a recent *New York Times* article say that Iraqi authorities are taking illegal commissions on contracts for food, medicine, and other essential goods. Humanitarian groups say that, whether the allegations are true or not, the Iraqi people, who have no control over any of this, are paying the human price of these sanctions. But there is plenty of blame to go around. The sanctions committee at the U.N. wields a mighty sword. It is currently blocking hundreds of contracts for items such as spare parts (which could repair refrigerated vehicles that transport medicines), ambulances, X-ray machines, medical swabs, syringes, and stethoscopes. The U.S.—through its security council status—has placed holds on approximately $700 million worth of contracts for food and medical supplies.

Current conditions in Iraq are tragic, but the particular tragedy for women is that before the embargo, they enjoyed arguably the highest status in the Arab world. They benefited from subsidized health care and education. Female as well as male students were regularly sent abroad to complete their education. Mothers who worked outside the home used state-subsidized day care. According to some estimates, nearly half the doctors in Iraq were women, and it was the first country in the Arab world to produce a woman judge, ambassador, and government minister. Now Iraqi women's lives have been reduced to a basic struggle for survival.

At the beginning of my trip, Nasra al-Sadoun had not wanted to reveal too much of this. "Go out," she said, "and see for yourself how it is. Make up your own mind." But making up one's own mind as a journalist in Iraq is a complicated process that involves a government minder, or "guide" as they prefer to call themselves. My minder, Khaled, somewhat of a rookie, is particularly vigilant in his quest to keep me on the "officially approved" straight and narrow.

Happily, there is a place where Khaled cannot filter everything I hope to learn about women and their lives: namely, the beauty parlor, where men do not venture. On previous visits to Baghdad, I had befriended a beautician named Ahlam, who worked in a salon near the al-Rashid. I phone her to make an appointment to see her. The salon is in Mansour, a relatively prosperous area of town, where Ahlam once lived. Now her home is 40 minutes away, in a formerly middle-class area that has been reduced, as has Ahlam's life, to poverty.

The salon is decorated with posters advertising European shampoos, and postcards—one of Paris, one of the Austrian Alps. I sit in the back with two women. One, dressed in blue jeans, is getting a pedicure, while the other, wearing a T-shirt and a long cotton skirt, waits her turn, leafing idly through a dog-eared copy of a fashion magazine. We drink coffee and smoke cigarettes, exchange gossip, and laugh at each other's jokes.

We could be anywhere; only the ubiquitous portrait of Saddam Hussein betrays our location. Our conversation is mainly about beauty products from Europe that are no longer available. No one talks about the other goods that are hard to find in embargoed Iraq. Sanctions fatigue seems to have set in, and unlike even a few years ago, no one wants to discuss it. The two women, who are sisters, are friendly and curious about me. I tell them that I am Canadian, but after they catch a glimpse of my thigh, as Ahlam prepares to strip the hair away with a sugar mixture, one exclaims, "But you have legs like an Arab woman!" There is a sense of freedom here. The sister's responses to my probing questions are not met with Baathist platitudes and sudden, inexplicable silences. And so, Ahlam's tone is almost casual as she discusses her husband, who died during the Gulf War on the "highway of death" (the desert highway where retreating Iraqi soldiers and civilians were massacred by U.S. forces). Now, like many other war widows, she is raising her children alone, on a salary of less than $150 a month.

At the time of her husband's death, Ahlam had a house and all the conveniences of middle-class life, including, she relates with a certain longing in her voice, a large freezer, a microwave oven, a washing machine, a television, and a VCR. The first thing to go was the living room sofa. "Then the armchairs," Ahlam says. She ticks off the household items she has sold over the years, a litany of loss. The last thing was the VCR, which she sold in 1996 to pay for an operation for her daughter. Soon after that, she had to sell her house and move into a small apartment.

As Ahlam paints her client's toenails blood red, her hands tremble. She apologizes, saying she is a little nervous about a pending operation to remove ovarian cysts. When pressed, she confides, "I'm worried that there won't be enough anesthetic," then changes the subject. She begins to sing quietly to herself as she stirs, on a small gas stove, the sugar mixture she will use as a depilatory. Sugar has become affordable again since rations were increased a year ago, she tells me. Now her children can sometimes eat sweets.

Most nights, she says, she can't sleep: stress and worry, as well as migraines and chronic pain in her abdomen keep her awake. I brought her bottles of extra-strength Tylenol on this trip, which she goes through at an alarming rate.

A few days later, I visit Ahlam at home. Her apartment, in a building on a street of open sewers and discarded garbage, is grim. She serves Khaled and me coffee in a small living room, beyond which is the bedroom where she and her two children, ages 9 and 11, sleep. Despite her drastic change in economic status, Ahlam clings to a fierce belief in the value of education. Out of her small earnings, she is supporting several of her siblings who are at Baghdad University. She is also adamant that her children stay in school and not work in the markets as many kids now do. She brings them to the salon after school, where they hang out upstairs, doing their homework. State-subsidized day care is a dream from the past, and private programs are "only for the rich."

Ahlam is hanging on by the tips of her beautifully manicured fingernails. In a few months, the building she lives in will be torn down, and current rents in the neighborhood are double what she pays now. She has undergone a series of operations for her ovarian cysts, but the underlying cause of these cysts is still unknown. Every time she needs another operation at the private clinic she goes to, she has to make impossible choices between food, rent, and bills. Public hospitals, which she relied on exclusively before the embargo, are now out of the question: "You only go there to die," she says.

Ahlam has no desire to remarry. When we'd been alone in the salon, I had asked her about that. "The situation is rough these days, so the men are rougher," she'd said. But now, with Khaled around, she is stiffer, and answers another question with what seems to be the "official" response: "The embargo has made women stronger, and the men have become more sympathetic to our suffering."

On another day, Khaled and I go to the Saddam Hussein Pediatric Hospital in central Baghdad, where we are given a tour and a briefing by two young interns. You can tell by their manner and dress that they are from well-to-do families, while most of the patients are poor. I have the sense that as soon as they finish their internship, they will go to a private clinic or perhaps, if they have the right connections, to a Western nation. Their state salaries are almost worthless now, in addition to which, the public hospitals, from their own description and from what I can observe, are devoid of even basic medicines.

We visit a ward where several babies and young children lie ill, their families hovering over them in great distress. One of the interns tells me that some women come into the ward so malnourished they can't produce breast milk to feed their babies. I approach a woman whose baby, I am told, is suffering from an acute upper respiratory infection as well as malnutrition. She cradles her tiny child in her arms. I ask where she is from. "Saddam City," she replies, referring to the traditionally working-class area of Baghdad that, even before the embargo, was a rough place, but now is so desperately poor that it is virtually sealed off to journalists. She has eight other children waiting at home with her husband, who hasn't worked since he had a heart attack in 1997.

Later, I talk to a woman who has come from the outskirts of Baghdad with her seven-year-old daughter, who has a form of meningitis. The mother says she has five other children; her husband died from injuries he sustained during the Gulf War. The hospital is lacking the specific antibiotics needed for a secondary infection the girl has developed. The prognosis is not good. What, I ask, did your daughter like to do when she was well? "She always dreamed of going to school," the woman says. "But she never had the chance. She has to work in the market with me."

In the far corner of the ward, a baby is dying. Surrounded by his parents and several other relatives, the baby is hooked up to a pulsing machine. A woman lies on the next bed quietly weeping. As I watch, a delegation of international officials sweeps into the ward surrounded by an entourage of flunkies and a camera crew. There is a whirl of lights and flashes, official photographs. And then, within perhaps a minute and a half, they are gone. The baby in the far corner is dead, and his female relatives are weeping in long wailing sobs.

Most Iraqis get their food through the "oil-for-food" program, which allows the government to use a set amount of oil money to buy U.N.-approved food and medicine. Before the war, oil revenues guaranteed a healthy diet for most Iraqis, but the destruction of the environment, as well as the embargo on animal vaccines and fertilizers, decimated the farming and fishing industries. Oil-for-food was started by the U.N. in 1996, to bring some relief from the embargo. Initially, the rations included tea, rice, sugar, flour, and lentils but no animal proteins, dairy products, or fresh produce. They were just enough to stop starvation, but not sufficient to prevent malnutrition. There has been a slight improvement over the years, but many Iraqis sell their rations to meet needs they consider more pressing, whether fuel for heat, textbooks for a student, or medicine for a sick child. It is a situation that Denis Halliday, the former U.N. humanitarian coordinator in Iraq, and one of several U.N. officials who resigned in protest over sanctions, has called "genocide."

The al-Gaylani mosque in Baghdad is an exquisite example of Islamic architecture. It is also, as are many mosques, the site of a food distribution center. With its cool balconies and incense-perfumed breezes, it is, in both a real and metaphysical way, a sanctuary. On previous visits, I met all kinds of women here, not just religious *hajis* but "modern" women—engineers, doctors, lawyers—who had started to pray again after the Gulf War. "It gives us strength," they told me. "It helps us to survive the situation."

I enter the mosque shortly before the Friday afternoon prayer, dressed in a black *chador* belonging to Khaled's mother. I'm hoping to have a brief audience with the imam. I had met him on previous visits and found him to be helpful. But when he receives me, he is far from friendly. "You journalists from the West," he snarls, "you say you want to help us, but you go home and write lies." He forbids me any contact with the women collecting food, but then relents slightly and allows me to photograph them. "But do not speak to any of them," he warns. Fumbling with my chador and camera straps in the bright winter sunlight, my situation becomes increasingly absurd. I leave Khaled behind and once again take refuge among women, this time in a courtyard prayer area set aside for them. I am taken up by a kind, old haji with a tattooed chin. "I am a journalist from Canada," I tell her, "and a Muslim." She extends part of her prayer mat to me.

The haji introduces me to her friends, who smile, holding their hands to their hearts, before the prayer begins. I pray shoulder to shoulder with the women and prostrate myself beside them. The imam's sermon is about the *"jihad"* of the Iraqi people—their struggle for survival. He prays for the lifting of the embargo. Some of the women weep as they listen. As I watch their faces, I feel the strength and solidarity they share. There is no spiritual crisis here, I think. Only a material one.

After the prayer, I return to see the imam, who seems calmer now. I explain again about my article. His initial reluctance may have had something to do with a recent government request that journalists refrain from reporting on extreme poverty and begging, which has become endemic in most areas of town. Or it may have just been anger and confusion. "Why," he asks me, "after all the reports you have made about the situation here, are the sanctions still in place?" Eventually he agrees to let me interview the women queuing up for the rations of soup and yogurt.

Many are young, barely out of their teens. They all have the pallid look I've come to associate with malnutrition. I ask about their lives before and after the embargo, but many have trouble remembering what "before" was like. They are a generation that has come of age knowing only war and sanctions. One woman gives me a bland look when I ask about life before 1990, and then says, "Um . . . we had a television that I remember." She smiles sheepishly and stares at the mosque's stone walls as if in a mild state of shock.

When I describe to the imam my conversation with the women, he responds, "They are only thinking of Paradise now."

If things are bad in Baghdad, they are worse in Basra, which bore the brunt of both the Iran/Iraq and Gulf wars, and has been the site of some of the worst post-war pollution. This once prosperous port town had been full of clubs and oil-rich sheikhs gambling and deal-making the night away. Now, Basra is a shadow of its former self, a jewel on the Gulf flooded with despair. On the drive from the newly re-opened airport, the first thing we notice is the floodwater mixed with open sewage seeping through the streets. These murky waters are everywhere—in rich and poor areas, in residential suburbs and the heart of downtown. During the Gulf War, U.S. planes bombed sewage and water-treatment facilities. They are slowly being restored, but the pace of work is hampered by the many goods withheld by the sanctions committee.

There is no other economy to speak of beside the oil industry. Some residents are trying to revive fishing, but the waters are too polluted. The rates of cancers and birth defects are soaring. Khaled and I and my Basran minder (now I will have two guides) head to the general hospital for a tour of the cancer ward. I meet with Dr. Abdul Karim, a gynecologist, who after taking a few minutes to welcome me, launches into a grim description of women's health issues. "Since the war," he begins, "there has been a huge increase in stillbirths, miscarriages, and congenital malformation and diseases like spina bifida." This could be partly explained, he suggests, by the severe anemia and widespread malnutrition in women of childbearing age, but not entirely. "We suspect it is also due to depleted uranium," he says.

It is estimated that at least 300 tons of the stuff was dropped on Iraq during the Gulf War, and Basra and its surrounding oil fields were heavily bombed. While there is no absolute proof that depleted uranium causes cancer and birth defects, the evidence is quickly mounting. British scientists have shown that even one atom of uranium lodged in the body can set off genetic mutations that can lead to cancer. One of the researchers on that study added that although there is a risk from radiation emitted by a uranium atom, "it may well be that the radiation is less harmful than chemical effects of the metal in the cell." The British Ministry of Defense has also recently acknowledged that depleted uranium weapons may also contain traces of plutonium, which increase the risk of cell damage for anyone exposed to it. Meanwhile, Dr. Karim's staff has kept records, including photos of babies born with two heads or missing limbs and vital organs.

"Cancers in women and children have increased dramatically," continues Dr.

Karim. "In children, the main cause of death after malnutrition and waterborne diseases is leukemia. Among women, there's been a huge rise in ovarian cancer, especially women in their twenties. Also uterine cancer, which is common in women over 60, is now occurring in women under 30. There's also been a pronounced increase in breast cancer and leukemia."

The doctor interrupts his narrative with a brief anecdote. "You know after the Gulf War, I remember we had three days of black rain. The sky was dark, and you could barely see in front of you." He is silent for a long moment. "We used to be called, here in Basra, 'The Venice of Iraq.' We were known then for our canals and palm trees. But after the Gulf War, most of the palm trees died."

We tour the cancer wards with a female intern, Amalid Abdul Jalim. There are about eight beds in each room, bare except for sheets and blankets and single lightbulbs hanging from the ceilings. The wards are not full. "Most of the cancer patients," explains Jalim, "go home to die. There's not much we can do for them here." The hospital lacks chemotherapy drugs, she says, as well as pain killers and often doesn't have syringes to administer IV fluids. "If I'd known it would be like this," she confides, "I would never have gone into medicine. I feel useless."

I speak with a patient. Her name is Zikra Abdul Hassan. She is 26, the mother of one boy. "Last year," Hassan tells me, "I started to see blue spots on my stomach." Then she developed severe menstrual bleeding and was diagnosed with ovarian cancer. A few months ago, she had her ovaries removed. Today she is back for a blood transfusion. "I was 16 at the time of the Gulf War," Hassan says. "My house was bombed."

For many Iraqis, their experience of bombing is in the present, not the past. For Iqbal Faous, an elementary school teacher in Basra, who is referred to by everyone as Um Hydir (mother of Hydir), the war is still going on. On January 25, 1999, her two young boys, ages 2 and 4, were playing outside when a U.S. missile was dropped into her residential neighborhood, killing seven people, wounding 36, and destroying several homes. Um Hydir remembers the morning with great clarity. "We were just finishing breakfast," she says, "when we heard a big boom that shook the whole house. I was in the kitchen, and all the cups and dishes fell out of the cupboards onto the floor. Everything was shaking. Then I remembered that my boys were outside. I ran out; the sky was dark and full of smoke. The whole neighborhood was out on the street and everyone seemed to have panic in their eyes. I went to look for my children and saw a small mound of earth mixed with blood and missile parts. There were my sons, Mustafa and Hydir. I called their names, but only Mustafa responded."

Hydir, the older boy, was lying face down in a pool of blood. A doctor in the neighborhood was on hand and broke the news that Hydir was dead. "But I already knew."

Mustafa underwent a series of operations on his hands—two of his fingers were destroyed—and to remove missile parts," says his mother. A U.S. charitable organization called LIFE wants to bring him to the U.S. where he can receive better medical care, but they haven't yet found a hospital willing to treat him. And without a commitment from a hospital, he isn't eligible for a "humanitarian" visa. Mustafa plays nearby as his mother recounts her story. "He's very nervous," she says, glancing over at him. "He can't sleep at night; he's always having nightmares."

Um Hydir still has hope, she says, thanks to her work as a teacher. It is a job she loves, despite the hardships of working in a school that has "no water, no books, no electricity, no blackboards, and no pencils." On top of that, "the children have a shorter attention span, less imagination," because of malnutrition. But she sees her role as vital. "I have to fight with the parents sometimes, to convince them to keep their children in school. One father tried to keep his little girl away so she could sell things in the market. I said to him, 'What kind of future will she have?' The father replied, 'Soon she will be married anyway.'" Such attitudes toward girls and education were much less prevalent before the embargo, says Um Hydir.

She is slowly adjusting to her losses. Her faith in Islam has helped her. She began wearing hijab in the mid 1990s, and she prays and fasts. "Before the embargo, I used to dress in Western clothes. But now this," she says, pointing to her voluminous black chador, "is my protection." I am not the first Western journalist she has met with, and now she asks me to deliver one more message to U.S. women: "What quarrel does your government have with our children? Stop the bombing, stop the sanctions, because they are destroying the lives of innocents.

"I know that many Americans are kind, good people who care about what is happening to us here," she adds, and then in a faint voice, " . . . they must."

As we drive back to the hotel, dusk comes and each neighborhood we pass through is enveloped in darkness, with only sporadic points of electric light. Soon, I think, if this embargo goes on, Iraq really will live up to its CNN image: an empty wasteland populated only by Saddam Hussein, the Republican Guard, and a broken populace too hungry to resist, too angry to forgive.

Bibliography

Bengio, Ofra, ed. *Saddam Speaks on the Gulf Crisis: A Collection of Documents.* Tel-Aviv: Moshe Dayan Center for Middle Eastern and African Studies, Shiloah Institute, Tel-Aviv University, 1992.

Ditmars, Hadani. *Dancing in the No-Fly Zone: A Woman's Journey through Iraq.* Moreton-in-Marsh, U.K.: Arris, 2006.

Eames, Andrew. *The 8:55 to Baghdad.* Woodstock, N.Y.: Overlook Press, 2005.

Gall, Sandy. *A Year in Kuwait.* Edinburgh, U.K.: Morrison Construction Group, 1992.

Hadithi, Naji. *Iraq 1990: An Official Handbook.* Iraq: Ministry of Information and Culture, 1989.

Hassig, Susan M. *Iraq: Cultures of the World.* Singapore: Times Books International, 1992.

M.E.N.A. Enterprises. *Saddam's Iraq: A Look before the War.* S.l.: M.E.N.A. Enterprises, 2001.

Owen, Nicholas, and Chris Sheridan. *Saddam Hussein Defying the World.* London: I.T.N., 1992.

Roberts, Paul William. *The Demonic Comedy: Some Detours in the Baghdad of Saddam Hussein.* New York: Farrar, Straus and Giroux, 1998.

Schwarzkopf, Norman. *It Doesn't Take a Hero: The Autobiography of General H. Norman Schwarzkopf.* New York: Bantam, 1993.

Thornhill, Teresa. *Sweet Tea with Cardamom: A Journey through Iraqi Kurdistan.* London: Pandora, 1997.

United States. *Tips for Travelers to the Middle East and North Africa.* Department of State Publication, 10167. Washington, D.C.: U.S. Dept. of State, Bureau of Consular Affairs, 1994.

United States Institute of Peace, Robert M. Perito, and Keith Bowen. *The Iraq Experience: A Briefing on Living and Working in Iraq.* Washington, D.C.: United States Institute of Peace, Professional Training Program, 2004.

Vincent, Christine. *Iraq: A Cultural Profile.* Ottawa: Catholic Information Centre, 1998.

Vine, Peter, and Paula Casey. *Kuwait: A Nation's Story.* London: Immel, 1992.

9

The Invasion of Iraq, 2001–2003

President George W. Bush and most members of his administration strongly believed that Saddam Hussein should be overthrown in order to protect American interests. The events of September 11 and President Bush's subsequent declaration of a "war on terror" provided an opportunity to advance this agenda. The "war on terror" was to be waged against any and all opponents who had "the will and the means to launch terrorist attacks like those of 11 September" (Tripp, 271). In December 2001, the United States ousted the Taliban from Afghanistan, because this West Asian country harbored the al-Qaeda terrorists responsible for 9/11. That very month, the Department of Defense submitted a plan to invade Iraq and overthrow the Ba'thist regime of Saddam Hussein.

After the quick victory in Afghanistan, plans to invade Iraq accelerated. In January 2002, President Bush gave his famous "Axis of Evil" speech, which identified Iran, North Korea, and Iraq as other countries that threatened U.S. security. President Bush and his advisors, however, drew particular attention to Saddam Hussein's Iraq, insisting that it was actively developing weapons of mass destruction (WMDs). (It was an allegation that would be proven false in January 2004.) By summer 2002, the administration had a draft of plans for the invasion, and its members now focused attention on gaining the approval of congressmen. Such approval was important since many members of the international community—particularly Russia, France, Germany, and China—refused to endorse a war with Iraq.

The Bush Doctrine emerged from the decisions of this time. Preemptive military action was one component of this foreign policy. Another was unilateralism, a term signifying that the United States need not adhere to multilateral action whereby the international community acted in concert. The neoconservatives who hammered out this doctrine believed that military intervention was a means of protecting American interests and also of spreading American values, such as democracy and free markets. The policymakers holding a neoconservative ideology generally felt contempt for international institutions, thinking instead that the United States must make the most of a unipolar world.

The U.S. Congress passed a joint resolution allowing for the use of force on 11 October 2002. The United States would lead what the Bush administration deemed a "Coalition of the Willing," which included the United Kingdom, Italy, Spain, Australia, and Poland. Hussein, clearly unnerved by the growing din of war drums, allowed Hans Blix to inspect Iraq for weapons of mass destruction, though the U.N. Monitoring, Verification, and Inspection Commission (UNMOVIC) team found no evidence of such. As a result, they made generally positive reports on Iraq in the early part of 2003. Nevertheless, Secretary of State Colin Powell went before the United Nations in February 2003 in order to convince the international community that Iraq had such weapons, which would then make Hussein and his Ba'thist cohort a global threat.

Five months after Congress passed a resolution allowing for the use of force in Iraq, President Bush began the war. On 17 March 2003, he announced that Hussein and his sons had forty-eight hours to leave Iraq, specifying that Iraq faced military action if they did not do so. They did not leave, and Operation Iraqi Freedom began two days later. Coalition forces bombed major military centers from the air and then coordinated a ground force assault, referred to as a "Shock and Awe" strategy. The ground force consisted of 173,218 troops, of which 150,816 were American. In anticipation of an easy victory, the Pentagon flew the Shi'i Ahmad Chalabi, the exiled and hand-chosen Hussein successor, to the region. By 9 April, the Coalition took over Baghdad. Two days later, the United States and its Kurdish allies had taken the northern city of Mosul. The Ba'th regime was no more, and the country was now under U.S. control. On 1 May, President Bush appeared—wearing a flight suit and helmet—on the *USS Lincoln* and, speaking under a banner that read "Mission Accomplished" declared a military success in Iraq.

This chapter challenges readers to consider whether the United States should have engaged in this war. It starts with a chilling response by Saddam Hussein to the events of 9/11. The chapter then moves to an op-ed piece by Brent Scowcroft, who argued against war in Iraq. After, a speech by George W. Bush is included, so that readers can see how the president argued that war was a necessary component of a larger War on Terror. As soon as the Iraq War began, one exiled Iraqi wrote a nostalgic (and somewhat anti-American) poem to his hometown of Baghdad. There follows a description of the Battle of Nasiriyah by an embedded journalist who makes it clear that the line between civilian and combatant was not always clear to American troops. Anne Garrels, foreign correspondent for National Public Radio (NPR), describes the occupation of Baghdad. Once occupied, the National Museum was looted, and its director describes the stealing of its precious artifacts. This chapter also includes Saddam Hussein's response to the invasion. This chapter ends with the infamous "Mission Accomplished" speech given by President Bush on 1 May 2003.

Saddam Hussein Responds to 9/11

Saddam Hussein and his Ba'thist regime did not have a hand in al-Qaeda's attack on 11 September 2001. Nevertheless, Hussein's response to these events aggravated tensions between the two countries. Many in the administration of George W. Bush were neoconservatives who already thought that it would be best to change regimes in this country. Hussein was the only leader in the world who did not condemn this attack; in fact, he suggested that the United States brought on the attack with its bad behavior in the international arena. Hussein gave the following speech on 12 September 2001. He gave it to members of his government, including the Deputy Prime Minister and the Minister of Military Industry. It was published in English in *America Reaps the Thorns Its Rulers Sowed in the World* (Baghdad: Iraqi Ministry of Information, 2001), 9–10. As you read his speech, you should consider the following: What arguments does Hussein use to condemn the United States? How does he use history in the service of condemning the actions of the United States?

> Regardless of the conflicting humanitarian emotions over what happened in America yesterday, America is only reaping the thorns sowed by its rulers in the world, the thorns that not only made the feet of those concerned bleed, but also the eyes of those who shed a lot of tears over their dead whose lives were taken away by America. The US has left no place without a memorial set up by its people to remind them of a criminal act by the US against them, be it in Japan which was the first to experience American nuclear weight which Washington has boasted, Vietnam and Iraq, its action against the Russian submarine let alone the crime it is perpetrating by supporting the criminal racist Zionism against our heroic Palestinian people....
>
> Would the American peoples save themselves and the world ... from the malice of their rulers, their terrorist crimes against the world? Or, would their rulers, who have become a toy in the hands of the criminal international Zionism and its poignant entity which usurped the land of Palestine and Arabs, turn against the world as would cater for the Jewish Zionist greed for illicit wealth and innocent blood?
>
> Let the American peoples remember that none has crossed the Atlantic to

reach them all throughout history, wielding arms against them. It is America that has crossed the Atlantic carrying with it death . . . and insatiable exploitation. . . .

We . . . remind the peoples of America that the lives that have perished under American weapons, American scheming and conspiracies, can ascend to the Lord of Heavens and Earth to complain the injustice of America. . . . God Almighty can see for Himself. When He decides to strike, nobody can deter His power.

Who does not want to reap evil, has to sow no evil. Anyone who cares for the lives of his own peoples as being . . . dear, must remember that the lives of people in the world are dear too. America is exporting evil . . . and crime, not only to spots where its armies deploy but also to whomever its films can reach.

American peoples have, therefore, to remember all this. If they choose to remember it, they would rescue their own security, the security of the world, and their rulers. If what happened to America is an internal affair, the household would be in a better position than others in diagnosing the disease.

Brent Scowcroft Opposes Invasion of Iraq

As the din of war drums grew louder, at least one key political actor tried to convince neoconservative politicians and the public whom they served not to go to war in Iraq. As National Security Advisor to George H. W. Bush, Brent Scowcroft had helped to construct the policy that led to the Persian Gulf War. He was, however, though Republican, a realist, not a neoconservative. Thus, he believed in fighting only if the United States was directly threatened by the actions of another country. In terms of Iraq, he did not think this was the case. He said as much in an op-ed piece in the *Wall Street Journal* on 15 August 2002. As you read it, you should evaluate the recommendations of this political insider: Why does he believe that the United States should not go to war with Iraq? What may be the costs of such a war? What does Scowcroft recommend as a foreign policy focus?

Our nation is presently engaged in a debate about whether to launch a war against Iraq. . . . The Bush administration vows regime change, but states that no decision has been made whether, much less when, to launch an invasion.

It is beyond dispute that Saddam Hussein is a menace. He terrorizes and brutalizes his own people. He has launched a war on two of his neighbors. He devotes enormous effort to rebuilding his military forces and equipping them with weapons of mass destruction. We will all be better off when he is gone.

That said, we need to think through this issue very carefully. We need to analyze the relationship between Iraq and our other pressing priorities—notably the war on terrorism—as well as the best strategy and tactics available were we to move to change the regime in Baghdad.

Saddam's strategic objective appears to be to dominate the Persian Gulf, to control oil from the region, or both.

That clearly poses a real threat to key U.S. interests. But there is scant evidence to tie Saddam to terrorist organizations, and even less to the September 11 attacks. Indeed Saddam's goals have little in common with the terrorists who threaten us, and there is little incentive for him to make common cause with them.

He is unlikely to risk his investment in weapons of mass destruction, much less his country, by handing such weapons to terrorists who would use them for their own purposes and leave Baghdad as the return address. Threatening to use these weapons for blackmail—much less their actual use—would open . . . his . . . regime to a devastating response by the U.S. While Saddam is thoroughly evil, he is above all a power-hungry survivor.

Saddam is a . . . dictatorial aggressor, with traditional goals for his aggression. There is little evidence to indicate that the United States itself is an object of his aggression. Rather, Saddam's problem with the U.S. appears to be that we stand in the way of his ambitions. He seeks weapons of mass destruction not to arm terrorists, but to deter us from intervening to block his aggressive designs.

Given Saddam's aggressive regional ambitions, as well as his ruthlessness and unpredictability, it may at some point be wise to remove him from power. Whether and when that point should come ought to depend on overall U.S. national security priorities. Our pre-eminent security priority—underscored repeatedly by the president—is the war on terrorism. An attack on Iraq at this time would seriously jeopardize, if not destroy, the global counterterrorist campaign we have undertaken.

The United States could certainly defeat the Iraqi military and destroy Saddam's regime. But it would not be a cakewalk. On the contrary, it . . . would be very expensive—with serious consequences for the U.S. and global economy—and could . . . be bloody. In fact, Saddam would be likely to conclude he had nothing left to lose, leading him to unleash whatever weapons of mass destruction he possesses.

Israel would . . . be the first casualty, as in 1991 when Saddam sought to bring Israel into the Gulf conflict. . . . [U]sing weapons of mass destruction, he might succeed, provoking Israel to respond, perhaps with nuclear weapons, unleashing an Armageddon in the Middle East. . . . [I]f we are to achieve our strategic objectives in Iraq, a military campaign . . . would have to be followed by a large-scale, long-term military occupation.

But the central point is that any campaign against Iraq, whatever the strategy, cost and risks, is certain to divert us for some indefinite period from our war on terrorism. Worse, there is a virtual consensus in the world against an attack on Iraq at this time. So long as that sentiment persists, it would require the U.S. to pursue a virtual go-it-alone strategy against Iraq, making any military operations . . . difficult and expensive. The most serious cost, however, would be to the war on terrorism. Ignoring that clear sentiment would result in a serious degradation in international cooperation with us against terrorism. . . . [W]e simply cannot win that war without enthusiastic international cooperation, especially on intelligence.

Possibly the most dire consequences would be the effect in the region. The shared view in the region is that Iraq is principally an obsession of the U.S. The obsession of the region, however, is the Israeli-Palestinian conflict. If we were seen to be turning our back on that bitter conflict—which the region, rightly or wrongly, perceives to be clearly within our power to resolve—in order to go after Iraq, there would be an explosion of outrage against us. We would be seen as ignoring a key interest of the Muslim world in order to satisfy what is seen to be a narrow American interest.

Even without Israeli involvement, the results could well destabilize Arab regimes in the region, ironically facilitating one of Saddam's strategic objectives. At a minimum, it would stifle any cooperation on terrorism, and could even swell the ranks of terrorists. Conversely, the more progress we make in the war on terrorism, and the more we are seen to be committed to resolving the Israel-Palestinian issue, the greater will be the international support for going after Saddam.

If we are really serious about the war on terrorism, it must remain our top priority. However, should Saddam Hussein be found to be clearly implicated in the events of September 11, that could make him a key counterterrorist target, rather than a competing priority, and significantly shift world opinion toward support for regime change.

. . . [W]e should be pressing the United Nations Security Council to insist on an effective no-notice inspection regime for Iraq—any time, anywhere, no permission required. . . . [S]enior administration officials have opined that Saddam Hussein would never agree to such an inspection regime. But if he did, inspections would serve to keep him off balance and under close observation, even if all his weapons of mass destruction capabilities were not uncovered. And if he refused, his rejection could provide the persuasive *casus belli* which many claim we do not now have. Compelling evidence that Saddam had acquired nuclear-weapons . . . could have a similar effect.

In sum, if we will act in full awareness of the intimate interrelationship of the key issues in the region, keeping counterterrorism as our foremost priority, there is much potential for success across the entire range of our security interests—including Iraq. If we reject a comprehensive perspective, however, we put at risk our campaign against terrorism as well as stability . . . in a vital region of the world.

President Bush Argues for War

Members of the Bush administration purported that Iraq's making of WMDs as well as its enmity made the Ba'thist regime a grave threat. Bush made the following speech four days before Congress was to vote on a resolution allowing for the use of force in Iraq. For this reason, this speech provides critical insights into President Bush's argument for war. "The Joint Resolution to Authorize the Use of United States Armed Forces Against Iraq" passed on 11 October 2002 with a vote of 373 for and 156 against. In reading this speech, you should reflect on the rhetorical means used to convince Americans to support the use of force in Iraq: What purpose do the historical precedents cited by President Bush serve in justifying a war? How does the president show Iraq to be a direct threat to the United States? How does President Bush make use of September 11 in his argument for the use of military force? Does he directly blame Iraq for it?

> Tonight, I want to take a few minutes to discuss a grave threat to peace, and America's determination to lead the world in confronting that threat.
>
> The threat comes from Iraq. It arises directly from the Iraqi regime's own actions—its history of aggression, and its drive toward an arsenal of terror. Eleven years ago, as a condition for ending the Persian Gulf War, the Iraqi regime was required to destroy its weapons of mass destruction, to cease all development of such weapons, and to stop all support for terrorist groups. The Iraqi regime has violated all of those obligations. It possesses and produces chemical and biological weapons. It is seeking nuclear weapons. It has given shelter and support to terrorism, and practices terror against its own people. The entire world has witnessed Iraq's eleven-year history of defiance, deception and bad faith.
>
> We also must never forget the most vivid events of recent history. On September 11th, 2001, America felt its vulnerability—even to threats that gather on the other side of the earth. We resolved then . . . to confront every threat, from any source, that could bring sudden terror and suffering to America.

Members of the Congress of both political parties, and members of the United Nations Security Council, agree that Saddam Hussein is a threat to peace and must disarm. We agree that the Iraqi dictator must not be permitted to threaten America and the world with horrible poisons and diseases and gases and atomic weapons. Since we all agree on this goal, the issue is: how can we best achieve it?

Many Americans have raised legitimate questions: about the nature of the threat; about the urgency of action—why be concerned now; about the link between Iraq developing weapons of terror, and the wider war on terror. These are all issues we've discussed broadly and fully. . . . And tonight, I want to share those discussions with you.

First, some ask why Iraq is different from other countries or regimes that also have terrible weapons. While there are many dangers in the world, the threat from Iraq stands alone—because it gathers the most serious dangers of our age in one place. Iraq's weapons of mass destruction are controlled by a murderous tyrant who has already used chemical weapons to kill thousands of people. This same tyrant has tried to dominate the Middle East, has invaded and brutally occupied a small neighbor, has struck other nations without warning, and holds an unrelenting hostility toward the United States.

By its past and present actions, by its technological capabilities, by the merciless nature of its regime, Iraq is unique. As a former chief weapons inspector of the U.N. has said, "The fundamental problem with Iraq remains the nature of the regime, itself. . . . Hussein is a homicidal dictator . . . addicted to weapons of mass destruction."

Some ask how urgent this danger is to America and the world. The danger is already significant, and it only grows worse with time. If we know Saddam Hussein has dangerous weapons today—and we do—does it make any sense for the world to wait to confront him as he grows even stronger and develops even more dangerous weapons?

In 1995, after . . . years of deceit by the Iraqi regime, the head of Iraq's military industries defected. It was then that the regime was forced to admit that it had produced more than 30,000 liters of anthrax and other . . . biological agents. The inspectors . . . concluded that Iraq had likely produced two to four times that amount. This is a massive stockpile of biological weapons that has never been accounted for, and capable of killing millions.

. . . [T]he regime has produced thousands of tons of chemical agents, including mustard gas, sarin nerve gas. . . . Hussein . . . has experience in using chemical weapons. He . . . ordered chemical attacks on Iran, and on . . . forty villages in his . . . country. These actions killed or injured at least 20,000 people, more than six times the number of people who died in the attacks of September the 11th.

And surveillance photos reveal that the regime is rebuilding facilities that it had used to produce chemical and biological weapons. Every chemical and biological weapon that Iraq has or makes is a direct violation of the truce that ended the Persian Gulf War in 1991. Yet, Saddam Hussein has chosen to build and keep these weapons despite international sanctions, U.N. demands, and isolation from the civilized world.

Iraq possesses ballistic missiles with a likely range of hundreds of miles—far enough to strike Saudi Arabia, Israel, Turkey and other nations—in a region where more than 135,000 American civilians and service members live and work.... Iraq has a ... fleet of manned and unmanned aerial vehicles that could be used to disperse chemical or biological weapons across broad areas. We're concerned that Iraq is exploring ways of using these UAVS for missions targeting the United States.... [S]ophisticated delivery systems aren't required for a chemical or biological attack; all that might be required are a ... container and one ... intelligence operative to deliver it.

And that is the source of our urgent concern about Saddam Hussein's links to international terrorist groups. Over the years, Iraq has provided safe haven to terrorists such as Abu Nidal, whose terror organization carried out more than 90 terrorist attacks in 20 countries that killed nearly 900 people, including 12 Americans. Iraq has also provided safe haven to Abu Abbas, who was responsible for seizing the *Achille Lauro* and killing an American passenger. And we know that Iraq is continuing to finance terror and gives assistance to groups that use terrorism to undermine Middle East peace.

We know that Iraq and the al Qaeda terrorist network share a common enemy—the United States of America. We know that Iraq and al Qaeda have had high-level contacts that go back a decade. Some al Qaeda leaders who fled Afghanistan went to Iraq. These include one very senior al Qaeda leader who received medical treatment in Baghdad this year, and who has been associated with planning for chemical and biological attacks. We've learned that Iraq has trained al Qaeda members in bomb-making and poisons and deadly gases. And we know that after September the 11th, Saddam Hussein's regime gleefully celebrated the terrorist attacks on America....

Some have argued that confronting the threat from Iraq could detract from the war against terror. To the contrary; confronting the threat posed by Iraq is crucial to winning the war on terror. When I spoke to Congress over a year ago, I said that those who harbor terrorists are as guilty as the terrorists themselves. Saddam Hussein is harboring terrorists and the instruments of terror.... And he cannot be trusted. The risk is simply too great that he will use them, or provide them to a terror network.

Terror cells and outlaw regimes building weapons of mass destruction are different faces of the same evil. Our security requires that we confront both. And the United States military is capable of confronting both.

Many people have asked how close Saddam Hussein is to developing a nuclear weapon.... [W]e don't know exactly, and that's the problem. Before the Gulf War ... intelligence indicated that Iraq was eight ... years away from developing a nuclear weapon. After the war, international inspectors learned that the regime has been much closer—the regime in Iraq would likely have possessed a nuclear weapon no later than 1993. The inspectors discovered that Iraq had an advanced nuclear weapons development program ... and was pursuing several different methods of enriching uranium for a bomb....

The evidence indicates that Iraq is reconstituting its nuclear weapons program. Saddam Hussein has held several meetings with Iraqi nuclear scientists, a group he calls his "nuclear mujahideen"—his nuclear holy warriors. Satellite photographs reveal that Iraq is rebuilding facilities at sites that have been part of its nuclear programs in the past. Iraq has attempted to purchase high-strength aluminum tubes and ... equipment needed for gas centrifuges, which ... enrich uranium for nuclear weapons.

If the Iraqi regime is able to produce, buy or steal ... enriched uranium a little larger than a single softball, it could have a nuclear weapon in less than a year.... Saddam Hussein would ... blackmail anyone who opposes his aggression. He would be in a position to dominate the Middle East. He would be in a position to threaten America. And Saddam Hussein would be in a position to pass nuclear technology to terrorists.

Some citizens wonder, after 11 years of living with this problem, why do we need to confront it now? ... We've experienced the horror of September the 11th. We have seen that those who hate America are willing to crash airplanes into buildings full of innocent people. Our enemies would be no less willing ... to use biological or chemical, or a nuclear weapon.

Knowing these realities, America must not ignore the threat gathering against us. Facing clear evidence of peril, we cannot wait for the final proof—the smoking gun—that could come in the form of a mushroom cloud. As President Kennedy said in October of 1962, "Neither the United States of America, nor the world community of nations can tolerate deliberate deception and offensive threats on the part of any nation, large or small. We no longer live in a world," he said, "where only the actual firing of weapons represents a sufficient challenge to a nation's security to constitute maximum peril...."

Some believe we can address this danger by simply resuming the old approach to inspections, and applying diplomatic and economic pressure. Yet this is precisely what the world has tried to do since 1991. The U.N. inspections program was met with systematic deception. The Iraqi regime bugged hotel rooms and offices of inspectors to find where they were going next; they forged documents, destroyed evidence, and developed mobile weapons facilities to keep a step ahead of inspectors. Eight so-called presidential palaces were declared off-limits to unfettered inspections. These sites actually encompass twelve square miles, with hundreds of structures, both above and below the ground, where sensitive materials could be hidden.

The world has ... tried economic sanctions—and watched Iraq use billions of dollars in illegal oil revenues to fund ... weapons purchases, rather than providing for the needs of the Iraqi people.

The world has tried limited military strikes to destroy Iraq's weapons of mass destruction ...—only to see them openly rebuilt, while the regime denies that they even exist.

The world has tried no-fly zones to keep Saddam from terrorizing his own people—and in the last year alone, the Iraqi military has fired upon American and British pilots more than 750 times.

After eleven years during which we have tried containment, sanctions, inspections, even selected military action, the end result is that Saddam Hussein still has chemical and biological weapons and is increasing his capabilities to make more. And he is moving ever closer to developing a nuclear weapon....

The time for denying, deceiving, and delaying has come to an end. Saddam Hussein must disarm himself—or, for the sake of peace, we will lead a coalition to disarm him.

Many nations are joining us in insisting that Saddam Hussein's regime be held accountable. They are committed to defending the international security that protects the lives of both our citizens and theirs. And that's why America is challenging all nations to take the resolutions of the U.N. Security Council seriously.

... [T]hese resolutions are clear. In addition to ... destroying all ... weapons of mass destruction, Iraq must end its support for terrorism. It must cease the persecution of its civilian population. It must stop an illicit trade outside the Oil for Food program. It must ... account for ... Gulf War personnel, including an American pilot, whose fate is ... unknown.

By taking these steps ... the Iraqi regime has an opportunity to avoid conflict. Taking these steps would ... change the nature of the Iraqi regime.... America hopes the regime will make that choice. Unfortunately, at least so far, we have little reason to expect it. And that's why two administrations—mine and President Clinton's—have stated that regime change in Iraq is the only certain means of removing a great danger to our nation.

I hope this will not require military action, but it may. And military conflict could be difficult. An Iraqi regime faced with its own demise may attempt ... desperate measures. If ... Hussein orders such measures, his generals would be well advised to refuse those orders. If they do not refuse, they must understand that all war criminals will be ... punished. If we have to act, we will take every precaution that is possible. We will plan carefully; we will act with the full power of the United States military; we will act with allies at our side. ...

There is no easy or risk-free course of action. Some have argued we should wait. ... In my view, it's the riskiest of all options, because the longer we wait, the stronger and bolder Saddam Hussein will become. We could wait and hope that Saddam does not give weapons to terrorists, or develop a nuclear weapon to blackmail the world. But I'm convinced that is a hope against all evidence. As Americans, we want peace—we work and sacrifice for peace. But there is no peace if our security depends on the will and whims of a ruthless ... dictator. I'm not willing to stake one American life on trusting ... Hussein.

Failure to act would embolden other tyrants, allow terrorists access to new weapons and to new resources, and make blackmail a permanent feature of world events. The United Nations would betray the purpose of its founding, and prove irrelevant to the problems of our time. ... [T]hrough its inaction, the United States would resign itself to a future of fear.

That is not the America I know. That is not the America I serve. ... This nation, in world war and in Cold War, has never permitted the brutal and lawless to set history's course. Now, as before, we will secure our nation, protect our freedom, and help others to find freedom of their own.

Some worry that a change of leadership in Iraq could create instability and make the situation worse. The situation could hardly get worse, for world security and for the people of Iraq. The lives of Iraqi citizens would improve ... if Saddam Hussein were no longer in power. ... The dictator ... is a student of Stalin, using murder as a tool of terror and control, within his ... cabinet, within his ... army, and ... within his ... family. ...

America believes that all people are entitled to hope and human rights, to the non-negotiable demands of human dignity. People ... prefer freedom to slavery; prosperity to squalor; self-government to the rule of terror and torture. America is a friend to the people of Iraq. Our demands are directed ... at the regime that enslaves them and threatens us. When these demands are met, the . . . greatest benefit will come to Iraqi men, women and children. The oppression of Kurds, Assyrians, Turkomans, Shi'a, Sunnis and others will be lifted. The long captivity of Iraq will end, and an era of new hope will begin. . . .

I have asked Congress to authorize the use of America's military, if it proves necessary, to enforce U.N. Security Council demands. Approving this resolution does not mean that military action is . . . unavoidable. The resolution will tell the United Nations . . . that America speaks with one voice and is determined to make the demands of the civilized world mean something. Congress will also be sending a message to the dictator in Iraq: . . . his only choice is full compliance, and the time remaining for that choice is limited. . . .

The attacks of September the 11th showed our country that vast oceans no longer protect us from danger. Before that tragic date, we had only hints of al Qaeda's plans and designs. Today in Iraq, we see a threat whose outlines are far more clearly defined, and whose consequences could be far more deadly. Saddam Hussein's actions have put us on notice, and there is no refuge from our responsibilities.

We did not ask for this present challenge, but we accept it. Like other generations of Americans, we will meet the responsibility of defending human liberty against . . . aggression. By our resolve, we will give strength to others. By our courage, we will give hope to others. And by our actions, we will secure the peace, and lead the world to a better day.

An Iraqi Elegy to Baghdad

Salah Al-Hamdani was an Iraqi exile, and he watched the conquest of Baghdad from his home in France. Members of the Ba'th regime had imprisoned Al-Hamdani in the 1970s, and he began his career as an author in prison, where he kept journals. After his release, he moved to France. In 2003, he was fifty-two years old, and he hadn't seen his home country in over thirty years. Although Al-Hamdani was a strong opponent of Hussein's Ba'thist state, he still had very strong feelings about the U.S. decision to invade Iraq. Al-Hamdani wrote the following poem on 25 March 2003. C. Dickson translated it, and the poem is found in the Words without Borders anthology *Literature from the "Axis of Evil": Writing from Iran, Iraq, North Korea, and Other Enemy Nations* (New York: New Press, 2006), 56–59. As you read this poem, you should consider the following: What does the imagery suggest about Al-Hamdani's conception of Iraqi identity? How does the poem suggest what the author feels in regard to the U.S. occupation of his homeland?

You needn't crucify yourself
either on the edge of a page
of history that is not your own,
or to atone for the dead born of your suffering
for nowhere is there a cry to soothe your pain.

You needn't crucify yourself on the banks of the bloody
torrents
that gush from your body,
as the Euphrates bares the secrets of its soul
at the dawn of a new defeat.
I know,
no wound can justify war.

You needn't crucify yourself at the end of day,
when you have not concluded your prayers
over the fallen palms
for there can be no honorable killer.

You needn't crucify yourself for the ashes of disaster
for the tombs of your Gods,
or for the beliefs of a dying humanity.

Baghdad, my beloved,
neither father, nor son, nor God,
no prophet crowned by the church will save your soul,
neither the one from Mecca,
nor the prophet of those who refuse
to share olive branches in Palestine.

Here is my war notebook
years of exile
folded into a suitcase;
abandoned far too long to the dreams of the condemned.

Here is my share of victims
my share of moon
my harvest of emptiness
my share of dust, of words, and of cries.

Here is my sorrow
like a comma barring off an ink mark.

Baghdad, my beloved,
I was squatting in a corner of the page
Sheltered from barren days
far from bloody rivers
that swept away the names of the dead
and people's silence.

Baghdad, my beloved
sitting like a Bedouin in a mirage
stretched along my shores, I cherished my own death shroud
far from the cross, from the hand of Fatma
and the star of David
far from their books, from their wars
wandering through the sandy dunes
from the wasteland to the town
I drag my body from season to season
and you from the couch to the mirror,
from my bedroom to the street
between my writing and my loneliness
far from their cemeteries,
from their martyrs, from their morgues.

Baghdad, my beloved,
you did not stand shivering in the doorway of the ruined days,
a whole civilization geared to killing
has robbed you of your innocence.
Baghdad, you who never submitted to Saddam, the brute
you have no reason to groan
at the simple revelation of that iron fist
those who busy themselves about your agonizing body,
those "liberators," become his henchmen.

Baghdad, my aching heart,
my father, a laborer, never knew joy
my mother lost her youth in the mirror
and the sole witness to my
first heartbroken sobs upon your breast is the blowing sand, the
starry sky and God's gaze as prayer is being called.

Madinat al-Salam
city of peace
love in the essence of the written word.

How I wish today
that man had never discovered fire
and I curse him for tramping on through his own deafening din.

The earth that gave me life is being put to death today
oh! mother! Let me return to your flesh
So I might listen to the beating of your soul
and drink in the murmur of your breath.

The Battle of Nasiriyah

Some of the heaviest fighting during the Iraqi invasion took place at Nasiriyah. This city is on the Euphrates River. It is—after Basra, Baghdad, and Mosul—the fourth largest city in Iraq. It was an important target for the United States, because the Ba'thist regime had set up a regional military headquarters there. As one of the south's largest cities, most residents were Shi'i. Despite being members of a beleaguered majority, not all residents welcomed U.S. troops with open arms. Some paramilitary groups fought troops. In the fighting that took place between 23 March and 1 April, over four hundred Iraqis were killed. Twenty-nine U.S. soldiers also died (six from friendly fire).

Evan Wright was a journalist, and he traveled with 1st Reconnaissance Battalion of the U.S. Marine Corps during the invasion of Iraq. Journalists who traveled with U.S. soldiers during combat are referred to as being "embedded" with the troops. Wright wrote of his experiences in Nasiriyah in the award-winning article "The Killer Elite," *Rolling Stone*, no. 925 (26 June 2003) (accessed 21 February 2010, http://www.rollingstone.com/politics/story/5938873/the_killer-elite). He later turned this article into the book *Generation Kill* (New York: Berkley Trade, 2008). As you read his account of frontline fighting, you should consider the following: Do the Marines know who is an enemy and who is a friend? How do they respond to being in a foreign land? What are the challenges that the Marines face? Are they prepared for them?

> Colbert's team is part of a twenty-three-man platoon in Bravo Company. Along with First Recon's other two line companies—Alpha and Charlie—as well as its support units, the battalion's job is to hunt the desert for Iraqi armor, while

other Marines seize oil fields to the east. During the first forty-eight hours of the invasion, Colbert's team finds no tanks and encounters hundreds of surrendering Iraqi soldiers—whom Colbert does his best to avoid, so as not to be saddled with the burden of searching, feeding and detaining them, which his unit is ill-equipped to do. Fleeing soldiers, some of them still carrying weapons, as well as groups of civilian families stream past Colbert's vehicle . . . on his team's second night in Iraq. Colbert delivers instructions to Garza, who is keeping watch on the Mark-19: "Make sure you don't shoot civilians. We are an invading army. We must be magnanimous. . . ."

There's an inescapable sense among Colbert's team that this is going to be a dull war. All that changes when they reach Nasiriyah on their third day in Iraq.

On March 23rd, Colbert's team, in a convoy with the entire First Recon Battalion, cuts off from the backcountry . . . and heads northwest to Nasiriyah, a city of about 300,000. . . .

By late afternoon, the battalion becomes mired in a massive traffic jam of Marine vehicles about thirty kilometers south of the city. The Marines are given no word about what's happening ahead, though they get some clue when, before sundown, they begin to notice a steady flow of casualty-evacuation helicopters flying . . . from Nasiriyah. Eventually, traffic grinds to a halt. The Marines turn off their engines and wait. . . .

Fick tells his men that the Marines have been taking heavy casualties in Nasiriyah. Yesterday, the town was declared secure. But then an Army supply unit traveling near the city came under attack from an Iraqi guerilla unit of Saddam Hussein loyalists called fedayeen. These fighters . . . wear civilian clothes and set up positions in the city among the general populace, firing mortars, rocket-propelled grenades (RPGs) and machine guns from rooftops . . . and alleys. They killed or captured twelve soldiers from the Army supply unit. . . . Overnight, a Marine combat team from Task Force Tarawa attempted to move into the city across the main bridge over the Euphrates. Nine Marines lost their lives, and seventy more were injured.

First Recon has been ordered to the bridge to support Task Force Tarawa, which barely controls its southern approach. Fick can't tell his men exactly what they're going to do when they get to the bridge, as the plans are still being drawn up at a higher level. What he does tell the men is that their rules of engagement have changed. Until now, they've let armed Iraqis pass, sometimes even handing them food rations. Now, Fick says, "Anyone with a weapon is declared hostile. If it's a woman walking away from you with a weapon on her back, shoot her."

At 1:30 p.m., the 374 Marines of First Recon form up on the road and start rolling north toward the city. Given the news of heavy casualties during the past twenty-four hours, it's a reasonable assessment that everyone in the vehicle has a better than average chance of getting killed or injured....

Cobras clatter directly overhead, swooping low with the grace of flying sledgehammers. They circle First Recon's convoy, nosing down through the barren scrubland on either side of the road, hunting for enemy shooters. Before long, we are on our own. The helicopters are called off because fuel is short. The bulk of the Marine convoy is held back until the Iraqi forces ahead are put down. One of the last Marines we see standing by the road pumps his fist as Colbert's vehicle drives past and shouts, "Get some!"

We drive into a no man's land. A burning fuel depot spews fire and smoke. Garbage is strewn on either side of the road as far as the eye can see. The convoy slows to a crawl, and the Humvee fills with a black cloud of flies....

There is a series of thunderous, tooth-rattling explosions directly to the vehicle's right. We are even with a Marine heavy-artillery battery set up next to the road, firing into Nasiriyah, a few kilometers ahead. There's a mangled Humvee in the road. The windshield is riddled with bullet holes. Nearby are the twisted hulks of U.S. military-transport trucks, then a blown-up Marine armored vehicle. Marine rucksacks are scattered on the road, clothes and bedrolls spilling out.

We pass a succession of desiccated farmsteads—crude, square huts made of mud, with starving livestock in front. The locals sit outside like spectators. A woman walks past with a basket on her head, oblivious to the explosions....

We reach the bridge over the Euphrates. It is a ... broad concrete structure. It spans ... a kilometer and arches up gracefully toward the middle. On the opposite bank, we glimpse Nasiriyah. The ... city is a jumble of irregularly shaped two- and three-story structures. Through the haze, the buildings appear as a series of dim, slanted outlines, like a row of crooked tombstones....

While two First Recon companies are instructed to set up positions on the banks of the Euphrates, Bravo Company waits at the foot of the bridge, about 200 meters away from the river's edge. No sooner are we settled than machine-gun fire begins to rake the area. Incoming rounds make a zinging sound, just like they do in Bugs Bunny cartoons. They hit palm trees nearby, shredding the fronds, sending puffs of smoke off the trunks. Marines from Task Force Tarawa to our right and to our left open up with machine guns. First Recon's Alpha and Charlie companies begin blasting targets in the city with their heavy guns. Enemy mortars start to explode on both sides of Colbert's vehicle, about 150 meters distant. "Stand by for shit to get stupid," Person says, sounding merely annoyed....

While Person talks, there's a massive explosion nearby. An errant Marine artillery round hits a power line and detonates overhead, sending shrapnel into a vehicle ahead of ours. A group of six Marines is also hit. Two are killed immediately; . . . four others are injured. Through the smoke, we . . . hear them screaming for a medic. . . .

For nearly six hours, we are pinned down, waiting, we think, to storm into Nasiriyah. But after sunset, plans are changed, and First Recon is called back from the bridge to a position four kilometers into the trash-strewn wastelands south of the city. When the convoy stops in relative safety, away from the bridge, Marines wander out of the vehicles in high spirits. First Recon's Alpha Company killed at least ten Iraqis across the river from our position. They come up to Colbert's vehicle to regale his team with exploits of their slaughter, bragging about one kill in particular, a . . . fedayeen in a bright-orange shirt. "We shredded him with our .50-cals," one says. . . .

Just after sunrise, First Recon's seventy-vehicle convoy rolls over the bridge on the Euphrates and enters Nasiriyah. It's one of those . . . Third World mud-brick-and-cinder block cities that probably looks pretty badly rubbled even on a good day. This morning, smoke curls from collapsed structures. Most buildings facing the road are pockmarked and cratered. Cobras fly overhead spitting machine-gun fire. Dogs roam the ruins.

The convoy stops to pick up a Marine from another unit who is wounded in the leg. A few vehicles come under machine-gun and RPG fire. The Recon Marines return fire and redecorate an apartment building with about a dozen grenades fired from a Mark-19. In an hour, we clear the outer limits of the city and start to head north. Dead bodies are scattered along the edges of the road. Most are men, enemy fighters, some with weapons still in their hands. The Marines nickname one corpse Tomato Man, because from a distance he looks like a smashed crate of tomatoes in the road. There are shot-up cars and trucks with bodies hanging over the edges. We pass a bus, smashed and burned, with charred human remains sitting upright in some windows. There a man with no head in the road and a dead little girl, too, about three or four, lying on her back. She's wearing a dress and has no legs. . . .

We are at a bend in the road, with a five-foot-high berm to the left. Shots are fired directly ahead of us. "Incoming rounds," Person announces. . . .

Colbert picks up a 203 round—an RPG—kisses the nose of it and slides it into the lower chamber of his gun. He . . . climbs up the embankment to observe a small cluster of homes on the other side. He signals for . . . the Marines to come out of the vehicle and join him on the berm. Marines from another platoon fire into the hamlet with rifles, machine guns and Mark-19s... Colbert does not clear his team to fire. He can't discern any targets. About two kilometers up the road, where First Recon's Alpha Company is stopped, suspected fedayeen open up with machine guns and mortars. Alpha takes no casualties. The battalion calls in an artillery strike on the fedayeen positions.

The team gets back in the Humvee. Trombley sits in the back seat eating spaghetti directly out of a foil MRE pack, squeezing it into his mouth from a hole in the corner. "I almost shot that man," he says excitedly, referring to a farmer in the hamlet on the other side of the berm....

Fifteen minutes later, we start moving north. Everyone in Colbert's vehicle believes we are taking a route that bypasses the hostile town, Al Gharraf. Then word comes over the radio of a change in plan. We are driving straight through.

Colbert's vehicle comes alongside the walls of the town, which looks like a smaller version of Nasiriyah. The street we are on... bears left. As Person makes the turn, the wall of a house... to my right and no more than three meters from my window erupts with muzzle flashes and the clatter of machine-gun fire. The vehicle takes twenty-two bullets, five of them in my door. The light armor that covers much of the Humvee (eight-inch steel plates riveted over the doors) stops most of them, but the windows are open and there are gaps in the armor. A bullet flies past Colbert's head and smacks into the frame behind Person's. Another round comes partially through my door....

We pass dead bodies in the road again, men with weapons by their sides, then more than a dozen trucks and cars burned and smoking by the road. Many have a burned corpse or two of Iraqi soldiers who died after crawling five or ten meters away from the vehicle before they expired, hands still grasping forward on the pavement. Just north of here... Marines... machine-gun four men in a field who appear to be stalking us. It's no big deal. Since the shooting started in Nasiriyah forty-eight hours ago, firing weapons and seeing dead people has become almost routine.

We stop next to a green field with a small house set back from the road. Marines from a different unit suspect that gunshots came from the house. A Bravo Marine sniper observes the house for forty-five minutes. He sees women and children inside, nobody with guns. For some reason, a handful of Marines from the other unit opens fire on the house. Soon, Marines down the line join in with heavy weapons....

Colbert, who believes the house contains only noncombatants, starts screaming, "Jesus Christ! There's fucking civilians in that house! Cease fire! Encino Man pops off a 203 grenade that falls wildly short of the house. Colbert, like other Marines in Bravo, is furious. Not only do they believe this Recon officer is firing on civilians, but the guy also doesn't even know how to range his 203.

Colbert sits in the Humvee, trying to rationalize the events outside that have spiraled beyond his control: "Everyone's just tense. Some Marine took a shot, and everyone has just followed suit."

The Occupation of Baghdad

By 9 April 2003, U.S. troops entered Baghdad and easily occupied it. Anne Garrels was a foreign correspondent for National Public Radio (NPR) at that time, and she had been subjected to the bombing of the city in order to report on the war. It was not the first time she had covered military conflicts, for she had also been a reporter in Chechnya, Bosnia, Kosovo, and Afghanistan. The Palestine Hotel where she was staying is located in Firdos Square, where American troops helped Iraqis tear down a bronze statue of Saddam Hussein on the first day of the occupation. Garrels recorded the following account of the U.S. occupation of Baghdad and the ripping down of the statue in *Naked in Baghdad: The Iraq War and the Aftermath as Seen by NPR's Correspondent* (New York: Picador, 2003), 186–90. As you read this account, you should consider the following: How do Iraqi residents of Baghdad respond to the occupation of their city? What problems does Garrels perceive? Should the U.S. military have helped tear down the statue of Saddam Hussein? Why? Or why not?

> April 9, 2003
> ... If there is to be a last-ditch fight by the Republican Guard ... or by fanatical irregular forces, they are nowhere to be seen today. In neighborhood after neighborhood the Baath Party members, steely-eyed security, and police have vanished. Iraqi troops have fled their sandbagged trenches. Under a bridge I saw surface-to-air missiles left unmanned. An army jacket and a pair of military boots lay strewn across an intersection. No one knew the fate of Saddam, but suddenly it didn't matter.
> Reporters looking for U.S. troops tripped on them in the eastern suburbs, where they found themselves face to face with Abram tanks. Marines moved quickly into abandoned Iraqi bunkers. Told there were no Iraqi military units anywhere between them and the city center, the Marine company commander reportedly chortled, "Love it, love it."
> What has followed has been an orgy of looting. First, there were just a few clusters of young men on the streets, but as people realized there was nothing

stopping them anymore, the crowds grew, their fury focused on the symbols of Saddam's power. Groups broke into government . . . warehouses, taking everything that wasn't nailed down . . . : chairs, air conditioners, computers, even doors. I see a yacht being pulled along downtown Sadoun Street. Vehicles are stolen from government parking lots. [My translator] Amer points to people . . . pushing cars because they can't get them started. He watches all this with growing distress. He is devastated at the damage.

Defense Secretary Donald Rumsfeld says we are watching history, the unfolding events that will shape the fate of a people and . . . the future of the region, but it doesn't look good from here. Government buildings across the street are on fire. We pass the Olympic headquarters, which looters have set ablaze. This building symbolizes the sick brutality of Saddam and his family, for it was here that his elder son Uday tortured disappointing athletes or those who merely displeased him. Outside the Oil Ministry, a young man stands in front of a statue of Saddam imitating his grand gesture. A friend snaps a photo. Such a lark would have cost him his life just yesterday.

Amer and I stop on a bridge as a column of Marines approach on the highway underneath. I jump out of the car and lean over the balustrade. I can almost touch the kids sitting on top of their tanks. Before I can stop myself, I shout down at them, "Hey, guys!" One guy turns around with an M16 pointed at me. I raise my hands and hear myself screaming "No! No! I'm an American." For so many days I had felt the bombs. . . . Suddenly, I am face-to-face with American troops and peering down a muzzle. I hadn't realized how threatened I felt by the recent . . . events and how relieved I was that the Americans are . . . here, and also how relieved I am to think that this phase of the war might be over soon. Just last week it seemed the war could go on for . . . months, and I was having trouble imagining how I would last.

Another column of Marines moves through Saddam City, the poor, predominantly Shiite Muslim area, where they are greeted with plastic flowers and cheers of "Welcome, welcome." People dance in the streets, waving rifles and defaced posters. Tongues are suddenly unleashed. Shiites pack into the al-Mokhsin Mosque, which has been closed ever since Saddam's agents murdered their much beloved imam three years ago. Sheikh Amar al-Musadawi told the rapt audience that Saddam Hussein had betrayed Islam. He spoke of thirty years of oppression. He urged Muslims to save the country, not loot and destroy it. He said nothing about the Americans passing by outside.

Amer is wracked with conflicting emotions. "What happened to the Republican Guard?" he wonders. Though a Sunni himself, he says Saddam sealed his doom by refusing to allow Shiites into the Republican Guard, but included only

Sunni Muslims largely drawn from his hometown and tribe. Amer lashes out at Saddam for fostering a hollow army rife with corruption and unable to defend the country. Bitterness bubbles to the surface as he speaks of the humiliation and worse that Iraqis have suffered at the hands of arrogant Republican Guards. He calls them puffed-up bastards who were good at throwing their weight around but couldn't fight like real men when the time came.

It's become evident from all he has said to me, and how he deals with people, that Amer has risen above divisions of tribe and Muslim sect to be first and foremost an Iraqi. . . . Exhausted, we grab fried chicken from a take-out place. I am sitting in Amer's room about to chow down when we hear a commotion out the window. The Marines have . . . approached the Palestine [Hotel]. . . .

I am stunned at how many Marines are packed into one Bradley. One after another emerges from its depths to take up guard duty around the hotel. Given the lawlessness in the city, it is reassuring to know they are here. Too many people, among them our former keepers, must know how much cash and equipment we have, and I had feared we would be a tempting target for thieves.

As more . . . tanks lumber forward to the hotel, crowds begin to gather in nearby Firdos Square. A fifty-four-year-old taxi driver tosses his shoes at a statue of Saddam, a deeply insulting gesture in the Arab world. "We were surrounded by fear," he tells me. "Even fathers and sons were afraid to speak openly to each other." He recalls a friend who was arrested in 1978 and never seen again. "Thank you, America," he says, "for removing this dictator." He then joins a small group that tries to pull down the statue. After attempts with . . . sledgehammers fail, the Marines move in a tank with a long boom to assist. The statue folds, falling to its knees, as the regime has.

The street scenes are nothing like as joyous as the cameras make them out to be. There are plenty of people standing around, numb or shocked at the events. Dr. Sa'ad Jawad, an Iraqi political scientist, watches sadly as the Marines help topple Saddam's statue, calling the scene humiliating. No fan of Saddam, he nonetheless warns of wounded pride. He acknowledges that now the Americans are here, they must be in . . . control, but he says their control will quickly be resented.

When I get back upstairs, Amer confesses that he wept as he watched the scene below. Though he too hated Saddam, he says seeing American troops in Baghdad is more than he can bear. . . .

Pulling down statues makes for good television, but as I saw in Moscow in 1991, it doesn't ultimately signify much. It doesn't begin to answer the deeper questions. Wiping out the past doesn't mean coming to terms with it. That's what Amer is struggling with: Who are the Iraqis? How did they get a Saddam? How did they tolerate the fear Saddam created? And where do they go from here?

At dusk a group of men sits outside their shuttered shops, hoping their presence will deter the growing number of looters. They too are in shock at the sudden collapse of the regime. "I've never known freedom," thirty-three-year-old Ali al-Abadi says, the tremor in his voice revealing a jumble of mixed emotions. "We want a just government, but we want a just Iraqi government," he adds. Asked if they can name Iraqis they would like to lead them now, these men all shake their heads. That's the problem, they say. The Iraqi opposition in exile which has been courted by the United States inspires no confidence. Each of them just wants power for himself, they agree. They want nothing to do with anyone who has just come back from living in luxury abroad while they themselves have suffered at home. And they all fear paroxysms of revenge as past scores are settled.

The Pillaging of the National Museum

Looting began as soon as the Coalition ousted the Ba'thist regime in Baghdad. The Coalition troops, however, did not have orders to stop the looting. They only had orders to protect the airport and the oil ministry. Much as happened at the end of the Thirty Days War in 1941, the policymakers and war managers perceived looting to be an internal problem that was not in the purview of military conflict. Afterwards, again much like in 1941, they acknowledged that this perception was wrong. The looting, after all, caused a sense of insecurity that did not help the Coalition's long-term interests. Later, the Coalition Provisional Authority (CPA) led by Paul Bremer estimated that the looting had cost the country of Iraq $12 billion.

One of the most horrifying examples of looting-run-rampant occurred at the National Museum of Iraq. As the heart of Ancient Mesopotamia and the capital of Abbasid Empire, Iraq has a profound cultural heritage. Recognizing this, the British administrator Gertrude Bell had set up this museum in the 1920s in order to display the wonders of Iraq's ancient past. Since its establishment, the museum had continued to collect ancient treasures. When U.S. forces took over Baghdad, some members of the Iraqi army engaged the enemy from the museum. The next day, with the city occupied by the Coalition, the looting of the museum began. Over the next two days 15,000 artifacts were stolen. The U.S. government was later criticized for this event.

Donny George Youkhanna was chairman of Iraq's State Board of Antiquities and Heritage (SBAH) and the Director General of the National Museum. He was fifty-three years old in 2003, so he had come into his maturity under the Ba'th regime. Dr. Youkhanna worked hard to recover the stolen items, but he did not, as recounted below, feel safe in post-Ba'thist Iraq. In 2006, he fled to Syria. The Scholar Rescue Fund helped Dr. Youkhanna to find a position as a visiting professor at Stony Brook University in New York. He recounted his experiences after the Coalition occupation of Iraq in Carl Mirra's *Soldiers and Citizens: An Oral History of Operation Iraqi Freedom from the Battlefield to the Pentagon* (New York: Palgrave Macmillan, 2008), 176–80. This account, given five years after the invasion, describes the looting of the museum and life in occupied Iraq. As you read his account, you should consider the following: Who does Youkhanna blame for the looting of the museum? What does his account tell you of the early occupation? How does he feel about Ba'thism? Why did he finally feel compelled to leave?

> I was director general of research and studies in SBAH in Baghdad. We had to leave the museum in April 2003 during the invasion. There was firing in the street. And, there were people in civilian clothes, we don't know if they were militia, but they had RPGs . . . and Kalashnikovs [Russian assault rifles]. They were firing and shooting at the American tanks. Then after a week or so, I think it was Sunday, April 15, 2003, we were able to return to the museum. In my office, there was two feet of debris on the floor and those were my documents, my reports, and so on. My computer and cameras were gone. When we went into the galleries, it looked like a hurricane hit it. I was thinking, "Why? Why could all this happen to a museum?" It could have very easily been prevented by placing one or two tanks in front of the museum. Even when we returned to the museum we did not have any protection. I myself have seen cars passing by the museum, flashing their Kalashnikovs.
>
> Almost a year before the invasion and looting, I had some information from London. Two people were sitting in a private meeting; one of them said to me, you know, Iraqis are not so good to have all these precious antiquities. People might steal these things and bring them to us in London. The second one said something like "I am waiting for the day that the American Army is going to invade Iraq and I will be with them, I will go to the Iraq museum and get what I want." I was surprised. In a meeting with the Board of Directors, I told the chairman that we need to protect the museum. We should do what the Lebanese did. They put everything in storage and sealed the doors. The directors said, "You know you are exaggerating. No one will come into Baghdad." Again, I raised the issue and said "For God's sake, let's do something." One administrator said no one will dare come into Baghdad while Saddam is here.

From my own investigations—archeologists are investigators—I understood that there might be three types of groups who entered the compound of the museum and stole artifacts. Group Number One we might call the normal people. They went into the museum, smashed the doors and took everything: furniture, computers, copy machines, and telephones. You name it; they took anything they could get their hands on. Group Number Two went through a glass window that had been blocked for, say, ten years. It was a small window that one could not see from the outside. Nobody would know the window was there unless somebody studied the plan of the museum or had investigated how to get into the museum. Thus Group Number Two had some knowledge of antiquities because they passed by some replicas in the galleries. I found glass cutters left around here and there that they prepared to cut the showcases. We had some showcases on the wall that showed a series of stamped bricks of all the history of Mesopotamia. They picked up nine pieces of those, which means they knew what to take. They knew what they wanted. I saw some smashed empty showcases, which contained masterpieces before the evacuation of the small items from the museum. All over the world museums are known for containing treasures and maybe this was the opportunity for people who had an eye on these things for some time. Now, Group Number Three were the ones who went into the store rooms that were located in the cellars. They entered through a small door in the Hatra gallery. I never knew there was a door there. They went through a door that goes to the basement of the museum; it was blocked by bricks. They smashed the bricks and the door. They entered the first room and they touched nothing there. They went through boxes in the second room, where they took small items: jewelry and related precious items. This group might have had information from the inside. There was no electricity; no light, but they knew where to go. . . .

Scholars in the United States provided coordinates of the museums to the Pentagon with instructions on how to protect them. I was told by these scholars that they said to the Pentagon if you go to the museum you will find someone called Donny George. He is cooperative and he will help you, but they never came. I am not blaming the soldiers who were in the streets of Baghdad. If they don't have orders, they won't act. They were there, but they did not protect the museum. One of the museum staff told me that he went to a U.S. tank that was very close to the museum. He pleaded with them to move the tank in front of the museum. He remembers that there were a few hundred people in front of the museum with guns, tool bars and hammers in their hands. The man in charge of the tank made a phone call, and he said "I'm sorry, we can't move the tank, we have orders." Later that same tank and the same tank commander would protect the museum. I spoke to them both together. The tank commander said, "Yes, this man came to me. I made a phone call, but I did not have orders to move my tank." I asked him who he called, and he said "I can't tell you that." But, I am not blaming him. . . . Now we have to work together to restore what was lost. We did restore some 4,000 objects that were stolen.

Maybe the forces did not . . . understand. They did not have sufficient information on the museum and on the history of the country. There was a picture of a looter in the Western media holding a vase and few people realized it was a sacred work. It goes back 3,200 years before Christ. Scholars say the bands on the vase represent the Sumerian philosophy of life on earth; it is one of the most important masterpieces in the world.

Whatever was happening in Saddam's time, the security situation was much better. He had half-a-million security people just for Baghdad. Of course, he had his heavy hammer and killed opponents. But now thousands of people are coming into the country and nobody is stopping them. I used to live in a place called Dora; it is just five minutes driving distance from the Green Zone [also called the International Zone, it is a heavily fortified complex in central Baghdad, where U.S. officials reside]. They say that Sunnis announced an Islamic Republic from Dora. Can you imagine this is happening only five minutes from the Green Zone? The situation is deteriorating; no one feels safe; there are no projects; and unemployment rates are huge. Most people stay at home unless it is . . . necessary to go out. I talked to someone there who told me that twenty liters of gasoline to fill a car costs 25,000 dinars [Iraqi currency], which is . . . double the normal cost. And, you can't find it; there is a huge black market in gasoline.

You see, first there were the Sunnis and Shiites. Now they are questioning the Christians. They say simply if you are a Christian, then you must be with the Americans. In my town, Dora, there was a high concentration of Christians. I am told they are walking door to door, telling people that you have twenty-four hours to leave. You either convert to Islam or you pay a tax to us or you leave. If you don't, you will be killed. People are leaving their homes and they are not allowed to take their belongings. I heard that there was talk of doing to the Christians what they did to the Jewish in the 1940s.

I had to leave the country. I was an official at the museum, of course, and they created a new ministry of antiquities that was given to the al-Sadr party. I was under pressure. First, I was chairman of the Board of Antiquities and they would not allow me to appoint any personnel. I then received an official letter, which withdrew all my . . . authority as chairman. I was told by someone that the order has come that Donny should not stay because he is Christian. But, before I heard this, there was a letter dropped on the driveway of my parents' house, where my two sons had lived. They mentioned that my sons were teasing Muslim girls and making trouble. But this was a lie, they were friends, they grew up together. My son spoke Arabic and the Muslims spoke our language. The letter also said that we know that your father works with the Americans. This was a serious accusation; it meant killing immediately. We managed to get a car and get to Damascus [Syria]. I applied for retirement and was approved immediately.

Iraq is my country. As an Assyrian Christian, my ancestors were there even before the Arabs. I am not saying this negatively. We had many wonderful Arab friends, they were brothers. I am concerned now about the Muslim gangs who are butchering the country. We never had problems among the Christians, Sunnis, and Shiites. In my second year of college, my friend asked where I was from. He never knew. He never had the idea of dividing people into Sunni, Shiite, or Christian. He never knew that I was a Christian, nobody worried too much about it.

I would say this sectarian division is the most dangerous thing that has happened in Iraq. The Iraqi Governing Council was set up, I think, under Paul Bremer [led the CPA]. The problem was that seats were given according to this division: a certain number for Shia, Sunni, Kurds, Turkmen, and so on. It ironically fueled these sectarian divisions. Despite the hardship of living under Hussein, everybody was living together. If you did not have anything to do with Saddam, you would never feel anything. Little by little things improved. Politically, of course, he crushed any kind of criticism. This was not democracy or a healthy environment for the country. But . . . you could go to work, go out at night, and feel safe. The normal life of Iraqis was to travel, plan vacations at summer resorts. . . . I am talking about the Iraqi people. We had a bad government. But the people lived a normal life. . . . Imagine a country with fine arts institutes and a . . . symphony orchestra. Every month I went to see the orchestra. This was the normal life in Iraq. . . . Iraq was not, and is not, simply a desert country. Yes, we have deserts, but we are sometimes portrayed as riding camels. We have cities and universities and I'd say the best doctors and poets in the Middle East.

That the United States got rid of Saddam Hussein is a very good thing. But all that has happened afterward, it is the responsibility of the United States. You can't leave a country of 20 million people burning. . . .

Saddam Hussein Responds to Invasion

Saddam Hussein left Baghdad as soon as U.S. troops came in sight of the capital city. According to Charles Tripp, Hussein "fled the city, pausing only to give a brief speech exhorting resistance until victory to a somewhat bemused crowd in al-'Adhamiyya" (Tripp, 274). Victory was not to be completely clear-cut for U.S. forces. On 28 April, demonstrators near Baghdad protested the U.S. presence. American soldiers fired into the crowds, killing thirteen and wounding seventy-five others. Undoubtedly sparked on by this, Saddam Hussein issued a statement that day, and this called on Iraqis to continue the struggle. Hussein would not be captured until December 2003. After his capture, the Iraqi Special Tribunal would find him guilty of crimes against humanity on 5 November 2006. Hussein was hanged the following month.

The following is a translated text of Saddam Hussein's last message to the Iraqi people. Brian Whitaker translated this response by the Iraqi leader for the *Guardian* on 30 April 2003 (accessed 21 November 2008, www.guardian.com.uk/world/2003/apr/30/iraq.brianwhitaker). As you read it, you should look at the rhetoric. How does Hussein use and manipulate history? If Ba'thism is a secular ideology, why does he start with a quote from the Quran? And with what effect?

> In the name of God, the compassionate, the merciful. "They had made a covenant with God that they would not turn back in flight, and a covenant with God must be answered for." [Koranic verse]
>
> Iraq, 28 April 2003
>
> From Saddam Hussein to the great Iraqi people, the sons of the Arab and Islamic nation, and honourable people everywhere.
>
> Peace be upon you, and the mercy and blessings of God.
>
> Just as Hulaku entered Baghdad, the criminal Bush entered it, with Alqami, or rather, more than one Alqami.
>
> They did not conquer you—you who reject the occupation and humiliation, you who have Arabism and Islam in your hearts and minds—except through betrayal.
>
> Indeed, it is not a victory while there is still resistance in your souls.
>
> What we used to say has now become reality, for we do not live in peace and security while the deformed Zionist entity is on our Arab land; therefore there is no rift in the unity of the Arab struggle.
>
> Sons of our great people:
>
> Rise up against the occupier and do not trust anyone who talks of Sunni and

Shia, because the only issue that the homeland—your great Iraq—faces now is the occupation.

There are no priorities other than driving out the infidel, criminal, cowardly occupier. No honourable hand is held out to shake his, but, rather, the hand of traitors and collaborators.

I say to you that all countries surrounding you are against your resistance, but God is with you because you are fighting unbelief and defending your rights.

The traitors have allowed themselves to declare their treachery, even though it is shameful, so declare your rejection of the occupier for the sake of great Iraq, for the nation, for Islam and for humanity.

Iraq—together with the sons of the nation and the people of honour—and we shall restore the stolen relics and rebuild Iraq which they (may God bring shame upon them) wish to split into pieces.

Saddam has no property in his own name and I defy anyone to prove that there were palaces except in the name of the Iraqi state. I left them a long time ago to live in a small house.

Forget everything and resist the occupation, because error begins when there are priorities other than the occupier and his expulsion. Remember that they are aiming to bring in those who will fight one another so that your Iraq will remain weak and they can plunder it as they have been doing.

Your party, the Arab Ba'ath Socialist party, is proud that it did not extend its hand to the Zionist enemy and did not give in to the cowardly American or British aggressor.

Whoever stands against Iraq and plots against it will not prosper in peace at the hands of America.

Greetings to everyone who resists, to every honourable Iraqi citizen, and to every woman, child and sheikh in our great Iraq.

United, and the enemy and the traitors who came in with him will flee. Know the one with whom the invading forces came, whose planes flew to kill you, will send nothing but poison.

God willing, the day of liberation and victory will come, for us, for the nation, and above all for Islam. This time, as always when right triumphs, the days to come will be more beautiful.

Take care of your possessions, your departments, and your schools. Boycott the occupier. Boycott him, for this is a duty towards Islam, religion and the homeland.

Long live great Iraq and its people.

Long live Palestine, free and Arab from the river to the sea.

God is greatest.

May the despicable ones be despised.

Saddam Hussein 26 Safar, 1424

President Bush's "Mission Accomplished" Speech

American spirits were high when the war ended after only thirty-seven days of fighting. Iraq had been conquered in less than five weeks, and the mortality rate for the Coalition was fairly low. Iraq's Deputy Prime Minister Tariq Aziz officially surrendered to U.S. forces on 24 April, and the invasion, in theory, then ended. In all, 140 American and 33 British had been killed in combat. The casualties on the Iraqi side were, of course, much more severe. The war killed as many as 12,000 soldiers and as many as 7,000 civilians (Tripp, 275). It seemed only a matter of time before Saddam Hussein would be caught and democracy would take root in Ba'thist Iraq.

To celebrate what seemed a stunning victory, President Bush decided to go to the Persian Gulf and give a speech aboard the aircraft carrier the *USS Lincoln*. Wearing a flight suit and helmet, which thereby emphasized his role as Commander-in-Chief, the president stood under a banner that pronounced "Mission Accomplished." The speech was given on 1 May 2003, and the *Guardian* put it on its web page (accessed 21 November 2008, http://www.guardian.co.uk/world/2003/may/01/usa.iraq). According to Hala Fattah, "in declaring a victory, the president had reiterated two falsehoods: that Iraq possessed WMD and that Hussein was in alliance with bin Laden" (Fattah, 250). As you read this speech, you should evaluate Fattah's statement: Does President Bush directly link Saddam Hussein and Osama bin Laden? Does he assert that WMDs exist in Iraq? How does the president use history in the service of this war? What benefits does President Bush propose the United States has won with this war?

> Thank you all very much. Admiral Kelly, Captain Card, officers and sailors of the USS *Abraham Lincoln,* my fellow Americans: Major combat operations in Iraq have ended. In the battle of Iraq, the United States and our allies have prevailed. And now our coalition is engaged in securing and reconstructing that country.
>
> In this battle, we have fought for the cause of liberty, and for the peace of the world. Our nation and our coalition are proud of this accomplishment— yet, it is you, the members of the United States military, who achieved it. Your courage, your willingness to face danger for your country and for each other,

made this day possible. Because of you, our nation is more secure. Because of you, the tyrant has fallen, and Iraq is free.

Operation Iraqi Freedom was carried out with a combination of precision and speed and boldness the enemy did not expect, and the world had not seen before. From distant bases or ships at sea, we sent planes and missiles that could destroy an enemy division, or strike a single bunker. Marines and soldiers charged to Baghdad across 350 miles of hostile ground, in one of the swiftest advances of heavy arms in history. You have shown the world the skill and the might of the American Armed Forces.

This nation thanks all the members of our coalition who joined in a noble cause. We thank the Armed Forces of the United Kingdom, Australia, and Poland, who shared in the hardships of war. We thank all the citizens of Iraq who welcomed our troops and joined in the liberation of their own country. And tonight, I have a special word for Secretary Rumsfeld, for General Franks, and for all the men and women who wear the uniform of the United States: America is grateful for a job well done.

The character of our military through history—the daring of Normandy, the fierce courage of Iwo Jima, the decency and idealism that turned enemies into allies—is fully present in this generation. When Iraqi civilians looked into the faces of our servicemen and women, they saw strength and kindness and goodwill. When I look at the members of the United States military, I see the best of our country, and I'm honored to be your Commander-in-Chief.

In the images of falling statues, we have witnessed the arrival of a new era. For a hundred of years of war, culminating in the nuclear age, military technology was designed and deployed to inflict casualties on an ever-growing scale. In defeating Nazi Germany and Imperial Japan, Allied forces destroyed entire cities, while enemy leaders who started the conflict were safe until the final days. Military power was used to end a regime by breaking a nation.

Today, we have the greater power to free a nation by breaking a dangerous and aggressive regime. With new tactics and precision weapons, we can achieve military objectives without directing violence against civilians. No device of man can remove the tragedy of war; yet it is a great moral advance when the guilty have far more to fear from war than the innocent.

In the images of celebrating Iraqis, we have also seen the ageless appeal of human freedom. Decades of lies and intimidation could not make the Iraqi people love their oppressors or desire their own enslavement. Men and women in every culture need liberty like they need food and water and air. Everywhere that freedom arrives, humanity rejoices; and everywhere that freedom stirs, let tyrants fear.

We have difficult work to do in Iraq. We're bringing order to parts of that country that remain dangerous. We're pursuing and finding leaders of the old regime, who will be held to account for their crimes. We've begun to search for hidden chemical and biological weapons and already know of hundreds of sites that will be investigated. We're helping to rebuild Iraq, where the dictator built palaces for himself, instead of hospitals and schools. And we will stand with the new leaders of Iraq as they establish a government of, by, and for the Iraqi people.

The transition from dictatorship to democracy will take time, but it is worth every effort. Our coalition will stay until our work is done. Then we will leave, and we will leave behind a free Iraq.

The battle of Iraq is one victory in a war on terror that began on September the 11, 2001—and still goes on. That terrible morning, 19 evil men—the shock troops of a hateful ideology—gave America and the civilized world a glimpse of their ambitions. They imagined, in the words of one terrorist, that September the 11th would be the "beginning of the end of America." By seeking to turn our cities into killing fields, terrorists and their allies believed that they could destroy this nation's resolve, and force our retreat from the world. They have failed.

In the battle of Afghanistan, we destroyed the Taliban, many terrorists, and the camps where they trained. We continue to help the Afghan people lay roads, restore hospitals, and educate all their children. Yet we also have dangerous work to complete. As I speak, a Special Operations task force, led by the 82nd Airborne, is on the trail of the terrorists and those who seek to undermine the free government of Afghanistan. America and our coalition will finish what we have begun.

From Pakistan to the Philippines to the Horn of Africa, we are hunting down al Qaeda killers. Nineteen months ago, I pledged that the terrorists would not escape the patient justice of the United States. And as of tonight, nearly one-half of al Qaeda's senior operatives have been captured or killed.

The liberation of Iraq is a crucial advance in the campaign against terror. We've removed an ally of al Qaeda, and cut off a source of terrorist funding. And this much is certain: No terrorist network will gain weapons of mass destruction from the Iraqi regime, because the regime is no more.

In these 19 months that changed the world, our actions have been focused and deliberate and proportionate to the offense. We have not forgotten the victims of September the 11th—the last phone calls, the cold murder of children, the searches in the rubble. With those attacks, the terrorists and their supporters declared war on the United States. And war is what they got.

Our war against terror is proceeding according to principles that I have made clear to all: Any person involved in committing or planning terrorist attacks against the American people becomes an enemy of this country, and a target of American justice.

Any person, organization, or government that supports, protects, or harbors terrorists is complicit in the murder of the innocent, and equally guilty of terrorist crimes.

Any outlaw regime that has ties to terrorist groups and seeks or possesses weapons of mass destruction is a grave danger to the civilized world—and will be confronted.

And anyone in the world, including the Arab world, who works and sacrifices for freedom has a loyal friend in the United States of America.

Our commitment to liberty is America's tradition—declared at our founding; affirmed in Franklin Roosevelt's Four Freedoms; asserted in the Truman Doctrine and in Ronald Reagan's challenge to an evil empire. We are committed to freedom in Afghanistan, in Iraq, and in a peaceful Palestine. The advance of freedom is the surest strategy to undermine the appeal of terror in the world. Where freedom takes hold, men and women turn to the peaceful pursuit of a better life. American values and American interests lead in the same direction: We stand for human liberty.

The United States upholds these principles of security and freedom in many ways—with all the tools of diplomacy, law enforcement, intelligence, and finance. We're working with a broad coalition of nations that understand the threat and our shared responsibility to meet it. The use of force has been—and remains—our last resort. Yet all can know, friends and foe alike, that our nation has a mission: We will answer threats to our security, and we will defend the peace.

Our mission continues. Al Qaeda is wounded, not destroyed. The scattered cells of the terrorist network still operate in many nations, and we know from daily intelligence that they continue to plot against free people. The proliferation of deadly weapons remains a serious danger. The enemies of freedom are not idle, and neither are we. Our government has taken unprecedented measures to defend the homeland. And we will continue to hunt down the enemy before he can strike.

The war on terror is not over; yet it is not endless. We do not know the day of the final victory, but we have seen the turning of the tide. No act of the terrorists will change our purpose, or weaken our resolve, or alter their fate. Their cause is lost. Free nations will press on to victory.

Other nations in history have fought in foreign lands and remained to occupy and exploit. Americans, following a battle, want nothing more than to return home. And that is your direction tonight. After service in the Afghan—and Iraqi theaters of war—after 100,000 miles, on the longest carrier deployment in recent history, you are homeward bound. Some of you will see new family members for the first time—150 babies were born while their fathers were on the Lincoln. Your families are proud of you, and your nation will welcome you.

We are mindful, as well, that some good men and women are not making the journey home. One of those who fell, Corporal Jason Mileo, spoke to his parents five days before his death. Jason's father said, "He called us from the center of Baghdad, not to brag, but to tell us he loved us. Our son was a soldier."

Every name, every life is a loss to our military, to our nation, and to the loved ones who grieve. There's no homecoming for these families. Yet we pray, in God's time, their reunion will come.

Those we lost were last seen on duty. Their final act on this Earth was to fight a great evil and bring liberty to others. All of you—all in this generation of our military—have taken up the highest calling in history. You're defending your country, and protecting the innocent from harm. And wherever you go, you carry a message of hope—a message that is ancient and ever new. In the words of the prophet Isaiah, "To the captives, 'come out,'—and to those in darkness, 'be free.'"

Thank you for serving our country and our cause. May God bless you all, and may God continue to bless America.

Bibliography

Atkinson, Rick. *In the Company of Soldiers*. New York: Henry Holt, 2005.

Blix, Hans. *Disarming Iraq*. New York: Pantheon, 2004.

Bogdanos, Matthew, and William Patrick. *Thieves of Baghdad: One Marine's Passion for Ancient Civilizations and the Journey to Recover the World's Greatest Stolen Treasures*. New York: Bloomsbury Publishers, 2005.

Bremer, L. Paul, and Malcolm McConnell. *My Year in Iraq: The Struggle to Build a Future of Hope*. New York: Simon and Schuster, 2006.

Brennan, Shane. *In the Tracks of the Ten Thousand: A Journey on Foot through Turkey, Syria and Iraq*. London: Robert Hale, 2005.

Claiborne, Shane. *Iraq Journal 2003*. Indianapolis: Doulos Christou Press, 2006.

Ferner, Mike. *Inside the Red Zone: A Veteran for Peace Reports from Iraq*. Westport, Conn.: Praeger, 2006.

Filipovic, Zlata, and Melanie Challenger. *Stolen Voices: Young People's War Diaries, from World War I to Iraq*. New York: Penguin Books, 2006.

Folsom, Seth W. B. *The Highway War: A Marine Company Commander in Iraq.* Dulles, Va.: Potomac Books, 2007.

Garrels, Anne, and Vint Lawrence. *Naked in Baghdad: The Iraq War and the Aftermath as Seen by NPR's Correspondent.* New York: Picador, 2003.

Hussein, Saddam. *America Reaps the Thorns Its Rulers Sowed in the World.* London: Ministry of Peace, 2005.

Hussein, Saddam, and Robert Lawrence. *Zabiba and the King.* College Station, Tex.: Virtualbookworm.com, 2004.

Lacey, Jim. *Take Down: The 3rd Infantry Division's Twenty-One Day Assault on Baghdad.* Annapolis, Md.: Naval Institute Press, 2007.

Livingston, Gary. *Fallujah with Honor: First Battalion, Eighth Marine's Role in Operation Phantom Fury.* North Topsail Beach, N.C.: Caisson Press, 2006.

Malinowski, Jon C., Wendell C. King, and Eugene J. Palka. *Iraq, a Geography.* West Point, N.Y.: U.S. Military Academy, 2002.

Pax, Salam. *Salam Pax: The Clandestine Diary of an Ordinary Iraqi.* New York: Grove Press, 2003.

Pritchard, Tim. *Ambush Alley: The Most Extraordinary Battle of the Iraq War.* New York: Presidio Press Mass Market Edition, 2005.

Seierstad, Åsne, and Maggie Mash. *A Hundred and One Days [a Baghdad Journal].* Translated by Ingrid Christophersen. Leicestershire, England: Perseus Books Group, 2006.

West, Bing, and Ray Smith. *The March Up: Taking Baghdad with the 1st Marine Division.* London: Pimlico, 2003.

Wilson, Peter. *Long Drive through a Short War: Reporting on the Iraq War.* South Yarra, Australia: Hardie Grant Books, 2004.

Windawi, Thura al-, and Robin Bray. *Thura's Diary: My Life in Wartime Iraq.* New York: Viking, 2004.

Wright, Evan. *Generation Kill: Devil Dogs, Iceman, Captain America and the New Face of American War.* New York: Putnam Adult, 2004.

Zucchino, David. *Thunder Run: The Armored Strike to Capture Baghdad.* New York: Grove Press, 2004.

10

The Occupation of Iraq under the Coalition Provisional Authority, 2003–2004

Once the Coalition invaded Iraq, the United States expressed its intent to rule directly for a year. It did so first under the Office of Reconstruction and Humanitarian Assistance (ORHA), which was set up in mid-April. By mid-May, however, the United States replaced the ORHA with the Coalition Provisional Authority (CPA) headed by Lt. Paul Bremer, who immediately implemented two policies that, in retrospect, were extremely problematic. He enforced the de-Ba'thification of government, which took 30,000 experienced administrators out of the political structures of the country. He also disbanded the armed forces, which left 300,000 men—all highly trained and familiar with the Iraqi terrain—unemployed (Tripp, 282). The CPA then set out to establish the institutions of a liberal democracy, which, since weapons of mass destruction were never found, became the legitimizing justification for the invasion. Thus, Bremer and the CPA formed the Iraqi Governing Council (IGC) in July 2003, and its twenty-five members served in an advisory role to Bremer and his team.

Despite the efforts of the CPA—or, as more likely, because of them—an insurgency began, and fighting intensified during its period of direct rule. Some Iraqis fought in order to express their anger at rule by a foreign military power, and popular resentment grew as the country struggled with high unemployment and low access to basic utilities, like electricity. Added to the general angst, there was a struggle to ensure that different parties had access to the future political life of their country as well as the resources that the state distributed. Many Sunnis feared that the United States was privileging Shi'is and Kurds. And some Shi'is feared that the United States was imposing a secular form of democracy. Ethnic and sectarian divisions became more prominent in Iraqi political and social life, thereby undermining the liberal reforms sought by the United States. By the time the CPA disbanded and handed over sovereignty to Iraq in June 2004, a full-scale insurgency had come into being.

As a result, the fighting between Iraqis and Coalition forces continued and worsened in the first year after the invasion. This Iraq War was not a military engagement in which there was a designated front line and enemy soldiers fought each other. Instead, all of Iraq became a front line, putting this country's entire population of 26 million at risk. This was true during the actual invasion, and it remained true once the insurgency began. By October 2004, the estimates regarding civilian deaths at the hands of Coalition forces ranged from a conservative 30,000 (proposed by Iraqis and Americans) to 100,000 (Tripp, 295). Civilian deaths are not easy to count. There are not only the casualties resulting from combat and violence; there are also those who die as a result of deteriorating conditions of daily life. A diabetic who dies because he does not have access to insulin is a victim of war. Three years after the war began, CNN reported that 655,000 deaths had occurred, 2.5 percent more than if there had not been a war (accessed 4 October 2011, http://www.cnn.com/2006/WORLD/meast/10/11/iraq.deaths/).

This chapter deliberately eschews formal documents in order to focus on the lives and deaths of individual Iraqis under the CPA and during the insurgency. It begins with an Iraqi perspective of the invasion and subsequent occupation based on the author's work with nongovernmental organizations. The chapter continues with a description by Lt. Paul Bremer on the choice of members for the IGC, which reflects the way the United States perceived Iraqi society. It then moves on to a journal by one young woman in Baghdad who lost her job—and so, her economic independence—due to the war. Anthony Shadid provides insight into one Sunni insurgent who died fighting the occupation. This chapter also addresses Shi'i concerns, particularly after the Ashura bombings of March 2004, which sparked Shi'i resentment because the Coalition proved unable to protect them. In light of the rising insurgency, this chapter also includes the "rules of engagement" for U.S. troops, and these show that children and women were potential targets. This account is then followed by the memoir of a soldier who needed to decide whether or not to kill an Iraqi teenager. Armed Iraqis, however, were not the only victims of fighting. An account by a Marine demonstrates that innocent civilians were also victims of this war. The chapter ends with an account by an exiled teenager whose Ba'thist father was killed by paramilitary groups that had formed in Baghdad.

Civilians and the Front Line

Salam Pax is the moniker of an Iraqi blogger who documented the effects of the Iraq war on the civilian population. As a resident of Baghdad when the war began, he felt the fear that comes with having American bombs aimed at your neighborhood. Though trained as an architect, his mastery of English allowed him to work at times as a translator for foreign journalists during the early days of the war. In May 2003, he traveled with the Campaign for Innocent Victims in Conflict (CIVIC), which was researching the trials of ordinary Iraqis. He broadcast some of their stories on his blog, which was later published as *Salam Pax: The Clandestine Diary of an Ordinary Iraqi* (New York: Grove Press, 2003), 170–72. As you read this account, you should consider the following: Why is it important to have women on the CIVIC team? Who does Salam Pax highlight as victims of war?

Monday, 19 May 2003

One of the biggest surprises when we got to Karbala was that Raed has a girl on his CIVIC team there. She had sent her brother to ask if it was OK for a woman to join. She keeps a notebook for the cases she wants CIVIC to try to help as fast as they can. She told us about um-Khudair, who is a thirty-year-old mother with six children. Her husband was fifty, but he died when their house was bombed. The house has been destroyed. Um-Khudair and her six children now live in one room in a *khan* (these are hotel-like buildings managed by mosques). She is pregnant as well. Sabah, the girl on the CIVIC team, tried to make Raed promise that he will do something, but he can't promise anything really. There is nothing worse than giving people false hope in situations like these and we remind the team not to give the people they interview any promises. CIVIC . . . can only collect information and . . . forward the info to an organization that has the funds and capability to help. . . .

Riyadh, one of the older volunteers, tells about an army training camp where families have taken shelter after their houses were bombed or couldn't pay the rent the last two months, when the country came to a standstill. Since this is one of the things CIVIC is looking into, Raed decides to take a look.

At the camp we get to meet Saif al-Deen, a huge name for a little kid who has a problem with "S"s (if you ask him, he'll tell you his name is "Thaif") and Ibrahim with his little brother. Saif al-Deen . . . and his family had to move to the army training camp when his father, a soldier in the Iraqi army, couldn't pay the rent for the last two months: $10 per month.

In total there are eight families at the camp. They say they have been moved from other places. They have squatted within the city, until they got this army center in the outskirts. When we asked who moved them out of the places they were in, they said it was usually the new political parties. These buildings were NOT given to these parties by the "coalition forces." The Americans . . . have decided to not look at that situation for now. I think that when ministries and other public institutions start functioning again, they will ask for their property back. I can't see why the Dawa Party should take the place of a public library. Anyway, both the newly homeless and the parties are competing to occupy public buildings.

The problem in the one we went to was that this training center is full of ammunition. And one unexploded thingy that has been fired at the camp from a helicopter. The kids run around showing us where the grenades and other stuff lies. There is no use putting up the warnings (given to organizations by the coalition forces to put at places where there are unexploded objects—mainly cluster bombs), because no one in this place can read or write. The only thing to do is to ask the families that are living near the back of the camp to move away from ... where the ammunition is. They tell us that this is just training ammunition and not dangerous. And they won't move out of this place, because they have nowhere else to go.

Lt. Paul Bremer Forms a Governing Council

Lt. Paul Bremer headed the Coalition Provisional Authority, so he reported directly to Secretary of Defense Rumsfeld. Before heading the CPA, he had served for twenty-three years as a diplomat in the U.S. Foreign Service, but he had never been stationed in the Arab world. Although the CPA originally intended to rule directly over Iraq, Bremer quickly came to the realization that the legitimacy of the system of government put in place by this organization needed the imprimatur of Iraqis. And so, Bremer decided to form an Iraqi Governing Council. The following account of the IGC's formation is taken from Lt. Paul Bremer's memoir *My Year in Iraq: The Struggle to Build a Future of Hope* (New York: Simon and Schuster, 2006), 90–95. As you read it, you should consider the following: What challenges does Bremer perceive in forming the IGC? What types of identities is the CPA fostering? Communal or civic? Can a distinct Iraqi identity emerge from Bremer's efforts?

> As part of our effort to find suitable tribal representation for the Governing Council, I had a meeting with leaders from the large Shammar tribe that same week. My years as a diplomat in Afghanistan and Malawi had shown me the ... role tribes still play in many countries. ...
>
> Iraqi tribes are a paradox. ... On the surface, they would appear to be relatively unimportant because more than 70 percent of Iraq's population lives in urban areas. And it's true that tribal leaders have less authority than they did

when the British occupied the country.... Nonetheless, tribes still play an important role in the social and political life of the country. Even Iraqis who have been city dwellers for several generations need little encouragement to discuss their tribal ancestry. Many still ... proclaim their tribe's roots as their ... last name.

But the tribes also had a reputation for respecting power and had always been ... aware of who was up and who was down. They were likely to support whoever exercised authority in Baghdad, until someone stronger came along.

My meeting June 24 at CPA headquarters with about a dozen Sunni sheiks of the Shammar tribe was a memorable encounter with this fact. The Shammar is one of Iraq's largest tribes and has both Shia and Sunni members, though the ... leadership is Sunni.

The members came to the session in their ... white robes. Most were over sixty, but among them was a younger member, Sheik Ghazi al-Yawar, whom we were considering as a candidate for the Governing Council. About forty years old, American educated, Ghazi was a ... businessman in Saudi Arabia. His uncle was the paramount chief of the tribe, and lived just outside Mosul. In deference to his elders, Ghazi said nothing at this meeting....

Like most tribal leaders, these men talked a lot. They were fond of their historic role in Iraq, recalling with pleasure the days when they had alternately fought and supported the British. Toward the end of the three-hour meeting, and after much tea and mutual congratulations on the liberation of Iraq, the ruling sheik spoke.

"Hakim," he said (using the Arabic term for "governor," for this is how the tribes saw me), "I want to assure you of the everlasting loyalty of the Shammar tribe to you and to the governments that have freed us...."

Warming to his theme, he continued, "Our loyalty is constant and unshakeable." Touching his chest, he added that this sentiment was in his mind, but more important was written on his heart and the hearts of his colleagues....

"Through the decades, we have always shown our loyalty and we will be faithful to this ancient tribal tradition." More sounds of agreement.

"If," he concluded, "we should ever decide to betray you, I pledge my word that we will give you a month's notice."

With this reassuring message written on my own heart, I returned the next day to meet the Kurdish leaders....

The Kurds are mountain people, tough-minded and independent. For the better part of a century, they were in rebellion against the rulers of Baghdad, whether British or Iraqi. The two leaders, Jalal Talabani, whose area was the northeast, and Massoud Barzani, in the west, had been at war with Saddam, and with each other, for decades.

My purpose was to persuade both to join the Governing Council. . . . [T]he Kurds had expressed reluctance to submit ever again to rule from Baghdad.

For years before 1991, the Kurds had insisted that a free Iraq must have a federal structure respectful of the unique Kurdish people. And the independence they had won after the Gulf War—represented by the Kurdistan Autonomous Zone, which Coalition air power had protected for years from Saddam's army—symbolized their ambition for an autonomous state.

I knew from my earlier visit that both Kurdish leaders welcomed Liberation and the dissolution of the Baath Party . . . But neither wanted to be on the Governing Council. Talabani even had the madcap idea of rushing off to Asia and Europe . . . at precisely the time we were to pull the Council together.

At his headquarters in Sulaymaniya, I told him that we were "determined to support the creation of a federal Iraq." Talabani was pleased that the Coalition now endorsed this long-standing Kurdish goal, but was still skeptical about serving on the Council.

"The Governing Council will have real political power," I emphasized. . . .

"Ambassador," he finally said over a glass of sweet local wine, "I will agree to serve on the Governing Council based on your personal appeal."

One down. One to go.

The next day I tackled Barzani. He was less urbane than Talabani, more a classic Kurdish tribal leader. Barzani dressed in traditional Kurdish clothing, was enamored beyond words with life at his lovely house atop the mountains at Salahuddin, surrounded by his tribesmen and apple trees. . . .

"I hate Baghdad," Barzani told me. "I don't want to have to live or . . . travel there. But, if you insist, I will agree, with great reluctance, to serve on the Council."

"I do insist."

"Then I agree."

The pace now picked up. John Sawers and I started . . . daily meetings of our large Governance Team. We had announced a goal of establishing the Governing Council by July 15. There were plenty of candidates by now. The job was to . . . sort them, bearing in mind the need for the Council to be representative yet small enough to be effective. We calculated that this would yield a Council of between twenty-five and thirty men and women. Because of the fragmented nature of Iraqi society, this was proving to be an extremely complicated task. . . .

First, we assumed that the Shia would have to be a majority of the Council since they were believed to make up 60 percent of the population. Next, we wanted to ensure that women—downtrodden under Saddam as in many other Arab countries—were well represented. We also needed to find effective, patriotic Sunni members. Finding them brought us face to face with a major structural problem inherent in Iraq's post-Liberation politics: a lack of credible Sunni leaders. Almost all politically active Sunnis had been co-opted into Saddam's security services or Baath Party, or killed as traitors. The Kurds would require representation in rough proportion to the Kurdish/Arab population, about 20 percent. There were Christians, Turkmen, and other minorities whom it was important to include in some way. And as if this were not complicated enough, we hoped that each of Iraq's eighteen provinces could be represented, and we did not want Islamists to dominate the secular majority of the country.

. . .

[Ahmad] Chalabi told me that he had recently met with Grand Ayatollah Ali Husseini Sistani, the most revered Shia cleric in Iraq, an Iranian. The Shiites had a clerical hierarchy who achieved prominence through theological scholarship and whose leaders, the *marjaiya*, spoke with authority for their followers. The Sunnis lacked this clear line of authority over their clerics. Sistani was reputed to be a true man of God, who lived a Spartan life and led his people by example. He had told Chalabi he did not care how the Council was pulled together, but insisted that Iraqis, not the Coalition, should write Iraq's constitution.

"Sistani has read that General Douglas MacArthur wrote Japan's constitution," Chalabi told me. "The Grand Ayatollah is concerned that the Coalition will do the same here."

Several days earlier, the ayatollah had issued a fatwa insisting that the constitution be written by Iraqis and the constitutional conference must be elected, not appointed by the Coalition.

"The Coalition has no intention of writing the constitution," I told Chalabi, "and I'll make sure that Sistani understands this."

Chalabi said that [Sergio] de Mello had apparently told Sistani that he saw no reason elections could not be held soon in Iraq. After all, when he was the UN representative to East Timor, de Mello had noted, his organization had conducted elections soon after arriving.

I replied that de Mello's analogy with East Timor—a former Portuguese colony in the Indonesian archipelago—didn't fit. Iraq had some 25 million citizens to East Timor's 1,000,000, and a much more complex social structure. Holding elections in Iraq under the present circumstances was simply not possible. . . .

As we worked to broaden the Governing Council . . . the British came up with the idea of including someone from the Iraqi Communist Party. In the 1950s and 1960s, the party had attracted many Iraqi intellectuals and artists and it still had a following in these circles. Saddam had let the party stagger along, calculating that its avowed atheism would be a useful counter to Islamism....

So, on July 8, I was in Sawers's office facing the recently retired general secretary of the Iraqi Communist Party, Aziz Mohammed. He was a seventy-nine-year-old Kurd, who clearly felt and showed his age. After describing our plans for the Council, I asked him what he had learned from the fall of Soviet communism.

In reply, Aziz wandered off into a long rumination about how Brezhnev had received letters he never read and sent letters he never wrote.

His comments left me with the distinct impression that he thought Brezhnev was still running the show in Moscow. I didn't have the heart to tell him that Leonid had not been too well recently. We struck Aziz from the list.

Fortunately, a couple of days later, Sawers and I interviewed Aziz's replacement as party leader, Hamid Majid Moussa. He was an energetic roly-poly man in his mid-forties who clearly understood the need to encourage a private sector in Iraq. Moussa, a Shiite, was to prove one of the most effective and popular members of the Governing Council.

Women during the Iraq War

The deteriorating lot of women since the Coalition's occupation of Iraq is a case of horrifying irony. The United States organized the invasion of Iraq in order to foster a stable democracy; and yet, the instability induced by the war has forced women outside of the economic and political life of their own country. By definition, a liberal democratic system includes not only elections, but also, equality of all citizens, rule of law, political pluralism, minority rights, social mobility, and freedom of expression. Free elections have technically been held in Iraq, but, with women afraid to leave their home, real democracy, some argue, has yet to be achieved.

The post-Hussein Iraqi state—even under American administration of the Coalition Provisional Authority—was all too willing to endorse this situation. The twenty-five members of the Iraqi Governing Council consisted of only three women. Since 2003, women have become victims of gender-based violence as well as organized kidnappings. The rise of Islamic fundamentalism has retracted some of the rights earned under Saddam Hussein. And the CPA, which ran Iraq after the first year of occupation, seemed willing to endorse women as second-class citizens. Thus, Paul Bremer initially acquiesced to Resolution 137 in

December 2003, which called for replacing the personal status law in Iraq with a conservative form of Islamic law. (See Isobel Colemen, "Women, Islam, and the New Iraq," in *Foreign Affairs* [January/February 2006] [accessed 8 November 2006, www.foreignaffairs.org].)

In this account, an Iraqi calling herself Riverbend recounts the backward slide of women's rights in her country after the Coalition's occupation of it. Riverbend is a twenty-four-year-old woman from a middle-class background, and she grew up in an English-speaking country. In August 2003, she began to post a blog in order to share her experiences in wartime Iraq, and she later published her account. This excerpt is taken from Riverbend, *Baghdad Burning: Girl Blog from Iraq* (New York: Feminist Press at the City University of New York, 2005). As you read this text, you should consider the situation of women before and after the Coalition occupation of Iraq. In what ways does Riverbend feel that the U.S. occupation has hurt women? How specifically was her life affected by the Iraq War? How does her situation differ from that of her brother E.?

Saturday, August 23, 2003: We've Only Just Begun

Females can no longer leave their homes alone. Each time I go out, E. and either a father, uncle, or cousin has to accompany me. It feels like we've gone back 50 years ever since the beginning of the occupation. A woman, or girl, out alone, risks anything from insults to abduction. An outing has to be arranged at least an hour beforehand. I state that I need to buy something or have to visit someone. Two males have to be procured (preferably large) and "safety arrangements" must be made in this total state of lawlessness. And always the question: "But do you have to go out and buy it? Can't I get it for you?" No you can't, because the kilo of eggplant I absolutely have to select with my own hands is just an excuse to see the light of day and walk down a street. The situation is incredibly frustrating to females who work or go to college.

Before the war, around 50% of the college students were females, and over 50% of the working force was composed of women. Not so much anymore. We are seeing an increase of fundamentalism in Iraq which is terrifying.

For example, before the war, I would estimate (roughly) that about 55% of females in Baghdad wore a hijab—or headscarf. Hijabs do not signify fundamentalism. That is far from the case—although I, myself, don't wear one, I have family and friends who do. The point is that, before, it didn't really matter. It was *my* business whether I wore one or not—not the business of some fundamentalist on the street. . . .

I am female and Muslim. Before the occupation, I . . . dressed the way I wanted to. I lived in jeans . . . and comfortable shirts. Now, I don't dare leave the house in pants. A long skirt and loose shirt (preferably with long sleeves) has become necessary. A girl wearing jeans risks being attacked, abducted, or insulted by fundamentalists who have been . . . liberated!

Fathers and mothers are keeping their daughters stashed safe at home. That's why you see so few females in the streets (especially after 4 p.m.). Others are making their daughters, wives, and sisters wear a hijab. Not to oppress them, but to protect them. . . .

Girls are being made to quit college and school. My 14-year-old cousin (a straight-A student) is going to have to repeat the year because her parents decided to keep her home ever since the occupation. Why? Because the Supreme Council of the Islamic Revolution in Iraq overtook an office next to her school and opened up a special "bureau." . . .

Sunday, August 24, 2003: Will Work for Food. . . .

The story of how I lost my job isn't unique. It has actually become very common—despondently, depressingly, unbearably common. It goes like this. . . .

I'm a computer science graduate. Before the war, I was working in an Iraqi database/software company located in Baghdad as a programmer/network administrator. . . . Every day, I would climb three flights of stairs, enter the little office I shared with one female colleague and two males, start up my PC and spend hours staring at little numbers and letters rolling across the screen. It was tedious . . . it was geeky and it was . . . wonderful. . . .

I loved my job—I was *good* at my job. I came and went to work on my own. At 8 a.m. I'd walk in lugging a backpack filled with enough CDs, floppies, notebooks, chewed-on pens, paperclips and screwdrivers to make Bill Gates proud. I made as much money as my two male colleagues and got an equal amount of respect from the manager (that was because he was clueless when it came to any type of programming and anyone who could do it was worthy of respect . . . a girl, no less—you get the picture).

What I'm trying to say is that no matter *what* anyone heard, females in Iraq were a lot better off than females in other parts of the Arab world (and some parts of the Western world—we had equal salaries!). We made up . . . 50% of the working force. We were doctors, lawyers, nurses, teachers, professors, deans, architects, programmers, and more. We came and went as we pleased. We wore what we wanted (within the boundaries of the social restrictions of a conservative society).

During the first week of June, I heard my company was back in business. It took several hours . . . [and] thousands of family meetings, but I . . . convinced everyone that it was necessary for my sanity to go back to work. They agreed that I would visit the company (with two male bodyguards) and ask them if they had any work I could possibly take home and submit later on, or through the internet.

. . . I packed my big bag of geeky wonders, put on my long skirt and shirt, tied back my hair and left the house with a mixture of anticipation and apprehension.

We had to park the car about 100 meters away from the door of the company because the major road in front of it was cracked and broken with the weight of the American tanks as they entered Baghdad. I half-ran, half-plodded up to the door of the company, my heart throbbing in anticipation of seeing friends, colleagues, secretaries . . . just generally something familiar again in the strange new nightmare we were living.

The moment I walked through the door, I noticed it. Everything looked shabbier somehow—sadder. The maroon carpet lining the hallways was dingy, scuffed and spoke of the burden of a thousand rushing feet. The windows we had so diligently taped prior to the war were cracked in some places and broken in others . . . dirty all over. The lights were shattered, desks overturned, doors kicked in, and clocks torn from the walls.

I stood a moment, hesitantly, in the door. There were strange new faces— fewer of the old ones. Everyone was standing around, looking at everyone else. . . . And I was one of the only females. I weaved through the strange mess and made my way upstairs, pausing for a moment on the second floor where management was located, to listen to the rising male voices. The director had died of a stroke during the second week of the war and . . . we had our own little "power vacuum." At least 20 different men thought they were qualified to be boss. . . .

I continued upstairs, chilled to the bone, in spite of the muggy heat of the building which hadn't seen electricity for at least 2 months. My little room wasn't much better off than the rest of the building. The desks were gone, papers all over the place . . . but A. was there! I couldn't believe it—a familiar, welcoming face. He looked at me for a moment, without really seeing me, then his eyes opened wide and disbelief took over the initial vague expression. He congratulated me on being alive, asked about my family and told me that he wasn't coming back after today. Things had changed. I should go home and stay safe. He was quitting—going to find work abroad. Nothing to do here anymore. I told him about my plan to work at home and submit projects. . . . [H]e shook his head sadly.

I stood staring at the mess . . . trying to sort out the mess in my head, my heart torn to pieces. My cousin and E. were downstairs waiting for me—there was nothing more to do, except ask how I could maybe help? A. and I left the room and started making our way downstairs. We paused on the second floor and stopped to talk to one of the former department directors. I asked him when they thought things would be functioning, he wouldn't look at me. His eyes stayed glued to A.'s face as he told him that females weren't welcome right now—especially females who "couldn't be protected." He finally turned to me and told me, in so many words, to go home because "they" refused to be responsible for what might happen to me.

A Sunni Insurgent

An insurgency against the occupying forces would begin by summer 2003. The so-called Sunni Triangle was a major center of insurgency. This term signifies a region of approximately 400 square miles northwest of Baghdad. Most people there are Sunni and Arab. This area includes Tikrit, the hometown of Saddam Hussein. Saddam Hussein's regime privileged nepotistic ties and thus Sunni Arabs, so this area had been a bastion of Ba'thist support. After the invasion, many in this region felt threatened by the increased political participation of the Shi'i majority. Nevertheless, do not assume that the insurgency was a monolithic movement. In fact, it was an unstructured set of fragmented groups acting in a very disjointed fashion.

Participants in this amorphous insurgency may never publish their memoirs, so their motivation in fighting Coalition forces cannot easily be gauged. For this reason, Anthony Shadid's account of his time in Iraq provides important insight into the insurgency. Shadid was in Iraq between March 2003 and June 2004 as a reporter for the *Washington Post*. He differs from most Western reporters who rely on translators, for he speaks Arabic. In this way, he talked with Iraqis and found out intimate details of their life after the Coalition invasion. He traces the life story of insurgents who died fighting the United States through interviews with friends and family. The following account is taken from *Night Draws Near: Iraq's People in the Shadow of America's War* (New York: Henry Holt, 2005), 349–57. As you read the following account, you should consider the following: What were all the possible reasons that Omar Ibrahim Khalaf opposed the United States and gave his life to the insurgency? Was he a Ba'thist? Or, indeed, did he even benefit from Ba'thist rule? How did the occupation affect him economically? Is Shadid's account of his life story an objective one?

Around the time that Fahdawi and his men were undergoing an awakening, Omar Ibrahim Khalaf, who lived in a village down the road from Fahdawi's town, was plotting his own act of resistance. His story was, in a way, more complicated than Fahdawi's, his motivations less clear. Beyond Khalaf's home of Albu Alwan, his death was little more than a footnote in a simmering guerilla war. But like the lives of Fahdawi and his comrades, Khalaf's was a unique part of the tapestry of post-Saddam Iraq, life defined by occupation and resistance. He was recognized by his community—his family, his village, and his local preacher—the way that Fahdawi and his colleagues were. He was seen as a devout Muslim, his death as sacred. His fight was viewed through the lens of faith, the construct through which the aftermath of Saddam's fall made sense.

Thirty-two years old, Khalaf was the second youngest in a family of six brothers and six sisters who belonged to the Albu Alwan, a Sunni tribe that gave its name to the village. He was known for his hot temper, but also for his sense of humor. He had curly black hair and a patchy beard more the product of oversight than grooming....

Albu Alwan was a hardscrabble village of a few thousand, its dirt roads bordered by olive trees, date palms, and muddy canals. Khalaf's education, like that of many boys in the village, ended with elementary school, and he soon began farming hay, barley, wheat, and sunflowers on an eight-acre plot he inherited from his father. He was drafted during the war with Iran, but deserted his post after serving six months in Heet. He married young and struggled to make money.

A few years before Saddam's fall, he landed a $600 contract hauling construction material to the resort of Sadamiya on Tharthar Lake.... But he spent most of his life eking out a living, driving a truck back and forth to Jordan and herding his fifteen sheep and one cow. His brother Abdel-Latif said that before the war he managed to make about $90 a month.... During the chaotic aftermath, as burdens mounted after the government's fall, he was making no more than $6 a month. His house, started four years before, remained an empty shell of concrete floors and unfinished tan brick walls. A month earlier, his wife had given birth to their sixth child, a boy named Radwan. "He had no money," said Khaled Mawash, a neighbor who knew the family.

Everybody knew everybody else's business; neighbors said Khalaf was devastated when Baghdad fell in just hours. One shopkeeper said Khalaf told him that he had wept at home all day. Others recalled the anger that he loudly voiced as U.S. patrols barreled down the highway that ran next to his house and fields. The sight, they said, was so repugnant that he quit playing soccer in a dusty field adjacent to the bridge that the convoys transited. A childhood friend, Mawlud Khaled, recalled that as the vehicles passed Khalaf said, "If I had a grenade, I would kill myself and take them with me."

Neighbors said his behavior grew increasingly erratic as the weeks progressed. In vain, he once fired a Kalashnikov at a U.S. helicopter flying overhead in the month after Saddam's fall. One morning a week before his death . . . he ran at a passing convoy dressed only in shorts, neighbors recalled. His family had to restrain him. "He hated the Americans," his friend said. "He didn't care whether he died or not." In late July, neighbors said, Khalaf wrote the names of three people on a piece of paper. He owed each one money—between ten and thirty dollars. A few days later, on August 1, he woke up early and dressed in gray pants and a plaid shirt. A little before seven a.m., as was his custom, he was seen taking his sheep to graze in a nearby pasture. He left without saying a word to his wife . . . or anyone else in the village. . . ."Nobody knew where he went," his cousin Nawar Bidawi told me.

A nine-vehicle convoy of the 43rd Combat Engineering Company was passing just a few miles outside of Fallujah when the attack began. It was 7:15 a.m. The assailants were hidden about fifty yards from the well-traveled road. . . .

Khalaf and at least ten others seem to have chosen their spot for the sake of the canals, which provided cover. They lay waiting in one, and another snaked behind it. Both were filled with stagnant water and overgrown with reeds as much as ten feet tall. The village of Falahat was less than a mile away, but the area of the ambush had only fields of clover and orchards of apricot trees and palms laden with ripening dates.

With a loud hiss, the attackers' first volley sent three rocket-propelled grenades at the convoy. Two missed their mark; a third hit the road underneath a Humvee, damaging the . . . transmission and disabling the vehicle. . . . [T]he soldiers returned fire with .50-caliber machine guns, along with lighter weapons and grenade launchers. The . . . return fire was so intense that even villagers in Falahat . . . sought cover. The U.S. troops . . . called in reinforcements, and Lieutenant Noah Hanners, the platoon leader of Heavy Company, arrived within ten minutes in a tank from a base about six miles away.

The assailants in the canal fired their Kalashnikovs wildly and lobbed badly aimed grenades every couple of minutes. But they were out-gunned and out-trained, and the U.S. soldiers were on higher ground. Khalaf and the others, all in civilian clothes, were concealed by the canal vegetation but had no avenue of escape, no way to get away. "You could see the cattails move as they tried to run, so we just put a large volume of fire down on the canals," Hanners said.

The lieutenant said he believed that Khalaf was one of the first to die. When he raised his head above the canal's reeds, he was struck by a .50-caliber round.

"His head was pretty much missing," the lieutenant said. Machine-gun fire almost detached his left arm and ankle; his torso was riddled with bullets and smeared with blood and the powdery dirt of the Euphrates valley. One or two more of the men were killed at about the same time. As the assailants tried to escape through the canals, wearing plastic sandals, another two or three were killed. In the lopsided fight, so intense villagers would later call it a glimpse of hell, no U.S. soldiers were hurt.

By the time a second tank arrived at about 7:30 a.m., the fight was over, and the soldiers took the body of Khalaf and two others to the U.S. base near a town called Habbaniya. At least one other corpse, too badly mangled to move, was left behind. The air stagnant, the heat tactile, Khalaf's body and the other two that had been recovered were stored in black body bags in a small cement room for three days. The stench was so overpowering that soldiers at the front gate, about a hundred yards away, burned paper to fend off the smell.

Khalaf's oldest brother, Abdel-Latif, and his brother-in-law were escorted by Iraqi police to the base. Soldiers gave them blue surgical masks, but a stench they compared with that of dead livestock on their farms threw them back out the door. "It was an ugly smell. It was unbearable," Abdel-Latif recalled as we sat in his house in Albu Alwan. He smoked cheap cigarettes and thumbed a string of amber worry beads. "When you faced it, you wanted to vomit."

Soldiers suggested they take all three bodies, but Abdel-Latif said he claimed only his brother, whom he identified by his bloodied clothes and his chipped front tooth. The rest of his face, he said, was unrecognizable.

Once again, the gulf between occupier and occupied, the almost certainly unintended and perhaps unavoidable slights: Khalaf's family was outraged by the fact that his body had been left lying on its stomach, rather than its back: his head had faced the ground, rather than the holy city of Mecca. The body had been left in a hot, windowless room, rather than refrigerated. And it was riddled with maggots. Mohammed Ajami, Khalaf's brother-in-law, said, "The treatment was inhuman," perhaps forgetting that it was his brother, after all, who had instigated the attack.

Khalaf's kinsmen returned in a blue Volvo at 3:30 p.m. and, before dusk, buried Khalaf in a wood coffin at the Kiffa cemetery. Because he was a martyr, he was interred as he had died, in his clothes and unwashed. The wounds, according to tradition, bore witness to his martyrdom.

His family said a convoy of a hundred cars carrying 250 people accompanied Khalaf's body. And in the mourning that ensued, Khalaf went from angry spectacle to hero. The sheikh at the village mosque, Omar Aani, told me that the three men to whom Khalaf owed money forgave their loans. Neighbors collected money for his children.... A family that had battled with Khalaf for a year over the rights to water from an irrigation canal apologized to his family and expressed shame at their enmity. "They recognized that he was a true hero," said Khaled, the childhood friend. "They regretted not talking to him."

On a sun-drenched plain along a bluff of barren cliffs, a cheap headstone made of cement marked Khalaf's grave. His name had been hastily scrawled on it in white chalk; below was the invocation "In the name of God, the most merciful and compassionate." This was followed simply by the date of his death: Friday, August 1, 2003. One word on the marker distinguished his resting place from the scores of others that dug into the rocky soil. Khalaf's epitaph declared him a *shaded*, a martyr.

Why did he choose to die?

Hanners, the American lieutenant, speculated that Khalaf was at the end of a chain that began with a paymaster—in the lieutenant's words, "someone we've pissed off lately who has money." The paymaster, in turn, would have been linked to someone else who could find weapons and plan the ambush, usually a military officer from Iraq's disbanded army. Hanners was confident that Khalaf had been paid. But as for motives other than money, Hanners told me, one could only guess: "Pretty much anything you can come up with, any motive you can come up with, is a possibility."

In private, a few residents of Albu Alwan passed on rumors that Khalaf might have been motivated in part by money, desperate as he was for a way to mitigate his grinding poverty. Others vigorously, sometimes angrily shook their heads at this suggestion—a denial based, perhaps, more on respect than reality. "The most important thing is that he was so upset by them. Money wasn't important, because he knew he would be killed," said his neighbor Muwaffaq Khaled. "If I'm Muslim and I respect God, I can't die for money. It's *harram*, forbidden."

"I know him well," his brother Mawlud insisted. "It wasn't a matter of money."

In the villages like Albu Alwan, bound by tradition and populated by Sunnis who bristled most at the day-to-day humiliations (perceived and real) of occupation, many insisted in those days that they were actually perplexed by the question of who was behind the attacks on U.S. troops. Were the insurgents driven by Islam, or by loyalty to Saddam? At one house, a neighbor of Khalaf remarked on fresh graffiti in nearby Fallujah, calling Saddam "the hero of heroes." Other graffiti read, "God bless the holy fighters of the city of mosques," "Fallujah will remain a symbol of jihad and resistance, and more bluntly, "We have the right to kill the foreign American occupiers...."

For many of the people I interviewed in Albu Alwan that week, Khalaf's death seemed to bring clarity to that question. They knew him, they said, and they knew why he would die. A week after his death, it seemed that Khalaf had been transformed into a symbol of his friends' and neighbors' dismay over the occupation. In words as heated as the village's scorched streets, some of the most outspoken townspeople insisted that he had acted out their own grievances. Through him, they found a certain element of catharsis. A shopkeeper along the village's main road called Khalaf a hero motivated by hatred of the occupation, which all of them felt was an awful humiliation. The speaker was Muslim; the Americans were infidels. There was not the slightest shading of hesitation to diminish the absoluteness of the division. What would follow, the speaker said, was clear. "Revenge is part of our tradition," he said; maybe it was with these words that I knew for certain that whatever the American intentions, that gulf was unbridgeable.

Khalaf's brother enumerated the promises that he believed had been broken by the Americans—a share of Iraq's oil he and others had supposedly been assured of receiving, one-hundred-dollar payments that would accompany better rations each month, jobs and prosperity that were supposed to follow the nearly thirteen years of sanctions. His brother-in-law complained of the daily degradations. U.S. soldiers had often made men bow their heads to the ground, for example, an act that he emphasized should only be performed before God. He recalled American soldiers pointing guns at Iraqi men in front of their terrified children and wives. Khalaf, they insisted, had stood up for his countrymen against these degradations.

As we chatted at the house of Aani, the village sheikh, which adjoined the mosque where he led prayers, he acknowledged that, after Khalaf died, he had to ask friends just who the man was.... But what he found out about Khalaf's life paled before what he came to understand about his death. "Omar sacrificed his soul for the sake of his faith, for the sake of his country, for the sake of oppressed people, not for the sake of the previous regime or for the Baath Party. He has become a model for everyone to follow," he said. "The person who resists this situation becomes an example."

He looked at me for a few moments. He seemed to be trying to read my face, trying to read whether I was more Arab or Western. "He's equal to half the Americans in Iraq," he said, his own face expressionless. I didn't know whether I was being insulted or not.

Shi'i Disillusionment

A majority of Iraqis are Shi'i, but this religious group had historically been treated by the government as a marginalized minority. This was as true under the Ottomans, who feared their links to the Persians, as it was under the British, who favored the established elite loyal to King Faysal. Saddam Hussein also favored Sunnis, especially since Shi'i groups had begun to form political groups that questioned Ba'thist legitimacy.

Once the Coalition forces ousted Saddam Hussein, many Shi'is hoped that they could practice their religion freely and integrate into the new political structures of Iraq. Some Sunnis, however, felt threatened by the idea of democracy simply because the Shi'i majority might threaten their privileged position within the state. The lot of Shi'is seemed uncertain, especially after the exiled leader Ayatollah Baqir al-Hakim was assassinated by a car bomb in summer 2003. American politicians, however, hoped to create a system of governance that incorporated Shi'is. Thus, the twenty-five members of the Iraqi Governing Council appointed in fall 2003 included thirteen Shi'is, including the brother of the assassinated al-Hakim.

Nevertheless, the first year of occupation exhibited a growing number of attacks on Shi'is. Haider Ala Hamoudi provides the reader with special insight into the Shi'i community of post-Saddam Iraq. He is an American-Iraqi who is Shi'i. Once the Coalition forces secured Iraq, he decided to return to his country—where his family still resided—in order to help with reconstruction. He hoped that his law degree would allow him to be a constructive intermediary between Iraqis and their foreign occupiers. He published this account of the holiday of Ashura in *Howling in Mesopotamia: An Iraqi-American Memoir* (New York: Beaufort Books, 2008), 125–30. As you read it, you should consider the following: What is Ashura? How did Iraqi Shi'is celebrate it? Why does its celebration sour Haider?

> In a better world, this chapter would be about the unfortunate security situation that prevented me from seeing my first Ashura commemoration in Baghdad—the first Ashura commemoration that had taken place in Iraq in my lifetime.
>
> The Ba'ath had prohibited, or at least severely restricted, the commemoration of this most important of Shi'i religious holidays for obvious reasons. What we are commemorating is the death of Muhammad's grandson Hussein, called by the Shi'a the "Leader of the Martyrs" and the rightful leader of the Muslim community, which at the time in Shi'i legend was in the hands of a tyrannical,

usurping, and unjust caliph Yazid. The cries that day, to the usurping caliph, of *far from us is your indignity* and *the oppressors shall see what punishment awaits them* would naturally disturb Saddam Hussein; the historical parallels could readily be drawn between him, a Sunni dictator seeking to subject the majority Shi'a of Iraq, and Yazid, the murderer of Muhammad's grandson Hussein. So the commemoration was banned for thirty-five years. . . .

I have seen commemorations to Hussein in the United States, Britain, and Iran, but never in Iraq where the original indignity had taken place, and never at the tomb in Kerbala. It was with a mixture of happiness (ironic given that the commemoration itself revolves around mourning and grief) and anticipation that we Shi'a looked forward to Ashura in March of 2004, when we would be free to commemorate as we wished. Still, there was a palpable sense of foreboding as well. The country was not safe. The Americans had proven themselves incapable of protecting it, or unwilling to do so. Al-Qaeda had suggested they would seek to provoke us in a civil war with our fellow countrymen through incendiary attacks, and nothing would be more provocative than an attack on this occasion. My brother and I had discussed the matter, and decided that we would participate in some of the evening celebrations in our paternal grandfather's home, and would certainly be involved in the massive cooking preparations that would take place the day before, but we would not go to the holy sites themselves. . . .

The food preparations on the night before Ashura in 2004 revived generations-old traditions that had been banned for more than two decades. They were a sight that warmed the heart. Food on the day of Ashura basically is of two types: a lamb and lentil stew . . . and a porridge known as *hareesa*. Families prepared these dishes the night before Ashura on the streets of Shi'i neighborhoods in pots large enough to hold a person. Families . . . share these foods with each other the next day.

Meanwhile . . . in the streets of Baghdad and at the holy site of Kerbala itself, processions of black-clad men wearing headbands with the script "O Hussein," and women covered head-to-toe in black chadors, marched through the streets. Children dressed like the men scurried back and forth between the two groups. Cries for the legends surrounding the dead Imam were heard, men walked and hit their chests rhythmically, men and women alike wept frantically and urgently for the orphans and widows of Kerbala—for Fatima the daughter of the Prophet and mother of the murdered grandson, for the Leader of the Martyrs' sister, Zainab, who carried the tale of the injustice throughout the Arab lands, ensuring that the stain which hung on the name of the Umayyad dynasty for this killing would remain forever.

And, as the news reported, in a custom more honored in the breach, many of the men and even some of the children carried with them sharpened knives tied on links of a chain. They then threw the chain on which the knives were hung over their backs in hard succession, cutting themselves in the process. Some fathers cut the foreheads of their very young children with razor blades, and the children, sometimes as young as two, cried uncontrollably as blood poured down their faces. Some believed that this would endear them to the grand martyr himself. The scene was frenzied, bloody, and somewhat frightening, though less so from where I was, which tended to be some distance away from those who were actually hurting themselves. The more extreme varieties of commemoration are not encouraged by our clerics, and nobody I knew chose to partake in the actual bloodletting, instead keeping themselves a fair distance away from it. Still today, nobody criticizes the practice, and no cleric dares to issue an outright ban....

All of this we witnessed, in sorrow and mourning as was the custom in honor of the dead grandson, but also with a strange mix of contentedness. We were free on the streets of Baghdad to practice our religion for the first time in decades. The blood was excessive, the fear was pervasive, the crowds hesitant, but each cry ... each thump on the chest was a cry of freedom, at last, from a savage tyranny that had at once seemed unending.

On the streets that night I ran into Abu Abbas, the friend of a relative. He was busy preparing *qima* with his family. "Look at these pots, look at this one ..."

"I see it Abu Abbas, it's great."

"No, look, this other one, see how big it is. And watch, if you touch the top, it's not hot. Touch it...."

"I don't really need to touch your pots, I believe you."

"And this one is even bigger, look at it!"

... I felt that perhaps my time was better spent watching the throngs in commemoration.

"I found these after my father passed away, Allah's mercy on him. I had never seen them before, but I knew what they were for. Ashura. Now I can use them."

Abu Abbas had on an apron that his uncle had brought him from England, which read, "The Chef is in, everyone else out," and it was stained with the *qima* he was preparing. We walked along together for a bit, he beating his chest more vigorously than I. He wept deeply as he heard over a loudspeaker the story of Zainab bidding farewell to her brother Imam Hussein for the final time before he left his tent on the night of Ashura.

After the story came to an end, Abu Abbas wiped away his tears ... and asked about my family. I could not tell if he was mourning the dead Imam or celebrating his freedom to commemorate. I didn't know which I was doing either.

I should be writing more about this. I should also be writing about the processions I watched on television the next morning as they culminated in a large gathering at holy sites in Baghdad and Kerbala, and reenactments took place of the events in Kerbala itself. Some unfortunates were conscripted to play the role of the soldiers in the caliph's army, charged with the task of murdering Imam Hussein, though in this case they were in greater dangers, as the audience spent a fair amount of energy damming them to hell, cursing them ... and in extreme cases throwing shoes at them. I should be writing about my feelings that day, those of mourning for a hero of my childhood, those of joy that we could breathe again the sweet air of freedom in Shi'ism's home, those of disappointment that security concerns kept me at home watching it all on television.

But then the "insurgents" struck again and for me everything changed—forever. The so-called Islamic resistance on that day, never regarded by me as a positive force, became my deepest enemy.

Mortars and grenades and suicide bombs were ... arranged throughout holy sites in Iraq to ensure the maximum damage to human life. Dozens were killed in Baghdad, dozens of others in Kerbala. ... On television, all that we could see were bloody limbs, terrorized people running frantically, buildings falling apart, ambulance sirens blaring, and chaos everywhere. We could make no sense of it, though we knew the substance of what had happened. On its holiest day and at its holiest site and at various places throughout the region, Shi'is were attacked for no reason other than because they were intending to practice their faith in freedom for the first time in decades. I have never been more despondent or more frustrated in my life. More than this, however, I was angry.

I was angry at the Americans, and the ... sight of watching a ... U.S. Army or CPA spokesman express ... outrage at the attacks turned my stomach. Though they insisted that they would shepherd the country to ... democracy, they had proven themselves ... unable to provide the one elemental service a sovereign must provide: security. If this was how they wanted to rule, they were better off going home. Nothing good could come from this type of governance. It was not governance at all, only its illusion to satisfy a discontented American public.

I heard the CNN spokespeople, I heard the experts explain how impossible it was going to be to protect so many people in so small an area, and I could only think one thing—if it was the Olympics, if it was the anniversary of September 11, if it was the Oscars, if it was the Super Bowl, an event not one-tenth as important as Ashura, America would have found a way. Whatever the problems, whatever the obstacles, the U.S. would make sure its people were protected. But when it came to Iraq, they sounded like Yasser Arafat. It was no surprise to me that the tanks that approached the mosques after the attacks were greeted by hails of rocks and shoes....

I went to the Ashura commemorations later that evening as I had committed myself to do; it never occurred to my brother or me that we would not. Before the events of the day, it was a matter of participating in an important religious ritual, but now it was political, and personal, and nobody was going to scare me into staying home. I saw Abu Abbas that night, and understandably he was crushed. His hopes for a grand Ashura celebration had been destroyed; something he had wait his whole life had been denied him for one more year. Looking at him—his downcast eyes, wearing the shirt he had on the night before, his cheeks streaked with tears—I remembered an image from a school educational film that would stay with me forever. It was of a young black man in a southern cafeteria sitting down and asking to be served while some rural whites poured ketchup on top of his head and jeered at him. He looked at them despondently and asked, "Why do you hate me so much? I just want lunch." I saw that same look, of incomprehensibility, of confusion, of despair at such an overwhelming injustice that seems entirely unprovoked, on the face of Abu Abbas that night.

The Rules of Engagement

The most notorious site of insurgency in the Sunni Triangle was Falluja. On 31 March 2004, four security contractors working for Blackwater were ambushed. These men were beaten and set on fire. Afterwards, their burned corpses were hanged from a bridge. The images of this tragedy sparked a strong reaction in the United States. There followed the first and second battles of Falluja (April–May and November–December respectively), when, the Coalition struggled to regain control over the city. In order to re-assume this control, the Coalition in conjunction with Ayad Allawi, the prime minister, ordered the entire population of the city to evacuate their homes. In a city of 600,000 people, 80 percent left their homes.

The following is an account of the rules of engagement as told to U.S. soldiers before the First Battle of Falluja. Dexter Filkins covered the war as an embedded reporter for the *New York Times*. He was in Iraq between March 2003 and August 2006. This excerpt is taken from Filkins's book about his experiences, *The Forever War* (New York: Alfred A. Knopf, 2008), 186–88. As you read it, you should consider the following: What problems do military personnel perceive in taking Falluja? What are some of the moral issues with which U.S. soldiers must grapple?

> The legal adviser walked to the front of the room, holding a sheet of paper. The marines . . . were assembled before him. The assault on Falluja was about to begin.
>
> "Okay, guys, these are going to be the rules of engagement," the adviser, Captain Matt Nodine, said. He looked across the room. "It's going to be slightly different this time, so everybody listen up."
>
> He glanced down at his paper. "First, you can engage the enemy wherever he engages us, or where you determine there is hostile intent," Nodine told the men.
>
> "Your response needs to be proportional to the attack," Nodine said. "That means you use the minimum amount of force to remove the threat and continue the mission. Let me give you an example. You may come under fire from a building. If you can kill the guy with an M-16 or an M-240, do that. But don't call in an airstrike—take him out yourself. If you need a grenade launcher or a machine gun to do it, that's okay, as long as you don't cause unnecessary collateral damage. A TOW missile might be a later resort. Just remove the threat and continue the attack. . . ."
>
> "There are some circumstances under which you will need specific permission to fire," Nodine told the marines. "If you are taking fire from mosques and minarets, you're going to need permission from your C.O. before you can engage. The one exception for that is if the loudspeakers are being used to call men to battle. In that case, you're free to engage. Take out the loudspeaker.
>
> "Okay, hostile intent," Nodine said. "You can fire if you determine there is hostile intent. What's hostile intent? Let me go through some of the situations.
>
> "If you see a guy carrying a gun," Nodine said, "that's hostile intent. It's assumed. You are free to shoot.
>
> "If the guy drops his weapon and runs, you can engage him," Nodine said. "But if he drops the weapon and puts his hands up and indicates that he's surrendering, you cannot engage. You have to detain him."
>
> He glanced down again at his card. Some of the men had begun looking at theirs. "If you see a guy on a cell phone—and he's talking on the phone and looking around like he's a spotter," he said, "that would be hostile intent. Use your judgment, but you can shoot.
>
> "Okay," Nodine said, looking up, "if a guy comes out of a building with a white flag, obviously you can't shoot him. Unless he starts to run back and forth

with the white flag," Nodine said. "We've had a lot of insurgents try to use white flags to maneuver. If he tries to use the flag to maneuver, that's hostile intent. You can shoot."

He glanced down at his note card again.

"Okay, ambulances," Nodine said. "You shouldn't be seeing any ambulances out there—the Red Crescent has withdrawn. But, as you know, we have had instances where enemy forces have used ambulances to transport their guns and wounded, and just to move around. So if you see an ambulance out there, fire a warning shot. If they don't stop, that's hostile intent. Use your discretion, but you can engage.

"Okay, now, listen up, this is important," Nodine said. "You might find yourself in a firefight where there are civilians around. You can't indiscriminately shoot civilians, obviously. But it's also possible that you're going to see women and children acting in hostile ways—carrying ammo to the enemy, or placing themselves between you and the enemy. We've seen that. We've had cases where the enemy tries to use civilians for cover. We saw that in Mogadishu, guys hiding behind women and children to shoot at us. In those cases, use your best judgment about whether or not to engage," Nodine said.

"And, if you have women and children engaging you—exhibiting hostile intent," Nodine said, "you are going to need to prepare yourself mentally beforehand for the possibility that you might have to engage them.

"Any questions?"

The Coffins of Muqdadiyah

Muqtada al-Sadr was a Shi'i religious student—only thirty years old—when the Coalition invasion began. He was the nephew of the cleric Muhammad Baqir al-Sadr killed by the Ba'thist regime in 1980. After claiming that the Iraqi Governing Council was not a truly representative body for Iraqis, al-Sadr formed his own army, which was called the Mahdi militiamen. According to Charles Tripp, "he emerged as a populist leader, claiming to protect and provide for his community, whilst using systematic violence against those who opposed him" (Tripp, 280). At first, his power rested in Baghdad's Sadr City (formerly Saddam City), but his influence spread quickly to other parts of Iraq, including Muqdadiya, a city in the northeastern Diyala province.

It was in Muqdadiya that Staff Sergeant David Bellavia was stationed along with the Third Platoon, Alpha Company in April 2004. The majority of its 300,000 residents are Sunni Arabs, though there are also Kurds and Shi'i Arabs in Muqdadiya. The mission of Third Platoon was to take out Mahdi militiamen loyal to al-Sadr. His memoir provides a grisly account of fighting, which took place among a civilian population. The following is from David Bellavia, with John R. Bruning, *House to House: An Epic Memoir of* War (New York: Pocket Star Books, 2007), 6–10. It represents the graphic horror of the Iraq War and the implementation of the "rules of engagement."

> The men moved for the door. As they forced their way inside, I peered around the corner and caught sight of a gunman on a nearby rooftop. I studied him for a moment, unsure whose side he was on. He could be a friendly local. We'd seen them before shooting at the black-clad Mahdi militiamen who infiltrated this part of the city earlier in the fight. Not everyone with a rifle was an enemy.
>
> The gunman on the roof was a teenaged boy, maybe sixteen years old. I could see him scanning for targets, his back to me. He held an AK-47 without a stock. Was he just a stupid kid trying to protect his family? Was he one of Muqtada al-Sadr's Shiite fanatics? I kept my eyes on him and prayed he'd put the AK down and just get back inside his own house. I didn't want to shoot him.
>
> He turned and saw me, and I could see the terror on his sweat-streaked face. I put him in my sights just as he adjusted his AK against his shoulder. I had beaten him on the draw. My own rifle was snug in my shoulder, the sight resting on him. The kid stood no chance. My weapon just needed a flick of the safety and a butterfly's kiss of pressure on the trigger.
>
> *Please don't do this. You don't need to die.*
>
> The AK went to full ready-up. Was he aiming at me? I couldn't be sure, but the barrel was trained at my level. Do I shoot? Do I risk not shooting? Was he silently trying to save me from some unseen threat? I didn't know. I had to make a decision.
>
> *Please forgive me for this.*
>
> I pulled my trigger. The kid's chin fell to his chest, and a guttural moan escaped his lips. I fired again, missed, then pulled the trigger one more time. The bullet tore his jaw and ear off. Sergeant Hall came up alongside me, saw the AK and the boy, and finished him with four shots to his chest. He slumped against the low rooftop wall.
>
> "Thanks, dude. I lost my zero," I said to Hall, explaining that my rifle sights were off-line, though that was the last thing going through my mind.
>
> Now a day later on a street surrounded by coffins and mourning families, their grief is too much for us to witness. These poor people had been caught in the middle, abused by the fanatics who chose to fight us. Muqtada al-Sadr's Mahdi militiamen are the foot soldiers of the Shia uprising. They're the ones

who have created this chaos in Muqdadiyah. They use innocent people's homes and businesses as fighting positions. . . .

The angst-filled scenes on the street cannot compare to what we find inside these battle-scarred houses. Yesterday, my squad kicked in one door and stumbled right into a woman wearing a blood-soaked apron. She was sitting on the floor, howling with grief. She looked to be in her mid-forties and had Shia tattoos on her face. When she saw us, she stood and grasped Specialist Piotr Sucholas by the shoulders and gave him a kiss on his cheek. Then she turned and laid her head on Sergeant Hall's chest as if to touch his heart.

I stepped forward and said in broken Arabic "La tah khaf madrua? Am ree kee tabeeb. Weina mujahadeen kelb?" *Do not be afraid. Injured? American doctor. Where are the mujahadeen dogs?*

She . . . kissed my wedding ring. "Baby madrua. Baby madrua." The despair in her voice was washed away by the sound of a little girl's laughter. When the giggling child came in from the kitchen and clutched her mother's leg, we . . . realized she had Down syndrome. I was struck by the beauty of this child. Specialist Pedro Contreras, whose heart was always the biggest in our platoon, knelt . . . and gave her a butterscotch candy. Contreras loved Iraqi kids. He had a six-year-old nephew back home, and seeing these little ones made him ache for the boy.

We didn't see the injured baby at first—we still had a job to do. I moved upstairs, searching for an insurgent who had been shooting at our Bradleys. Halfway up, I discovered a smear of blood on the steps. Then I found a tuft of human hair. Another step up, I saw a tiny leg.

Baby madrua.

Ah, fuck. Fuck.

The child was dead. She was torn apart at the top of the stairs. Specialist Michael Gross had followed me partway up the stairs. I turned to him and screamed, "Get back down! I said get the fuck back down!" Gross stopped suddenly, then eased off the stairs, a wounded look on his face. I was overly harsh, but I didn't want him to see what was left of this dead child.

Leaving the squad on the first floor, I went to clear the roof alone. Three dead goats lay bleeding on the rooftop next to a dead Mahdi militiaman dressed in black with a gold armband. He had died with an AK in hand, a rocket-propelled grenade launcher leaning against the wall at his side. My stomach churned. Was this the woman's husband? Had he really endangered his family by shooting at us from his own rooftop? What kind of human does this? Revolted, I fled downstairs. The rest of the squad found shell casings in the children's bedroom. The Mahdi militiaman had been shooting from the window there. . . .

I'll never forget that house. The woman kissed each of us good-bye. As she touched her lips to my cheek, I pointed to my wedding ring and asked her where her husband was.

"Weina zoah jik? Shoof nee, shoof nee." *Where is your husband? Show me, show me.*

She spat onto the floor and cried, "Kelb." *Dog.* I guessed he was the corpse on her roof. I touched my heart and tried to convey my feelings, but the language barrier was too great.

Operation Devil Siphon

During the occupation, the line between combat soldier and peacekeeper quickly began to blur. It was day-to-day circumstances, and not policy, that determined the role of Coalition troops after the invasion. Commanders and politicians needed to stop and ask themselves: Were troops to remain combat-ready, even though the invasion was complete? Or were they to engage in peacekeeping and nation-building activities? In the southern provinces, the British tried for the latter, keeping soldiers out of kevlar. In the U.S.-controlled provinces throughout the rest of Iraq, troops continued to wear kevlar, but they were often given tasks that were not military in nature. Given the rising insurgency in the year after the invasion, this blurry line became problematic. The infantry, for example, whether in the Army or Marines, was trained to be intimate killers who engaged the enemy in hand-to-hand combat.

Donovan Campbell throws light on the difficulties faced by members of the infantry who were expected both to engage in urban combat with insurgents and to police the activities of civilians. Donovan led an infantry platoon of 40 Marines in Ramadi from March to September 2004. In contrast to Falluja, he writes: "We ... fought a much blurrier battle, a classic urban counter-insurgency, a never-ending series of engagements throughout the heart of a teeming city where our faceless enemies blended seamlessly into a surrounding populace of nearly 350,000 civilians" (Campbell, 7). Donovan recorded the following in *Joker One: A Marine Platoon's Story of Courage, Leadership, and Brotherhood* (New York: Random House, 2009). In the following account, he reveals the unintended consequences of sending a convoy of highly armed American troops to stop a black marketer, a decision forced on the infantry by politicians. As you read the account, you should consider the following: What role did Donovan want the infantry to play? What role did the politicians force on it? And with what effect?

Five days later, the platoon was out on Michigan again, but this time we weren't protecting the road or hunting IEDs or their makers. Instead, we were executing Operation Devil Siphon, another of the many Coalition Provisional Authority-driven tasks that probably made sense to the twenty-six-year-old political appointee who drafted it in the safety of the Green Zone but that seemed completely illogical to those of us tasked with its execution. The theory behind Devil Siphon was fairly straightforward: The legitimacy of the provincial government was being undermined by a robust black market that had sprung up to distribute gasoline, so coalitional forces needed to dismantle said market because the Iraqi police were incapable of doing it themselves. In Ramadi, control of all official fuel stations seemed to be firmly in the hands of the government, and the twin levers of fuel supply and gasoline prices were potent ones indeed. Anything that diminished the power of those levers or that made the ... government look incompetent ... seemed a threat worth eliminating in the eyes of our overseers in Baghdad.

However, like everything else in Iraq, sweat-soaked, blood-soaked reality was more complex than disconnected theory composed neatly in air-conditioned rooms. The vast majority of downtown Ramadi was supplied by a single gas station with restricted hours, and whenever we patrolled past it, lines of cars stretched for hundreds of meters along Michigan, waiting for hours with their engines turned off for just a brief chance at the pump. In response to the overwhelming demand and sharply restricted supply, dozens of local entrepreneurs had set up shop along the highway, selling gasoline (cut with varying amounts of water) out of plastic jerry cans, empty glass Pepsi bottles, and any other container they could scavenge. Though the sales were technically illegal, these newly minted businessmen were serving a serious need, and, it could be argued, helping to keep the overall level of popular resentment down. To those of us routinely subjected to the glares of stranded motorists, the rationale behind eliminating what seemed a fairly robust safety valve was suspect ... and threatened to alienate the locals further. Besides, for every jerry can we slashed, five more took its place immediately. Nevertheless, we had our orders (and they weren't immoral or illegal, just illogical), so we were constantly trying to disrupt the operations of anyone selling substantial quantities of black-market gasoline.

On May 22, we spotted a particularly egregious offender. At the time, the whole platoon was rumbling east down Michigan after having inspected the one official fuel station.... As the Ox was in charge of contracting and other inspection work for the company, he had come along with us, bringing with him

George and a radio operator. Now the Ox was traveling in our second vehicle, along with Leza and Raymond. As the convoy neared the Saddam mosque, Leza called over the PRR.

"Sir, we just spotted a guy selling a lot of gas right in that little field next to the mosque. Do you want us to get him?"

"Yeah, have Raymond jump out and take care of business." Our Devil Siphon plan called for Raymond and his team to leap out of our vehicles, hustle over to whatever target we had spotted, and quickly slit or otherwise irreparably damage the fuel containers. The rest of us would wait near the Humvees—the idea was to be maximally time-efficient so that our stationary convoy didn't present too much of a target and so that the truly important missions, like patrolling, could continue with a minimum of Devil Siphon–imposed interruption.

The whole convoy screeched to a halt in a nearly five-hundred-meter-long line along the south side of Michigan, and Raymond's team launched themselves out of the back of their Humvee without bothering to wait for it to come to a halt. Unbeknownst to me, the Ox also decided to launch himself on the quick fuel-spill mission. As the convoy ground to a complete halt, Raymond's team, augmented by the Ox and his radio operator, sprinted as fast as possible across Michigan. Quickly, they closed the distance on the fuel salesman and his assistant, a male relative who appeared to be in his early teens. . . . It didn't take long for both of them to catch sight of the six armed Marines charging across the busy four-lane highway, and it took even less time for the salesman to realize that he was the intended target. As Raymond's team jumped the concrete median divider, the salesman bolted for a nearby yellow-and-orange taxi that was parked near his enterprise, leaving the teenage male to fend for himself.

By the time the Ox and Raymond made it completely across the street, the salesman had already revved up his car. As the Marines closed, he suddenly bolted with it, nearly running them over as the taxi fishtailed out onto Michigan. However, the street was jam-packed with cars, and the fleeing salesman ground to a halt before traveling even one block. Raymond's team pursued on foot, so the salesman pulled his car up onto the sidewalk and started driving crazily along it at what must have been well over thirty miles per hour. Shouting civilians frantically dived left and right as the vehicle upended a few tea tables that had been set up on the sidewalk. The taxi may even have hit a few of the pedestrians, and as the vehicle continued its crazy course down the sidewalk, the driver gained at least a block of distance between himself and Raymond's team.

As the gap widened, the Ox yelled out an order, the substance of which we will never know. He (and his radio operator) claimed that he screamed out

"Stop him!" to get the Marines at the back end of our convoy to take action, but, in all the confusion—the madly honking horns, the screaming citizens, the helmets flopping back and forth across the Marines' heads, the fogged glasses—Raymond and the other three Marines heard "Shoot him!" from their superior officer.

So they knelt and began firing at the rear window of the vehicle, imploding it. The car continued driving, and as it passed the last two vehicles of our convoy, the Marines there opened fire as well. They hadn't heard the order, but as soon as Raymond's gunshots rang out, they had reasonably assumed that this taxi, like so many other taxis in recent days, had just performed a drive-by shooting on our convoy. Staff Sergeant put three well-aimed rounds through the driver's side window as the car hurtled past him on the sidewalk. Others hammered the door with their SAWs. Just after it passed our final Humvee, the taxi veered off the sidewalk, cut across two lanes of traffic, and slammed head-on into the concrete median divider, where it came to an immediate, jarring halt. The driver's side window was spiderwebbed and spattered with darkness.

Nearly four hundred meters away, at the front of the column, I saw none of this. Instead, I heard a few quick M-16 pops, then the swelling roar of fully automatic weapons fire. Immediately, I assumed that our stationary convoy had just been ambushed—Flowers and fourth platoon had been hit at this exact same spot yesterday by roughly ten men armed with rockets and small arms. I started running along the convoy toward the sound of the fire, and I mentally braced myself for the horrible double explosions of armed RPGs.

They never came. Instead, silence descended as all the horns shut off and most of the pedestrians disappeared from the sidewalk. Bewildered, I arrived at the crash site to find the salesman dangling upside down out of the open driver's side door. Docs Smith and Camacho were tugging at him, trying to pull him out of the vehicle to provide first aid. The man's . . . tongue hung out of the side of his mouth, clenched firmly between his teeth. Seeing him, my first thought was that the cabdriver looked just like the deer that we used to shoot back home. My next thought was, "What have we just done?"

At the time, I knew nothing of the Ox's order, and I had no idea why the platoon opened fire. All I knew was that an apparently unarmed Iraqi was hanging out of the door of his car, breathing shallowly with ropy streams of mucus, spittle, and blood dangling from his mouth and nose.

The docs wrestled the unconscious man out of the car and went to work, but he was bleeding pretty heavily from the midsection, and a dark pool quickly formed on the pavement beneath him. Meanwhile, I set the squad leaders, all of whom were as confused as I, to assembling a 360-degree cordon around the area. The pedestrians were returning, and they were eagerly gathering in large numbers around the macabre scene. As soon as the cordon was set, I moved back to the docs, and this time it was Smith who looked up at me and shook his head. I nodded back at him and instructed both docs to keep working nonetheless, to try to keep the man alive until an ambulance showed up. We weren't allowed to medevac Iraqis ourselves—scarce American medical resources had to be husbanded . . . for American use—but Iraqi emergency care vehicles, we had learned, usually showed up quickly at the scene of any shooting.

I was still confused about what had caused us to open fire, so I started walking the platoon's perimeter to find Raymond and his team. Halfway through the circuit, an agitated Ox approached me and said something . . . approximating the following:

"Hey, One, I never told them to open fire. Someone gave an order to start shooting, but it wasn't me. You've gotta believe me. I have no idea why they started shooting. . . . It was someone else. Someone else told them to open fire."

I stared at the Ox uncomprehendingly. I still didn't know of his impromptu foray out with Raymond, and I had no idea why the company XO would have been ordering my men to be doing anything, let alone opening fire, from the back of the Humvee where I assumed he had been. Why was the Ox so vehemently defending himself? Puzzled, I blinked at him and moved on. . . .

Just a little bit farther down, I found the Marine I was looking for and asked pointedly why he had started shooting. Taken aback, Raymond stared placidly at me for a second, then said simply, "Sir, Joker Five ordered us to."

"What? Why in the hell was Joker Five with you guys?"

"I don't know, sir. He just jumped out with us and started running. When the guy started getting away in that car, he told us to shoot him."

"Joker Five did?" I was incredulous. Now the Ox's bizarrely preemptive self-defense was starting to make some sense.

"Yes, sir."

I interviewed the other three Marines, and they all gave the same story. Joker Five told us to shoot, sir, so we did. You sure you heard right? Oh yes, sir, it was unmistakable. That's why we started shooting, sir. We wouldn't have otherwise, but he told us to.

Furious, I made a beeline back for the Ox, but my assault was checked in midstream by an outbreak of sharp, agonized wailing. The teenage relative had arrived on scene. Taking one look at the bloody mess that had been the fuel salesman, he started crying violently, and when I approached, the kid was trying to shoulder his way through the crowd and through our cordon. Seeing him, my anger at the Ox died, and in its place was born deep sadness at the whole messy situation. George managed to calm the kid enough to talk with him, and when they had finished up George informed me that the young man was the fuel salesman's son. We let him through our lines. Right at that time, the Iraqi ambulance finally arrived, and two stretcher bearers ran over to take our grisly cargo. Glad to quit the scene, I ordered the man transferred to them and the platoon to mount the Humvees. We headed back to the Outpost....

I took two sedatives that evening, but sleep still came only fitfully.

A subsequent investigation cleared both my platoon and the Ox of any willful wrongdoing. My men testified truthfully as to the order they thought they had heard, and the Ox and his radio operator testified truthfully as to the order they thought he had given. In the end, the investigators concluded that no one had failed due to negligence, laziness, or malice. The Devil Siphon incident was just another of the tragedies that inevitably occur during the fog and the chaos of war, tragedies that affect anonymous individuals on all sides of the conflict.

Their stories are usually crushed out by the larger narratives of nations, and history doesn't even record their names. Their children still cry, though.

The Lot of Children

Children are the most pitiable victims of war, though their lot is often overlooked by the mainstream media. The Iraq War degraded the situation of children in this country. According to a 2008 report by UNICEF, only 50 percent of primary-school-age children attend school. This same report noted that 60 percent of children did not have access to safe water. Tens of thousands of children have lost family members to violence. Many, given the loss of wage earners, must work. During the first year of the war, for example, UNICEF estimated that 15 percent of all children under the age of fourteen years old worked to support their families. Malnutrition threatens two million Iraqi children. Given these traumatic conditions, these children may very well be the "walking time bombs" of the future.

Many children became displaced refugees, and their lot is particularly horrific. In 2008, UNICEF estimated that the war displaced 1.2 million Iraqis. (This is a conservative estimate, for Deborah Ellis feels more comfortable with a number between 3 and 5 million.) UNICEF counts 600,000 children among these refugees. Some are internal refugees, moving to other parts of Iraq. Still others are exiled to foreign countries, where they often live as illegal aliens. In this way, it is difficult—if not impossible—for children to attend school.

Hibba is one Iraqi refugee. She recounted her story to Deborah Ellis, who traveled to Jordan to meet Iraqi children displaced by the war. At that time, 2008,

Hibba was sixteen years old. Her story provides insight into the fate of some Ba'thists, a party of which, as she readily admits, her father was a member. Hibba's story is recorded in Deborah Ellis's *Children of War: Voices of Iraqi Refugees* (Toronto: Groundwood Books, 2009), 20–24. As you read this account, you should identify why Hibba became a refugee. What class is she from? What sect? How does her story suggest how Ba'thists fared under the Coalition?

> My mother is Sunni. My father was Shia. This is the way it used to be, before we became divided. Sunni, Shia, no difference, no enemies.
>
> We left Iraq in July of 2003, just a few months after the invasion.
>
> Our father was working with the foreign ministry at the time, so he was part of the government of Saddam Hussein. At the time of all the bombing, he was stationed in Djbouti, at the Iraqi embassy there. We were living with just our mother. I have two older brothers, Saed and Akmed, who are now twenty and nineteen.
>
> The bombing was a terrible time. How would you feel? We were all crowded together in one room. If anything hit our house, we wanted to know where everyone was. We wanted to be able to get to each other. We huddled together and waited to die. Overhead we heard the aircraft, felt the ground shake, heard the world around us exploding.
>
> People watch war in the movies and they think they know what it's like. They don't know. If they knew, they wouldn't allow it to happen. Only very sick, bad people would want to make war.
>
> Paul Bremer came to Iraq and said, "We will make de-Ba'athification." So everyone who ran the country before the Americans came was fired. The Americans didn't understand that people didn't have a lot of choice about joining the Ba'ath Party. You joined if you wanted to get a job in your profession. A lot of good people joined, like my parents.
>
> We managed to stay a few more months in Baghdad until people started making death threats against us. We heard rumors at first, then a group of men in masks came to our house. They told us to get out or we would die.
>
> Even then, we didn't want to leave. Iraq is our home. Why should we leave our home? Then the men came again to our house, and yelled and shot guns at our feet—not to shoot our feet but to scare us, to give us one final message to get out.
>
> This time we left. We joined our father in Amman.
>
> I didn't like leaving Iraq, but at this time I was happy to be in Amman because my father was with us. He was away from us so much with his work that I didn't often get to see him, so to be able to spend so much time with him, even

though we were in exile, was wonderful. I was very close to my father. As the youngest of his children I was special in his heart.

In 2006, my father went alone back to Baghdad, leaving us behind in Jordan. Time had passed, and he thought it would be safe. We were running out of money where we were, and he went back to deal with some of our property so that we could pay our bills and keep on eating. He also needed medical treatment, which was too expensive in Jordan. He kept in touch with us by telephone as he moved from one relative's house to another. He thought it was safe, but he wasn't taking any chances.

My oldest brother went back to Baghdad to be with our father, to look out for him and help him.

For a while we heard nothing. Then the kidnappers called our relatives and said, "You will find him in the morgue."

My brother went to look, but our father wasn't inside the morgue. He was outside of it, lying on the ground on a rubbish heap on the street. He had a bullet in his head.

My brother tried to get back into Jordan, but he wasn't allowed. They said, "You have no legal residency here. You have no papers allowing you to enter." Even if he had papers, they probably still would have said no. Jordan doesn't like to let in young Iraqi men in case they turn out to be terrorists.

Now my brother is in Egypt. We can't go there to visit him because we will not be allowed back into Jordan. And he cannot come here and visit us, so we are separate, and my mother wears widow's black.

My other brother earns a bit of money for the family by jumping from job to job, helping people in the market, cleaning, hauling things, jobs like that. He never works at one place for very long because he's afraid the immigration police will catch him and deport him back to Iraq.

I'd like to be able to finish my schooling and do something about my life, but I don't know how it will be possible to do that the way we live now. The important thing is to try to get the family united again. That won't happen in Jordan....

We have applied for asylum to the United States. They have accepted us, at least to this stage, so now we have to just wait. It's possible that we may soon be living in America. My mother hopes that my brother can join us there. She says, "If my son is there and we are there and we are all together, that's all we need to be happy," but I don't know.

I don't know how I will feel about living in America, seeing the American flag every day. These are the people who destroyed my country, and they are over there across the ocean living a good life. They destroy things, then they forget about it and have a good supper and watch television. And I will be among them, and will have to get along with them for the good of my family. I don't know if I can do it.

I have nothing in common with American children. How could I? They are raised up with peace and fun and security. They have nothing to worry about. We are raised with war and fear. It's a big difference. They won't know how to talk to me, and I will have nothing to say to them. Except, maybe, that they should keep their soldiers at home.

Bibliography

Afong, Milo S. *Hogs in the Shadows: Combat Stories from Marine Snipers in Iraq.* New York: Penguin Group, 2007.

Anthony, Lawrence, and Graham Spence. *Babylon's Ark: The Incredible Wartime Rescue of the Baghdad Zoo.* New York: Thomas Dunne Books, 2007.

Baker, James A., Lee Hamilton, and Lawrence Eagleburger. *The Iraq Study Group Report.* New York: Vintage Books, 2006.

Bird, Christiane. *A Thousand Sighs, a Thousand Revolts: Journeys in Kurdistan.* New York: Ballantine Books, 2004.

Bond-Gunning, Heyrick. *Baghdad Business School: The Challenges of a War Zone Start-Up.* Singapore: Marshall Cavendish Editions, 2006.

Braithwaite, Al. *Off Screen: Four Young Artists in the Middle East; Al Braithwaite, Henry Hemming, Stephen Stapleton, Georgie Weedon.* London: Booth-Clibborn, 2004.

Campbell, Donovan. *Joker One: A Marine Platoon's Story of Courage, Leadership, and Brotherhood.* New York: Random House, 2009.

Conner, Seth A. *Boredom by Day, Death by Night: An Iraq War Journal.* Chicago: Tripping Light Press, 2007.

Crawford, John. *The Last True Story I'll Ever Tell: An Accidental Soldier's Account of the War in Iraq.* New York: Riverhead Books, 2005.

Ellis, Deborah. *Children of War: Voices of Iraqi Refugees.* Toronto: Groundwood Books, 2009.

Engel, Richard. *War Journal: My Five Years in Iraq.* New York: Simon and Schuster, 2008.

Etherington, Mark. *Revolt on the Tigris: The Al-Sadr Uprising and the Governing of Iraq.* Ithaca, N.Y.: Cornell University Press, 2005.

Fahmy, Mohamed Fadel. *Baghdad Bound: An Interpreter's Chronicles of the Iraq War.* Victoria, B.C.: Trafford, 2004.

Fasshi, Farnaz. *Waiting for an Ordinary Day: The Unraveling of Life in Iraq.* New York: Public Affairs, 2008.

Feiler, Bruce S. *Where God Was Born: A Journey by Land to the Roots of Religion.* New York: William Morrow, 2005.

Fisher, Scott. *Axis of Evil World Tour: An American's Travels in Iran, Iraq, and North Korea.* New York: IUniverse, 2006.

Haas, Richard N. *War of Necessity, War of Choice: A Memoir of Two Iraq Wars.* New York: Simon and Schuster, 2009.

Hamoudi, Haider Ala. *Howling in Mesopotamia: An Iraqi-American Memoir.* New York: Beaufort Books, 2008.

Hoyt, Mike, and John Palattella. *Reporting Iraq: An Oral History of the War by the Journalists Who Covered It.* New York: Melville House, 2007.

Jaber, Hala. *The Flying Carpet of Small Miracles: A Woman's Fight to Save Two Orphans.* New York: Riverhead Books, 2009.

Jadick, Richard, and Thomas Hayden. *On Call in Hell: A Doctor's Iraq War Story.* New York: NAL Caliber, 2007.

Janega, James. *The Pocket Idiot's Guide to Surviving Iraq.* New York: Alpha, 2006.

Khashan, Nesreen, and Jim Bowman. *Encounters with the Middle East: True Stories of People and Culture That Help You Understand the Region.* Palo Alto, Calif.: Solas House, 2007.

LeBleu, Joe. *Long Rifle: A Sniper's Story in Iraq and Afghanistan.* New York: Lyon's Press, 2009.

LeMoine, Ray, Jeff Neumann, and Donovan Webster. *Babylon by bus: Or, the true story of two friends who gave up their valuable franchise selling Yankees suck t-shirts at Fenway to find meaning and adventure in Iraq, where they became employed by the occupation in jobs for which they lacked qualification and witnessed much that amazed and disturbed them.* New York: Penguin, 2007.

Mansoor, Peter R. *Baghdad at Sunrise: A Brigade Commander's War in Iraq.* New Haven: Yale University Press, 2008.

Marozzi, Justin. *The Man Who Invented History: Travels with Herodotus.* London: John Murray, 2008.

Martinkus, John. *Travels in American Iraq.* Melbourne, Victoria, Australia: Black, 2004.

Mirra, Carl. *Soldiers and Citizens: An Oral History of Operation Iraqi Freedom from the Battlefield to the Pentagon.* New York: Palgrave Macmillan, 2008.

Naidoo, Beverley. "Iraq." In *Making It Home: Real-Life Stories from Children Forced to Flee,* 39–47. New York: Dial Books, 2005.

O'Donnell, Patrick K. *We Were One: Shoulder to Shoulder with the Marines Who Took Fallujah.* Cambridge, Mass.: Da Capo Press, 2006.

Prouse, Anna, and Elizabeth Griffin. *Two Birthdays in Baghdad: Finding the Heart of Iraq.* Washington, D.C.: Compass Press, 2005.

Riverbend. *Baghdad Burning: Girl Blog from Iraq.* New York: Feminist Press at the City University of New York, 2005.

Rosen, Nir. *In the Belly of the Green Bird: The Triumph of the Martyrs in Iraq.* New York: Free Press, 2006.

Shadid, Anthony. *Night Draws Near: Iraq's People in the Shadow of America's War.* New York: Henry Holt, 2005.

Sheeler, Jim. *Final Salute: A Story of Unfinished Lives.* New York: Penguin Group, 2008.

Stewart, Rory. *Occupational Hazards: My Time Governing in Iraq.* Rearsby, England: W. F. Howes, 2007.

———. *The Prince of the Marshes: And Other Occupational Hazards of a Year in Iraq.* Orlando, Fla.: Harcourt, 2006.

West, Francis J. *No True Glory: A Frontline Account of the Battle for Fallujah.* New York: Bantam Books, 2005.

Winter, Jeanette. *The Librarian of Basra: A True Story from Iraq.* Orlando, Fla.: Harcourt, 2005.

Wismer, Frank E. *War in the Garden of Eden: A Military Chaplain's Memoir from Baghdad.* New York: Seabury Books, 2008.

Woods, Trish. *What Was Asked of Us: An Oral History of the Iraq War by the Soldiers Who Fought It.* New York: Bay Back Books, 2007.

Zangana, Haifa. *City of Widows: An Iraqi Woman's Account of War and Resistance.* New York: Seven Stories Press, 2007.

Secondary Source Material

Abdullah, Thabit. *A Short History of Iraq: From 636 to the Present.* London: Longman, 2003.

Al-Ali, Nadje Sadig. *Iraqi Women: Untold Stories from 1948 to the Present.* New York: Zed Books, 2007.

Al-Ali, Nadje, and Nicola Pratt. *What Kind of Liberation: Women and the Occupation of Iraq.* Berkeley: University of California Press, 2010.

Bashkin, Orit. *The Other Iraq: Pluralism and Culture in Hashemite Iraq.* Palo Alto, Calif.: Stanford University Press, 2008.

Batatu, Hanna. *The Old Social Classes and the Revolutionary Movement in Iraq.* 1978. Reprint, London: Saqi Books, 2004.

Bengio, Ofra. *Saddam's Word: Political Discourse in Iraq.* London: Oxford University Press, 2002.

Bernhardsson, Magnus Thorkell. *Reclaiming a Plundered Past: Archaeology and Nation Building in Modern Iraq.* Austin: University of Texas Press, 2006.

Cleveland, William. *A History of the Modern Middle East,* 3rd ed. Boulder, Colo.: Westview Press, 2004.

Cole, Juan R. I. *The Ayatollahs and Democracy in Iraq.* Amsterdam: Amsterdam University Press, 2007.

Davis, Eric. *Memories of State: Politics, History, and Collective Identity in Modern Iraq.* Berkeley: University of California Press, 2005.

Dawisha, Adeed. *Iraq: A Political History from Independence to Occupation.* Oxford: Princeton University Press, 2009.

Dodge, Toby. *Inventing Iraq: The Failure of Nation-Building and a History Denied.* New York: Columbia University Press, 2003.

Farouk-Sluglett, Marion, and Peter Sluglett. *Iraq since 1958: From Revolution to Dictatorship.* London: I. B. Tauris, 1987.

Fattah, Hala. *A Brief History of Iraq.* New York: Checkmark Books, 2008.

Ghareeb, Edmund. *Historical Dictionary of Iraq.* Lanham, Md.: Scarecrow Press, 2004.

Lutz, Catherine, and Jane L. Collins. *Reading National Geographic.* Chicago: University of Chicago Press, 1993.

Marr, Phebe. *The Modern History of Iraq.* Boulder, Colo.: Westview Press, 2003.

McDowall, David. *A Modern History of the Kurds.* London: I. B. Tauris, 1996.

Mufti, Malik. *Sovereign Creations: Pan-Arabism and Political Order in Syria and Iraq.* Ithaca, N.Y.: Cornell University Press, 1996.

Nakash, Yitzhak. *Shi'is of Iraq.* Princeton, N.J.: Princeton University Press, 1994.

Polk, William Roe. *Understanding Iraq: The Whole Sweep of Iraqi History, from Genghis*

Khan's Mongols to the Ottoman Turks to the British Mandate to the American Occupation. New York: Harper Perennial, 2006.

Shiblak, Abbas. *Iraqi Jews: A History of the Mass Exodus*. London: Saqi Books, 2005.

Shields, Sarah D. *Mosul Before Iraq: Like Bees Making Five-Sided Cells*. New York: State University of New York Press, 2000.

Steet, Linda. *Veils and Daggers: A Century of National Geographic's Representation of the Arab World*. Philadelphia: Temple University, 2000.

Tripp, Charles. *A History of Iraq*. New York: Cambridge University Press, 2002.

Wien, Peter. *Iraqi Arab Nationalism: Authoritarian, Totalitarian and Pro-Fascist Inclinations, 1932–1941*. London: Routledge, 2006.

Yildiz, Kerim. *The Kurds in Iraq: The Past, Present, and Future*. London: Pluto, Kurdish Human Rights Project, 2004.

Acknowledgments

Many people and organizations contributed to this anthology, and I would like to thank them all. I was lucky enough to have two undergraduate and graduate research assistants, who made the process of collecting and editing these documents much easier. For this reason, I will begin my acknowledgment with thanks to Emily Louise Dawes and Beau Gaitors. They exhibited laudable patience with all my detailed—and usually last-minute—requests.

I would also like to thank the people who read all or part of this manuscript. The introduction, in particular, was a bear to write, and it is better for the input of my colleague Will Gray as well as the very gifted graduate students Sanket Desai and Brandon Ward. I would also like to thank Eric Davis for offering comments on an earlier draft of this manuscript. My deepest gratitude goes to the anonymous reviewer no. 3, who took the time to read and to comment on two complete drafts of this anthology.

This book benefited from the assistance of Purdue University. A Purdue Alumni Association grant allowed me to hire research assistants. And the Center for Undergraduate Instructional Excellence awarded me a semester leave in order to complete the manuscript. I thank this university for its support of my project.

Finally, I would like to thank friends who listened to me think through aspects of this manuscript over the course of two years. Randy Roberts listened to my worries and offered terrific advice on choosing the documents for this anthology. Dawn Marsh provided a well-needed intellectual sounding board, especially in the final stages of this manuscript's editing. And Mark Bernstein listened to all my concerns throughout writing and editing this book. I hope that this book reflects the valuable advice and support of these wonderful people and organizations.

* * *

Sati' al-Husri excerpt translated from the Arabic by Sylvia G. Haim and included in her *Arab Nationalism: An Anthology* (Berkeley: University of California Press, 1962), 147–53. Reprinted by permission of Sylvia Kedourie (née Haim).

Baghdad Burning: Girl Blog from Iraq, by Riverbend (New York: Feminist Press at the City University of New York, 2005). Reprinted by permission of the publisher.

From *Baghdad Diaries,* by Nuha al-Radi. Copyright © 1998, 2003 by Nuha al-Radi. Used by permission of Vintage Books, a division of Random House.

"Baghdad My Beloved," by Salah Al-Hamdani, and translated by C. Dickson. Published in *Literature from the "Axis of Evil": Writing from Iran, Iraq, North Korea, and Other Enemy Nations,* edited by Words without Borders. Copyright © 2006 by Words without Borders. Reprinted by permission of Words without Borders (http://www.wordswithoutborders.com).

British Documents on Foreign Affairs: Reports and Papers from the Foreign Office Confidential Print (Series B: Turkey, Iran, and the Middle East, 1918–1939), edited by Robin Bidwell (Ann Arbor, Mich.: University Publications of America, 1985), 12: 16–20. Used by permission of ProQuest LLC.

Extract from *Children of War,* by Deborah Ellis. Copyright © 2009 by Deborah Ellis. Reprinted by permission of Groundwood Books Limited (http://www.groundwoodbooks.com).

Contemporary Iraqi Fiction: An Anthology, by Shakir Mustafa (Syracuse, N.Y.: Syracuse University Press, 2008), 185–90. Reprinted by permission of the publisher.

"Dying at the Edge of Death," by Ghassan Kanafani, and translated by Diana Der-Hovanessian and by Lena Jayyusi (first translator) in *Modern Arabic Poetry: An Anthology,* edited by Salma Khadra Jayyusi, 398–99 (New York: Columbia University Press, 1987). Copyright © 1987 by Columbia University Press. Reprinted by permission of the publisher.

From *The First Evidence: A Memoir of Life in Iraq under Saddam Hussein.* Copyright © 2003 by Juman Kubba by permission of McFarland and Co., Box 611, Jefferson, N.C. 28640 (http://www.mcfarlandpub.com).

From *The Forever War,* by Dexter Filkins. Copyright © 2008 by Dexter Filkins. Used by permission of Alfred A. Knopf, a division of Random House, Inc.

From *Guests of the Sheikh,* by Elizabeth Warnock Fernea. Copyright © 1965 by Elizabeth Warnock Fernea. Used by permission of Doubleday, a division of Random House, Inc.

Hell Is Over: Voices of the Kurds after Saddam, by Mike Tucker (Guilford, Conn.: Lyons Press, 2004), 108–10. Copyright © 2004 by Lyons Press. Reprinted by permission of the publisher.

From *House to House: A Soldier's Memoir,* by Staff Sergeant David Bellavia with John R. Bruning. Copyright © 2007 by David Bellavia. Reprinted by permission of Free Press, a division of Simon and Schuster, Inc. All rights reserved.

Howling in Mesopotamia: An Iraqi-American Memoir, by Haider Ala Hamoudi (New York: Beaufort Books, 2008), 125–30. Reprinted by permission of the publisher and author.

Instructions for American Servicemen in Iraq during World War II, by the United States Army (Chicago: University of Chicago Press, 2007), 1, 3–5, 11–14, and 16–17. Reprinted by permission of the publisher.

From *Iraqi Jews: A History of Mass Exodus*, by Abbas Shiblak (London: Saqi Books, 2005), 171–72. Reprinted by permission of Saqi Books.

"The Iraq-Iran Front: Bodies," from *Baghdad without a Map*, by Tony Horwitz (New York: Penguin, 1991). Copyright © 1991 by Tony Horwitz. Used by permission of Dutton, a division of Penguin Group (USA).

Iraqi Women: Untold Stories from 1948 to the Present, by Nadja Sadig Al-Ali (London: Zed Books, 2007), 95–101. Reprinted by permission of the publisher.

Iraq's Last Jews: Stories of Daily Life, Upheaval, and Escape from Modern Babylon, edited by Tamar Morad, Dennis Shasha, and Robert Shasha (Hampshire, U.K.: Palgrave Macmillan, 2008), 130–38. Reprinted by permission of the publisher.

Iraq's Last Jews: Stories of Daily Life, Upheaval, and Escape from Modern Babylon, edited by Tamar Morad, Dennis Shasha, and Robert Shasha (New York: Palgrave Macmillan, 2008), 66–69. Reprinted by permission of the publisher.

Iraq under General Nuri: My Recollections of Nuri Al-Said, 1954–1958, by Waldemar J. Gallman, 200–218. Copyright © 1964 by Johns Hopkins Press. Reprinted by permission of Johns Hopkins University Press.

"Iraq—Where Oil and Water Mix," by Jean Shor and Franc Shor, in *National Geographic Magazine* (October 1958): 443, 449, and 473. Reprinted by permission of National Geographic Society.

Jews and Muslims: Images of Sephardi and Eastern Jewries in Modern Times, edited by Aron Rodrigue (Seattle: University of Washington Press, 2003), 277–78. Reprinted from the 2003 edition by permission of the publisher.

From *Joker One: A Marine Platoon's Story of Courage, Leadership, and Brotherhood*, by Donovan Campbell. Copyright © 2009, 2010 by Donovan Campbell. Used by permission of Random House, Inc.

Journey among Brave Men, by Dana Adams Schmidt (Boston: Little, Brown, 1964), 172–75 and 221–24. Reprinted by permission of Dana Schmidt, Jr.

Excerpt from "The Killer Elite," by Evan Wright from *Rolling Stone*, issue date June 26, 2003. Copyright © 2003 by Rolling Stone. All rights reserved. Excerpt reprinted by permission.

Kurds, Arabs and Britons: The Memoir of Wallace Lyon in Iraq, 1918–1944, edited by D. K. Fieldhouse (London: I. B. Tauris, 2002), 92–96. Reprinted by permission of I. B. Tauris Publishers.

From *The Last Jews in Baghdad*, by Nissim Rejwan. Copyright © 2004. By permission of the University of Texas Press.

From *Leap of Faith: Memories of an Unexpected Life,* by Queen Noor. Copyright © 2003 Her Majesty Queen Noor. Reprinted by permission of Miramax Books. All rights reserved.

"Life and Death in Iraq," by Hadani Ditmars, in *Ms.* (June/July 2001): 47–57. Reprinted by permission of *Ms.*, copyright © 2001.

Letter by Gertrude Bell dated 28 April 1909. Robinson Library Special Collections, Newcastle University, United Kingdom. This material is used by permission of the librarian, Robinson Library, Newcastle University.

Letter by Saddam Hussein, translated by Brian Whittaker, the *Guardian*, 30 April 2003 (http://www.guardian.co.uk/world/2003/apr/30/iraq.brian whitaker). Reprinted by permission of Guardian News and Media Ltd.

Letter to the editor, by Brent Scowcroft, *Wall Street Journal*, 15 August 2002. Reprinted from the *Wall Street Journal*, copyright © 2002 by Dow Jones and Co. All rights reserved.

"Lullaby for the Hungry," by Muhammad Mahdi al-Jawarhiri, translated by Mr. John Heath-Stubbs and Issa Boullata in *Modern Arabic Poetry: An Anthology*, edited by Salma Khadra Jayyusi (New York: Columbia University Press, 1987), 80–81. Copyright © 1987 by Columbia University Press. Reprinted by permission of the publisher.

Memories of Eden: A Journey through Jewish Baghdad, by Violette Shamash (London: Forum Books, 2008), 21, 24, and 61–63. Reprinted by permission of Tony Rocca and Mira Rocca and Northwestern University Press (http://www.memoriesofeden.com).

Mustafa Barzani and the Kurdish Liberation Movement, by Massoud Barzani (New York: Palgrave Macmillan, 2003), 340–43. Reprinted by permission of the publisher.

From *My Father's Paradise,* by Ariel Sabar. Copyright © 2008 by Ariel Sabar. Reprinted by permission of Algonquin Books of Chapel Hill. All rights reserved.

Excerpt from *My Year in Iraq: The Struggle to Build a Future of Hope,* by Ambassador Lt. Paul Bremer III with Malcolm McConnell. Copyright © 2006 by Lt. Paul Bremer III. All rights reserved. Reprinted by permission of Simon and Schuster, Inc.

Out of Iraq: Escape from Saddam and Al-Qaeda, by Mahmoud Albayati (Baltimore, Md.: PublishAmerica, 2006). Reprinted by permission of the publisher.

Excerpt from *Princesses' Street: Baghdad Memories,* by Jabra Ibrahim Jabra, and translated by Issa J. Boullata. Copyright © 2005 by University of Arkansas Press. Reprinted by permission of the publisher (http://www.uapress.com).

Princeton Readings in Islamist Thought: Texts and Contexts from al-Banna to Bin Laden, edited by Roxanne L. Euben and Muhammad Qasim Zaman (Princeton, N.J.: Princeton University Press, 2009). Reprinted by permission of Princeton University Press.

Excerpt from *Salam Pax: The Clandestine Diary of an Ordinary Iraqi.* Copyright © 2003 by Salam Pax. Used by permission of Grove/Atlantic, Inc.

"Sanctions Have an Impact on All of Us," by Denis Halliday, 6 October 1998 (http://www.merip.org/mer/mer209/hallid.htm). Reprinted by permission of MERIP.

Socialist Iraq: A Study in Iraq Politics since 1968, by Majid Khadduri (Washington, D.C.: Middle East Institute, 1978). Reprinted by permission of Middle East Institute.

Soldiers and Citizens: An Oral History of Operation Iraqi Freedom from the Battlefield to the Pentagon, by Carl Mirra (New York: Palgrave Macmillan, 2008), 176–80. Reprinted by permission of the publisher.

A Soldier's Story: From Ottoman Rule to Independent Iraq: The Memoirs of Jafar Pasha Al-Askari (1885–1963), translated by Mustafa Tariq Al-Askari and edited by William Facey and Najdat Fathi Safwat (London: Arabian Publishing, 2003), 19–22 and 27–28. Reprinted by permission of Omar Z. Al-Askari.

The Tragedy of the Assyrians, by R. S. Stafford (Piscataway, N.J.: Gorgias Press, 2006), 167–62. Reprinted by permission of Gorgias Press.

La vie de l'ayatollah Mahdî al-Khâlisî par son fils, translated by Pierre-Jean Luizard (Paris: Editions de la Martinière, 2005), 261–66. Used by permission of Pierre-Jean Luizard (http://halshs.archives-ouvertes.fr/halshs-00408063).

Winston S. Churchill: His Complete Speeches, edited by Robert Rhodes James (New York: Chelsea House Publishers, 1974), 3: 3095–96 and 3: 3098–102. Reprinted by permission of the publisher.

From *A World Transformed,* by George H. W. Bush and Brent Scowcroft. Copyright © 1998 by George H. W. Bush and Brent Scowcroft. Used by permission of Alfred A. Knopf, a division of Random House.

A Year in Baghdad, by Albert V. Baez and Joan C. Baez, Sr. (Santa Barbara, Calif.: John Daniel, 1988), 31–32, 71–72, and 181–83. Used by permission of Joan C. Baez, Sr.

Index

Aani, Sheikh Omar, 350, 352
Abad (Sayid), 156
Abadan (Basra province), oil refineries of, 39
al-Abadi, Ali, 323
abaya (garment), 183–85
Abbas, Abu (Ashura celebrant), 355–56, 357
Abbas, Abu (PLF leader), 308
Abbasite dynasty, 97; Iraq during, 34
Abd al-Ilah (regent), 89, 125
Abdul Aziz-al-Saud (king of Saudi Arabia), 101
Abdul Hamid II, Sultan: deposition of, 18, 29–30, 34; patronage networks of, 30; Young Turks and, 24, 53
Abdul Karim (Sayid), 156
Abdulla, Hussein Ahmad, 180
Abdullah, Emir, 73
Abdullah, Ibtisam: Iran-Iraq War fiction of, 254–58
Abu, Sha'alan, 63
Abu Timman, Ja'far, 56, 60
Achille Lauro (ship), seizure of, 308
Adib, Albert, 139
al-Adib (monthly magazine), 139
Afghanistan, U.S. military in, 332
Aflaq, Michel, 10, 11, 193
Ahali group, reformers in, 107
al-'ahd (sacred society), 26
Ahlam (beautician), 291–93
Ajami, Mohammed, 350
Alamin (Ba'thist police), 223, 224, 225, 227
Albayati, Mahmoud: on Ba'thist Party, 245; *Out of Iraq*, 244–48
Albu Alwan (village), 348, 350; Khalaf's symbolism for, 351–52
Album Hessian (village), in Revolt of 1920, 65
alcohol consumption, Muslim: British on, 41, 78
Algiers Agreement (1975), 232, 234, 258
Ali (Sayid), 157

al-Ali, Nadje Sadig, 209; *Iraqi Women*, 182–87
Allah, Mal, 177
Allawai, Ayad, 357
Allenby, Edmund, 73
Alliance Israelite (school), 1, 114; anti-Semitism concerning, 115; civilizing mission of, 19–21
al Qaeda: and Ashura celebrations, 354; Bush's invocation of, 332, 333; Hussein and, 308
Amini, Ali, 189
Amiriyah, Coalition bombing of, 266
al Anfal (anti-Kurdish campaign), 12, 230, 258–61; chemical warfare during, 259; Iraqi military during, 259; survivors' accounts of, 259–61
Anglo-French Declaration (1918), 58
Anglo-Iraqi Joint Defence Board, 136
Anglo-Iraqi Thirty Days War (1941), 8, 125, 127, 323
Anglo-Iraqi Treaty (1922), 54
Anglo-Iraqi Treaty (1930), 89, 133
anti-Semitism, Iraqi: in Baghdad, 7, 8–9, 90, 113–15, 126–30; causes of, 114–15
anti-Semitism, pan-Arabism and, 114
Arab Congress (proposed), 99–102; agenda for, 101; British attitude toward, 101–2
Arabic language: official status of, 91, 92; suppression of, 36
Arab-Israeli War (1948), 147
Arab Revolt, 78, 114; al-Askari in, 26; al-Husri in, 93; Lawrence of Arabia in, 66; Sunnis in, 81
Arabs: British promises to, 69–71; Syrian, 101
Arabs, Iraqi: British policy on, 72–73; British reprisals against, 67, 68; concept of honor, 61; effect of British mandate on, 66; under Ottoman Constitution, 38. *See also* Shi'is, Iraqi; Sunnis, Iraqi
Arabs, Palestinian, 114; displacement of, 147

Arafat, Yasser, 284, 357; and Persian Gulf War, 278
Arif, Abd al-Rahman, 160; Ba'thist overthrow of, 193; patronage networks of, 193
Arif, Abd al-Salam, 163, 171; death of, 160; overthrow of Ba'thists, 11
Arif, Rafiq, 162
artists, Iraqi, 138–39
Ashaar (Ottoman Mesopotamia), European occupation of, 40
Ashura (Shi'i celebration), 90, 115–21; al Qaeda and, 354; at Baghdad, 355–56; Ba'thist targeting of, 223, 225–27, 353–54; bombings during, 15, 356; British accounts of, 116–21; during Coalition occupation, 353–57; flagellation during, 116, 118–20, 355; food celebrating, 354, 355; at Karbala, 225–27, 354, 356; U.S. protection for, 356
al-Askari, Jafar, 18; assassination of, 26, 107; and Bakr Sidqi coup, 111; career of, 25–26; on Ottoman corruption, 25–29; support for Faysal, 78
Assyrian Affair (1933), 89, 102–7; Kurdish looting during, 103, 104; tribal role in, 103, 106
Assyrian Empire, 174
Assyrians, Iraqi: under British mandate, 102; conflict with Kurds, 103, 104; self-determination for, 7, 8, 89–90, 102
al-Attar, Leila, 289–90
Autonomy Law (1974), 216
Azayrij tribe, 82
Aziz, Tariq, 270, 277
al-Aziz, Siddique Abd: on al-Shawwaf Conspiracy, 176–81

Babylon, 174
Baez, Albert V. and Joan: *A Year in Baghdad*, 140–43
Baez, Joan (daughter), 140, 141
Baghdad: Abu Sifain neighborhood, 128; Al-A'dhamiyya neighborhood, 128; anti-Semitism in, 7, 8–9, 90, 113–15, 126–30; attitudes toward women in, 182; during Bakr Sidqi coup, 108–9, 110, 112; during British mandate, 60, 73; class distinctions in, 182–83; Clinton missile attack on, 290; Coalition bombing of, 273–78, 279, 290; College of Arts, 138; el-Karrada al-Sharqiyya neighborhood, 128; Farhud in, 125, 126–30, 144; al-Gaylani mosque, 294–95; governmental corruption in, 169–70; intellectual life in, 137–40; Iranian air attacks on, 245; during Iran-Iraq War, 245, 246, 249, 257; land speculation around, 169–70; Mansour district, 292; al-Mokhsin Mosque, 321; Naqib of, 77–78; during Persian Gulf War, 273–78; poverty in, 140–43, 171; power outages in, 274–76; Proclamation of (1917), 18, 45–47; Ras el-Tchol neighborhood, 128; Saddam City, 321; Saddam Hussein Pediatric Hospital, 293; Scud missile attacks on, 246; Shi'i pilgrims to, 117; street vendors of, 142; Al-Wazira district, 140–41. *See also* National Museum (Baghdad)
Baghdad (Coalition-occupied), 301, 312, 320–27; Ashura celebration at, 355–56; Green Zone, 326; in Iraqi poetry, 312–15; looting in, 14, 320–21, 323–27; Sadr City, 359; sectarianism in, 326, 327–28, 368, 369
Baghdad (Ottoman Mesopotamia): British occupation of, 45–47, 49–50; cosmopolitanism of, 18–19; Jewish community of, 1, 3–4, 19–21, 45–50, 113–15, 126–30; Kutchet el-Nasaara district, 50; liberalism of, 18; reform movements in, 33–38; suburbs of, 47; trade with Great Britain, 46; during World War I, 45–50
Baghdad Pact, Iraqi withdrawal from, 173
Baghdad Petition (1910), 33–38, 167; on Arabic language, 36; Ottoman loyalty in, 38; street-widening project in, 36–37
Baghdad province (Ottoman Mesopotamia), 2, 17; British occupation of, 53
al-Bakr, Ahmad Hasan, 193, 196
Bakr Sidqi coup (1936), 8, 90, 107–13, 121; al-Askari and, 111; Baghdad during, 108–9, 110, 112; British attitudes toward, 108–13; manifesto of, 113; targets of, 107
Balfour Declaration, 114

Barzani, Massoud: IGC membership, 341; *Mustafa Barzani and the Kurdish Liberation Movement*, 176

Barzani, Mustafa, 7, 161, 206; anti-British attitude of, 189; assassination attempt against, 216; on Autonomy Law of 1974, 216; in Kurdish Revolt, 187–91; leadership of KDP, 176; return to Iraq, 10, 187; revolt of 1974, 11; view of Americans, 190

al-Barzani, Idris, 206

Basra: under British mandate, 59; Coalition bombing of, 296, 297–98; following Persian Gulf War, 296–98; in Iran-Iraq War, 230, 249

Basra (Ottoman Mesopotamia): Anglo-Indians in, 41; British occupation of, 53; living standards in, 39–40; roads of, 40; Westerners' conduct in, 40–42

Basra province (Ottoman Mesopotamia), 2, 17; British military rule in, 39–42; during World War I, 39

Basra Times, 41

Ba'thist Constitution, Iraqi (1970), 11, 195–98; rights and duties under, 197–98; state and society in, 196

Ba'thist Party: authoritarianism of, 160; creation of, 193; pan-Arabism of, 10, 11, 193, 207; populism of, 193; Syrian, 195; Women's Organization of, 209, 210

Ba'thist Party, Iraqi: censorship by, 224–25; coup of 1963, 10–11, 160; coup of 1968, 193, 194–95; executions, 224; executions of Jews, 198, 204; foreign policy of, 212; foreign wars of, 12–13; influence in education, 212–14; Jewish exodus under, 198–206; modernization under, 185; overthrow of Arif, 193; patriarchal ideologies of, 185; patronage networks of, 11; popular appeal of, 193; prisoners of, 198, 199–203; Revolutionary Command Council (RCC), 196; Shi'i protests against, 223–27; Shi'is under, 11–12, 220–27; soldiers' view of, 245; stance toward Israel, 206–8; Sunnis in, 194; targeting of Ashura celebration, 223, 225–27, 353–54; totalitarianism of, 212–14; tribal ideologies of, 185; use of torture, 199, 201; U.S. support for, 239–44; violence under, 11, 194, 199, 201; women's dress under, 185; women under, 20–12; youth under, 212. *See also* Hussein, Saddam; Republic of Iraq, Ba'thist

Bazirqan, Ali, 60

Baz tribe, 104

Begin, Menachem, 233

Bell, Gertrude, 54; account of Abdul Hamid, 29–30; establishment of National Museum, 323; on Iraqi nationalism, 55, 62; on San Remo Agreement, 55–61; support for Faysal, 76, 78

Bellavia, David, 359; *House to House*, 360–62

Belshazzar, fall of, 174

Bengio, Ofra, 231

Bidawi, Nawar, 349

Bidwell, Robin: *British Documents on Foreign Affairs*, 108

binbashis (Ottoman offiers), 31, 32

black market, Iraqi: fuel in, 363–67

Blix, Hans, 301

bombing, aerial: during Kurdish Revolt, 190–91; during al-Shawwaf mutiny, 179

bombing, Coalition, 272, 301; of Amiriyah, 266; of Baghdad, 273–78, 279, 290; of Basra, 296, 297–98; of Jordan, 280; during Persian Gulf War, 266

bombing attacks: during Ashura, 15, 356; on Baghdadi Jews, 148; on Kurds, 188; by suicide bombers, 356; at Waziriyah, 232–33

Bragg, H. V., 64

Brazilian Café (Baghdad), 139–40

Bremer, Paul, 15, 323, 327; de-Ba'athification under, 336, 368; formation of IGC, 337, 339–43; leadership of CPA, 336; *My Year in Iraq*, 339–43; and Resolution 137, 343

British mandate: Churchill on, 70; cost of, 71–72; effect on Great Britain, 66; Iraqi provinces under, 75–76; in Middle East, 53–54, 69–74

British mandate (Iraq), 5, 6–7, 15; Assyrians under, 102; Baghdad under, 60, 73; British Political Officers of, 75, 76; Civil Administration of, 57–59, 60, 67–68; constitutional monarchy under, 54; cost of, 72; end of, 89; freedom of the press under, 58; General Assembly under, 58, 59, 72; indirect rule under, 54, 154; Iraqi nationalism during, 55–61; Kurds under, 62, 74–78; Lawrence of Arabia on, 54, 66–68; and League of Nations, 58; provisional government under, 57, 72, 80; provisions of, 58, 59; purpose of, 68; religious minorities during, 57; resistance in Rumaithah, 63–66; Revolt of 1920 against, 61, 62–66; sheikhs under, 60–61, 62; Shi'is under, 62, 81–86, 353; state formation under, 73; Sunnis under, 81, 116; tribes under, 56–57, 73, 75; troop commitments in, 67–68, 70, 71; Turkish Chamber of Deputies and, 59–60. *See also* San Remo Agreement

brotherhood, Muslim: and Muslim unity, 96, 97

Burdett, A. L. P.: *Arab Dissident Movements*, 99

Bush, George H. W., 13, 279; coalition against Iraq, 266; *A World Transformed*, 282–84. *See also* Persian Gulf War, second

Bush, George W.: on al Qaeda, 332, 333; arguments for Iraq invasion, 306–12; "Axis of Evil" speech, 300; invocation of September 11th, 300, 306, 308, 309, 312, 332; invocation of World War II, 331; "Mission Accomplished" speech, 14–15, 301, 302, 330–34; regime change under, 303, 311–12; use of history, 330; war on terror of, 300, 301, 332–33; on weapons of mass destruction, 306, 307–10, 330

Bush Doctrine, 300–301

Cairo, British Arab Bureau in, 76, 77

Cairo Conference (1921), 5, 69–74; attendees at, 69; Kurdish question at, 74

Campaign for Innocent Victims in Conflict (CIVIC), 338

Campbell, Donovan: *Joker One*, 362–67

Caractacus (pseudonym), *Revolution in Iraq*, 167–72

chadors (clothing), 295, 354

Chalabi, Ahmed, 287, 301

Chemchemal (Mesopotamia), Hamavand raid on, 31

chemical warfare: Bush on, 307; during Iran-Iraq War, 259, 262

Cheyney, Richard, 284

children, Iraqi: during Coalition occupation, 360–62, 367–70; effect of U.N. sanctions on, 285–86, 290, 293–94, 297; fatalities among, 360–62; malnutrition among, 14, 267, 281, 285, 290, 294, 295, 298, 367; poverty among, 141, 142; UNICEF on, 367

Christian Church, political unity under, 96

Christian sects, Iraqi, 90; Assyrian, 7, 8; in Coalition-occupied Baghdad, 326, 327; Yazidis, 2, 3

Churchill, Winston: at Cairo Conference, 5, 69–74; and Faysal I, 73, 79

civilians, Iraqi: during Battle of Nasiriyah, 316–17, 318, 319; casualties of Muqdadiyah, 359–62; during Coalition occupation, 337–39, 358–59; fatalities among, 337, 360–62, 365–67

clerics, Shi'i: exile of, 6; influence of, 3, 11–12, 61, 342

Cleveland, William L., 13, 266

Clinton administration, missile attack on Baghdad, 290

Coalition Provisional Authority (CPA), 14, 323, 336; Ba'thists during, 368; civilians under, 337; disbanding of, 336; Iraqi identity under, 339; and Kurdish autonomy, 341; women under, 343–44. *See also* occupation of Iraq, U.S./Coalition (2003–2004)

coffeehouses, Iraqi: intellectual life in, 137, 139–40

Cold War, in Middle East, 161, 194

Communist Party, Iraqi, 143–47; IGC representation, 343; Jews in, 146; minority coalition in, 143, 145–46; role in social change, 183; Shi'is in, 143, 147, 221

Contreras, Pedro, 361

Cornwallis, Kinahan, 77, 78
coup d'états, Iraqi: Bakr Sidqi's (1936), 8, 90, 107–13, 121; Ba'thist (1963), 10–11, 160; Ba'thist (1968), 193, 194–95; al-Kaylani's (1941), 8, 125, 127, 128; Qasim's (1958), 10, 160–66, 220
Cox, Sir Percy, 58; and arrest of Talib Pasha, 76–77; and Faysal's coronation, 78; on Kurdish autonomy, 74
cultural production, pan-Arab, 206–8
culture, Iraqi: antiquities of, 323; marriage in, 187; U.S. soldiers and, 130–33. *See also* gender segregation
Cursetjee, C. M.: *The Land of the Date*, 39–42

Daghistani, Ghazi, 162
Dahuk prison, Kurdish prisoners at, 260, 261
Dallal, Sasson, 146
Dallall, Oddil, 206
Dallall, Yitzhak, 200
Daly, Major C., 63
Damanloudgi, Colonel, 164, 165
Dannoos, Eli, 203–8
Daud, Shaikh Ahmad, 60
Davis, Eric, 137, 139–40; on Ba'thist Party, 206–7, 212; on Iraqi women, 209
Dawa Party, 220–21, 339; outlawing of, 229
Denaturalization law. *See* Law No. 1 (1950)
Desert Shield (defensive operation), 13, 266; Arab supporters of, 278
Desert Storm (1991), 13; Arab supporters of, 278. *See also* Persian Gulf War, second
Dhawalim tribe, in Revolt of 1920, 63
Ditmars, Hadani, 267; *Dancing in the No-Fly Zone*, 288–98
al-Douri, Abd al-Aziz, 138
al-Duroubi, Hafiz, 138
Dyer, Reginald Edward Harry, 68

economy, Islamic: basic elements of, 222; al-Sadr on, 221–23; social justice in, 221–23
education, Iraqi, 92, 93, 94; Ba'thist influence in, 212–14; of postwar era, 138–39; women's, 210, 344, 345

Egan, Eleanor: *The War in the Cradle of the World*, 42–45
Eisenhower doctrine, 161
Ellis, Deborah, 367; *Children of War*, 368–70
El Nahra (Shi'i village): gender segregation in, 154; Sayids of, 154–58
Esam, Abu, 224

Fadhila (Sayid), 156–57
Fallujah, insurgency in, 351, 357–59
Faous, Hydir, 297–98
Faous, Iqbal, 297–98
Faous, Mustafa, 297–98
Farhud (Baghdad, 1941), 125, 126–30, 144; Baghdad police during, 128; blame for, 127; looting during, 129–30; military during, 144
Farouk-Sluglett, Marion, 235
Fattah, Halah, 121, 330; on Ba'thist ideology, 193
Faysal bin al-Hussein I (king of Iraq), 5; Churchill and, 73, 79; Constituent Assembly under, 81, 82, 83; constitutional monarchy of, 54, 73, 74, 81; coronation of, 77–78; coronation speech of, 54, 78–81; death of, 89; "Declaration... on the Occasion of the Termination of the Mandatory Regime," 91–93; election of, 74–78, 81–86; nationalism of, 80–81; pan-Arabism of, 6–7, 90, 99–102; policy on minorities, 90–93; and proposed Arab Congress, 99; Shi'i opposition to, 81–86; supporters of, 76, 77, 78. *See also* Hashemite monarchy
Faysal II (king of Iraq), 153
fedayeen (fighters), 316
Fernea, Elizabeth Warnock: *Guests of the Sheik*, 154–58
Filkins, Dexter: *The Forever War*, 357–59
Foster, John W., 195
France: influence in Syria, 99, 100, 101; in San Remo Agreement, 53
fundamentalism, Islamic: rise in Iraq, 343; women's dress under, 344–45

Gallman, Waldemar J.: *General Nuri*, 161–66; meetings with Qasim, 164, 165

Gardiner, C. C., 64
Garrels, Anne, 301; *Naked in Baghdad*, 320–23
gender segregation: in El Nahra, 154; Hussein on, 211; liberalization of, 186–87
General Federation of Iraqi Women, 209, 210
Geneva Convention (Third, 1949), 262
Georges-Picot, François, 22
Ghazi (king of Iraq), 89; during Bakr Sidqi coup, 109–10, 111, 112, 113
Glaspie, April, 12; meeting with Hussein, 265, 267–70
Golden Square (military junta), 8
Great Britain: aid to Ottoman Empire, 98; and Bakr Sidqi coup, 108–13; "civilizing mission" of, 22; in Coalition occupation of Iraq, 362; direct rule of Iraq, 5, 8, 9, 53, 69; Iraq's relationship with, 79, 81, 89, 116; Middle East policy of, 69–74; Ministry of Defense, 296; occupation of Baghdad (first), 45–47, 49–50; occupation of Baghdad (second), 125; in Ottoman Mesopotamia, 4, 17, 18, 39–47; postcolonial politics of, 99; in postwar Iraq, 133–37; presence in Basra, 39–42; presence in Mosul, 39; and proposed Arab Congress, 101–2; trade with Baghdad, 46; War Office, 68, 70; wartime occupation of Iraq, 125, 130. *See also* British mandate
Great Powers, European: mandate system of, 54; and Ottoman Empire, 17, 21–22
Gross, Michael, 361
Gulli tribe, 149

Habbaniya (town), 350
Haim, Sylvia G., 95
Hajee, Issa, 259, 260–61
al-Hakim, Baqir: assassination of, 353
Halabja, chemical warfare on, 259
Haldane, Aylmer L., 53; *The Insurrection in Mesopotamia*, 63–66
Halliday, Denis, 14; protest against U.N. sanctions, 285–87, 294
Hamavands (Kurds), rebellion against Ottomans, 30–33
Al-Hamdani, Salah: elegy to Baghdad, 312–15; Iraqi identity of, 312

Hamid, Abdul, 35
Hamid, sheik, 154
Hammurabi, code of, 174
Hamoudi, Haider Ala: *Howling in Mesopotamia*, 353–57
Hanners, Noah, 349–50, 351
Harper, E. W. L., 66
Hashemite monarchy, 5, 54, 89–123; anti-Semitic violence during, 125, 126–30; Communist Party under, 143–47; corruption of, 9, 160, 167–72; elitist system of, 166; fall of, 125, 160–66; foreign policy of, 107; land speculation in, 169; opposition to, 133; Parliament under, 89; political violence during, 125; social divisions under, 125–26, 142, 169, 171; Sunnis in, 176; trade under, 169; and Treaty of Portsmouth, 133–37; view of Zionism, 145. *See also* Faysal bin al-Hussein I; postwar era, Iraqi
Hassan, Zikra Abdul, 297
Healey, J. J., 64
health care, Iraqi: effect of U.N. sanctions on, 285, 290, 293–94, 296–97. *See also* malnutrition, Iraqi
Helms, Richard, 215
Herdoon, Saeed: escape from Iraq, 203–5; imprisonment by Ba'thists, 198–203
Hibba (Iraqi refugee), 367–70
hijab, Iraqi women's use of, 344
Horesh, Charles, 203
Hormuz Straits, in Iran-Iraq War, 234
Horowitz, Tony: *Baghdad without a Map*, 248–53
Howe, Jonathan, 240
Humphreys, F.: on proposed Arab Congress, 99–102
al-Husri, Sati,' 7, 90, 121; career of, 93–94; pan-Arabism of, 93–99
Hussein (grandson of the Prophet), murder of, 116, 117, 120, 353
Hussein (king of Jordan), and Persian Gulf War, 278–81
Hussein, Saddam: and al Qaeda, 308; *America Reaps the Thorns Its Rulers Sowed in the World*, 302–3; ascent to power, 11, 193, 229;

on Ba'thist educational curriculum, 212–14; bombings under, 279; capture of, 328, 330; exiled opposition to, 287, 288, 323; fear of Khomeini, 237; following Persian Gulf War, 282–84; on gender segregation, 211; hanging of, 328; helicopter force of, 284; and international terrorism, 308–9; invasion of Kuwait, 12–13, 265–73, 281; invocation of Islam, 234–35, 328, 329; on Iran-Iraq War, 230–35, 269; under Iraqi Liberation Act, 287–88; on Iraqi nationalism, 214; Iraqis' toleration of, 323; on Iraqi unity, 210, 213, 214; leadership style of, 236; manipulation of history, 230, 231, 328; meeting with Glaspie, 265, 267–70; meeting with Khayralla, 237–39; military inexperience of, 235; military under, 230, 235, 245; on minority self-rule, 213–14; Muslawis' threat to, 238; palaces of, 200, 202, 310, 329; patronage networks of, 194, 288; "People's Army" of, 245; perceived threats from, 269, 306–7; public images of, 290, 292; regional ambitions of, 304; response to Coalition invasion, 328–30; response to September 11th, 301, 302–3; Shi'is under, 12; toppling of statue, 322; torture parties of, 201; vice-presidency of, 193; "Women—One Half of Our Society," 209–12; on Zionism, 209, 210, 211, 302, 328, 329. *See also* Ba'thist Party, Iraqi; Republic of Iraq, Ba'thist

Hussein, Uday, 321

Hussein bin Ali, Sharif, 46, 78, 79; Arab Revolt of, 26; Churchill on, 73

Hyatt, P. T., 63

Ibrahim, Jajji, 150–51

identity, Iraqi, 1, 16; communal, 2, 15, 91; CPA's fostering of, 339; ethnic, 2; under Faysal I, 91; Jews,' 114, 127, 147–48; national, 91, 93; role of poetry in, 14; unity in, 14

al-Ilah, Abd, 8

Imamate, doctrine of, 3

Impressionists Group (Baghdad), 138–39

insurgencies, Iraqi, 336–37, 347–52, 362; in Fallujah, 351, 357–59; Mahdi militiamen in, 359–61; Sunni, 337, 347–52, 357–59; in Tikrit, 347

intellectuals, Iraqi: appeal of Communism to, 143–44; of Baghdad, 137–40; reading of Marx, 145

International and Regional Treaties and Agreements: Iraq, Kuwait, 133

invasion of Iraq, U.S./Coalition (2001–2003), 14–15, 300–334; battle of Nasiriyah in, 14, 301, 315–20; bombing during, 301; Bush's arguments for, 306; "Coalition of the Willing" in, 301; consequences for Middle East, 305–6; cost of, 303, 304; effect on Israel, 304; effect on war on terror, 304, 305, 308–9; fatalities during, 334; occupation of Baghdad during, 320–27, 328; preemptive military action in, 300; Republican Guard during, 320; Scowcroft's opposition to, 301, 303–6; sectarianism during, 326, 327–28; "Shock and Awe" strategy, 301. *See also* military, U.S.; occupation of Iraq, U.S./Coalition

Iran: aid to Northern Iraq, 233; expansionism of, 232, 233–34; in Iraqi air space, 233; ousting of Shah, 229, 233; relations with Iraq, 230–32; theocracy in, 229, 232; threat to Ba'thist Iraq, 229

Iran-Iraq War (1980–1990), 12; al Anfal during, 12, 230, 258–61; Baghdad during, 245, 246, 249, 257; Basra during, 230, 249; Ba'thist propaganda during, 248, 249–53; beginning of, 229, 236–37; beginnings of, 229, 231; border clashes preceding, 233; cease-fire (1991), 13, 269; chemical warfare during, 259, 262; cost of, 230; effect on families, 230, 244, 254–58; end of, 230, 261–63; fatalities during, 230, 246, 249, 251–53; front line of, 248–53; home front during, 254–58; Hormuz Straits in, 234; Hussein's justification of, 230–35; international awareness of, 261; Iraqi debt following, 265, 268; Iraqi military's view of, 235–39; Iraqi oil reserves in, 241, 243, 244; Iraqi "People's Army" in, 245; Iraqi soldiers' view of, 244–48; journalistic coverage of, 248–53; Kurds in, 248, 258–61;

Iran-Iraq War—*continued*
poison gas use in, 230, 252; pre-military army of, 247–48; refugee crisis following, 13; Shatt al-Arab waterway in, 229, 234, 248; travel during, 245; U.S. role in, 230, 239–44; women during, 254–58, 259
Iraq: during Abbasite dynasty, 34; American perceptions concerning, 131; anti-American sentiment in, 162–63, 164, 274, 277, 369; British direct rule of Iraq, 5, 8, 9, 53, 69; British mandate in, 5, 6–7, 15, 53–86; British military access to, 89; Central Intelligence Department, 146; CNN images of, 289, 298; Coalition bombing of, 266, 272, 279, 280; creation of, 4–5; cultural heritage of, 323; de-Ba'thification of, 336, 368; Development Board, 171; education in, 92, 93, 94, 138-39, 210, 212–14, 344, 345; foreign threats to, 99–100; humanitarian aid to, 288; humanitarian crisis in, 267; in interwar years, 7–8; land reform in, 160, 167, 187; in League of Nations, 89, 93, 101; liberal institutions of, 89; patriarchal networks of, 209; relationship with Great Britain, 79, 81, 89, 116; relations with Iran, 230–32; religious diversity in, 113; Revolutionary era, 160–66, 173–87; rise of fundamentalism in, 343; U.N. sanctions against, 13–14; U.S. invasion of, 14–15, 300–334; water-damming projects in, 171; Western influences in, 1, 4, 17–21; during World War II, 8, 126, 130–33. *See also* Hashemite monarchy; invasion of Iraq, U.S./Coalition; Mesopotamia, Ottoman; occupation of Iraq, U.S./Coalition; postwar era, Iraqi; Republic of Iraq; women, Iraqi
Iraq-First policy, 107
Iraqi Governing Council (IGC), 336; Communist Party representation, 343; formation of, 339–43; Kurds in, 340–41; Resolution 137, 343; Shi'is in, 342, 343; Sunnis in, 342; tribal members of, 339–40; women in, 343. *See also* occupation of Iraq, U.S./Coalition
Iraqi National Congress, 287
Iraqi poetry: occupation of Baghdad in, 312–15; pan-Arab, 207–8; traditional forms of, 121
Iraqi poetry, nationalist, 14, 61–62; al Jawahiri's, 121–23
Iraqi Special Tribunal, trial of Hussein, 328
Iraq Liberation Act (U.S., 1998), 14, 287–88
Iraq Petroleum Company, 214
Iraq's Last Jews (2008), 144, 198
Iraq war. *See* invasion of Iraq, U.S./Coalition; occupation of Iraq, U.S./Coalition
The Iraq War Reader (Sifry and Cerf), 268
al-Isfahani, Sayyid Abu I-Hasan, 84, 86
Ismail, Kamil, 177
Israel: aid to Kurds, 206; Ba'thist Party on, 206–8; conflict with Palestine, 305; effect of Iraq invasion on, 304; Hussein's bombing of, 279; immigration to, 148–51, 205–6; Law of Return, 147; U.S. protection of, 194–95

Jabra, Ibrahim Jabra, 144; *Princesses' Street*, 137–40
Jalim, Amalid Abdul, 297
Jangana, Joseph, 199
Jawad, Sa'ad, 322
al-Jawahiri, Muhammad Mahdi: elegy to the poor, 121–23; political ideals of, 121
Jayyusi, Salma Khadra, 121; *Modern Arabic Poetry*, 207
Jewish Agency, aid to emigrants, 206
Jews, Baghdadi, 1, 3–4, 19–21, 45–50, 113–15; bomb attacks on, 148; civic participation by, 127; during Farhud, 125, 126–30
Jews, Iraqi, 3–4; Ba'thist execution of, 198, 204; Communist, 146; emigration, 9, 16, 48, 49, 125, 144, 147; emigration under Ba'thists, 198–206; imprisonment by Ba'thists, 198, 199–203; Iraqi identity of, 114, 127, 147–48; Kurdish aid to, 198, 204–6; numbers of, 114; religious tolerance toward, 113–14; Turkish violence against, 48; in twenty-first century, 15–16; violence against, 8–9, 125, 126–30; during World War II, 145. *See also* Law No. 1
Jews, Kurdish, 4; anti-Semitic experiences of,

153; emigration of, 148–53; reaction to Law No. 1 (1950), 149
Jomart, Apo, 190
Jordan: anti-American feeling in, 279, 280, 281; Coalition bombing of, 280; expatriate returnees to, 281; Iraqi refugees in, 369; during Persian Gulf War, 278–81; population of, 278; rationing in, 280
journalists: coverage of Iran-Iraq War, 248–53; embedded, 315–23, 357–59; on U.N. sanctions, 295
Joyce, Colonel P., 77, 78

Kamil Pasha, 35
Kanafani, Ghassan: assassination of, 207
Karbala: Ashura celebrations at, 225–27, 354, 356; battle of, 116, 117, 223
Karim, Abdul, 296
al-Karim, Mikhael Abd, 177
Kasr al-Nahaya prison, 203
al-Kailani, Rashid Ali, 111, 112; coup of 1941, 8, 125, 127, 138
Kemal, Mustafa, 75
Kennedy, John F., 309
Khadduri, Majid: *Socialist Iraq*, 196
Khafaja tribe, 82
Khalaf, Abdel-Latif, 348, 350
Khalaf, Omar Ibrahim, 347; death of, 349–52; early life of, 348; as martyr, 350, 351–52; motives of, 351; in Sunni insurgency, 348–49
Khalaf, Radwan, 348
Khaled, Mawlud, 349
Khaled, Muwaffaq, 351
Khalid, Ayyob, 180
al-Khalisi, Mahdi, 6, 54; on elections, 82, 83–85; exile of, 81; son's account of, 81–86
Khater, Akram Fouad: *Sources in the History of the Modern Middle East*, 212
Khayralla, Adnan, 236–39; death of, 235; meeting with Hussein, 237–39; moral authority of, 237
Khomeini, Ayatollah Ruhollah, 229; Hussein's fear of, 237; military rebellion against, 236
Kiernander, Major, 64

Kissinger, Henry, 215
Kubba, Amer, 224, 225; at Ashura demonstration, 225–27
Kubba, Juman: *The First Evidence*, 223–27
Kubba, Mohammad Mahdi, 162
Kubba, Zeena, 224–25
Kurdish-Iraqi conflict (1974–1975), 215–20; cease-fire in, 203; effect on social relations, 216
Kurdish language, official recognition of, 91, 92–93
Kurdish Revolt (1961–1963), 161, 187–91; aerial bombing during, 190–91; Barzani in, 187–91
Kurdistan: Autonomous Zone, 341; under Autonomy Law of 1974, 216; during Iran-Iraq War, 258–61
Kurdistan Democratic Party (KDP), 176
Kurds, Iraqi: aid to Jewish emigrants, 198, 204–6; in al Anfal, 230; autonomy for, 187, 188, 283; under Ba'thist Party, 258–61; bombing of, 188; under British mandate, 62, 74–78; conflict with Assyrians, 103, 104; under Faysal I, 5–6; and Faysal's election, 74–78; following Persian Gulf War, 282–83; hospitality of, 174; on IGC, 340–41; in Iran-Iraq War, 248, 258–61; Israeli aid to, 206; Jewish, 4, 148–53; under Ottoman Empire, 2, 3; at Paris Peace Conference, 74; under Qasim, 187; revolt against Hussein, 13; revolt of 1935, 7; secessionism of, 3, 12; self-rule for, 6, 74, 258, 341; during al-Shawwaf mutiny, 176; Sunni, 3, 90; U.S. assistance to, 214–15. *See also* Hamavands
Kut (Ottoman Mesopotamia), during World War I, 42, 45
Kuwait: ground war in, 266; Hussein's invasion of, 12–13, 265–73, 281; Marine advance into, 282; oil production in, 265; perceived threat from, 268–69; sovereignty of, 266, 267

land reform, Iraqi, 160; under Law No. 30, 167
Law No. 1 (1950), 125, 126; Kurdish reaction to, 149; provisions of, 147–48

Law No. 30 (1958), 167, 187
Law No. 188, 182
Lawrence, T. E., 5, 131; al-Askari and, 26; on British mandate, 54, 66–68; support for Faysal, 76
League of Nations, 70; British mandate and, 58; Iraq in, 89, 93, 101
Lebanon, U.S. intervention in (1958), 161, 162, 165
LIFE (U.S. charitable organization), 298
Literature from the "Axis of Evil" (2006), 312
looting: during Farhud, 129–30; by Kurds, 103, 104
looting (occupation of Baghdad), 320–21; of National Museum, 14, 302, 323–27; opportunistic/planned, 324
Lorimer, John, 33
Luizard, Pierre-Jean, 81
Lyon, Wallace, 54; *Kurds, Arabs, and Britons*, 75–78

Madrid, Middle East peace conference in, 284
al-Majid, Ali Hassan (Chemical Ali), 258
Majnoon, during Iran-Iraq War, 251
malnutrition, Iraqi: among children, 14, 267, 281, 285, 290, 294, 295, 298, 367; among women, 294, 295; under U.N. sanctions, 267, 285–86, 293–94, 295, 297, 298
al-Manassifi, Ahmed, 111
March Manifesto (1970), 216
Marines, U.S.: 1st Reconnaissance Battalion, 315–20; during occupation of Baghdad, 320, 321, 322; in Operation Devil Syphon, 362–67. *See also* military, U.S.
Marr, Phebe, 8; on Bakr Sidqi coup, 108; on Ba'thist Constitution, 196; on Glaspie-Hussein meeting, 268; on Iraqi minorities, 90–91; on Iraqi poverty, 140; on Oil-For-Food Program, 285; on U.N. sanctions, 267; on al-Wathba, 133
marriage, Iraqi, 187
Marriott, Lieutenant, 64
Marshall, Major, 77
Marx, Karl: Iraqi intelligentsia's reading of, 145
Maude, Sir Stanley, 4; occupation of Baghdad, 45; Proclamation of Baghdad (1917), 18, 45–47; at Sunnaiyat, 43
Mauluds (Sunni celebrations), 55–56; forbidding of, 60
Medina (Sayid), 155–56
Meir, Eliahu, 49
Mello, Sergio de, 342
Mesopotamia, Ottoman, 2–3, 17–50; British influence in, 4, 17, 18, 39–47, 69; corrupt government of, 25–29; freedom of press in, 36, 38; Jewish population of, 113–14; leadership of, 17; population of, 17, 60; poverty in, 26; Shi'is of, 2–3, 116–17, 353; Sunnis of, 2–3, 116–17; taxation in, 27; Westernization of, 4, 17–18; during World War I, 4, 18, 42–47. *See also* Ottoman Empire
Michael, Sami: on Communist Party, 144–47; novels of, 144
Middle East: Ba'thism in, 193; British policy on, 69–74; Cold War in, 161, 194; consequences of Iraq invasion for, 305–6; state formation in, 5; U.S. intervention in, 284
Mileo, Jason, 334
military, Iraqi: during al Anfal, 259; in Assyrian Affair, 103–7; in Bakr Sidqi coup, 107–13; dominance of, 8; during Farhud, 144; following Persian Gulf War, 283; under Hussein, 230, 235, 245; from Mosul, 238; "People's Army" of, 245; political power of, 90; of postwar era, 9–10; view of Iran-Iraq War, 235–39
military, U.S.: in Afghanistan, 332; embedded journalists with, 315–23, 357–59; 43rd Combat Engineering Company, 349–50; infantry duties, 362–67; in Operation Devil Syphon, 362–67; peacekeeping role of, 362; political decisions governing, 362, 363; preemptive action by, 300; rules of engagement for, 337, 357–49, 360–61; World War II occupation of Iraq, 130–33. *See also* Marines, U.S.
minorities, Iraqi, 113; American promises to, 74; appeal of Communism to, 143, 145–46; under British mandate, 57; civic institutions of, 92; educational rights of, 92;

under Faysal I, 90–93; Hussein on, 213–14; identity of, 7; under Ottoman Empire, 2–3; religious, 3–4; role in nation-building, 90; self-rule for, 213–14; sociopolitical role of, 1; Young Turks and, 24–25. *See also* Assyrians, Iraqi; Jews; Kurds, Iraqi

Miran, Yousif, 177

Mofid, Kamran, 230

Mohammed, Aziz, 343

Morton, H. V.: *Middle East*, 116–21

mosques, Iraqi: unbelievers in, 132

Mosul (Iraq): Assyrian massacre in, 89; during Bakr Sidqi coup, 108–9; Coalition occupation of, 301; foreign claims to, 99–100; military leaders from, 238; al-Shawwaf mutiny in, 176–81; Sunnis of, 239

Mosul (Ottoman Mesopotamia), 2, 17; British in, 39; decline of, 22–23; living conditions of, 22, 23; railway to, 22, 23; riot of 1908, 24; Sykes on, 21–23; tribal rebellion near, 30–33; Vali of, 31

Mosul province: under British mandate, 75; in Ottoman Mesopotamia, 53

Moussa, Hamid Majid, 343

Muharram, celebrations during, 116

Muntafik province (Iraq), 82

Muqdadiyah, civilian casualties of, 359–62

al-Musadawi, Sheikh Amar, 321

Mustafa, Shakir, 254

al-Mustansiriya University (Baghdad), bombing at, 232

Nadhim Pasha (governor of Baghdad), 28; autocratic behavior of, 35; civil officials under, 38; petition against, 33–38; removal of Arab officers by, 37–38; street-widening project of, 36–37; suppression of Arabic language, 36

al-Na'ini, Mirza Husayn, 84, 86

Najaf, religious university in, 220

Nakash, Yitzhak: *The Shi'is of Iraq*, 61–62

Naqshbandi, Khalid, 162

Nasiriyah, Battle of (2003), 14, 301, 315–20; casualties in, 316; civilians during, 316–17, 318, 319

Nasiriyah, U.S. occupation of, 318

Nasser, Gamal Abdel, 161, 174

National Geographic: Orientalism of, 173; view of Iraq, 160–61, 173, 175

nationalism, Kurdish, 77

nationalism, Iraqi: during British mandate, 55–61; Churchill on, 73; Faysal I's, 80–81; following Bakr Sidqi coup, 107–8; Hussein on, 214; in Revolt of 1920, 61; Young Turks,' 47

nationalism, pan-Arab, 6–7, 8, 93–99; Hameed Said's, 11. *See also* pan-Arabism

National Museum (Baghdad): Bell's work with, 323; looting of, 14, 302, 323–27; restoration of objects to, 326; security for, 326

nation-building, Iraqi: role of minorities in, 90. *See also* state formation, Iraqi

Nazif Bey (Vali of Bussorah), 35

neoconservatism, American, 287, 301; on regime change, 302

Ninevah (Assyrian Empire), 174

Nodine, Matt, 358–59

Noor (queen of Jordan), 13; *Leap of Faith*, 278–81

Nuri, Abdul Latif, 109, 110–11, 112–13

occupation of Iraq, U.S./Coalition (2003–2004), 15, 336–70; anti-American feeling during, 369; Ashura celebration during, 353–57; black market in, 363; British troops in, 362; children during, 360–62, 367–70; civilians during, 337–39, 358–59; civilians' fatalities during, 337, 360–62, 365–67; de-Ba'thification during, 336, 368; infantry's role in, 362–67; insurgency against, 336–37, 347–52, 357–59; Iraqi blogs during, 337–39; in Iraqi poetry, 312–15; Office of Reconstruction and Humanitarian Assistance, 336; popular resentment of, 336; rules of engagement during, 337, 357–59, 360–61; sectarian divisions during, 336; Shammar tribe during, 339; sheikhs during, 340; Shi'i disillusionment with, 353–57; shortages during, 336; suicide bombings during, 356; tribes during, 339–40;

occupation of Iraq—*continued*
  women during, 338, 343–47, 361–62; women's employment during, 345–47. *See also* Coalition Provisional Authority; invasion of Iraq, U.S./Coalition; Iraqi Governing Council
Office of Reconstruction and Humanitarian Assistance (ORHA), 336
oil, Iraqi, 53, 171; exports of, 241, 244; in Iran-Iraq War, 241, 243, 244; nationalization of, 214; price of, 270; refineries, 39
Oil-for-Food Program, 13–14, 285, 294; benefits for Ba'thists, 287, 288
Operation Devil Siphon, 362–67; casualties during, 365–67
Operation Iraqi Freedom, 301, 331
Organization of Petroleum Exporting Countries (OPEC), 265
Organization of the Islamic Conference, 231
Orientalism, 173
Ottoman Empire, 2–3; British aid to, 98; Constitution of, 24–25, 28, 36, 38; extent of, 17; fall of, 4; government of, 17; Hamavand rebellion against, 30–33; Jewish population of, 113–14; patronage networks of, 30; political system of, 4, 33; religious tolerance in, 4, 113–14; Russian threat to, 98; spread of news in, 29; wars with Persia, 3; during World War I, 4, 42. *See also* Mesopotamia, Ottoman

Palestine: conflict with Israel, 305; Iraqi sympathy toward, 207; Jewish immigration to, 114, 144
pan-Arabism, 6–7; among literate classes, 95; and anti-Semitism, 114; Ba'thist, 10, 11, 193, 207; British view of, 100; Faysal I's, 6–7, 90, 99–102; al-Husri's, 93–99; of interwar years, 8; and Muslim unity, 94–99. *See also* nationalism, pan-Arab
Paris Peace Conference (1919), 74
patriarchy, Iraqi, 1; Ba'thist, 185; networks of, 209
Peace Partisans (leftist group), 176, 177
Persian Gulf: access to, 229; balance of power in, 283; U.S. presence in, 240

Persian Gulf War, first. *See* Iran-Iraq War
Persian Gulf War, second (1991), 266; anti-American feeling in, 274, 277, 279, 280, 281; and Arab democracy, 278; Baghdad during, 273–78, 290; Basra following, 296–98; cease-fire in, 281–84; Coalition bombing during, 266; effect on Arab states, 278; effect on Arab unity, 277; effect on bird life, 275; fatalities during, 266, 280; humanitarian cost of, 281; Jordan during, 278–81; Kurds following, 282–83; power outages during, 274–76; Saudi Arabia during, 279, 280; Scowcroft's role in, 303; Shi'is following, 282–83; shortages during, 274–76
Philby, Harry St. John, 76–77
pishmorga (freedom fighters), 205
postwar era, Iraqi: British military presence in, 133–37; Communism in, 9; education during, 138–39; institutional failures during, 126; military in, 9–10; tribal sheikhs during, 154; Western influence in, 9. *See also* British mandate; Hashemite monarchy
poverty: among Iraqi children, 141, 142; in Baghdad, 140–43, 171; in Iraqi poetry, 121–23. *See also* malnutrition, Iraqi
Powell, Colin, 284; on WMDs, 301
Pratt, Nicola, 209

al-Qadisiya, Battle of, 230–31
Qasim, Abd al-Karim, 10; and Baghdad Pact, 173; Iraqi women under, 182–87; Kurdish revolt against, 187–91; Law No. 30 under, 160; meetings with Gallman, 164, 165; opposition to, 176; populist reforms of, 160; during al-Shawwaf mutiny, 178; Soviet aid to, 189; Soviet alliance of, 173; Sunni opposition to, 161
Qasim coup d'état (1958), 10, 160–66, 220; American businessmen during, 166; American Embassy evacuation during, 163–64; American response to, 161–66; mob violence during, 163–64; promises of, 166–67; reasons for, 167
Queen Aliya College for Girls (Baghdad), 138

al-Radhwani, Abd al-Majeed Abd al-Hakim, 180, 181
al-Radi, Nuha: *Baghdad Diaries*, 273–78
Radio Cairo, anti-Western broadcasts of, 173
al-Rahman, Abd, 160, 179
Rakib (newspaper), 36
al-Rashid, Harun, 174
Regina (Baghdadi woman), 15; baby of, 20; wedding of, 1–3, 18–21
Rejwan, Nissim: *The Last Jews in Baghdad*, 127–30
Republican Guard, Ba'thist, 289, 298; following Persian Gulf War, 282; during invasion of Iraq, 320; makeup of, 321–22
Republic of Iraq (1958–1968): American view of, 173–76; anti-Western views in, 174, 175; class distinctions in, 182–83; DDT use during, 189; decrees establishing, 162; Kurds under, 187; land reform in, 167, 187; modernization during, 183, 184; professional classes of, 183; Soviet alliance with, 173; urbanization during, 183; U.S. recognition of, 166; women during, 182–87
Republic of Iraq, Ba'thist, 193–227; Autonomy Law (1974), 216; Coalition occupation of, 195–96; exiled opposition to, 287, 288, 323; following Persian Gulf War, 282–84, 289–90; health care in, 290; human rights violations in, 286; implementation of UN SC Res 598, 261; Iranian threat to, 229; under Iraqi Liberation Act, 287–88; Kurds under, 215–20, 258–61; Ministry of Information, 249, 289; Republican Guard, 282, 289, 298, 321–22; sanctions against, 13–14, 266–67, 271, 285–87; secret police of, 260; Shi'is under, 353; Soviet influence in, 214; State Board of Antiquities and Heritage (SBAH), 323–24, 326; U.S. aid to, 241–42; U.S. military assistance to, 242–43, 244; U.S. relations with, 240; war debts of, 230, 268, 365. *See also* Ba'thist Party, Iraqi; Hussein, Saddam
Revolt of 1920, 62–66, 209; Album Hessian during, 65; Iraqi nationalism in, 61; Lawrence of Arabia on, 67–68; motives for, 63

Reza Pahlavi, Shah: ousting of, 229, 233; U.S. support for, 239, 252
Riverbend (Iraqi woman), *Baghdad Burning*, 344–47
Riyadh (CIVIC volunteer), 338
Rodrigue, Aron: *Jews and Muslims*, 19, 114
Rubay'i, Najib, 162
Rumaithah, resistance to British in, 63–66
Rumsfeld, Donald, 321, 331
Rush, Alan de L.: *Records of the Hashimite Dynasties*, 79

al-Sa'adun, Abd al-Muhsin, 82
Sabar, Ariel, 126, 148; *My Father's Paradise*, 149–53
Sabar, Rahamim: on emigration, 148–50; emigration of, 151–53
Sabar, Yona, 148–53; emigration of, 152–53
Sada, Georges Hormis, 230; career of, 235; *Saddam's Secrets*, 235–39
Sadoula, Mohammed, 189
al-Sadoun, Nasra, 290, 291
al-Sadr, Muhammad Baqir, 12, 56, 224, 359; assassination of, 221; Dawa Party of, 220–21; on Islamic economics, 221–23; and social justice, 220–23
al-Sadr, Muqtada: Mahdi militiamen of, 359–61
Safwan, cease-fire negotiated at, 281–82, 283–84
Sa'id, Hameed: *Dying at the Edge of Death*, 207–8
al-Said, Nuri: agreement with British, 171; Arab nationalism of, 99, 172; on corruption, 168; death of, 163, 165; exile of, 107; political repression under, 172; power over Ministers, 172; role in corruption, 171–72
Salamiyah, during al-Anfal, 260
Saleem, Hiner: *My Father's Rifle*, 216–20
Salem Pax (Iraqi blogger), 337; *The Clandestine Diary of an Ordinary Iraqi*, 338–39
Samawah (Iraq), in Revolt of 1920, 63, 64
sanctions, United Nations, 13–14, 266–67, 271, 281; child mortality under, 285–86, 290, 294, 297; effect on families, 286; effect on health care, 285, 290, 293–94, 296–97;

sanctions, United Nations—*continued*
effect on Iraqis, 267; effect on women, 288–98; encouraging of fanaticism, 286, 291; Halliday's protest against, 285–87, 294; *jihad* under, 295; journalistic accounts of, 295; malnutrition under, 267, 285–86, 293–94, 295, 297, 298; profiteering in, 291; social effect of, 286

San Remo Agreement (1920), 53; Bell on, 55–61; Delegates' response to, 57–59, 60; Iraqi response to, 55; religious minorities and, 57; Sunni-Shi'ah agreement on, 55–56; supporters of, 55; tribal violence and, 56–57. *See also* British mandate

Saudi Arabia: Hussein's bombing of, 279; during Persian Gulf War, 279, 280; U.S. protection of, 266

Saunders, Harold H., 214–15

Sawers, John, 341

Sayids (descendants of the Prophet), 154–58; support of sheikhs for, 156

Schmidt, Dana Adams: *Journey among Brave Men*, 188–91; sources of, 188

Scholar Rescue Fund, 324

Schwarzkopf, H. Norman, 281–82, 284

Scowcroft, Brent, 14, 284; opposition to Iraq invasion, 301, 303–6; role in Persian Gulf War, 303; on WMDs, 303, 304; *A World Transformed*, 282–84

sectarianism, Iraqi: in Coalition-occupied Baghdad, 326, 327–28, 368, 369; of interwar years, 7–8

September 11 attacks: Bush's invocation of, 300, 306, 308, 309, 312, 332; Hussein's response to, 301, 302–3

Shadid, Anthony, 337; *Night Draws Near*, 347–52

Shamash, Violette: *Memories of Eden*, 45–50

Shammar tribe, during Coalition occupation of Iraq, 339

Shar'iah law, 61

Sharif, Hajee Omar, 259–60

Shatt al-Arab waterway, in Iran-Iraq War, 229, 234, 248

Shawkat Pasha, Mahmoud, 28

al-Shawwaf, Abd al-Wahhab, 10, 176

al-Shawwaf mutiny (Mosul, 1959), 176–81; aerial operations during, 179; arrests during, 177; ethnic issues in, 176; Qasim during, 178

Sheddir (Sayid), 157–58

sheikhs, Iraqi: under British mandate, 60–61, 62, 154; during Coalition occupation, 340; and election of Faysal I, 77; Ottoman taxation of, 27; during postwar era, 154; and San Remo Agreement, 56–57; support for Sayids, 156. *See also* tribes, Iraqi

Sheile Dze (Kurdish village), in Kurdish Revolt, 188–89

Sherifa (Sayid), 156, 157

Shiblak, Abbas, 147

Shields, Sarah D.: *Mosul before Iraq*, 24

Shi'is, Iraqi, 90; autonomy for, 283; under Ba'thist Party, 11–12, 220–27, 353; under British mandate, 5, 62, 81–86, 353; clerical influence among, 3, 11–12, 61, 342; during Coalition occupation, 337, 353–57; in Communist Party, 143, 147, 221; under Faysal I, 6; following Persian Gulf War, 282–83; Hussein's exile of, 12; in IGC, 342, 343; marginalization of, 115–16; marriage with Sunnis, 187; during occupation of Baghdad, 321; opposition to Faysal I, 81–86; of Ottoman Mesopotamia, 2–3, 116–17, 353; protests against Ba'thist Party, 223–27; protests against British, 5; in Republican Guard, 321; resistance to U.S., 15, 359–61; revolt against Hussein, 13; village life of, 154–58

Shi'is, Persian, 116

Shimun, Mar, 7, 104

Shor, Jean and Franc: "Iraq—Where Oil and Water Mix," 173–76

Sidqi, Bakr: coup of, 8, 90, 107–13, 121; manifesto of, 113; role in Assyrian Affair, 89–90

Simmel: Assyrian refugees in, 103; looting of, 104; massacre at, 105–7

Sindi tribe, 149

Sistani, Ayatollah Ali Husseini: fatwa on constitution, 342

Six Day War (1967), 193, 198; Israeli territory following, 207

Slivani tribe, 149
Sluglett, Peter, 235
Soane, Ely Banister: *To Mesopotamia and Kurdistan in Disguise*, 30–33
social justice, Islamic, 221–23; the Prophet on, 222
society, Iraqi: in Ba'thist Constitution, 196; effect of U.N. sanctions on, 286; fragmentation of, 9; militarization of, 244, 245–47; role of tribes in, 340
soldiers, American: rules of engagement for, 337, 357–49, 360–61; in World War II Iraq, 130-33
Soviet Union: aid to Qasim, 189; dissolution of, 287; influence in Iraq, 173, 214; Iraqi admiration for, 145
Stafford, R. S.: on Assyrian Affair, 103–7
state formation, Iraqi, 5–6, 91; under British mandate, 73; failures of, 15
Steet, Linda, 173
Sucholas, Piotr, 361
Suez Crisis, 161
Sulayman, Hikmat, 8; in Bakr Sidqi coup, 107–8, 109, 110, 111–12; role in Assyrian Affair, 89
Sumayyil, Assyrian massacre at, 103
Sunnaiyat: Arabs at, 43, 44; battlefield of, 42–45; Turks at, 44, 45–46
Sunnis, Iraqi: in Arab Revolt, 81; Ba'thist, 11, 194; during Coalition occupation, 336; Communist opposition to, 146; dominance of, 5, 6, 10, 12, 90; in Hashemite monarchy, 176; in IGC, 342; insurgents, 337, 347–52, 357–59; Kurdish, 3, 90; marriage with Shi'is, 187; in Mosul, 239; opposition to Qasim, 10, 161; of Ottoman Mesopotamia, 2–3, 116–17; Pan-Arabism of, 6–7, 15; protests against British, 5; relationship with British, 81, 116; in Republican Guard, 322
Sunni-Shi'i split, 7–8, 116, 223; and San Remo Agreement, 55–56
Sunni Triangle region, 15, 347, 357
Suwaid, Yusuf, 60
Sykes, Sir Mark, 4, 18; *The Caliphs' Last Heritage*, 22–23; career of, 21–22; on Mosul, 21–23
Sykes-Picot Agreement (1916), 22
Syria: Ba'thist Party of, 195; French influence in, 99, 100, 101

Taha, Khalid, 179, 181
Taili, Mustafa, 180
Talabani, Jalal, 340–41
Talib Pasha, Saiyid, 59; arrest of, 76–77; as Minister of Interior, 75
Task Force Tarawa (Marine combat team), 316, 317
Ta'ziyah (Shi'ah ritual), 56
Tel Aviv, Scud attack on, 279
al-Thaura (Ba'thist newspaper), 207
Thinaiyan, Abdul Latif Effendi, 36
Tikrit, Sunni insurgency in, 347
Tish'a-Bab (season of mourning), 48
Tofiq, Ahmed, 190–91
Tohalla, Ismail Abawi, 105–7, 111
Townshend, Charles, 43, 44
Treaty of Lausanne (1923), Kurds under, 74
Treaty of Portsmouth (1948), 9, 125; British military presence in, 133–37; Communist Party and, 146; Iraqi oil following, 171
Treaty of Sevres (1920), 6, 70
Treaty of Versailles (1919), 70
tribes, Iraqi: under British mandate, 56–57, 73, 75; under Coalition occupation, 339–40; organization of, 60; rebellion (Mosul, 1909), 30–33; respect for power, 340; in Revolt of 1920, 63–66; role in Assyrian Affair, 103, 106. *See also* sheikhs, Iraqi
Tripp, Charles, 13–14, 33; on Ba'thists, 194; on Coalition invasion, 328; on communal identities, 91; on Iraqi Communist Party, 143; on Oil-for-Food Program, 288; on Persian Gulf War, 266; on Revolt of 1920, 66; on al-Shawwaf mutiny, 176; on Shi'is, 81
Tucker, Mike: *Hell Is Over*, 259–61
Turkish language, sanctioned uses of, 91

Ubaid, Hatim, 178
Ummayyad dynasty, 116

UNICEF, report on Iraqi children, 367
United Arab Emirates, perceived threat from, 268–69
United Nations: Charter of, 262; Charter on Human Rights, 286; diplomatic aid to Iraq, 241–42; Food and Agriculture Organization, 267; Monitoring, Verification, and Inspection Commission, 301; sanctions against Iraq, 13–14, 266–67, 271, 281, 285–87; *The United Nations and the Iraq-Kuwait Conflict*, 271–72
United Nations Security Council, 262, 263, 312; Resolution 598, 12, 230, 261–63; Resolution 660, 271; Resolution 661, 265, 266, 271, 285–87; Resolution 662, 267, 271–72, 278; Resolution 678, 267, 272–73; Resolution 968, 285; Sanctions Committee, 271; unity on Iraq, 271; and WMDs, 305
United States: assistance to Kurds, 214–15; and Ba'thist coup, 194–95; humanitarian aid to Iraq, 88; intervention in Lebanon (1958), 161, 162, 165; intervention in Middle East, 284; interventionism of, 287; invasion of Iraq, 14–15, 300–334; Iraqi refugees in, 369; Iraq Liberation Act (1998), 287–88; "Joint Resolution to Authorize the Use of United States Armed Forces Against Iraq," 306; military assistance to Iraq, 242–43, 244; national security priorities of, 304; neoconservatism in, 287, 301, 302; preemptive military action by, 300; protection of Israel, 194–95; recognition of Republic of Iraq, 166; role in Iran-Iraq War, 230, 239–44; role in U.N. sanctions, 291; support for Iraqi Ba'thist Party, 239–44; support for Shah of Iran, 239, 252; unilateralism in, 300. *See also* invasion of Iraq, U.S./Coalition; occupation of Iraq, U.S./Coalition; Persian Gulf War, second
United States Army, *Instructions for American Servicemen in Iraq during World War II*, 130–33
United States Department of State, "Iran-Iraq War: Analysis of Possible U.S. Shift from Position of Strict Neutrality," 240–44
unity, Arab: effect of Persian Gulf War on, 277; linguistic, 95; versus Muslim unity, 94–99; political, 96; in proposed Arab Congress, 99, 100; social aspects of, 98
unity, Iraqi: challenges to, 7; effect of communal identity on, 2; Hussein on, 210, 213, 214; role of poetry in, 14
al-Usba (Communist newspaper), 146

valis (Ottoman governors), 2
Veliotes, Nicholas A., 240

war on terror (Bush administration), 300, 301, 332–33; effect of invasion of Iraq on, 304, 305, 308–9
al-Wathba ("the rising," 1948), 9, 125, 133; Communists in, 146
Waziriyah, bombing at, 232–33
weapons of mass destruction (WMDs) controversy: Bush in, 306, 307–10, 330; inspections in, 301, 309, 310; Scowcroft on, 303, 304; United Nations Security Council and, 305; U.S. claims in, 300, 301
Wilson, Arnold Talbot, 57–58, 68
women, Iraqi: advice to U.S. soldiers concerning, 132–33; as agents of change, 1; Assyrian, 103, 106–7; under Ba'thist regime, 11, 209–12; Campaign for Innocent Victims in Conflict, 338; cancer among, 296–97; during Coalition occupation, 338, 343–47, 361–62; under CPA, 343–44; doctors, 291; dress of, 183–85, 295, 298, 344–45; education of, 210, 344, 345; effect of sanctions on, 288–98; forced prostitution of, 286, 290; gender-based violence against, 343; *hajis*, 295; Hamavand, 32–33; IGC membership, 343; during Iran-Iraq War, 254–58, 259; in labor force, 209, 210, 344, 345–47; malnutrition among, 294, 295; marriage arrangements for, 187; poverty among, 142–43; in public sphere, 209, 289, 291; under Qasim regime, 161; in revolutionary era, 182–87; social influence of, 1, 211; socializing with men, 186–87; social life of, 182–87; in trade unions, 210; use of *chador*, 295, 298; war widows, 292; Westernization of, 19–21
women, Jewish: Westernization of, 19–21

women's rights, Iraqi, 161, 182; Hussein on, 209–12; in post-Saddam era, 343–47
World Health Organization (WHO), 285
World War I: Baghdad during, 45–50; Basra during, 39; British occupation during, 130, 145; Ottoman Mesopotamia during, 4, 18, 42–47
World War II: American occupation during, 130–33; Bush's invocation of, 331; Iraq during, 8, 126, 130-33; Iraqi Jews during, 145; poverty during, 140
Wright, Evan: "The Killer Elite," 315–20

Yasin (Cabinet Minister), 109–10, 111, 112
al-Yawar, Ghazi, 340
Yazid (Umayyad ruler), 223, 354
Yazidis (syncretic sect), 2, 3, 90
Youhanna, Donny George: directorship of National Museum, 324; *Soldiers and Citizens*, 323–27
Young Turks, 33; and Abdul Hamid, 24, 53; countercoup against, 29, 35; Proclamation of 1908, 18, 24–25; reforms of, 24–25, 53; and religious minorities, 24–25; territorial nationalism of, 47
Yusuf Pasha (military commander), 27–28
yuzbashis (Ottoman officers), 31, 32

Zakho (Kurdish village), 148–49; Jewish emigration from, 126, 151–52; Jews of, 148–50; middle class of, 151; Muslims of, 149, 152
Zaurah (newspaper), 36
Zilkha, Joseph, 199, 202, 204
Zionism, 114–15; versus Communism, 145–46; Hussein on, 209, 210, 211, 302, 328, 329; Iraqi Jews' support for, 145

Stacy E. Holden is associate professor of history at Purdue University. She is the author of *The Politics of Food in Modern Morocco*.

The University Press of Florida is the scholarly publishing agency for the State University System of Florida, comprising Florida A&M University, Florida Atlantic University, Florida Gulf Coast University, Florida International University, Florida State University, New College of Florida, University of Central Florida, University of Florida, University of North Florida, University of South Florida, and University of West Florida.